# European Integration and the Postmodern Condition

'This is the first book combining the debates about postmodernity and postmodernism in International Relations Theory on the one hand, and the transformation of Europe's political organization on the other. Peter van Ham's *European Integration and the Postmodern Condition* comes at the right time – many colleagues who teach European Studies will be eager to find a volume taking up this theme.'

*Thomas Diez, University of Birmingham*

'This is a lively and stimulating book and the first text which deals so explicitly with the implications of postmodernism for European politics/integration.'

*Robert Bideleux, University of Wales, Swansea*

This is the first book to look at the process of European integration by drawing on both established and novel trends in postmodern thinking and analysis. The book asks how we can study the process of European integration in the current period of paradigm shift, and maps out the central elements of the academic debate dealing with the future of integration and 'Europe' in general.

Peter van Ham argues that the European Union may develop into a postmodern entity characterized by decentered, complex policy formation based on a multi-level 'European' identity, a new notion of democracy, legitimacy and authority; and related in an open way to its 'Other', in the form of anarchy (embodied by Russia), cultural alterity (Islam) as well as a juxtaposition with the USA. Given that the state is now only one source of authority amongst several, this book explores the idea that the state, like other traditional spatial modes of representation, may gradually be paralleled by other forms of organization, which will have important implications for democratic theory and practice, as well as the place and role of the West in the world at large.

The process of European integration is shaped by a globalizing world order. Peter van Ham persuasively concludes that, in order to understand the qualitatively new nature of the emerging Euro-polity, a multi-faceted postmodern approach is required, and this book offers the first elements of such an approach. This book stimulates fresh readings of the European project, and encourages open thinking space for developing new analytical horizons. It will be a significant cutting-edge contribution to debates in international relations, comparative politics and European studies.

**Peter van Ham** is Professor of West European Politics at the George C. Marshall European Center for Security Studies in Garmisch-Partenkirchen, Germany. He recently co-edited *Mapping European Security after Kosovo* and co-authored *A Critical Approach to European Security*. He is the author of *The EC, Eastern Europe and European Unity; Managing Non-Proliferation Regimes in the 1990s*, and *Western Doctrines on East–West Trade*.

# Routledge Advances in European Politics

**Russian Messianism**
Third Rome, revolution, communism and after
*Peter J.S. Duncan*

**European Integration and the Postmodern Condition**
Governance, democracy, identity
*Peter van Ham*

# European Integration and the Postmodern Condition

## Governance, Democracy, Identity

**Peter van Ham**

London and New York

First published 2001
by Routledge
11 New Fetter Lane, London EC4P 4EE

Simultaneously published in the USA and Canada
by Routledge
29 West 35th Street, New York, NY 10001

*Routledge is an imprint of the Taylor & Francis Group*

© 2001 Peter van Ham

Typeset in Baskerville by Taylor & Francis Books Ltd
Printed and bound in Great Britain by Biddles Ltd, Guildford
and King's Lynn

*British Library Cataloguing in Publication Data*
A catalogue record for this book is available from the British Library

*Library of Congress Cataloging in Publication Data*
Ham, Peter van, 1963–
European integration and the postmodern condition: governance,
democracy, identity
Includes bibliographical references and index.
1. European Union. 2. Postmodernism–Political aspects. 3. Globalization.
4. Democracy. I. Title. II. Series.
JN30.H35 2001
341.242'2–dc21                    00-062728

ISBN 0–415–24699–7

**To Margriet, Lidewij and Thomas**

# Contents

# Preface

The ideas which this book presents on European integration and, more specifically, the new theoretical approach to understanding the nature of European politics, have been some time in the making. All scholars that want to make some sense of how the European Union (EU) is changing and shaping the economic, political, cultural and security landscape of the continent have to ask which perspectives are more useful than others, which metaphors may give us better insight in the complexity of integration, and which reading of the European political text is dominant.

Over the years, I have looked at (and through) a number of the conceptual 'lenses' that are available in the academic literature and found most of them too constricted or simply out of focus. It struck me that, although the process of European integration is unique and the developing Euro-polity without its equal, most theoretical approaches remain embedded within a pattern of traditional, state-centric concepts of politics and continue to take the classical inside/outside divide of domestic/international politics for granted. I am, however, convinced that the study of European politics requires a different, more open, eclectic and decentered approach. Such a postmodern perspective of European politics has been developed in this book, and I hope that it will serve as an intellectual springboard for those that are beginning to come to terms with the rapidly changing and expanding agenda of European political studies. Certainly, I expect to work along these lines of enquiry myself during the foreseeable future.

# Acknowledgements

I would like to express my thanks to all those who have contributed to my thinking on the study of European integration. Most of my colleagues and students (who must have heard more about this book than they would ever have chosen to) have persisted in pointing out the vague and imprecise aspects of the postmodern reading of European politics; I owe them all a large debt of gratitude, since they have helped me to escape from (at least some of) the pitfalls and hazards of postmodern analysis and made me formulate my arguments in a more lucid way. Although the book itself was written alone and in the relative solitude of the George C. Marshall Center's splendid isolation in a small-town *Kurort* in the Bavarian Alps, I want to offer my particular thanks to those who have helped in the different phases of transforming my ideas and work on European integration in this final book. I have presented different chapters (as sometimes rough drafts) during a number of conferences and seminars and have benefited from the comments and discussions that were provoked. I thank all those who offered many good suggestions, and ask their forbearance for the ones I ignored. My wife Margriet has done more than anyone else to help me over the inevitable rough spots on the always demanding road of writing a book, which is why I have dedicated it to her as well as our children.

PETER VAN HAM
Summer 2000
Garmisch-Partenkirchen

---

# 1 European integration and the challenge of postmodernity

## Global metamorphosis

In the study of International Relations (IR), most orthodox approaches have been put into question, and no coherent, new paradigm for explaining and understanding daunting recent political phenomena seems to emerge.[1] Absolute and *bona fide* scientific/ideological maxims about what the world is, how it should be understood and where it is heading for, have lost their credibility.[2] With the end of the Cold War, the central metanarrative for the West has collapsed. Globalization and the promise of a more cosmopolitan world based on a postperspectivalist compression of time/space has provoked a general crisis in the strategic discourse in the West, challenging the piety of conventional thought and politics.[3]

We (the 'we' in this book should be read as an open invitation to join me in this conversation) are plainly living in an era of no longer/but not yet. Students of politics are engaged in varied attempts to chart the end of the ancient and the beginning of the new, which have involved numerous pronouncements on the ongoing struggle to establish workable structures of governance on local, regional and global scales. This process has unleashed a vehement critique of the overly state-centric and power-oriented nature of mainstream IR, based on the argument that Realist grand theory has shown itself incapable of living up to its promises, namely predicting and adequately explaining the consequential changes in global politics (most notably, of course, the demise of the Soviet superpower and the subsequent end of the Cold War).[4] This book argues that the classic texts of IR are in many ways a lost cause and of little help in gaining a semblance of understanding of the serious challenges of contemporary European and global politics. The triviality of traditional approaches to IR is especially striking if we look at the new challenges facing mankind in an epoch where geographical entities will appear less fixed, solid and puissant than they once did, and where (most) no longer seem to control their destiny. Incessant societal transformation, embedded in a swirl of centralization and fragmentation, has problematized traditional 'problem-solving' rituals of mainstream theories, prompting a degree of intellectual vertigo that continues to bog the mind.

The 'billiard-ball' metaphor and its accompanying levels of analysis continues to look at complex political developments through the narrow lens of 'power politics', based on ahistorical assumptions and without a critical reflection of the fundamental philosophical premises of Western modernity.[5] Its traditional themes include the central role of anarchy and the balance of power, the relationship between state identity and national interests, and the (limited) possibility for change in the structures of global politics. The dichotomous conception of 'inside-outside' which underlies most accounts of mainstream IR, does not allow us to understand how the European Union (EU) is changing the economic, political, social and cultural landscape in Europe. These categorical schemes of IR theory represent knowledge of these political processes in terms of generalized and universalized systems of political behavior, reducing global events to a 'reflection' of a supposed anarchical struggle for power among states based on the rational pursuit of their national interests. This theoretical embodiment of modernist rationality has made mainstream IR theory 'the space in which knowledge and power, reason and violence are allowed, indeed encouraged, to converge'.[6]

There are few reasons to believe that these rigidly ordered patterns of understanding will be able to portray and elucidate the complex and turbulent global events we are witnessing today. Globalization and fragmentation are undermining traditional notions of community and reduce the moral significance of nation-states and inter-state boundaries. Add to the strong brew of uncertainty such factors as the end of the Cold War and a variety of other 'end' and 'post'-debates (from the 'end of' history, geography and the nation-state, to 'post'-modernism, sovereignty and positivism), and it becomes clear that what we need is a profound reappraisal of questions of ontology and epistemology – of the way we think and act in the world and how we come to understand 'reality'. This may be a global metamorphosis that not only erodes established paradigms, but that also calls for an alternative, more critical approach to the study of IR.[7] We find ourselves clearly engaged in a new debate and a new project that, depending on one's perspective, may lead us to renewal and intellectual insight and/or cause serious scientific havoc. Obviously, we are not yet able to articulate coherent concepts of politics that can capture the uniqueness of this postmodern world. But we should at least give it a try.

In this book I concern myself with the question how to study the process of European integration in the current period of paradigm shift. I do not intend to provide a comprehensive overview of contemporary approaches to the study of European integration. This has been done in a number of other places.[8] I will also not structure my work around a coherent research agenda which might offer 'empirical answers' that other scholars may use as the raw material in a process of accumulation of knowledge. My narrative of European integration is a personal one; it will result not in an all-embracing system but in nothing more (and nothing less) than an intellectual horizon that challenges and problematizes most traditional approaches. It is my intention to provide a cognitive map of the territory of academic debate which deals with the future of European integration, and 'Europe' in general. I will endeavor to delineate the changing forms of a rather chaotic surface, going back and forth between a range of disciplines, notably political science, European law and sociology. Despite this spatial disorientation, the rudimentary *leitmotif* of this book is that the nation-state as we know it today can no longer claim to be an exceptional actor in world politics; it is now one source of authority among several.[9] I argue that this requires new political and institutional frameworks beyond the state, which widen the boundaries of policy-making and the existing dialogic community. My effort is therefore closely linked to the critical project (as defined, for example, by Andrew Linklater),[10] which tries to identify the possibilities and needs for change in existing political structures and arrangements in order to create space for new political and cultural moves.

It is the progressive pressures of globalization which necessitate such a widening of the boundaries of existing political communities (most notably within the nation-state). Although globalization's risks and problems are clear (especially the deepening of material inequalities), it also opens up room to change contemporary social and political patterns and structures. For example, in much of the western world the competition for global markets has replaced the traditional quest for military power and territory. With the gradual shift of economic and political authority away from the nation-state, power has become only tangentially linked with territoriality. This gradual (and far from completed) disconnection of territoriality as a source of authority and prosperity raises a number of significant questions for the study of policy-making on the European level, and within the EU in particular. This implies that spatial modes of representation may gradually be paralleled by other forms of organization, with important implications for democratic theory and practice, the organization of European society and the place and role of Europe in the world at large. This book is concerned with all these elements of the debate and suggests how these developments and questions are interlinked and how the process of European integration takes shape in (and is itself shaped by) a globalizing world order.

Traditional theories of European integration try to explain why states have decided to integrate and have not merely opted to co-operate on an *ad hoc* basis, or chosen for other options of co-operation or even conflict.[11] They have tried to explain why the process of European integration started to take a concrete, institutionalized form after World War II, and not at an earlier or later date.

Three 'schools' have dominated the debate on these questions. First, there is the 'Idealist' school, which emphasizes the impact of persons and ideology to explain the origins and development of the European integration project. It argues, for example, that only after the destruction of World War II could a visionary political elite led by 'founding fathers' such as Jean Monnet, Robert Schuman and Konrad Adenauer, persuade European states to embark on a program of integration with the ultimate goal of European federalism. Second, there is the 'Functionalist' school (also labeled as the 'institutionalist' approach);

this emphasizes gradualism and a bottom-up approach to integration, based on the concept of 'spillover', which assumes that common policies in a 'low-politics' field will inevitably result in pressures to integrate in other policy areas, triggering a snowball effect that may well end in a federally structured Europe. Its main argument is that, although international integration may be initiated by governments, once established, they develop their own momentum and lock states into patterns of collective behavior in a search for supranational policy solutions.

Third, there is the 'Realist' school (also called the 'intergovernmentalist' approach), which emphasizes that European states have only decided to co-operate and integrate after a careful cost-benefit analysis based on clear conceptions of their 'national interests'. Each step on the way toward the current European Union has been deliberate; therefore the nation-state stays 'in control' through an ongoing process of bargaining in which the state is the principal actor. Andrew Moravcsik, one of the academic proponents of this view, argues that 'European integration resulted from a series of rational choices made by national leaders who consistently pursued their national interest ... When such interests converged, integration advanced'. This leads him to conclude that the European 'integration process did not supersede or circumvent the political will of national leaders, it reflected their will'.[12] From this Realist (or intergovernmentalist) point of view, the EU is little more than an association of convenience between a number of states that is keen on preserving national sovereignty and optimizing power and prosperity.

These two 'Why'-questions (why *integration?*, and why *now?*), continue to be central to the understanding of the European project. With only a few exceptions, scholars entering the debate on European integration have rooted their approach in one (or more) of these three traditions. Perspectives have changed over time and with academic fashion, but on the whole remain indebted to state-centric thinking and premised on stalwart notions of national interests, national sovereignty and state-based democracy. The scientific hegemony of these three 'schools' of thought has been established during the 1970s and 1980s, and much of the current intellectual vocabulary has been created during this timeframe. In the earlier phases of the academic debate, relatively few scholars have approached the EC/EU as a new and unique phenomenon, but have rather tried to understand the European project as a functional, intergovernmental structure aimed at co-operation. This attitude changed only gradually with the introduction of the Single European Act (SEA) in 1987 and the signing of the Maastricht Treaty on European Union in 1992. But these two documents are the clearest expression of an ongoing process that is now creating a new and incomparable Euro-polity: a European political community that in many cases eludes the explanatory powers of established, orthodox paradigms.[13]

In thinking through the nature and dynamics of European integration, one soon comes to realize that this process is unique. However one wants to read the EU[14] and assess what it is doing and how, it becomes apparent that the European project is quite distinct from efforts at regional co-operation and regionalization that we can see in other parts of the world. Among the multitude of regional co-operative entities (ranging from the North American Free Trade Association and Asia Pacific Economic Cooperation, to numerous subregional entities, such as the Association of Southeast Asian Nations and the *Mercado Comun del Sur* in Latin America), the EU stands out as the most cohesive, extensive and intensive form of regionalism. In contrast to other forms of regional co-operation, the EU represents a form of deep regionalism whose depth and breadth of involvement affects the daily lives of all its citizens. Despite the fact that the EU and its 'Brussels' bureaucracy may often seem detached from the concerns of Europe's wo/man 'in the street', it is the European project that is increasingly shaping the ordinary, everyday matters of households and individuals. Different also is the European rhetoric of working toward a still nebulous but certainly puissant 'ideal' of European unity – a notion that is without equivalent in any other part of the world. Europe's political and cultural convergence, in terms of democratic institutions, shared norms and secularism, has no counterpart. This European Idea(l) has its roots in historical experiences, a sense of cultural uniqueness and perhaps even a veiled missionary vision of Europe as a civilizing force in world politics. To express it more theoretically, we can say that the process of European integration is *sui generis* and that the EU represents an '*n* of 1' (i.e., there are no current analogies to the EU, which therefore escapes comparison with other international institutions).

The EU is further characterized by a conceptual ambiguity that can perhaps best be captured by the notion of 'betweenness'. It escapes traditional categories and analytical concepts, since it is neither a European government nor a straightforward common market, and falls in between politics and diplomacy, incorporating both the domestic and foreign policy agendas of its Member States. The Union also falls between IR and comparative politics theories: between democracy and autocracy, as well as between classical balance-of-power politics and a consensual system based on law and regularized procedures.[15] The European project has remained without precedent in its voluntarist approach to integration, its combination of pragmatic, piecemeal change with its long-range objective of a European federation of some sort. This is one of the reasons why Richard K. Ashley has placed the postmodern study of IR at the borders of the domestic and international realms of politics, a site which he labels a 'non-place'.[16] Both Ashley and Robert Walker have shown that the mainstream study of IR is part of the dichotomization of domestic and foreign policy. IR pictures international relations as the domain of violence and anarchy, whereas the domestic realm is seen as the place of order, progress and the peaceful resolution of conflicts.[17] Ashley and Walker further claim that IR and the study of domestic ('comparative') politics are therefore dependent upon each other. Walker even argues that IR is both cause and effect of this division, since it both reinforces and upholds the inside/outside-divide.[18] Reading the EU (as John Gerard Ruggie has done) as 'the first truly postmodern international political form',[19] means that traditional concerns of sovereignty, anarchy and power have to be revisited. Normative questions which have been reserved for the safe domain of domestic politics now also become relevant for 'Europe' as such.

All this implies that the best one can do is to approach the European integration process without preconceived notions and to analyze the EU without shoehorning its failures and shortcomings into a rigid theoretical framework that escapes scientific review. I would not like to suggest, as one scholar has urged us to do, to 'Forget IR Theory' altogether,[20] and examine the EU as a *tabula rasa*. Following Walker and Ashley, I will question (and ultimately reject) the notion that the EU can be usefully studied by accepting the classical IR inside/outside-divide. European Union studies have already gone beyond simple descriptions of IR themes which are produced as a negation of normative domestic politics; issues like 'justice', 'law', 'freedom' and 'social progress' have now gripped the 'nonplace' of EU politics. Given these developments, the main objective is to think creatively about the development of European integration and not contribute to the mass of mind-numbingly dull Euro-analysis that is hopelessly lost in bureaucratic detail, respectfully and meekly 'policy relevant', and usually remains blissfully unread, or is archived straight into the 'filing'-bin. Instead, the main objective should be to open up what has been called 'thinking space': the deliberate disposition to shed the chains of our conceptual habits.[21]

Wider thinking space and intellectual fresh air is especially looked for to make analytical sense out of current institutional developments in Europe. In these circumstances, each analyst builds his/her own personal narrative using the descriptive elements of European politics that fit his/her perspective. This should be regarded as a legitimate exercise, particularly since the political developments in contemporary post-Wall Europe offer researchers opportunities to study theoretical issues that are only just emerging and remain soft and fluid. This opens a new agenda of problems and questions that has its particular historical roots and precedents but is also new in the wide range of challenges it poses to European society. This list of issues is extensive and focuses most notably on the impact of globalization and regionalization on state sovereignty; the paradoxical and almost dialectic phenomenon of simultaneous integration and fragmentation to be witnessed in Western, Central and Eastern Europe; the development of a new European political community, characterized by multi-level governance, in which the state is making a desperate effort to cling to (and even tries to recapture) some of its legitimacy and problem-solving capacities through co-operation at the European level; and so forth. It is fair to say that these challenges still lack a new analytical framework, not just because they are different, atypical and dynamic, but perhaps first and foremost because the requisite freshness of thought, the intellectual thinking space that is so essential to make sense out of these new phenomena, has not yet been created.

David Campbell has argued that the study of international politics

> must address the basic question of whether it is adequate as a mode of understanding global life given the increasing irruptions of accelerated and nonterritorial contingencies upon our political horizons, irruptions in which

a disparate but powerful assemblage of flows – flows of people, goods, money, ecological factors, disease, etc. – contest borders, put states into question (without rendering them irrelevant), rearticulate spaces, and reform identities.

> (David Campbell, 'Political Prosaics, Transversal Politics, and the Anarchical World', in Michael J. Shapiro and Hayward R. Alker (eds), *Challenging Boundaries: Global Flows, Territorial Identities* (Minneapolis: University of Minnesota Press, 1996), p. 9)

This book makes an effort to adopt a critical attitude to the process of European integration and its discipline of European studies, trying to keep Campbell's question in mind. It does not follow a linear argument based on a number of 'testable' hypotheses, but instead attempts to sketch the contours of, and identify the key elements in, an intricate grid of often contradictory arguments and discourses. In the pages that follow I examine the contemporary condition of European integration from two general perspectives. I argue that Europe, like most of the western world, is in the midst of a shift from cultural modernity to postmodernity, and from economic modernity to postindustrial society. This dual shift affects the status and nature of knowledge and the ways we can gain some understanding of how this swirling change acts upon and transforms the role of the state, the development of a European identity and the nature and quality of democratic governance. I also argue that this phase of cultural and societal movement requires a more open and critical analysis of these new phenomena found in the body of literature captured under the catch-all term of postmodernism.

## Postmodernism and the humbling of knowledge

Postmodernism is the social, cultural and political air we breath. It permeates virtually all facets of contemporary life in the West. Like globalization, postmodernity is not merely a word or concept, it is what we are and think, how we play and enjoy. Postmodernism therefore means many things to many people. But, despite (or perhaps one should more accurately say because of) the frequent use of the term, the postmodern condition is inherently ambiguous and many-sided. Postmodernist thinkers are comfortable with this conceptual illegibility, since it illustrates their call for 'radical pluralism' with a multiplicity of voices and models of reality that all have a legitimate claim to our attention.[22] This sets the tone of postmodern thought and captures the crux of the postmodern condition. A broad spectrum of postmodern temperament offers a number of distinct insights into how to cope with the intellectual and moral uncertainty that has come to haunt western society with the passing of modernity and traditional society.[23] It would be impossible to capture the complexity and depth of postmodern thought in just a few pages, so I will summarize the main themes most relevant to our conversation on European integration and the development of European society, its culture and identity.

Postmodernism is both a condition of knowledge and the self-conscious stage in the evolution of modernity.[24] Although no causal link can be established either way, the epistemology and methodological dimensions of postmodernism and the crisis of late capitalist society have been parallel chronicles and are intimately connected.[25] Postmodernism bids farewell to the notion of comprehensive, rational knowledge and continuous progress which formed the basis of the Enlightenment. Its critique centers on the claim that the modern view explains the world in universal terms that are supposed to apply to all peoples in all places. It understands that these modern, reasoned arguments and claims to a 'universal truth' also lay at the root of catastrophes like the Gulag, the Holocaust, Hiroshima and the dubious sanctification of nuclear deterrence. Modernity is judged guilty by association of the alienation, violence and suffering which oppressive political regimes have visited upon their populations, working through modern rational planning and organization. Even Auschwitz was organized in a 'civilized' way, with the assistance of bureaucratic organization and instrumental rationality.[26] Modern scientific knowledge has lost much of its traditional credibility, since it is no longer legitimated by 'truth' but by performativity. Knowledge has degenerated and has been instrumentalized to produce an optimal input/output ratio; it is produced in order to be sold, rather than having value as an end in itself.[27]

Postmodernism can therefore be read as a shift away from the mainstream of 'modern' ways of thinking based on linear progress, rationality, and the possibility of acquiring and accumulating scientific knowledge.[28] It is at dis-ease with the assumption that history is an unending and logical process toward industrialization, urbanization, rationalization, bureaucratization and the growth of individualism within the context of state formation. Rather, it seeks to liberate modernity from its preoccupation with power, authority, hierarchy, efficiency and commercialized 'ethics'. In this sense, postmodernism declares the 'end of history' – not necessarily in the meaning of Hegel and Fukuyama, but by rejecting the notion of history as a unitary process with the 'West' at the political center of gravity. Instead, postmodernism points to a greater awareness: a different sense of historical past and of the plurality of histories from peoples that are marginalized and remain voiceless. The traditional and dominant voice of history (usually a white, male and European one) offers only a limited perspective of 'reality'. Modernity has been unable to give credence to anything it cannot perceive and sense, but today's postmodern science is postpositivist, since it 'speaks increasingly of the unseen, and does so respectfully. It tells us that matter derives from space (which is invisible until populated), and that 90 per cent of the universe is invisible'.[29] What is more, technology and speed now call for a more open and diverse approach to understanding and interpreting 'reality'. Paul Virilio, for example, claims that 'new technologies are substituting a virtual reality for an actual reality ... We are entering a world where there won't be one but two realities, just like we have two eyes or hear bass and treble tones'.[30] This also requires intellectual stereoscopy and stereophony.

Jean-François Lyotard has defined the postmodern as 'incredulity toward metanarratives'.[31] He associates the postmodern condition with the crisis in the language of the universal, the absolute, based on an eroding confidence in progress and scientific as well as religious truths. The title of this book alludes to the crises associated with the 'postmodern condition' and places them in the context of European integration. These metanarratives, or stories that claim universal status and that grant all other stories their true meaning, are now delegitimized. (Be honest: Do you know one Big Story that has not been laughed at – or, even worse, completely ignored?) Within society there is a marked decline in the credibility of the legitimating power of grand narratives or stories that people are used to telling each other about the nature of politics and science. This, Lyotard notes, has undermined the belief in the

> progressive emancipation of reason and freedom, the progressive or cata-strophic emancipation of labor ... the enrichment of all humanity through the progress of capitalist technoscience, and ... the salvation of creatures through the conversion of souls to the Christian narrative of martyred love.
> (Jean-François Lyotard, *The Postmodern Explained: Correspondence, 1982–1985* (Minneapolis: University of Minnesota Press, 1992), p. xxiv)

Postmodernism therefore rejects all totalizing world views, be they political, religious or social. Rather than Big Stories, it encourages personal(ized) *petits récits* based on individual experience and imagination. It also recognizes that (as William Pfaff has argued) 'governments as well as individuals want lies about history – or, as it may also be put, constructive oversimplifications – because these make history intelligible and seem to offer a view of the future'.[32] But there is no grand historical lie left, no grand metanarrative that can explain the world from a truly objective, disinterested perspective. There is no single, exceptional Archimedean fixed point of value-neutral pure reason from which one could credibly adjudicate rival claims and theories. There are merely particularistic and personal perspectives.[33] This follows Nietzsche's recurring insistence that 'all truth is perspectival, all seeing interpretive, all knowing interested, perspectival, and interpretive'.[34]

Perhaps the best we can hope for is to let things and people flourish in their multiple and different ways, but avoid pretending that we have the 'ultimate truth' based on scientific, general and knowable 'truth'.[35] This embraces what the Russian literary theorist Mikhail Bakhtin has termed the state of 'heteroglossia': the multiplicity of as many voices and perspectives as possible without seeking to reconcile them or to blend them into a consistent and unified story.[36] We should therefore accept and even emphasize this heteroglossia, this diversity and complexity of the multiple and overlapping concerns and readings of gender, class and other elements of identity. To accept the ineradicable plurality of global politics, not as a temporary state of demi-perfection but as a constitutive quality of political life, assumes a mental and intellectual shift in perspective. At the same time, valuing diversity does not necessarily presume incommensurability among discourses, a denial of the possibility of intersubjective understandings.[37] Rather, it calls for increased and intensified dialogue that does not aim at eliminating differences but leads to further understanding, cooperation and accommodation that can sustain differences within a broader context of tolerance and respect.[38] We shall see that these notions are especially relevant in a postmodern account of European identity (Chapter 3) and EU policy formation (Chapter 5).

Postmodernism further heralds the death of foundationalism and instead proposes *cultural relativism* (the notion that it is impossible to evaluate objectively the value of different cultures); *moral relativism* (the notion that it is impossible to evaluate different individual behavioral patterns objectively); and *truth relativism* (the notion that it is impossible objectively to evaluate competing truth claims).[39] It argues that the living community is the *locus* of any knowledge and should therefore decide for itself what is important, good and relevant. Any meaning of 'truth' is local and not universal. The emphasis should therefore be on hermeneutics (understanding and interpretation), rather than causal explanations. It argues that the only possible non-hierarchical and non-monolithic discursive approach is one that tries to decenter all claims to transcendental justifications (including its own). 'Theory', or any other form of knowledge, should therefore (merely) aim to provide persuasive narratives of specific events or offer a new horizon which includes everything that can be seen from a particular vantage point. What we accept as knowledge is always based on the private or public acceptance of a specific paradigm, mode of discourse or set of epistemological premises. Postmodernism calls for humility, since we can never know for sure that we are 'right', and we certainly can never prove to others that we are *always* 'right'. Lyotard's philosophical investigations are therefore based on the 'right to differ'. The only possible basis for politics is the protection of diversity and the support of universal doubt. Lyotard considers 'difference' as the fundamental element and central value of any political movement, disregarding the characteristic core values and issues of identity.[40] Postmodernism therefore opens the door to a radical notion of politics and identity and, once in a while, even walks through it.

Similarly, modern science is considered to be saturated with value judgements and unable to develop a 'true' picture of the 'real' world, or to discover causal networks of events. Modern science has traditionally justified the normative positions of any government it has served, using 'scientific facts' as the blunt weapons of its discourse to silence the dissenting voices of those who do not live up to their formal standards of inquiry. It is therefore 'spiritually corrosive, burning away ancient authority and traditions'.[41] Modern science is also considered to be too mechanical, being based on what Vaclav Havel has called the 'vain ratiocentrism' and the 'destructive impatience of contemporary technocratic civilization'.[42] Quite contrary to the modern notion that science can resolve uncertainties and problems of all sorts by the acquisition of knowledge, postmodernism argues that the current accumulation of knowledge actually *produces* uncertainty.[43] This undermines the possibility of manipulating society's 'variables', and thus controlling the outcomes of economic, social and political processes. Postmodernism, in short, does not whole-heartedly believe in politics. As Jean Baudrillard has claimed: 'Power itself has for a long time produced nothing but the signs of its resemblance. [It] is in essence no longer present except to conceal that there is no more power'.[44] By exposing the omissions of orthodox IR, postmodernism calls attention to a range of contemporary issues that are now exiled and find themselves beyond the boundaries of IR 'reality'. In doing so, it challenges the overwhelmingly positivist notions central to the study of IR – arguing that these epistemological questions matter, since they determine what we consider to be 'reality' in the first place, and hence what the study of global politics needs to understand and explain. In the study of global politics, postmodernists therefore tend to concentrate on what (they think) has been neglected, forgotten, subjugated, excluded, deferred and disjointed.

Postmodernism debates and produces openings for a critique of the underlying rules of contemporary political structures, thereby offering opportunities for new, radical approaches. In the study of European integration, it helps to undermine Realism as a straightforward 'problem-solving' approach and explains that Realism 'has the effect of assisting the reproduction of the very structures which many political actors regard as unjust and which they are evidently keen to transform'.[45] This not only applies to the realm of study of this book – the melange of politics, economics and society – but also to the arts (which is now proclaimed to be all-pervasive: in musea, in the street, in mass-culture as well as advertising), as well as sports and religion.[46] The erosion of all values has given way to the aestheticization of everyday life in which the (western) Protestant work ethic has been replaced by an all-dominant consumer ethic. It goes without saying that this significantly impacts upon the social fabric of society as well as the 'work' environment of the state and the very nature of politics.

## Unearthing the prosaic Europe

Postmodern Europe forms a remarkable puzzle for analysts who want to come to a better understanding of political life in all its variety and multiplicity. But in the light of the complexity of the European project, political scientists should be advised to refrain from formulating comprehensive and inclusive theories about the nature of the EU beast. Since it will be difficult to generate sufficient empirical data to 'test' hypotheses about the dynamics of European integration, accepting *one* set of theories will blind one to the multifarious evolution of Europe's political community. IR already has sufficient 'one-eyed monsters – one-eyed because they [are] oblivious of politics; monsters because they [are] so arrogant towards all outsiders'.[47] This book is therefore a call for theoretical eclecticism which takes into account the complex reality of Europe's political existence. We should be continuously on our guard, questioning *all* scientific methods of acquiring a sense of understanding of political life, since the discourse on 'knowledge' and 'truth' is open to manipulation by dominant societal interests. What we call 'reality' and 'realistic' today, may seem archaic and preposterous the day after tomorrow. Traditional grand strategies of thought and *modus operandi* should be replaced by more creative, innovative notions of authority, legitimacy, sovereignty, identity and power. The last thing we need is to replace established rational-scientific notions of global politics with another closed framework, philosophy or homogenized approach to political life.

The essence of the postmodern pursuit is therefore to develop and cultivate a new sensibility for competing interpretations of 'reality'. It accepts

> the notion that things are too complex to be grasped by any one theoretical account. The late-modern world is now variously understood to be composed of interpenetrating and multiple realities, where complexity in social, economic and political relationships is further compounded by a multitude of electronic images, disparate cultural influences, and changes in the dimensional referents of time and space due to advances in transportations and communications.
>
> (Darryl S.L. Jarvis, 'Postmodernism: A Critical Typology', in
> *Politics and Society*, vol. 26, no. 1 (March 1998), p. 105)

Every scholar of IR and European integration studies should be humbled by the mass of academic literature which tries to explain and understand new political and cultural developments. We are all truly postmodern in the sense that we accept that we can only take dip in a sea of information and ideas, failing to capture the full range of the 'true' and always dynamic features of contemporary political phenomena. As Baudrillard has noted: 'We live in a world where there is more and more information, and less and less meaning'.[48] Using multiple theoretical analytical methods and avoiding one single theoretical dimension will be essential to grasp the economic, political, social and cultural faces which represent today's world. Applying a diversity of typologies is not only heuristically useful but, I would argue, indispensable. What is left is philosophical laughter, laughter at oneself and the limits of human endeavor. Following Nietzsche's call for a 'Gay Science', only this philosophical laughter can liberate our quest for absolutes and make us accept the limits of our (postmodern) condition.[49]

Against this background, Jeffrey Anderson has claimed that 'the search for a single theoretical framework to explain the totality of institutionalized European co-operation has become a quest for the Holy Grail'.[50] A critical approach to the European project should accept the limits of any single 'theory of regional/European integration', and think in terms of open, flexible and fragmentary approaches to integration. But how should we appreciate this new openness and fragmentarity of European politics and society? Inspired by Bakhtin, Gary Saul Morson has introduced the notion of the 'prosaic' as a useful neologism for a postmodernist study of this complex political and cultural world. 'Prosaic' thinking about human events 'focuses on the ordinary, messy, quotidian facts of daily life ... [It] does not presume that behind all apparent disorder there lies a hidden order or system'. Morson further claims that such an approach 'resists the impulse of semiotic totalitarians who try to think away disorder by treating it as governed by an order not yet fully identified'.[51] This stands in stark contrast with the 'heroic politics' of Big Events, which has now come to function as the soothing drug to cure our postmodern trauma of a loss of referentials. History, with a capital H, has become a fetishism 'to escape this void, the leukemia of history and of politics, this hemorrhage of values'.[52] Heroic politics may return images of order and violence and offer illusory moorings to hitch mankind's historical progress to, but it says little about the daily lives of ordinary people, their needs and worries, their suffering and delights.

Michelangelo is said to have argued that his *David* had always been there: he just had to chip away the pieces of marble to make its artistic and physical splendor visible, to give life to beauty and order. This assumes the existence of order despite our cognitive understanding of disorder. A prosaic understanding of politics takes a different approach. It assumes that the natural state of the world – and of world politics in particular – is chaotic, and that it is order, not disorder, that needs to be explained, clarified, and at times even justified. Preference should be given to such a 'prosaic' disposition, which aims to demystify and analytically expose the delusions of grandeur of established 'grand theories' that have dominated the academic discourse. This is especially required because even a cursory examination of world politics shows that a global (or even a more modest regional) *David* does not exist. The economic and political forces chipping away 'disorderly' fragments to reveal a preordained 'order' are few and far between. A prosaic approach to politics is based on the understanding that if we do not pay attention to what is going on, ordered things get messy by themselves, but that these messy things *never* get ordered by themselves. Moreover, there are many more ways in which we can experience and imagine disorder than ways in which we can experience and imagine order. Only such a prosaic attitude can accept the panoply of voices, faces and the abundance of postmodern reality based on disorder. By thinking about human events first and foremost as unorganized, ordinary and quotidian, just like daily life, prosaics may be a useful approach to the study of global political phenomena, and to the grammar of contemporary European politics in particular.

This is why Morson argues that in

> contrast to most great systems, prosaics questions whether the most important events may not be the most ordinary and everyday ones – events that we do not appreciate simply because they are so commonplace ... Cloaked in their very ordinariness, the prosaic events that truly shape our lives – that truly *are* our lives – escape our notice.
>
> (Gary Saul Morson, 'Prosaics: An Approach to the Humanities',
> in *The American Scholar*, vol. 57, no. 4 (Autumn 1988), p. 519)

When Salman Rushdie was struck by the *fatwa* of Ayatollah Khomeini in 1989, normal routines such as shopping for groceries, taking a walk and driving a car were rendered impossible. Rushdie's testimony is illuminating: 'What I miss is just that, these tiny little things. When you have them you think they're completely unimportant or even chores ... But when you can't do them you realize that in fact that's what life is, that's real life'.[53] So with political life. Historians and political analysts obviously focus on the exceptional and dramatic events, the key moments of countries and institutions.[54] But it should be realized that they may be memorable *because* they are exceptional and outside standard and routine. It may be, however, that it is the standard and routine that is in the end shaping events and steering the process; exceptions are, after all, merely exceptions.

I would like to argue that such a postmodern, more prosaic approach to the study of contemporary political Europe, and of European integration in particular, is useful and opens up intellectual horizons. It is the EU, rather than other international organizations like NATO or the Organization for Security and Co-operation in Europe (OSCE), that is increasingly shaping people's existence and making a difference in the ordinary, familiar questions that affect quotidian life. It is the EU that is affecting the daily concerns of European citizens and denizens by dealing with such matters as food labeling, pension entitlements and maternity leave regulations. Moreover, I will also contend that the EU is developing as a prosaic political entity, rather than a standard European superpower. The archeology of European integration is bound to unearth only a prosaic Europe, a Union which focuses first and foremost on economic, social and cultural matters that concern its constituency on a daily basis. In the field of heroic politics, and especially in its efforts to develop a more cohesive European Common Foreign and Security Policy (CFSP), the EU has hardly been able to make its influence felt.[55] This may have to do with the rather simple reality that in this area Member States continue to guard their national sovereignty closely, and decisions continue to be made on the basis of unanimity (if at all). A European Common Defense Policy (CDP), as ordained by the Maastricht Treaty, remains remote, despite the advances made in the direction of a more robust and autonomous European defense capability in 1999/2000.[56]

In later chapters, I will emphasize that 'Europe', both in its cultural and political/institutional manifestation, is drenched in ambiguity, and that politics at the European level is a continuous clash between centrifugal and centripetal forces that seek to construct some meaning and order out of the disorder that has become regular reality. Europe's identity cannot be 'discovered' like Michelangelo's *David*. I will argue that the absolute dichotomy between the purported depth, fixed and final singularity of an identity which transcends and unifies spatial and temporal difference, and the surface of ephemeral human experience is not an adequate approach to the study of European politics. A critical inquiry into European integration should not look for a European 'natural structure' of identity, but should instead embrace the lack of an 'apocalyptic objectivity', of a true 'Europe'. I will also accept that in the study of

European integration, 'the recovery of a hidden identity is not the liberative enterprise it is so often proclaimed to be'.[57] Moreover, the EU decision-making process is not mechanical, is not a Newtonian, clockwork-like assemblage that can be taken apart and analyzed. Rather, if it can de described and understood at all, it is an organism with a distinct metabolism, absorbing a wide variety of power, influence, meanings and information, and ultimately returning rules, norms and action programs. Like most studies of metabolistic processes, this is neither necessarily pleasant nor, in the end, intellectually rewarding. I trust that nevertheless the reader will bear with me and join me on my theoretical journey in this book, in the hope that it will offer some academic rewards.

## Postmodern nations and other hallucinations

This (all too brief) introduction should make it clear that postmodernism not only stands for a scientific approach, but that it also refers to the *era* that parallels contemporary modernity. Again, a consensus on what this new postmodern era will have in store is adamantly lacking; it is equally unclear how the dawn of postmodernity will affect present-day international order.

The argument is made that European nation-states have developed from the late Middle Ages up to the middle of the twentieth century. These modern states were ruled first by monarchs, later by 'the people' in various forms of mass politics. Modern states have concentrated their power as clearly defined territorial and self-reliant political and cultural entities that have often developed mercantilist national programs in order to strengthen their grip on the industrial base and armed forces. In this context, nationalism has been instrumental in cultivating and forging strong, resilient and unified national identities, which made it rather easy to define the 'Other' and to mobilize the population for a wide range of military and political reasons.[58] This 'modern state', it is now widely argued, has had its day and is either 'withering away' (as Marx had already predicted in another context) or transforming itself beyond recognition. What seems to emerge from this process is a new, postmodern state. Although postmodern states still *look* very much like classical modern states, they are qualitatively different, most notably because they emphasize welfare rather than warfare.[59] In a postmodern environment, traditional concerns like borders, national identity and state sovereignty are of less concern than the pursuit of prosperity, democratic governance and individual well-being. This reflects the strong pluralist and individualist streak of postmodern society, which is tolerant to cultural and political dissent, stresses multiculturalism and legitimizes multiple identities and lifestyles. This goes hand in hand with a perceived loss of the sense of a shared historical past, which may in turn open up possibilities of forging more inclusive identities going beyond the rigid confines of the nation-state. The interconnectedness of the world also makes it difficult for individual states and societies to sustain possible illusions and fantasies of 'national superiority' and uniqueness.

The erosion of state control over the 'national' economy and civil society places limits on the range of policy options which governments can pursue in managing the state 'top-down'. In particular, the twin processes of economic globalization and European integration are accelerating the development of mature postmodern states in Western Europe; other parts of Europe and the world are still in different stages of societal formation. We should therefore not conceive the gradual major change from modernity to postmodernity as an 'epochal' or 'tectonic' shift, implying a total transformation of world politics in linear time. This would be too simple. Rather, we now witness premodern, modern and postmodern societies existing simultaneously, with some regions of the globe dominated by one phase of development, other regions by others.[60] That this may be a complicating factor in world politics, further fogging up our already hazy analytical lenses, is further discussed throughout this book.

Students of IR can no longer ignore that many orthodox concepts have lost much of their analytical value and therefore have to define their position *vis-à-vis* the challenge posed by postmodernity. Disregarding postmodernism (and other critical-reflective positions) as a potentially valuable approach is not acceptable, and it just will not do to argue that 'those who like this sort of thing will find this the sort of thing they like – those who do not, will not'.[61] It is clear that the postmodern challenge, or at least the debate about postmodernism and its analytical value and epistemic implications, is politically pertinent. Yet its intellectual importance remains clouded and highly contested. Criticism has focused on postmodernism's 'hidden claims in foggy formulations', 'vacuous linguistic affectations', and a tendency to formulate 'trivial, commonplace ideas banging at an open door'.[62] Part of this critique is certainly justified; part of it is unfounded. All in all, the intellectual muddle and elasticity of the postmodernist approach may be best explained by the intellectual premonition of change accompanied by a feeling of 'intellectual liberation', by an exultation of new scholarly approaches which transgress classical boundaries. This explains why we find postmodernist writings on architecture, geography, media, gender, religion, the study of science and philosophy, as well as within IR.

In the meantime, postmodernism offers a new, radical intellectual and political agenda. Its rejection of boundaries of any kind, whether as means of physical demarcation (separating peoples between 'us' and 'them') or as intellectual ordering devices (distinguishing between academic disciplines) should be read as a means to overcome modernist mechanisms of marginalization and exclusion of peripheral voices: the poor, women and children, racial and other minorities, artists and youth and other sub-cultures, as well as academic endeavors that try to go beyond the well-trodden path of orthodox discourse. It is broadly interdisciplinary in approach and denies that any particular methodology is better than another (although it may argue that some are more fruitful and less boring). As a result, postmodernism does not acknowledge monological interpretations of reality, rejects unifying and dominant actors like the nation-state, and has lost faith in ideas like 'progress', 'God', or any collectivist ideology. Instead, it calls attention to the multiple perspectives and overlapping identities, which necessitate a continuous process of questioning and problematization. It rejects modern science in its pursuit of categories, classifications and generalizations. In a postmodern world everything worth noting is unique and unrepeatable, which makes establishing causality problematic. Since our knowledge is grounded in language, postmodernism offers (only) interpretations and does not care for positivist considerations of locating patterns and 'hard' data. In this sense, modern universalism has been abandoned for postmodern particularism; general, *prêt-à-porter* theories and concepts have been discarded for micro-theories that are not really theories at all, but flexible approaches, analytical horizons and methods, perspectives that do not merely change, but are even *supposed* and *expected* to change almost continuously.

Attempts to capture the nature of the postmodernist movement in traditional terms tend to fail, since we might do better to imagine postmodernism not as a specific set of theories, but as a set of diverse social and intellectual tendencies whose parameters still remain to be identified. Postmodernism not only explains and understands, it largely *resists* traditional schools of thought and epistemic rules of the game. It disturbs, rather than merely comprehends. It is not so much a theoretical innovation as a means to infuse the established practices of western scholarship with some critical insight.[63] However, this continuous questioning and problematizing established truths, scientific approaches and epistemologies does not necessarily imply the negation of a workable level of knowledge and insight that offers a more comprehensive and sophisticated understanding of global space in a postmodern political context. Nor does it necessarily imply that all existing scholarly standards and methods should be thrown out of the window and exchanged for narratives that often read more like a piece of fiction than an academic tract.[64]

However, it should also be clearly said that reading the EU as a postmodern polity will not be an easy endeavor. Joseph Schumpeter once captured the liberal's dilemma by saying that s/he has to grant 'the relative validity of [his or her own] convictions and yet stand for them unflinchingly'.[65] Postmodernism's equivocality and discursiveness requires both open-mindedness and a certain intellectual tenacity. This is made even more complicated by the fact that I do not accept the postmodern understanding that human actors are powerless to implement meaningful social change and that the political dies have been cast.[66] My attempt to come to a non-positivist understanding of the European integration process is based on the acknowledgment of its complexity, and therefore seeks to construct (my) meaning from more diverse and localized points in the European political system rather than defining it in an abstract manner from above. This implies that I do not focus only on the 'real' but also on the normative aspects and issues in European politics which affect human action.

## Late/post-modernity and other critical-reflective positions

This book neither attempts to deconstruct 'Europe' or the EU, nor to use the vague postmodern vocabulary that deters and estranges so many readers who do not speak (or do not *want* to speak) 'postmodern'. Postmodernist semantics is often stilted in style and pedantic in tone. But many of the problems that are central to this book can hardly be satisfactorily analyzed within the classical frameworks of Idealist, Functionalist and Realist thinking about conflict, co-operation and integration. It can certainly be argued that, with the end of the Cold War and the onset of a new wave of globalization, the orthodox political discourse based on geographical entities, conflict and a Manichean view of world affairs has reached a terminal crisis. This, of course, explains why critical and postmodern approaches to global politics are increasingly challenging mainstream theory. This book is embedded in these new streams of international thought which comprise Critical Theory, post-structuralism, constructivism and other reflective research agendas. Although all these elements of the new debate within IR arose in reaction to the intellectual (and political) hegemony of the Realist (as well as, to a lesser extent, the Neoliberal) paradigm, the nature, degree and scope of their criticism differ markedly. Within the IR field, Critical Theory has been most successful in establishing itself as a full-fledged attack on prevailing social and power relationships. Critical Theory differs from traditional 'problem-solving' frameworks since it calls these existing structures into question, asks about their origins and investigates whether they might be in the process of changing.[67] By refusing the world as it is (or seems to be), Critical Theory is concerned with human emancipation and asks how this may be accomplished. Central figures in the articulation of the idea of Critical Theory are Jürgen Habermas and his *Frankfurter Schule*, dependency theorists, liberation theologists and many feminists, who all provide compelling arguments in support of societal and political change and insights into how this might be achieved.[68]

Constructivism is the other main challenger of Realism and Neoliberalism. Its main slogan is that 'ideas and discourse matter', and that norms, values and identity are concepts that heavily influence political life.[69] Although many (but not all) constructivists work within the conventional paradigm and use a positivist epistemology, the notion that the identities and interests of political actors are socially constructed and should not be considered as a 'given' is certainly relevant to our conversation.[70] Constructivism also implies that normative factors (including identities) shape the behavior of nation-states and that they may serve as road-maps or focal points for themselves as well as others.[71] Since identity and norms are exogenous to Realist and Neoliberal theory, constructivism helps to establish a link between postmodernism and mainstream IR by problematizing existing assumptions about how knowledge is created and anchored in politics.[72] The problem with orthodox IR is that it explains neither the processes for change in global politics nor the reasons why global politics should be constructed along Realist lines. It takes the nation-state, anarchy and sovereignty for granted, and fails to understand how change in global politics may come about (and why). Ruggie has argued that constructivism is no independent and full-fledged theory but a theoretically informed approach to the study of global politics; it does not prize deductive methods of theory-construction and does not seek to 'uncover' causalities.[73] Constructivism tries to grasp how social collectivities (nation-states as well as other political actors) give meaning to their roles and actions, adding a new spectrum of study to mainstream readings of global politics.

This book uses a broad definition of 'postmodernism'.[74] This is because I consider it useful to provide a broad orientation for the study of European integration, employing many critical perspectives, rather than being limited to one theoretical approach. I am comfortable using the label 'postmodernism', because I share its suspicion of universalizing claims, but am unwilling to replace any 'discredited' theory (even Realism) with new 'pomo'-flavoured 'certainties'. For those who consider that modernity has (at least partially) exhausted its energies for solving problems (which it has mostly created itself), the term 'late modernity' may be preferable. For those who follow the lines of thought of Derrida and Foucault, the notion of 'post-structuralism' may be better. Since these are all critical-reflective approaches to the problems of modernity and are (only) different responses to the crisis of modernity, this book celebrates them all under the heading of 'postmodernity', in the sense that they all prize difference over identity, and fragmentation over the illusion (and perils) of unity. Others may prefer the term 'reflectivist', since many of these critical approaches aim at 'first the disembedding and second the re-embedding of industrial social forms by another modernity'.[75]

However, for the time being the dominant IR discourse remains rooted in Realism (and, to a lesser extent, Neoliberalism), which consciously ignores 'non-useful' questions regarding culture, economy and identity. Instead, it focuses on the narrow goal of 'establish[ing] structure by abstraction from "concrete reality" '.[76] This Realist line of thinking remains open to critique, since it reflects a particular condition in world history, characterized by Cold-War bipolarity and modernity, which has now lost its claim to universal truth. The state-centric Realist model clearly provides the necessary analytical support for western structures of modernity and their aura of superiority and universality. By disregarding economic, societal and cultural factors, and by rejecting the power of ideas and tradition, Realism has come under attack for providing scholarly apologies for maintaining the status quo and for consciously discarding other approaches and explanations, thereby deliberately oppressing dissonant voices. Critics have argued that it provides the basic patterns of thinking which has been designed 'primarily for violent response and big-power coercion rather than for prevention and sensitive negotiation'.[77] Realism may have had its value for understanding and explaining the historical phase of modernity in which the nation-state and its ideological counterpart of nationalism were dominant, but it hardly offers the appropriate analytical tools for coping with the challenges posed by a new, postmodern era.

Our reasoning about sovereignty, the role of the state, democracy and citizenship, the development of a supra-national political polity, and federalism, order and chaos must therefore go beyond the intellectual horizons that have limited our perspective for so long. By applying specific analytic frameworks for analysis, scholars and policy-makers inevitably put on blinkers, instead of using multiple paradigms, skipping among frameworks. Ruggie has correctly argued that the 'prevailing modes of analytical discourse simply lack the requisite vocabulary'.[78] Orthodox theories of European integration have developed their own discursive boundaries and have established strict rules of intellectual exchange and defined methods of acceptable scientific analysis that excludes an array of other (equally legitimate) approaches. By their very nature, all discourses of European integration apply an analytical framework that in a subtle way determines our thinking process, and, by doing so, places certain boundaries on what can be thought and what can be written.

This is especially problematic because the dominance of existing categories of analysis (the state, sovereignty) tend to limit our creative ability when thinking about the future organization of a Europe that may go 'beyond the nation-state'. The orthodox IR idiom is marked with Cold-War tattoos of misplaced pride and prejudice that continue to blemish the global political tissue. Most analysts, and certainly most policy-makers, fail to reconceptualize the sovereign state on a transnational level, but instead tend to think about the EU as a 'state writ large' which merely mirrors the qualities and drawbacks of the traditional nation-state. The simple fact that we continue to formulate certain actors as 'something-national' (*sub*national, *supra*national, or *trans*national), indicates that our analytical thinking remains based on the hegemony of the 'nation-state'. The same applies to the use of concepts like *pre*modern and *post*modern, which testify to the continued centrality of the modern norm. Although this is not without reason (most importantly because it facilitates communication), one has to acknowledge that new concepts may be necessary to cope with a qualitatively different set of political problems. One alternative concept is the notion of 'transversal' politics (used by Foucault) to refer to relations that are not limited to one country. This term is useful, since it avoids reference to national boundaries and does not immediately focus our thoughts on the state-centered political problematic.[79] All in all, it should be clear that using a hammer and nails to fix your personal computer tends to be both frustrating and useless; bringing 'modern' concepts to bear on contemporary European politics will be equally unrewarding.

In many ways this is a quite normal process which should not be dramatized, albeit the 'requisite vocabulary' we have come to use in IR and the study of European integration should be upgraded. Lyotard has therefore argued that 'it is our business not to supply reality but to *invent allusions* to the conceivable which cannot be presented'.[80] If we are prepared to consider this IR vocabulary as the Microsoft Windows® of the dominant discourse – as the code we use for both analysis and communication – we must accept that such a regular 'upgrade' is hardly a revolutionary matter. Rather, it should be seen as a reformation, firmly grounded in day-to-day reality, which at the same time challenges the foundation of many core articles of the IR faith. Again, although no intellectual revolution may be required, we should accept that a number of concepts and basic elements of analysis must be questioned and problematized. We should be prepared to ask how relevant these concepts continue to be in providing some understanding of the contemporary world. Is it not necessary to add new dimensions to the dominant 'reality' and to analyze the power/knowledge nexus by *re*formulating the main questions of IR? Perhaps we should devise and enlarge the existing vocabulary, making it possible to think beyond lines that are now conceptual dead ends?[81]

Although this book will not try to introduce this 'requisite vocabulary' for the study of European integration, it will make an effort to go beyond the current intellectual perimeters that have been established by traditional IR concepts and semantics. I will especially problematize the European context of the inside/outside-dichotomy and the still prevailing notion that an anarchical world ('outside') contrasts sharply with the rational and ordered world of domestic life ('inside'). When we accept that policy-making in the EU is non-hierarchical, based on a continuous process of bargaining and power-brokering, that it is fragmented in different institutional settings, involves sub-state, state and transversal actors, that it is based on pragmatism and comitology and that it aims to embed the nation-state in Europe's deep regionalism, we are describing a political entity that has gone beyond the nation-state and that to all intents and purposes deserves qualification as 'postmodern'. This postmodern European proposition claims to be best suited to come to grips with the epochal changes we are witnessing today. These changes in the fields of technology, transportation, trade and culture all affect the political, economic and social 'realities' as we perceive them. This world – which is gradually shifting toward a postmodern condition, with 'new' economic, political, spatial and non-spatial modes of representation – requires a commensurate shift in conceptual approach and calls for a postmodern theoretical apparatus able to make sense of these new phenomena.

This book argues that the study of European integration should make a serious effort to come to terms with postmodernity. I realize that it is certainly not going to be an unembarrassing process to shed antiquated ideas and intellectual categories of thought and modes of work; nor will it be easy to assimilate new ones. Postmodern scholars have difficulty in breaking the pattern of traditional thought, and their critics in traditional IR have trouble in understanding what it is these postmodernists are actually talking about. Be that as it may, I consider it useful and necessary to imbue European studies with postmodern thinking, and I will argue that this can make our insight into contemporary European politics richer and more meaningful, and might ultimately establish a novel tradition of acquiring understanding by asking new questions, reformulating existing answers and reworking assessments based on new learning and new practical experiences.[82] In order to achieve this aim, European studies must recognize itself as a tradition in the postmodern sense. It should not consider itself the rival of other approaches, but merely as another way of looking at European events, as a particular way of analyzing and understanding human affairs, and one way of investigating policy. Although it should not shy away from making value judgements, postmodern European studies should remain aware of its own epistemological baggage, its belief system. It should continuously scrutinize its own notions of the good, true and beautiful, but realize that these represent merely one set of perspectives among many. It should not only try to come to a more profound and sophisticated understanding of European society and events, but should also be aware that its interpretations may (and almost inevitably will) be (ab)used for reconstructing politics, economics and new modes of social control. Finally, postmodern European studies should be, and should remain, open, allowing conversation to flourish and new phrases and moves to be made. There is no need to listen to His Master's Voice; there is no need for extended soliloquy.

In many ways postmodernists may behave like Toto, the small dog in *The Wizard of Oz,* 'who pulls back the curtains of the Holy of Holies and sees the all-too human wizard from Kansas generating his own *mysterium tremendum* at a microphone'.[83] Clearly, the Cartesian solemnity of modern science has now been unmasked and shown for what it is: an all-too-simple and hegemonic construct of reality, producing tremendous noise to make us believe in its ideology of transcendent omnipotence. Postmodern social science crosses these intellectual boundaries and offers a stage for the continuous interaction of 'old' and 'new' scientific traditions. This will in the first instance be a *philosophical* stage for living out theories in praxis and to consummate personal and societal self-realization through discourse. We will have to see what will happen next.

Campbell has redefined the study of international politics as a 'philosophical anthropology of everyday life on a global scale'.[84] This acknowledges that more space is required for the study of a contemporary Europe that goes beyond traditional power politics and imposed identity, but instead looks out for the Europe that is now engaged in the dynamic process of reframing its meaning and message. More modestly, this study makes an effort to come to an under-standing of the vastness of political life on a European scale, reading the process of European integration as a postmodern attempt at framing disorder. In doing so, it only scratches at the surface of many complex and varied problematics. But, as Zygmunt Bauman has argued, social science 'does not have any credentials to make prophetic statements. Social scientists who use their authority to make predictions are false prophets. All we can do is to speculate about various possibilities'.[85] This is what this book attempts to do.

### Notes

1 The term 'International Relations' (IR) refers to the traditional study of global political processes as understood in the West, and primarily in the Anglo-American part of the world. For many it has become synonymous with a universalized and essentialized 'reality' of global life and represented in a particular kind of theoretical framework based on 'Realism'.

2 For an acknowledgement from the Realist spectrum of IR, see Robert Jervis, 'The Future of World Politics: Will It Resemble the Past?', in *International Security*, vol. 16, no. 3 (Winter 1991), p. 39.

3 Pheng Cheah and Bruce Robbins (eds), *Cosmopolitics: Thinking and Feeling Beyond the Nation* (Minneapolis: University of Minnesota Press, 1998); Gearoid O Tuathail, 'At the End of Geopolitics? Reflections on a Plural Problematic at the Century's End', in *Alternatives*, vol. 22, no. 1 (January/March 1997), and Jane Flax, *Thinking Fragments: Psychoanalysis, Feminism, and Postmodernism in the Contemporary West* (Berkeley: University of California Press, 1991), p. 6.

4 John Lewis Gaddis, 'International Relations Theory and the End of the Cold War', in *International Security*, vol. 17, no. 3 (Winter 1992).

5 Kenneth N. Waltz's *Man, the State and War: A Theoretical Analysis* (New York: Columbia University Press, 1959) is obviously the classical text of this approach.

6 R.B.J. Walker, 'Genealogy, Geopolitics and Political Community: Richard K. Ashley and the Critical Social Theory of International Politics', in *Alternatives*, vol. 13, no. 1 (January 1988), p. 87.

7 Przemyslaw Grudzinski and Peter van Ham, *A Critical Approach to European Security: Identity and Institutions* (London: Cassell Academic, 1999).

8 For recent additions to a vast literature, see Carolyn Rhodes and Sonia Mazey, 'Introduction: Integration in Theoretical Perspective', and James A. Caporaso and John T.S. Keeler, 'The European Union and Regional Integration Theory', both in Carolyn Rhodes and Sonia Mazey (eds), *The State of the European Union: Building a European Polity?* (Boulder CO: Lynne Rienner, 1995).

9 For a strong case of this assertion, see Susan Strange, *The Retreat of the State: The Diffusion of Power in the World Economy* (Cambridge: Cambridge University Press, 1996).

10 Andrew Linklater's book *The Transformation of Political Community* (Columbia SC: University of South Carolina Press, 1998), is the most eloquent expression of the critical project to extend the concept of political community beyond the nation-state.

11 For a standard overview, see Andrew Moravcsik, *The Choice for Europe: Social Purpose and State Power From Messina to Maastricht* (Ithaca NY: Cornell University Press, 1998).

12 *Ibid.*, pp. 3, 4.

13 This case is made by Kenneth Armstrong and Simon Bulmer in their *The Governance of the Single European Market* (Manchester: Manchester University Press, 1998).

14 Thomas Diez, *Die EU Lesen: Diskursive Knotenpunkte in der britischen Europadebatte* (Opladen: Leske & Budrich, 1999).

15 Brigid Laffan, 'The European Union: A Distinctive Model of Internationalisation', in *European Integration online Papers (EIoP)*, vol. 1, no. 18 (1997); available HTTP: http://eiop.or.at/eiop/texte/1997-018a.htm (accessed 2 August 2000).

16 Richard K. Ashley, 'Untying the Sovereign State: A Double Reading of the Anarchy Problematique', in *Millennium: Journal of International Studies*, vol. 17, no. 2 (Summer 1988), pp. 227–49.

17 Lene Hansen, 'R.B.J. Walker and International Relations: Deconstructing a Discipline', in Iver B. Neumann and Ole Wæver (eds), *The Future of International Relations: Masters in the Making?* (London: Routledge, 1997), p. 317.

18 R.B.J. Walker, *Inside/Outside: International Relations as Political Theory* (Cambridge: Cambridge University Press, 1993).

19 John G. Ruggie, 'Territoriality and Beyond: Problematizing Modernity in International Relations', in *International Organization*, vol. 47, no. 1 (Winter 1993).

20 Roland Bleiker, 'Forget IR Theory', in *Alternatives*, vol. 22, no. 1 (January/March 1997).

21 Jim George, 'International Relations and the Search for Thinking Space: Another View of the Third Debate', in *International Studies Quarterly*, vol. 33, no. 3 (September 1989).

22  As Bleiker noted: 'One cannot eliminate the contradictory, the fragmentary, and the discontinuous. Contradictions are only contradictions if one assumes the existence of a prior universal standard of reference … Contradictions are to be preferred over artificially constructed meanings and the silencing of underlying conflicts'. See Bleiker, 'Forget IR Theory', p. 71.

23  For an overview of postmodern thought and its relevance for the social sciences, see Pauline Marie Rosenau, *Post-Modernism and the Social Sciences: Insights, Inroads and Intrusions* (Princeton NJ: Princeton University Press, 1992).

24  John W. Tate, 'Kant, Habermas, and the "Philosophical Legitimation" of Modernity', in *Journal of European Studies*, vol. 27, no. 3 (September 1997).

25  Fredric Jameson, *Postmodernism: Or, the Cultural Logic of Late Capitalism* (Durham NC: Duke University Press, 1992).

26  Zygmunt Bauman, *Modernity and the Holocaust* (Ithaca NY: Cornell University Press, 1989).

27  The uncertainty of science (even the 'hard' sciences) is now widely debated. See especially Andrew Pickering, *Constructing Quarks: A Sociological History of Particle Physics* (Chicago: University of Chicago Press, 1999); Bruno Latour, *Science in Action: How to Follow Scientists and Engineers Through Society* (Cambridge MA: Harvard University Press, 1987); and Bruce Mazlish, *The Uncertain Sciences* (New Haven CT: Yale University Press, 1998).

28  For critical comments on the traditional practice of IR theory, see Richard K. Ashley and R.B.J. Walker, 'Reading Dissidence/Writing the Discipline: Crisis and the Question of Sovereignty in International Studies', in *International Studies Quarterly*, vol. 34, no. 3 (September 1990); Andrew Linklater, 'The Question of the Next Stage in International Relations Theory: A Critical-Theoretical Point of View', in *Millennium: Journal of International Studies*, vol. 21, no. 1 (Spring 1992); Jim George, 'Of Incarceration and Closure: Neo-Realism and the New/Old World Orders', in *Millennium: Journal of International Studies*, vol. 22, no. 2 (Summer 1993); Chris Brown, 'Turtles All the Way Down: Anti-Foundationalism, Critical Theory and International Relations', in *Millennium: Journal of International Studies*, vol. 23, no. 2 (Summer 1994); John MacMillan and Andrew Linklater (eds), *Boundaries in Question: New Directions in International Relations* (New York: St Martin's Press, 1995); and Darryl S.L. Jarvis, *International Relations and the Challenge of Post-Modernism: Defending the Discipline* (Columbia SC: University of South Carolina Press, 2000).

29  Huston Smith, 'The Ambiguity of Matter', in *Cross Currents*, vol. 48, no. 1 (Spring 1998).

30  Interview by Louise Wilson with Paul Virilio, 'Cyberwar, God and Television: Interview With Paul Virilio' (1 December 1994). Online. Available HTTP: http://ctheory.com (accessed 29 March 2000).

31  Jean-François Lyotard, *The Postmodern Condition: A Report on Knowledge* (Minneapolis: University of Minnesota Press, 1984), p. xxiv.

32  William Pfaff, 'The Reality of Human Affairs', in *World Policy Journal*, vol. 14, no. 2 (Summer 1997), p. 89.

33  R.P. Peerenboom, 'Reasons, Rationales, and Relativisms: What's At Stake in the Conversation Over Scientific Rationality?', in *Philosophy Today*, vol. 34, no. 1 (Spring 1990).

34  C. Ellsworth Hood, 'Nietzsche Contra Postmodernism', in *Philosophy Today*, vol. 41, no. 3 (Fall 1997), p. 424.

35  Heikki Patomäki, 'How to Tell Better Stories About World Politics', in *European Journal of International Relations*, vol. 2, no. 1 (March 1996).

36  Mikhail M. Bakhtin, 'Discourse in the Novel', in Mikhail M. Bakhtin, *The Dialogic Imagination: Four Essays* (Austin: University of Texas Press, 1981), pp. 271–82.

37  Dean C. Hammer, 'Incommensurable Phrases and Narrative Discourse: Lyotard and Arendt on the Possibility of Politics', in *Philosophy Today*, vol. 41, no. 4 (Winter 1997).

38 Nicholas C. Burbules and Suzanne Rice, 'Dialogue Across Differences: Continuing the Conversation', in *Harvard Educational Review*, vol. 61, no. 4 (November 1991); and Iris Marion Young, 'The Ideal of Community and the Politics of Difference', in Linda J. Nicholson (ed.), *Feminism/Postmodernism* (London/New York: Routledge, 1990).

39 On these issues, see John Rothfork, 'Postmodern Ethics: Richard Rorty and Michael Polanyi', in *Southern Humanities Review*, vol. 29, no. 1 (Winter 1995), and Neta C. Crawford, 'Postmodern Ethical Conditions and a Critical Response', in *Ethics & International Affairs*, vol. 12 (1998).

40 For this element of Lyotard's work, see Tim Jordan, 'The Philosophical Politics of Jean-François Lyotard', in *Philosophy of the Social Sciences*, vol. 25, no. 3 (September 1995).

41 Bryan Appleyard, 'Post-Scientific Society', in *New Perspectives Quarterly*, vol. 10, no. 3 (Summer 1993).

42 Vaclav Havel, 'Speech to the Academy of Humanities and Political Science in Paris, France', 27 October 1992' available HTTP: http://www.hrad.cz/president/Havel/speeches/1992/2710uk.html (accessed 2 August 2000).

43 Ulrich Beck, *Risk Society: Towards a New Modernity* (London: Sage, 1992).

44 Jean Baudrillard, *Simulacra and Simulation* (Ann Arbor: University of Michigan Press, 1994), pp. 23, 26.

45 Linklater, *The Transformation of Political Community*, p. 21.

46 Neil Blain, Raymond Boyle and Hugh O'Donnell, *Sport and National Identity in the European Media* (Leicester: Leicester University Press, 1993) – especially Chapter 1; Paul Heelas and David Martin (eds), *Religion, Modernity and Postmodernity* (Oxford: Blackwell, 1998): and Edith Wyschogrod and John D. Caputo, 'Postmodernism and the Desire For God: An E-Mail Exchange', in *Cross Currents*, vol. 48, no. 3 (Fall 1998).

47 Susan Strange, 'An Eclectic Approach', in Craig N. Murphy and Roger Tooze (eds), *The New International Political Economy* (Boulder CO: Lynne Rienner, 1991), p. 33.

48 Baudrillard, *Simulacra and Simulation*, p. 79.

49 Friedrich Nietzsche, *The Gay Science* (New York: Vintage Books, 1974), and Noel O'Sullivan, 'Nietzsche and the Agenda of Post-Modernity', in *History of European Ideas*, vol. 20, nos 1–3 (1995).

50 Jeffrey J. Anderson, 'The State of the (European) Union', in *World Politics*, vol. 47, no. 3 (April 1995), p. 465.

51 Gary Saul Morson, 'Prosaics: An Approach to the Humanities', in *The American Scholar*, vol. 57, no. 4 (Autumn 1988), p. 516.

52 Baudrillard, *Simulacra and Simulation*, p. 44.

53 Quoted in Giles Gunn, 'Rorty's Novum Organum', in *Raritan*, vol. 10, no. 1 (Summer 1990), pp. 99–101.

54 Foucault has argued that 'A few years ago, historians were very proud to have discovered that they could write not only the history of battles, of kings and institutions, but also of the economy. Now they're all dumbfounded because the shrewdest among them learned that it was also possible to write the history of feelings, of behaviors and bodies. Soon they'll understand that the history of the West cannot be dissociated from the way in which "truth" is produced and inscribes its effects'. Quoted in Thomas R. Flynn, 'Foucault and the Spaces of History', in *Monist*, vol. 74, no. 2 (April 1991).

55 Jan Zielonka, *Explaining Euro-Paralysis: Why Europe is Unable to Act in International Politics* (New York: St Martin's Press, 1998).

56 For an overview, see Laurence Martin and John Roper (eds), *Towards a Common Defence Policy* (Paris: WEU Institute for Security Studies, 1995), and Peter van Ham, 'Europe's New Defense Ambitions: Implications for NATO, the US, and Russia', Marshall Center Paper Series, no. 1 (Garmisch-Partenkirchen, June 2000).

57  Richard K. Ashley, 'The Geopolitics of Geopolitical Space: Toward a Critical Social Theory of International Politics', in *Alternatives*, vol. 12, no. 4 (October 1987), p. 408.

58  'Otherness' (or the 'Other'), is mainly used to indicate the we have (in principle) no right to speak for (or perhaps even to speak *about*) others. But if we do speak about them, we always construct them in our own image, inevitably rereading the Other in our own grammar and overlooking the Other's difference and particularity.

59  Peter van Ham and Przemyslaw Grudzinski, 'Affluence and Influence: The Conceptual Basis of Europe's New Politics', in *The National Interest*, no. 58 (Winter 1999/2000).

60  Richard Falk, *Exploration at the Edge of Time: The Prospects for World Order* (Philadelphia: Temple University Press, 1993), p. 23.

61  Quoted in Darryl S.L. Jarvis, 'Postmodernism: A Critical Typology', in *Politics and Society*, vol. 26, no. 1 (March 1998).

62  Oyvind Osterud, 'Antinomies of Postmodernism in International Studies', in *Journal of Peace Research*, vol. 33, no. 4 (November 1996).

63  R.B.J. Walker and Richard K. Ashley, 'Speaking the Language of Exile: Dissidence in International Studies', special issue of *International Studies Quarterly*, vol. 34, no. 3 (September 1990).

64  Foucault, in a famous phrase, has noted that 'I am aware that I have not written anything but fictions'. See Michel Foucault, 'Two Lectures', in Colin Gordon (ed.), *Power/Knowledge: Selected Interviews and Other Writings* (New York: Pantheon, 1980), p. 193.

65  Quoted in Gunn, 'Rorty's Novum Organum', pp. 92–3.

66  For a feminist critique of postmodernism which shares this position, see Barbara Epstein, 'Why Poststructuralism is a Dead End For Progressive Thought', in *Socialist Review*, vol. 25, no. 2 (1995), and Val Codd, 'Postmodernism Obfuscates Reality: No Room For Activism', in *Off Our Backs*, vol. 29, no. 8 (August/September 1999).

67  Brown, 'Turtles All the Way Down'. For a concise introduction related to the study of security, see Michael C. Williams and Keith Krause, 'Preface: Toward Critical Security Studies', in Keith Krause and Michael C. Williams (eds), *Critical Security Studies* (Minneapolis: University of Minnesota Press, 1997).

68  Stephen T. Leonard, *Critical Theory in Political Practice* (Princeton NJ: Princeton University Press, 1990).

69  Yosef Lapid and Friedrich Kratochwil (eds), *The Return of Culture and Identity in IR Theory* (Boulder CO: Lynne Rienner, 1996); Alexander Wendt, 'Anarchy is What States Make of It: The Social Construction of Power Politics', in *International Organization*, vol. 46, no. 2 (Spring 1992); and Emanuel Adler, 'Seizing the Middle Ground: Constructivism in World Politics', in *European Journal of International Relations*, vol. 3, no. 3 (September 1997).

70  Alexander Wendt has tried to bridge Neorealism and the constructivist position in his *Social Theory of International Politics* (Cambridge: Cambridge University Press, 1999).

71  Ronald L. Jepperson, Alexander Wendt and Peter J. Katzenstein, 'Norms, Identity, and Culture in National Security', in Peter J. Katzenstein (ed.), *The Culture of National Security: Norms and Identity in World Politics* (New York: Columbia University Press, 1996).

72  Steve Smith, 'The Self-Images of a Discipline: A Genealogy of International Relations Theory', in Ken Booth and Steve Smith (eds), *International Relations Theory Today* (Cambridge: Polity Press, 1995), and Steve Smith, 'Positivism and Beyond', in Steve Smith, Ken Booth and Marysia Zalewski (eds), *International Theory: Positivism and Beyond* (Cambridge: Cambridge University Press, 1996).

73  John G. Ruggie, 'What Makes the World Hang Together? Neo-Utilitarianism and the Social Constructivist Challenge', in *International Organization*, vol. 52, no. 4 (Autumn 1998). See also Wendt, *Social Theory of International Politics*.

74  Mathias Albert, ' "Postmoderne" und Theorie der internationalen Beziehungen', in *Zeitschrift für Internationale Beziehungen*, vol. 1, no. 1 (1994), and Thomas Diez, 'Post-

moderne und europäische Integration: Die Dominanz des Staatmodells, die Verant-wortung gegenüber dem anderen und die Konstruktion eines alternativen Horizonts', in *Zeitschrift für Internationale Beziehungen*, vol. 3, no. 3 (1996).

75  Ulrich Beck, 'The Reinvention of Politics: Towards a Theory of Reflexive Modernization', in Ulrich Beck, Anthony Giddens and Scott Lash, *Reflexive Moderni-zation: Politics, Tradition and Aesthetics in the Modern Social Order* (Stanford CA: Stanford University Press, 1994), p. 2.

76  In his *Theory of International Politics* (New York: McGraw-Hill, 1979), p. 80, Kenneth N. Waltz here quotes the anthropologist Meyer Fortes.

77  Jim George, 'Understanding International Relations After the Cold War: Probing Beyond the Realist Legacy', in Michael J. Shapiro and Hayward R. Alker (eds), *Challenging Boundaries: Global Flows, Territorial Identities* (Minneapolis: University of Minnesota Press, 1996), p. 35.

78  Efforts to develop such a new vocabulary have been made by Philippe Schmitter. See Schmitter, 'The European Community as an Emergent and Novel Form of Political Domination', Juan March Institute Working Paper Series, no. 26 (Madrid, 1991); Schmitter, 'Representation and the Future Euro-Polity', in *Staatswissenschaften und Staatspraxis*, vol. 3, no. 3 (1992), and Franz Traxler and Philippe C. Schmitter, 'The Emerging Euro-Polity and Organized Interest', in *European Journal of International Relations*, vol. 1, no. 2 (June 1995). See also James A. Caporaso, 'The European Union and Forms of State: Westphalian, Regulatory or Post-modern?', in *Journal of Common Market Studies*, vol. 34, no. 1 (March 1996), and Ruggie, 'Territoriality and Beyond'.

79  Ashley, 'The Geopolitics of Geopolitical Space', note 7 on p. 430.

80  Lyotard, *The Postmodern Condition*, p. 81.

81  Zygmunt Bauman, for example, has offered a whole range of vocabulary to capture the postmodern experience, trying to liberate us from conventional sociological concepts such as 'society', 'socialization' and 'community'. See Bauman, *Intimations of Postmodernity* (London: Routledge, 1992). For some, therefore, postmodern accounts may be more theoretically elegant than politically plausible.

82  The following is inspired by the little checklist offered by Roland Hoksbergen in his 'Postmodernism and Institutionalism: Toward a Resolution of the Debate on Relativ-ism', in *Journal of Economic Issues*, vol. 28, no. 3 (September 1994).

83  Regina Schwartz, 'Monotheism and the Violence of Identities', in *Raritan*, vol. 14, no. 3 (Winter 1995).

84  David Campbell, 'Political Prosaics, Transversal Politics, and the Anarchical World', in Michael J. Shapiro and Hayward R. Alker (eds), *Challenging Boundaries: Global Flows, Territorial Identities* (Minneapolis: University of Minnesota Press, 1996), p. 24.

85  Zygmunt Bauman, 'Modernity, Postmodernity and Ethics – An Interview With Zygmunt Bauman' (no author), in *Telos*, no. 93 (Fall 1992).

# 2 Globalization and Europeanization

## Parallel processes (parallel puzzles)?

### Globalization: The dominance of a discourse

Robert Walker has rightly reminded us that it is a grand cliché of modernity to claim that we live in an 'era of rapid transformations': 'Ever since the possibility of a progressive history was elaborated during the European Enlightenment, modern thinkers have struggled to grasp the succession of events as an unfolding of a more or less reasonable, even rational process'.[1] More often than not, the process of globalization is portrayed as such an inevitable, unstoppable phenomenon, which will in due course encompass the world in its totality. Most western political leaders follow this line of argument, noting that 'globalization and the technology revolution are not policy choices; they are facts', adding that the 'forces of global integration are a great tide, inexorably wearing away the established order of things'.[2] Typically, these 'forces' are considered as anonymous, faceless and beyond the control of individual nation-states and (regional) organizations. Globalization is assumed to be fast making all existing maps of the political world useless, obsolete, and in the process is threatening to erode our understanding of international relations. The global market is rapidly reconstructed into a deity whose Invisible Hand is correcting the dysfunctions of late capitalism. The new catechism of global free trade is constantly reiterated by most western media and politicians, endowing it with a rather intimidating authority. Globalization now constitutes a dominant paradigm in international politics and has turned into a hegemonic discourse which gives meaning to both old and new categories of thought. As Ignacio Ramonet has argued, globalization is becoming a 'One Idea System', the new post-Cold-War dogma.[3] No western country harbors any illusions of halting this 'tidal wave' of globalization; Don Quixote clearly will not ride again.

Globalization as the inevitable course of history, bringing economic development, peace and stability to every corner of the world may soothe the western mind. But recent developments, recent academic publications and popular protestations have raised our awareness that the spread of a 'global culture' based on individualism and consumerism does not appeal to everyone. The bombing of US Embassies in Tanzania and Kenya in August 1998 (and the subsequent air strikes by the United States on alleged terrorist targets in Afghanistan and the Sudan), has dramatically highlighted how ferociously anti-American and anti-western Islamic extremist groups may react to what they perceive to be a threat of global American economic/cultural hegemony. The tens of thousands of protesters who descended on Seattle in December 1999, rallying against the World Trade Organization's attempts to push economic globalization forward, clearly made the point that these issues are no longer decided through back-room deals by an anonymous political elite.[4] Benjamin Barber's book called *Jihad vs. McWorld*, as well as Samuel Huntington's more controversial thesis of a looming 'clash of civilizations', provide provocative accounts of a dynamic struggle between 'the West' as the proponent of globalization, and an Islamic world in the 'South' which sees its religious and ethnic identity challenged.[5] It is clear that despite the apparent triumphalism of the globalization discourse, questions about the profits and costs – who benefits and suffers – are as relevant as ever.

This raises the question of the place of the process of European integration in the global context of increased economic interdependence. How do the global puzzle and the European puzzle relate to each other? One thing is immediately apparent: that the political rhetoric of proponents of European integration is also based on a notion of 'historical logic', a 'logic' that is working (on a more modest, regional scale) toward European unity and federalism. In this respect there is an analytical parallel to be drawn between the processes of globalization and European integration, each following the fundamental, unwritten but clearly understood laws of late capitalism.[6] But, before examining the characteristics of Europeanization, it will be necessary to come to grips with what globalization really means, what its societal implications are, how it affects the modern state-centric framework in general and the European system in particular.

Like postmodernism itself, 'globalization' has become something of a catch-all concept that 'serves to explain everything from the woes of the German coal industry to the sexual habits of Japanese teenagers'.[7] This is, indeed, a rather broad spectrum, and few concepts can claim to shed light on it. The dominant discourse of globalization is economic in nature, but it has dramatic and far-ranging political and societal consequences. The political economy of globalization is a booming academic discipline which (as Fredric Jameson has argued) has made the study of capital our true ontology, turning it into a 'new world system, the third stage of capitalism, which is for us the absent totality, Spinoza's God or Nature, the ultimate (indeed, perhaps the only) referent, the true ground of Being of our own time'.[8] Globalization has in many ways become a new and comprehensive narrative that aims to map the innumerable realities of world politics. Modernity's secular liberal ethos has demolished the bounds of human freedom, opening the door to a kaleidoscopic display of moral and intellectual chaos that comes from having all freedom without concrete boundaries. In this context, globalization has become an allegory for expressing the absent and unrepresentable totality of global processes.

More often than not, globalization refers to both the reality and the subjective feeling of a 'global compression', a condensation of time and space in which a world is increasingly perceived as 'one place'. To many, late capitalist society feels like a 24-hour economy that has lost its clock. The escalating density and speed of the flows of money, goods, information and images has a centrifugal effect on all aspects of human activity. It involves the notion that even the most prosaic economic, social, cultural and political activities are increasingly influenced by events happening on the other side of the world, so that the practices of small groups and institutions may sometimes have significant global consequences. With globalization, the sense of spatial separation between people is eroding – with the paradoxical consequence that increased awareness of the finitude of our planet and its humanity has not produced a commensurate sense of homogeneity, but instead has made us aware of the rich diversity of cultures, mores and ways of life.[9] Globalization goes hand in hand with a parallel process of individualization, which refers to 'the widening and deepening of the principle of individual self-determination accompanied by a dissolution of traditional alignments and the tendency to evaluate things on the basis of individual cost-benefit calculations'.[10]

Globalization may therefore be read (if you wish) as a dialectical process in which homogenizing forces may bring with them a new emphasis on difference and diversity. Globalization is most evident in the developed-market economies of the West and most visible in the relocation of industrial plants and companies around the globe (which might explain the 'woes of the German coal industry'). We are therefore witnessing the transmogrification of a world dominated by nation-based capitalism into a new phase of cosmopolitan capitalism, global in its scope and logic. At the same time, globalization should not be read as a static condition, nor as a linear process of capitalist development; it is not to be thought of as a final end point of social organization.

But globalization also encompasses a broad range of non-material aspects of production, management, finance and communication. It informs the pervasiveness of western-style consumer culture based on transnational images, signs, values and norms that urges the 'global citizen' to adopt western moral principles (which might explain 'the sexual habits of Japanese teenagers'). Globalization should be thought of as a multidimensional phenomenon which applies to most domains of human activity and includes economical, political and military, as well as cultural, legal, technological and ecological sites of social activity. New technologies like the Internet, email, satellite television and communication are changing the way that people relate to each other. We could therefore argue that in many ways the world has become a 'single place', not in terms of a unidimensional area of physical space but in terms of the social, political and technical conditions of community in the contemporary information society. In a sense, the world of bits is in the process of creating one world. Global television and its power of simulation has reconstructed itself as a potent cultural machine with an unprecedented capacity to homogenize cultural references around the globe through advertisement and 'entertainment'.[11] In this sense, globalization touches individuals and political communities at all levels around the globe, practically without exception. Although it does make a difference whether you are a high-flying manager collecting more air miles a year than s/he can ever make use of, or whether you live in a premodern society in the Amazon rainforest,[12] one could say – to paraphrase Trotsky's words on war – that although you might not be interested in globalization, globalization is certainly interested in you.

Understanding technological change is therefore absolutely essential in order to make at least some sense of our fast-paced postmodern era. New communications and information systems are playing a crucial role in reducing the costs of 'transportation' of services and goods. The reduction of obstacles for trade in general, and greater freedom for foreign direct investment (FDI) around the globe, in particular, have significantly increased economic activity. Since transnational companies now account for the bulk of FDI (and are both customers of and active participants in international financial markets), globalization has often been understood as development toward a borderless world dominated by stateless firms.[13] This notion has been strengthened by the fact that technological developments have also made many services tradable that previously were not. Knowledge-intensive industries (predominantly, but not solely, of a high-tech nature) involve the delocalization of research and development activities. Since the value of these services is no longer intrinsically linked to the amount of time spent, but rather value the creativity of the job or task, globalization compresses the time/space dyad of social and international relations. These delocalization strategies therefore necessitate a continuous search for markets where service industries (ranging from banking, finance and telecommunications to entertainment and education) are increasingly 'internationalized', which brings with it strong pressures to liberalize markets and develop new regional and international (free) trading arrangements. Inevitably, trade continues to grow rapidly in relation to the size of the national economy, and is reaching unprecedented levels. With a few exceptions, all national economies of the world are now locked in a dense network of highly competitive trade in goods and services and bound together by global financial flows.

The World Trade Organization (WTO), set up in 1995 to establish some rules for this new global capitalist game, has been celebrated by many as some sort of global messianic rebirth which will usher in a new era of even further expansion of world economic activity. Since the mid-1990s the WTO has been deliberating the so-called Multilateral Agreement on Investment (MAI).[14] The MAI would guarantee all transnational firms 'national treatment', which would imply that national governments could no longer discriminate against foreign companies. Were the MAI to be signed, this would open the door for a world of virtually free trade, flourishing FDI and a new qualitative arrangement of economic interdependence. As of today (the summer of 2000), a number of countries remain adamantly opposed to the MAI (among them France), but a revised and toned down MAI-like arrangement is bound to be agreed upon before too long. Such an agreement would introduce a new level of global economic and financial governance geared to facilitate a new stage of capitalist development, steamrollering non-economic categories and cultural identities which do not carry sufficient political clout to have their voices heard.

Globalization is therefore more than a fancy word for greater interdependence of all levels of human activity. In past centuries cities, regions, states and empires were always connected in one way or another, and their prosperity (at times their very existence) highly interdependent. But whereas previous historical periods knew extensive trading networks that cut across political and cultural boundaries, contemporary (hyper)globalization is unique because of its *geographical extensiveness*, its *intensity* in financial and trade flows, the *impact* these flows have on the behavior of states, societal groups and individuals, and the degree to which globalization relies on an *institutionalized technological infrastructure*.[15] Globalization's impact on the nature of world politics is still contentious and remains a matter of fierce debate. The increased importance of global processes does not inevitably and immediately signal 'the end of the state' as we know it; it does not necessarily imply that the Westphalian state-centric system will be eclipsed by the new 'global village'. This will certainly not be a traditional, face-to-face community on a global scale. Rather, it may develop into a global *virtual* community where the absence of others (as well as 'the Other') constitutes the dominant ontological meaning of the relationship between people(s), even when they are spatially together.

Globalization has undeniably pushed the nation-state from its almost mythical pedestal of political pre-eminence, redefining national power in more modest (unsentimental and sober) dimensions. This opens an era in which the state is only one important actor among several in a mixed global system involving premodern, modern and postmodern modes of governance. Globalization is changing the world by introducing new inequalities in power and wealth. It adds to the turbulence of late capitalism and mediatized social and political upheaval, and visualizes its ensuing pain and poverty. The liquid assets of power have shifted gradually (albeit not fully) toward the ability to establish norms, rules and regulations on a regional and/or global level, to control international institutions and networks and the access to information and regional and global media that shape world opinion. The ability to mobilize traditional military power resources remains of importance, but invariably less so. Given this spectrum of factors, we should therefore acknowledge that globalization is a much-contested and somewhat overworked concept that means many things to many people.

At the same time, globalization is not to be read as a neutral concept, but rather as an ideological usage in a new discourse which emphasizes the role of market forces and forecloses a wide range of alternative political options.[16] Globalization has not only measurably changed political life, it increasingly functions as a hegemonic discourse which 'itself alters the *a priori* ideas and perceptions which people have of the empirical phenomena which they encounter; in so doing, it engenders strategies and tactics which in turn may restructure the game itself'.[17] The discourse of globalization thrives on the image of economic and political inevitability, assuming global cultural homogenization and ignoring the boundless fragmentation and polarization among and between peoples. This is a totalizing vision of a global world in which we are all the same, regardless of culture, race, nationality and geography.[18] In this process of depolitieization, both the nation-state and the political process are presumed to play a subordinate role, because human problems are supposed to be addressed less through political mediation and more through technological fixation. This is not a minor change, since the decaying relevance of the political process will in the course of time affect all aspects of societal organization. Globalization also questions the basic premise of territoriality, which is the dominant political and psychological notion underlying statehood. It therefore calls for the recontextualization of the state within the global system. The dismay, or at times delight, of nearing 'end of politics' only illustrates the hegemony of the globalization discourse.

## Globalization as the end of politics

Novel notions of chronopolitics (government of time),[19] geo-economics and geo-governance have emerged, all claiming that geopolitics is a concept from a bygone epoch. The political implications of computerization, revolutions in transportation and communication, the dominance of commerce and money, and the search for workable governance structures on a regional/global scale have moved up the international agenda and compete with the orthodox security discourse based on *Realpolitik* and a balance-of-power conception of the world.

The dominant idea and emerging conventional wisdom is that these new and unprecedented technological developments have led to an irreversible level of economic integration among countries around the globe. The fundamental turbulence regarding both the level and the scope of political regulation is due to the complex dynamics of globalization and the shift toward a postmodern society. In their effects on economic, social, cultural and political organization, these developments resemble the great transformation that has affected Europe and the United States in the second half of the nineteenth century. Peter Drucker, America's top management guru, has heralded what he has labeled a 'post-capitalist world', a new global system in which the new resources of power will be neither 'labor' nor the allocation of capital to productive uses; instead it will center around 'productivity' and 'innovation'.[20] This is part of an increasingly dominant element in the globalization discourse, namely that the only way for national governments to maintain at least some control over their economies is to do what 'global business' demands from them: to observe the rule of law at home, to refrain from aggression abroad, and to open their economies and societies to the free play of global market forces. By integrating into the global economy, by opening themselves up to foreign investment and by giving more power to consumers, states are supposedly restricting their own capacity to wreak havoc both domestically and abroad. The old creed of 'peace through trade' has now been replaced by 'peace and democracy through globalization'.

In its most profane form, the globalization discourse has followed the Big Mac thesis of international politics, which claims that 'no two countries that both have a McDonald's have ever fought a war against each other'.[21] If anything, it is this argument which now seems to reach conceptual pre-eminence in the West, and in the United States in particular. Of the impending Russian elections in February 1996, the *New York Times*' Thomas Friedman noted: 'Sure, a Communist or radical populist in the Kremlin would be worrying. But their room for maneuver would be constricted – much more than we realize and much, much more than they realize, Russia today is connected with the global economy'.[22] This vision of global affairs is characteristic for a world in which 'politics', as a deliberate endeavor to shape events, hardly matters. It is a view that has surrendered a voluntaristic approach to politics in favour of a doctrine based on the positive effects of free trade and open minds mediated through new technology. Giovanni Agnelli, the former chairman of FIAT, has therefore claimed that the process of European integration 'is not so much the result of a utopian dream as it is the political recognition of economic reality; the reality of global markets, the reality of economic interdependence, and the reality of competitive pressures'.[23] Globalization and free trade are assumed to lead to an expansion of world economic activity, the 'new global tide [that] will lift all boats'. But, just as the rise of competitive capitalism was not a 'natural' affair, let alone a spontaneous one ('*Laissez-faire* was planned',[24] as Karl Polanyi has argued), the current wave of globalization, hailed by its ardent supporters as natural and spontaneous, is to a large extent driven by both political and economic actors who are benefiting from the uncontrolled dynamics of this transformation.

Hyperglobalism adopts a one-sided, unidimensional and rosy attitude toward human progress, intentionally or unconsciously overlooking and ignoring the drawbacks of globalization. It disregards the darker sides of a global economic crunch in which many communities and individuals are bound to fall through the cracks. It overlooks the fact that many will not be able to jump on the globalization bandwagon: the poorly educated, technologically marginalized social and ethnic groups, both in 'the West' and in other parts of the world. Even a scant reflection on the basic statistics of world poverty undermines the argument that globalization will benefit *all* individuals and *all* societies. UN figures indicate that more than half of humanity exists on less than US$2 a day; that 1.3 billion people are so poor that they live in shanty towns; and that 40,000 people die every day from preventable diseases and malnutrition; it is almost needless to add that 70 per cent of the world's poorest are women and children.[25] This is the structural violence of late capitalism.

Globalization therefore constructs the poor as being different from 'us', encouraging the construction of new identities around the benefits derived from the divine manifestation of the free market. But, by focusing on hard-nosed criteria of productivity and capability, the globalization discourse overlooks that the essence of politics is dialogue, compromise and continuous mediation, which gives it a flexible and in essence humane character. The globalized intrusions of technology, finance capital and mass media, on the other hand, involve a predetermined, almost mechanical application of apparently universal constructs. Globalization uses the yardstick of economic efficiency, but disregards notions of equity and ecology.[26] Relying on the market to address the problems of exclusion has proved illusory.[27] The decline of the political process therefore implies a concomitant decline of interest for the marginal and powerless voices of society.[28] This means that globalization does not imply an end to scarcity, an end to poverty, exploitation or a conflictual quest for power and wealth. It also does not mean that everyone will become more prosperous, although some countries, firms and individuals inevitably will.

As an *ersatz* foreign policy, this 'logic of globalization' has appealed especially to the US Clinton administration, as well as to Tony Blair's New Labour government in the United Kingdom and Gerhard Schröder's *Neue Mitte* in Germany. Lacking a concrete foreign policy agenda after having 'won' the Cold War, western policy-makers have embraced the discourse of globalization as the language and signs of a bright, novel future. The 1998 US National Security Strategy, for example, argues that underpinning

> our international leadership is the power of our democratic ideals and values. In designing our strategy, we recognize that the spread of democracy supports American values and enhances both our security and prosperity. Democratic governments are more likely to cooperate with each other against common threats, encourage free trade, and promote sustainable economic development. They are less likely to wage war or abuse the rights of their people. Hence, the trend toward democracy and free markets throughout the world advances American interests.
>
> (*A National Security Strategy For a New Century*,
> The White House (October 1998), p. 2)

Since the current speed of economic integration stems from technology, which is understood as both politically and culturally neutral, globalization is said to be in the interest of all countries in the world, benefiting all peoples sooner rather than later. This further assumes that the process of globalization will serve as both a stick and a carrot to induce renegade regimes to follow the rules of the 'international community'. It implies not so much that it is Washington and its allies that will have to impose sanctions on countries like China, as that the global market place will offer most countries a persuasive and powerful mixture of benefits and liabilities that will encourage 'responsible behavior'. (And those who don't are labeled 'rogue states', and treated accordingly).[29] It further implies that the US may well abdicate from its post-Cold-War status as the world's sole traditional superpower, a power that is both able and *willing* to intervene politically and militarily around the globe.

In this context, Barry Buzan has made a strong case for the argument that postmodern society is 'incompatible with great-power politics'.[30] His basic claim is that citizens of postmodern society do not put much trust in their own governments and are no longer prepared to die for their country (or at least not with the zeal of old). Individualism and a consumer ethic have turned western citizens into lethargic free-riders, looking (often in vain) to an illusory 'international community' to douse the political and military bush fires that continue to ignite around the globe. Post-Cold-War conflicts are often murky affairs which lack an ideologically sanctioned division between the forces of 'Good' and 'Evil'. The cases of Bosnia and Kosovo illustrate this ambiguity – as well as the US reluctance both to become militarily involved and, if it does, to incur massive casualties among American soldiers. What is more, the emphasis on ethical and moral issues, as well as the obligation to comply with international law, complicates efforts to conduct a resolute foreign and security policy. It has also become more difficult to engage cosmopolitan, postmodern society in a military conflict with a dehumanized Other before using force against it. Domestic concerns are considered more important than problems 'outside', especially given the conspicuous lack of a public consensus on what rights and responsibilities 'the West' has *vis-à-vis* other peoples in other continents.

Buzan clearly sees a shift toward postmodernism in Western Europe, but also to a limited extent in countries like Japan and the United States. The US is the only classical superpower left, with the capability and willingness to project its military power and political clout around much of the globe. However, Buzan claims the US is 'on the road to becoming a postmodern state for the same deep structural reasons as Britain and France', which is already reflected in Washington's 'neuralgia about casualties' (see Kosovo), and 'America's tendency toward isolation'. This societal shift toward a postmodern mentality and approach toward security may go far to explain why images of global integration as a tidal wave are so appealing to the political elites in western capitals. Especially for the US, globalization may be an instrument to keep the world safe for democracy as well as for capitalist development. As Peter Beinart has argued

> It allows American elites to imagine that the security won for their country is now protected by a force both unstoppable and benign ... Globalization is the narcissism of a superpower in a one-superpower world. It allows America to look at the world and see its own contentment and its own fatigue.
>
> (Peter Beinart, 'An Illusion For Our Time',
> in *The New Republic*, 20 October 1997)

Globalization is assumed to create peace and stability around the globe for a group of postmodern western countries that is increasingly reluctant to do the job itself. Beinart further claims that the US, as the world's *primus inter pares*, is looking at a globe in which its old rivals are dead and new rivals are yet beyond the horizon. In this spell of tranquillity, 'America can afford to dream of a world without conflict, of an End to History'.[31] For many postmodern countries, globalization therefore means the end of foreign policy. For most premodern and modern states, however, the process of globalization may mean something totally different: fragmentation, marginalization, the growth of inequality and increasingly harsh global competition.

A similar 'end-of-politics' argument now dominates the discourse on domestic politics, where globalization has become a helpful excuse to push through a liberal political program based on unfettered free markets. Domestically, globalization is often used as a fig-leaf to hide politicians' imagined or real impotence in the bright spotlights of global attention. New technologies, flatter borders and a growing consensus on the indispensability of international co-operation have confined national governments' room for maneuver in determining their economic and monetary policies. Financial markets and transnational firms are disciplining all western governments, without exception, 'punishing' deviations from the free-trading norm with forced currency devaluation and higher unemployment. In this post-political setting, political parties and specific ideological and moral commitments are gradually losing their societal relevance, bounded as they are by strong pressures to adapt to the functional requirements of regional and global markets. The argument flows along these lines:

> It is the survival of our economies and of our social systems in a fiercely competitive world which imposes budgetary restraint on us all. It is the global competition which makes it impossible to return to the Keynesian deficit spending of the 1930s or 60s as a way of creating jobs.
>
> (Klaus Hänsch, 'Reasserting the Political Will to Move Europe Forward'.
> The Robert Schuman Lecture at the European University Institute
> (Florence) 27 June 1996)

Pursuing Keynesian reflationary strategies has indeed become a non-option for western governments, limiting their political toolkit to scalpel and surgical clamps, rather than the traditional saw and screwdriver. Globalization has turned domestic policy into the art of micro-management rather than social engineering.

Despite its background of economic and technological change, the challenge that globalization poses is therefore most significant in the area of politics. Over the past few centuries a European states system developed in which nationalism and industrialization were closely linked to state sovereignty and democracy. In this national context, vertically organized structures of government, business, military and political authority corresponded closely with geographical boundaries and identities. On a more abstract level, traditional symbols of identification like language, laws and money have also been organized and defined along national lines. We could say that we have become used to a political system in which nationality, territoriality and sovereignty are to all intents and purposes quasi-congruent. This has now changed. The process of globalization has brought us in a new, postmodern era in which these traditional foundations of political order are being undermined, step by step. Vertically organized national cultures and national economies are gradually being replaced by new horizontal and global networks. These new networks are not simply pyramids of governance that rise from one level to the next – from local to regional to national to global. Instead, transversal politics has overtaken the classical inside/outside dyad and given new meaning to both the spheres of domestic and international politics.

In Europe these structural transformations have provoked an intense debate on how far globalization has stripped away power and decision-making capacity from the nation-state (allegedly) in favor of unaccountable transnational firms and finance houses as well as the Anglo-American (political) culture that is said to sustain them. This discussion has focused on a number of themes, ranging from the interface between the global and the national, the national and regional, to the deterritorialization of economic activity (and the supposed 'end of geography'). These developments have a far-reaching impact on the nature and quality of state sovereignty as well as the nature and quality of a democratic system that continues to take a hollowed-out state as its basis of reference. The key question that has hardly been raised (and never adequately answered), is what happens to the credibility of representative democracy when the ability of elected governments to shape the daily lives of their citizens are increasingly curbed by the movements and actions of unelected economic and financial actors who cannot be held responsible for their policies?

One could argue that globalization is an 'historical process' in which transnational firms are merely following the rules of a game they have not devised themselves and which they can hardly hope to alter. But ultimately people will ask what is the purpose of their 'national' economy? If it is not there for the well-being of the people who live in it, what is it for? We can answer that alongside globalization we can see a distinct process of localization; alongside homogenization, we see a parallel trend toward more differentiation; alongside integration, we can clearly detect many examples of fragmentation. We can say that national power is now dispersing upwards, downwards and sideways as well; that sovereignty is derogated to the international level, pooled among nation-states and transferred downwards to local authorities in an effort to satisfy local aspirations. But, ultimately, the questions about the legitimacy and efficiency of state-based democracies remains politically explosive. (See Chapter 6 for a conversation on the implications of globalization and Europeanization on the concept of postmodern democracy.)

Do all these new developments inevitably result in the 'end of politics' as we have known it? It is clear that transnational firms are not *truly* global, footloose and stateless operators, but that they have, through their extraordinary economic weight, shifted the balance between the costs and benefits of individual nation-states' domestic policies. Globalization renders particular national policies more problematic by imposing costs on certain political options. Certain social and economic policies that have underpinned the traditional European welfare state have therefore been undermined by globalization. This has limited government intervention intended to attract FDI to issues such as education, training and infrastructure, rather than classical tools like industrial policy, taxing and spending. The assumption of the 'end of politics' is therefore an integral element of the hegemonic discourse of globalization since it gladly accepts the international anarchy of late capitalism; it advises resignation to the violent consequences of the free market as if it were a resignation to an ordained political fate.[32]

It should also be recognized that the underlying assumptions of postmodernity, its rejection of metanarratives, its insistence that everything must be understood as socially constructed and its rejection of any claims of value, justice and truth, conflict with the assumptions that are necessary for radical politics. Postmodernism's celebration of difference, its acceptance of fragmentation and its open hostility to unity, makes it 'particularly inappropriate as an intellectual framework for movements that need to make positive assertions about how society could be better organized and that need to incorporate difference within a collective unity for social change'.[33] Postmodernism may have radical *intellectual* implications, but it may also be *socially and politically* conservative, since it implies that there is no subject (person or group) capable of acting with some degree of autonomy from the embedded social structures and ideologies. This problematizes the possibilities for any meaningful social actions and radical change. In a sense, therefore, the 'end-of-politics' debate reflects the political passivity, social inertia and acquiescence which follow from the postmodern premise. Postmodernism does not offer an agenda for social change and does not open *political* space for resistance. Late capitalism's expansion through globalization is assumed to encroach upon the whole of society, commodifying social and political relations. Postmodernism does not legitimize this global sway, but neither does it offer a moral and political guide to an alternative vision of political reality.[34] What it does offer, however, is a 'politics of resistance' by discovering points of opposition of forms of power through a continuous flow of critique. The problem is, however, that such a politics of subversion ultimately does not allow for a foundation of political commitment and for the institutional ossification of political positions, since such foundations, as soon as they become generally accepted, should again be resisted.[35] This is postmodernity's political irony. It also explains the wide variety of postmodernity's discontents.

## Commercialism@identity.org

But globalization also reflects a notable shift in how we live and learn to adapt to a more cosmopolitan and postmodern society based on a positive acceptance of uncertainty and difference.[36] There is no need to see Marx' classical dialectics at work here; these contradictory trends are partly a knee-jerk emotional reaction, as people respond to a perceived loss of control over their daily lives and their future; partly a matter of a conscious political choice to protect their local, regional and/or national identities against what is seen as the soulless and often violent mobility of capital. However, one can make too much of the pervasiveness (and inherent shallowness) of CNN, of the emergence of the English language as the *lingua franca* of the postmodern era, and of the development of a 'McWorld' that blankets the rich diversity of human civilizations that can (still) be found around the world in blandness, sterility and homogeneity.[37] But there is certainly serious concern for the viability of local cultures and the fear that in future everywhere will be the same as everywhere else. This would be an anti-utopia dominated by multi-lane highways and concrete skyscrapers, where all businessmen wear gray business suits, watch movies and TV series produced in Hollywood, and talk about them on mobile phones.

All these fears of vulgarization are not without foundation. Global entertainment has become vacuous mind-candy for many people, and in many places the 'local' seems to cede ground to the capitalist universal, sometimes with rather absurd results. The globalization of media imagery has now become the most effective means of shaping the world and making 'other' cultures compatible with the western corporate image. Global media is cloning western cultures, with as yet unknown consequences for the cultural and political DNA of world society. The continuous flow of modern media has now also resulted in an information sickness, an emotional anesthesia and psychic numbing caused by the demands placed on all of us to digest one global catastrophe after another.[38] Global media makes us all passive bystanders, in the process producing moral indifference and widening the gap between our 'knowledge' of world affairs and the possibilities of ethical action.[39]

At the same time we should also recognize that these concerns tend to be framed in a rhetoric that is often narrowly nationalistic and somewhat xenophobic. We should, for example, ask whether it is really inevitable that economic globalization should march in tandem with westernization and a cultural hegemony predominantly based on an American individualistic value system? (Are there no alternative options open to us?) Must the emerging borderless world of economic globalization also be a superficial and orderless word? And, if so, will this (b)orderless world bring peace and prosperity to more and more people, or will it return us to a Darwinian world of the survival of the fittest? These are just a few of the emerging questions on which the political debate in western countries is centered.

These critical questions should make it clear that globalization has its fair share of discontents, most notably on the political Left, among environmentalists and human-rights activists.[40] The most frequently repeated argument holds that this wave of globalization will not result in a universal free market, let alone global democracy and prosperity, but will instead lead to 'an anarchy of sovereign states, rival capitalisms and stateless zones'.[41] Globalization is considered to be a conscious project led by transnational firms intent on expanding business freedoms, circumventing democratic control and establishing effective corporate governance of global affairs. The elimination of national governmental control over global corporate activities and national currencies is considered a voluntaristic abdication of state responsibilities, which may ultimately result in the dismantling of local traditions and relatively autonomous economies. Since states increasingly see their role as facilitators in the process of adapting their national economies to the 'new realities' of globalization, many alternative political options are now foreclosed, bringing about an inevitable sense of societal homogenization. The state now seems to have shed its task of promoting a certain comprehensive model of (social) order, and looks upon the variety of available models with relative equanimity.

This trend toward the homogenization of culture based on similar lifestyles and technological immersion is bound to result in economies of scale in production, marketing and advertising for the transnational firms that are said to drive this process of globalization. This would be a world where the very notion of 'citizen' is undermined, and where individuals merely participate in society as 'consumers', watching TV where commercials sell Presidents as well as God. This will result in a commodification of both culture and politics in which social/political identity is acquired primarily by the purchase of commodities. Citizens and the electorate are thereby transmogrified into a mass audience of atomized individuals with a commensurate egocentric consumer consciousness.

This leads to the conclusion that '[e]conomic globalization involves arguably the most fundamental redesign and centralization of the planet's political and economic arrangements since the Industrial Revolution',[42] which poses 'a more formidable challenge to social cohesion than the Soviets ever did'.[43] For Europe, the pressures of globalization have given rise to a more flexible labor market with more part-time employment, one in which workers are expected to be prepared to change their job, their employer (or both), as well as the location of employment.[44] All this has resulted in increasingly noisy calls for novel and more radical forms of global governance that will bring a semblance of social justice and equality to the harsh world of financial markets and which will promote the cohesion of societies as well as the integrity of states.[45] Accepting a global *laissez-faire* is seen as jeopardizing the high level of peace and prosperity in the West and offering little hope for premodern countries (like Somalia, Liberia, Colombia and Pakistan), whose poverty and instability is due to the absence of effective government of *any* kind. In both cases we may talk about 'failed states': in the West because national governments are no longer able to guarantee their peoples' social protection and a strong sense of belonging; in the 'developing world' because governments provide their peoples neither with the basics of law and order, nor with water and rice. In this story of globalization the US is put forward as the main culprit: it is said that its free-marketeering spirit and turbo-capitalism are undermining the world's distinctive cultures, and that it is using the spread of new technologies not to advance freedom and democracy but simply to emancipate market forces from social and political control.

Susan Strange has referred to the problematic of global governance as 'Pinocchio's Problem' (which does not refer to the growth of the little boy's nose when he lied, but to the idea that, once he turned into a real boy, the strings that used to guide him were all of a sudden lacking).[46] The general systemic entropy of authority has resulted in conflicting sources of power and legitimacy, turning the nation-state into a mere quasi-sovereign political actor which is increasingly dependent on external circumstances. The governmental strings that hitherto guided the nation-state have now snapped, and it is – like the grown-up Pinocchio – now left to its own devices among multiple authorities, allegiances and identities. But Strange's crucial argument is that authority and political control have not just shifted from one actor (the state) to another. Rather, the 'diffusion of authority away from the national governments has left a yawning hole of non-authority, ungovernance'.[47] This implies that some of the authority in the postmodern system of governance has simply been lost, leading us toward at least *partial* 'ungovernance', to a 'governance vacuum' that has yet to be filled. Globalization's black holes do not merely create economic and political turbulence, they also absorb measures of governance that will be difficult to restore or replace. This would support the 'end-of-politics' thesis we explored earlier, since we could now go as far as to argue that the emerging 'governance vacuum' will not – and, more importantly, *cannot* – be filled.

There is obviously no consensus on these matters. An Organisation for Economic Co-operation and Development (OECD) study entitled *Towards a New Global Age* (published in 1997), argued that international security is expected to be enhanced as a result of the substantial increase in economic interdependence and a reduction in world poverty.[48] It is clear that an organization like the OECD, which aims at achieving the highest possible sustainable economic growth and improving the economic and social well-being of the populations of its member countries, based on the principles of the market economy, is unlikely to proclaim anything else. Others, like Daniel Drezner, have claimed that the forces of globalization 'impose stringent constraints on national governments, but they also empower them in a new way. Globalization does not imply the erosion of the nation-state's authority, but rather a change in state strategies and a redirection of state energies'.[49] His argument is that globalization forces states to focus on their core competencies, such as the provision of public goods and establishing the rules of international institutions. This leads him to conclude that '[e]ven if the nation-state is weakening in the face of global forces, it still has a few centuries of life remaining. Its death is likely to be as slow as its birth'.[50]

But, despite these qualifications and caveats, it can hardly be denied that by gradually handing over the levers that control basic elements of their economies to international financial markets and transnational firms, national governments now find themselves left with such weak and defective tools as fiscal policies, changing labor costs and rights, and possible weaker pollution controls. By doing so, states seriously risk becoming expendable actors in a complex process of geo-economics. The hyperglobalist argument further overlooks the fact that global capitalism also changes social expectations, values and institutions; it basically undermines its own enabling status and power structures. Japanese management writer Kenichi Ohmae, for example, has argued that materialistic motives and undiluted consumerism are necessary as well as sufficient human characteristics for organizing political society. Cultural and social identities play no role in Ohmae's globalized future; peoples' main interest in political organization will be the opportunity to increase their material wealth.[51] This is a problematic assumption, mainly because capitalism offers neither appealing social organizing principles (apart from efficiency) nor social or cultural 'we-concepts' as the basis for identity. Globalization destroys many an entrenched identity, national as well as cultural, but it does not necessarily offer opportunities for creating new solidarities on the basis of positive emotional communication.

Global capitalism is a powerful ideology, focused on individual prosperity, which disregards the consequences for the social order in which it is itself embedded. As Ulrich Beck has argued, 'as global capitalism divests itself of all responsibility for employment and for democracy, it is undermining its own legitimacy'.[52] It is here that a postmodern perspective will be needed to come to a better understanding of political existence. Globalization not only makes *physical* borders porous and unimportant, it also challenges our *conceptual understanding* of borders, making them ever more complex and problematic. It requires us to become cognizant of the effects of globalization on the spatial location of power and the ways in which new technologies and communications affect the social, economic and political relationships that are part of our daily lives. For the social sciences this translates into studies that pay attention to the new forms of (de)territoriality, state sovereignty, culture, technology and society, as well as a wide range of other facts and factors which suggest that classical notions like 'class', and perhaps also 'nationalism', may give way to splintered, networked identities. An emerging atomized political culture based on hyper-individualism will make it more difficult for the state to mobilize its citizens for 'collective', 'national' issues. But it may at the same time offer new opportunities for the development of a 'European identity' as one of a number of novel, alternative sites of identification. For the more imminent future, however, the question will be what vision may be realized of a more private, voluntary sphere of civil society than the universalization of the profane search for material wealth. What values, beliefs and shared hopes will constitute the basis of an emerging 'European identity', and will such an identity be able to offer Europeans a feeling of connectedness that reaches those parts of their souls that commercial satisfaction cannot reach? What idea may be capable of meeting the human needs for moral community and social cohesion?

## Europeanization as a response to globalization

A similar debate on the progressive and destructive sides of globalization can be found in the European context, embedded within the discussion on European integration and the future of 'Europe' in general.[53] One could therefore argue that the process of European integration is to be understood as globalization on a regional scale, as well as a defensive response to the world-wide trend of growing economic interdependence. Both aspects are of key importance to understanding these recent phenomena and are worth looking at in some detail.[54]

It is possible to identify advocates of two different, if at times also overlapping, approaches toward Europeanization: those who consider 'Europe' (however one wants to define it, but most often as a reference to the EU) to be a *sanctuary*, and those who consider 'Europe' mainly as a *proponent* of further globalization. The first line of argument often calls attention to the downsides of globalization. It is then suggested that Europeanization is the only remaining option, not so much as a way of riding the waves of global development, but more as a means to keep globalization at bay or to break up these waves to wavelets of more manageable and human proportions. There is certainly a tendency to see a strengthening of the EU, and European economic and political co-operation in general, as one of the few ways to overcome some of the drawbacks and challenges of the globalizing world economy. Europe's Left, in particular, argues that 'politics' must again try to regain a sense of control over the quasi-anarchic laws of globalization. If national politics cannot succeed in doing this, European politics may stand a better chance.

The hope is that the EU, by merging the power and influence of individual Member States, can rise to the challenge of restoring the preponderance of politics.[55] European Monetary Union (EMU) and the single European currency are seen as the paramount instruments for restoring a measure (if perhaps only a mere semblance) of political control over the financial markets that increasingly determine the monetary (as well as fiscal) parameters of national policy. Former president of the European Parliament, Klaus Hänsch, therefore noted that, since we can do little else than 'face the power of global forces, our great chance for self-determination is a united Europe'.[56] Helen Wallace further believes that

> European integration can be seen as a distinct west European effort to contain the consequences of globalization. Rather than be forced to choose between the national polity for developing policies and the relative anarchy of the globe, west Europeans invented a form of regional governance with polity-like features to extend the state and harden the boundary between themselves and the rest of the world.

(Helen Wallace, 'Politics and Policy in the EU: The Challenge of Governance', in Helen Wallace and William Wallace (eds), *Policy-Making in the European Union* (Oxford: Oxford University Press, 1996), p. 16)

Europeanization is thus perceived as a general means to protect Europe from the onslaught of global forces which threaten its uniqueness, its identity and the political, economic and monetary independence of its constituent states.

At the other end of the spectrum we find voices arguing that Europeanization is mainly a regional example of a world-wide phenomenon, a regional manifestation of a global pattern in which new technologies and methods of communication bring down national barriers. In this perspective, European integration just rides the waves of globalization, adapting European societies and economic and political systems, making them ready to survive and even prosper in an increasingly competitive world. This is the basic tenet of the liberal, free trade argument of Europeanization. Its proponents are not concerned that Europeanization might well result in a protectionist trading bloc in which preferential tariffs might cause trade to flow in inefficient ways (so-called 'trade diversion'), or distort the patterns of 'comparative advantage' that underlie the free trade-mechanism.[57] These potential shortcomings and liabilities are deemed to be generously compensated for by the impetus toward trade liberalization both within the EU and in the countries that are (temporarily) excluded (most notably the Central European applicant countries). More often than not, this view transforms the forces of globalization into a postmodern Hand of God, inducing political complacency and excluding a serious role for either national/regional government or the EU itself.

It is worth stressing that, except among an increasingly marginalized group of Euro-skeptics and extreme nationalists, Europeanization as a policy has become generally accepted for one (or, more often than not, a mixture) of the arguments outlined above. The political debate has now increasingly concentrated on the process, speed and means of Europeanization, rather than on the underlying question of whether we should proceed with European integration in the first place. This does not imply that all Europe's national actors have committed themselves whole-heartedly to the ideal of a federal European Union. Rather, they have come to understand that Europeanization is their only option for surviving in an increasingly interdependent world. This corresponds to the analytical arguments of Alan Milward, who has suggested that since World War II West European states have maintained and even strengthened their political authority in the eyes of their citizens by providing a wide range of social services and by promising economic prosperity.[58] Perhaps somewhat paradoxically, European states have thereby promoted a process that increasingly erodes their territorial sovereignty and undermines their claim to dominant political authority. As Milward has noted, 'To supersede the nation-state would be to destroy the [EU]. To put a finite limit to the process of integration would be to weaken the nation-state, to limit its scope and to curb its power'.[59] In contemporary Europe, it has become clear that, in order to sustain what is left of national 'sovereignty', nation-states try to recapture some of the lost political and economic control at the European level.

Intensive co-operation and integration within a European framework has become the only realistic option for regaining some political influence on the welfare and security of the state's citizens. Europeanization has therefore turned from a policy *option* to a political *necessity*. Robert Picht has argued that the market has created such a degree of complementarities that 'we already have the economic conditions that constitute a common European society. However, we do not have a government adapted to this society with all its problems of intercultural understanding and co-operation'.[60] Europeanization marks out important steps toward such a network of European governance. But with each step it becomes clearer that European politics is increasingly decentered: there is no longer a clear center of economic and political authority. Even the traditional state–market continuum no longer has an unquestioned conceptual validity. This uncertainty of boundaries, this blurring of practical and conceptual categories, reflects the postmodern European condition in which the social, economic and political are transformed into overlapping modes and locales for governance.

Philip G. Cerny's concept of the 'competition state' best captures this political decenteredness by focusing on the reinvention of the traditional welfare state as a 'quasi-enterprise association'.[61] Cerny argues that the state constitutes the main agency of the process of globalization, driven by its desire to remain relevant to 'its' people. Postmodern states have metamorphosed into political entities pursuing a premeditated policy of societal marketization in order to attract economic activities into their national space, thereby making themselves more competitive in international terms. Their central challenge is to combine a rudimentary domestic welfare system while at the same time promoting structural reform in order to improve international competitiveness. Cerny considers it a paradox that the development toward the competition state 'in turn hinders the capacity of state institutions to embody the kind of communal solidarity or *Gemeinschaft* which gave the modern nation-state its deeper legitimacy, institutionalized power and social embeddedness'.[62] The emerging dominance of the competition state certainly undermines the achievement of the communal goals that have constituted the *raison d'être* of the (European) state since the late nineteenth century. The western competition state now values efficiency above equity, competitiveness above solidarity. In so doing, the postmodern state utilizes the universal discourse of commerce, which now more than ever dominates the public sphere. Now that the nation-state agrees to play the game of late capitalism, the crude and violent logic of advertisement and consumerism in not challenged, it is legitimated. Both rhetorically and technologically, the postmodern state's role and place in society and global politics has been altered by its new *style* as well as its new *message*. As a consequence of these shifting priorities, it is prepared to sell its national sovereignty to other actors on the economic and political playing field(s) of global competition.

These transformations do not call for an *end* to politics, but rather turn many traditional state-based political institutions into semi-obedient servants catering to the tastes of the economic and financial performers of late capitalism. Cerny has therefore argued that the competition state has to do both *more* and *less*; it has to 'reinvent government' by fostering (or even imposing) adaptation to global competitive forces in return for (temporary) protection and legitimacy. It has become clear that globalization requires a tighter monetary policy alongside a looser fiscal policy through tax cuts. The competition state has to encourage mergers and industrial restructuring; promote research and development; encourage private investment and develop new forms of infrastructure; pursue a more active labor-market policy; and in general deregulate, while simultaneously imposing new regulatory structures designed to facilitate global market forces. These shifts in responsibilities do not suggest the end of the modern nation-state, but they certainly do alter the role and place of the nation-state in the overall system of international politics. What is more, the postmodern competition state will not come in one, uniform shape. In order to be effective and attractive, it will manifest itself in many guises (and will habitually perform as a market actor itself). The main point to make here is that the EU has now acquired a character similar to that of the many competition states that comprise it: the EU has become a *supra*competition state. The crisis of today's nation-state has matured the EU into a transversal economic and political *ninja*-fighter, fighting against emerging trading blocs around the globe on behalf of its Member States and sheltering them from global turbulence.

The best illustration of the dynamic and parallel processes of globalization and Europeanization is the decision to introduce the single European currency (Euro) within the context of a European Monetary Union.[63] In 1996 Germany's then Foreign Minister Klaus Kinkel referred to the Euro as 'Europe's big strategic reply to globalization',[64] which makes this point powerfully. The growing interdependence of the world economy and the world's financial markets has increased the competitive pressures on European companies. It has made it all too clear that Europe's fragmented financial structure, with its multitude of currencies, will be too vulnerable to the fluctuations of American, Asian and other regional markets and the future of the world economy in general. The turmoil in the European Exchange Rate Mechanism in 1992, the plunge in the value of the Mexican peso in 1994–5, and especially the financial instability of many Asian economies (as well as Russia) in 1998, have shown how the world of financial trading can 'punish' policy misalignments with an astounding alertness. This has strengthened the calls for inter/national controls on the financial markets to impose some moderation on the lightning-quick flows of capital across borders (for example by modest transaction taxes). In this context, EMU and the Euro are to be read as strategic answers to the process of economic and technological globalization, based on the understanding that only a consolidated monetary union in Europe will be strong enough to weather the global winds, and resilient enough to outlast the many global economic and financial viruses that have for so long infected West European economies.

With the launch of the Euro, it is clear that Europe will become economically as well as monetarily more self-contained.[65] Within the Euro-zone – which encompasses all EU Member States except Denmark, the United Kingdom and Sweden – what used to be intra-EU trade has now *de facto* become 'domestic' trade. This has come to mean that inside the Euro-zone the export share of GDP has shrunk to around 10 per cent (which is close to that of the US). In some respects the EU is therefore becoming more autarkic and less dependent on the economic and financial woes of other regional centers around the world. The Euro might also mark some serious steps toward 'emancipating' Europe both from the US dollar and from the powerful financial markets of Wall Street. It is widely expected that EMU will strengthen Europe's position in the world financial system and encourage the development of a consolidated, more cohesive European market that will attract more FDI, encourage structural change and thereby secure a politically sustainable level of employment.

Since January 1999, the European Central Bank (ECB) is the body having authority for setting interest rates for the Euro-zone with the prime objective of maintaining price stability (i.e., to limit inflation to a declared maximum of 2 per cent). The ECB's governing board, which consists of the six executive board members and the governors of the participating national central banks, meets once a month and takes all the important monetary policy decisions, most notably those concerning interest rates and exchange rate policy. The ECB is now one of the most independent central banks in the world, and its executives are not supposed to take political orders from any government. They are called upon to pursue a monetary policy in the interest of the EMU area as a whole, without favoring any individual country. In its organizational structure, as well as its primary objective of limiting inflation, the ECB emulates the functioning and priorities of the German Bundesbank. Unlike the US Federal Reserve Board, the ECB does not have the specific task of enhancing economic growth. The national governors (the presidents of the national central banks) will have to ensure that national interests will not be ignored within EMU and that all decisions will be based on the traditional recipe for European integration: compromise.

As a new institution setting monetary policy for a market approximately the size of the US, the ECB has to satisfy all participating Member States and their central banks, as well as earn the respect and confidence of their societies and the world's financial markets. Its decisions affect an economic space that is extremely diverse in terms of cyclical development and social and political expectations. It has now also become evident that the EMU will not merely affect monetary policy, but will inevitably set the tone as well as the limits for a wide range of other policy areas. For example, as early as July 1998 the ECB's first President, Wim Duisenberg, called upon the countries of the Euro-zone to run balanced budgets. Although officially the ECB has no say in the fiscal policies of EMU countries (and has no legal mechanism for imposing its views on national governments), it has become apparent that EMU will revolutionize economic cohesion within the Euro-zone. EMU countries can no longer claim to be the sole masters of either their monetary or fiscal policies, and have now accepted unprecedented intervention of the ECB in domains they have for so long guarded with great jealousy. The pressures to harmonize taxes among EMU countries further transfers traditional national prerogatives toward the European level. Karel van Miert, the former European Commissioner for Competition Policy, has noted that 'Ireland has a tax system which attracts investors and possibly causes relocations. This can no longer continue like that'.[66]

The debate on the Euro has exposed the wide spectrum of views on the nature of globalization and the need for commensurate Europeanization. Those who celebrate globalization obviously support the current arrangement based on an independent ECB fully focused on the prime goal of price stability. Critics of unabated global capitalism have from the outset called for political strings to be attached to the EMU by making the ECB accountable to the participating Euro-countries, for the sake of both national primacy and democracy. The so-called 'convergence criteria' for entry into the EMU (which were laid down at Maastricht) already called for limited budget deficits and a tight fiscal policy. EU Member States have had to tighten their economic belts for several years to qualify to join the EMU, which has raised many questions about whether the Euro would actually benefit European societies. Increasing competitive pressures on European firms have resulted in less rigid labor markets, but have failed to create the number (and kind) of new jobs that would make a serious impact on the painfully high level of unemployment within the EU. For those at the margins of Europe's labor market, the social safety nets now seem to be unraveling, creating a pool of unemployable people that forms globalization's new *lumpenproletariat* (citizens who are not socially responsible and active).

In this context, it is hardly surprising that nationalist forces in all EU Member States have been hostile toward the introduction of the Euro. Financial belt-tightening in times of high unemployment is never popular. Especially in the larger Member States (France, Germany and the United Kingdom), opposition has been fierce and loud. The UK has decided not to participate yet, but the Labour government has been supportive of the EMU project in general and might reconsider its position after a possible second term in office. In Germany, mainstream political parties across the board have adopted a co-operative stance toward the single European currency, but almost warlike noises against the Euro have been heard from the many (electorally small) extremist nationalist parties. As might have been expected, France has been the most vocal critic of an autonomous ECB, which some consider as nothing more than a ventriloquist's dummy for the Bundesbank. This has, of course, not so much been a theoretical discussion of purely economic merits as a political discourse reflecting the more *dirigiste* attitude of the French political elite toward all political questions. The very fact that the French electorate was split down the middle on the issue of EMU in the 1992 referendum on the Maastricht Treaty, illustrates the lukewarm French support for the single currency.

French ambiguity toward EMU has certainly not waned, but it has only strengthened the view that monetary union should be given a more 'human face' through active political intervention. President Jacques Chirac clearly reflected this attitude by saying that

> France would like the irreversible globalization of technologies and markets to be better organized and better controlled through the adoption and implementation of common rules and through the action of international organizations responsible for enforcing them ... This accelerated economic integration must be supplemented by new progress at a human level in Europe, in particular in terms of employment and the European social model. That is our answer to certain perverse effects of globalization, and it is a condition for our people's long-term support for the European project.
> (Jacques Chirac, 'Speech to Ambassador's Conference, Paris, France', 26 August 1998)

This would call for a *renaissance* of the political, albeit on the European level.

## Postmodern strangers and the end of work

According to official figures of EUROSTAT, around 10 per cent of the (working) population of the EU was officially looking for a job in 1999; youth unemployment (15–24 years of age) averaged 20 per cent.[67] With few indications that the number of jobless will decrease dramatically over the next few years, it should be clear that this level of unemployment is causing far-ranging social problems in Western Europe. It is threatening the social cohesion of European societies and, through falling living standards, is marginalizing a large part of the labor force. Since globalization is largely an impersonal process, it creates ill-feeling among many people based on a general concern about eroding social standards and a very concrete fear of unemployment. Their resistance to the catechism of the market is therefore understandable. Here again, Europeanization has been identified as the key solution.

But under Europe's condition of late capitalism unemployment is likely to be more structural in nature. Daniel Bell has argued that the culture of modernity does not only celebrate the transgression and erosion of established values, but through its new alliance with consumerism also emphasizes the central role of play and hedonism. In many ways the work ethic is gradually replaced by a consumption ethic.[68] Although inert politicians and labor and business leaders are still clinging to the myth of full employment, it is slowly dawning upon European society that the very definition of 'work' calls for a serious overhaul: it is very unlikely that the natural condition of all individuals from adulthood to retirement will be full-time employment in the same job with the same employer in the same place. Many European postindustrial societies are heading toward capitalism without work, without sufficient jobs to satisfy the 'needs' of society. The new stage of globalized capitalism calls for flexibility and short-term commitments to work, altering both the central role of 'work' as a point of reference for defining durable personal relationships and people's sense of self-worth. Late capitalism therefore not only erodes the basic fabric of European society, it also wears down the basic foundations of representative democracy. The consolidating consumer culture not only refers to the increasing production and salience of cultural goods but also to the way in which identity as well as other signifying practices become mediated by consumption. The activity of consumption, therefore, goes far beyond the simple use of values and goods; it has transformed the consumer into an appropriator of signs and images, and this unloosens the established social order by its aestheticization of prosaic life.

Ulrich Beck has argued that in the West, democracy has originally meant a 'democracy of work', in the sense that it rested on political participation in a form of gainful employment.[69] During this phase of democracy people could participate in the political process through trade unions and labor councils and could hope to use their influence as employees and members of the welfare state. Beck argues that over the decades the traditional welfare state has helped to legitimate the political existence of the nation-state, not only by preventing widespread poverty but also by offering the sense of social justice that now underlies European social democracy. But today it is the specter of unemployment and social uselessness, more than anything else, that overshadows the lives not only of the less-educated but increasingly also of the well-educated middle classes of western society. This social undertow, this nagging premonition of personal failure, adds to the understanding of uncertainty that is so characteristic of postmodern society. It adds to the erosion of social bonds and loyalty to employer as well as the nation-state: neither are any longer considered trustworthy social partners. It undermines the feeling of national belonging, since the traditional (nation-based) public realm no longer seems able to cope with the new, global economic tasks and challenges. As Richard Sennett has argued, 'this qualitative impoverishment makes increasing numbers of people feel that they personally have no footing in the process of economic growth'.[70]

This is also the central point of the critique by Bauman, who argues that globalization and the concomitant dismantling of the European welfare state have turned the unemployed, the poor and the socially marginalized into 'strangers', into new categories of 'dirt'. They are the 'flawed consumers', the 'people unable to respond to the enticements of the consumer market because they lack the required resources, people unable to be "free individuals" according to the sense of "freedom" as defined in terms of consumer choice'.[71] Whereas the European welfare state has in the past tried to manage this 'reserve army' of labor in order to get its members a job in the future, the prospect of full employment has now all but vanished. Bauman claims that the dominance of the economic logic within the public discourse has removed other senses of order; it has resulted in the absence of other senses, including the political, the social, and eventually also the downright human. Since consumption has become the main (if not sole) measure of a successful life, of happiness and human decency, those who cannot partake in this consumer feast are by definition suspect; they have become the 'inner demons' specific to the postmodern era of consumerism. Bauman claims that '*being poor* is seen as a crime; *becoming poor*, as the product of criminal predispositions or intention – abuse of alcohol, gambling, drugs, truancy and vagabondage'.[72] In many ways, the unemployed and poor, this broad category of flawed consumers, embody the sins of late capitalism. These are the people who do not benefit from the individualization and atomization of postmodern society; these are the people who are powerless, who lack the resources to adopt the routine of postmodern identity surfing, who cannot change masks and roles at will and as economic and social winds change. These are the weak and meek who are 'experiencing the world as a trap, not as an adventure park'.[73]

Bauman further makes the case that globalization does not erase the role of the nation-state, but has instead developed a vested interest in encouraging the emergence of a network of 'weak states'. These are nervous competition states searching for legitimacy and an ephemeral identity which, according to Bauman, 'can easily be reduced to the (useful) role of local police stations, securing the modicum of order required for the conduct of business, but need not be feared as effective brakes on the global companies' freedom'.[74] States continue to be essential for the main global actors of late capitalism as the unswerving and ardent providers of education and infrastructure, of social order, justice and policy. But, as Slavoj Zizek has stated, this emerges as 'the ultimate consequence of the post-political suspension of the political in the reduction of the state to a mere police agent servicing the (consensually established) needs of the market forces and multiculturalist tolerant humanitarianism'.[75]

This complex background informs Europe's immense employment challenge. Since the 1990s a wide European debate about unemployment has resulted in significantly more 'high-level' conferences and 'jobs summits' than practical results. In 1994 the European Commission issued an EU White Paper on *Growth, Competitiveness and Employment*, promising to create 15 million new jobs by the year 2000 (needless to say, this ambitious goal has not been reached). The Heads of State and Government further agreed, at the Amsterdam Summit of June 1997, to give employment policy a legal basis in the Treaty on European Union by introducing a Title on Employment. The European Commission now argues that this

> employment challenge must be met if the Union is to attain its ambitious objectives to provide for material well-being and social justice for all its citizens. Indeed, the challenge is to demonstrate that higher levels of employment and more flexibility in the labor markets can be achieved without abandoning the basic foundations of solidarity and social rights upon which the European societies are built.
>
> (Quoted from the European Commission's website
> www.europa.eu.int/com/dg05, accessed 25 August 1999)

This is part of a wide range of efforts to project on the EU a vision of political potency to assist its participating nation-states in their efforts to regain political legitimacy and credibility. The fact is that rising structural unemployment has shaken the faith of many people in the capacity of national governments to live up to their promise of prosperity and social security. Part of the problem can be attributed to the nature and dynamics of globalization, which stresses technological competence and skill-based technological change. Low-educated workers now often find themselves redundant, and their unemployment tends to be structural and permanent. The revolutions that are taking place in the global marketplace, especially in the fields of information technology and financial markets, have also emphasized the need for flexibility, deregulation and less government interference. Over the last ten years or so labor markets in continental Western Europe have become significantly more flexible, although they still lag somewhat behind the US and the United Kingdom. It has become easier to fire workers without having to go through a tiresome bureaucratic hassle. Most large West European firms have restructured and modernized their businesses, and complete sectors, such as telecommunications, have been privatized. Given that in this competitive European market blue-collar and relatively poor European citizens have more reason to fear the loss of their jobs and a decline in their wages, it may not come as a surprise that some scholars have claimed that 'class and related ideological positions remain crucial, even if not dominant, determinants of individual attitudes toward European unifica- tion'.[76] This, *ipso facto*, also applies to popular support for Europe's single currency.

Of course, the EMU has officially been hailed as the new engine *par excellence* for economic growth and employment across Europe. But at the same time, the EMU has been criticized as a blunt instrument and a slow-moving mechanism which in countries with above-average unemployment may contribute to interest rates higher than they would otherwise have been. The ECB is committed to the new religion of 'Central Bankism' (to use Edward Luttwak's phrase),[77] and so will not commit itself to deflationary policies which would be justified in high- unemployment countries. Such a 'one-size fits all'-policy by the ECB is likely to result in political inertia in Member States, who will conveniently shift public opprobrium from the domestic level to the European domain, blaming 'Brussels' for a wide range of woes that no doubt will befall them. Another outcome will be that high-unemployment countries will call for continued massive transfers of funds from other, wealthier EU Member States. This will press the widely acclaimed 'European solidarity' to its limits. It will also again accentuate the many problematic aspects of democracy at the European level, illustrating that Europe's many competition states now fight each other, while also co-operating on the European level to compete with even fiercer global challengers.

'We say yes to market economy, but no to market society'.[78] For many, this remark by French Prime Minister Lionel Jospin reflects the attitude of European society as well as Europe's postwar experience with a social market economy. The question is whether Europe will be capable of squaring this circle involving wealth creation, social cohesion and political freedom. Most European nation- states have come to realize that Europeanization is the only realistic formula for at least keeping up the appearance of social services that have earned welfare states both societal allegiance and democratic legitimacy. But will Europe be able to conform to the strict rule of the market while maintaining its traditional commitment to social solidarity and societal cohesion? Will Europe be able to develop an open, free-trading market economy without compromising its European identity, its cultural uniqueness? Will Europe be able to de-estrange the new strangers of the postmodern consumer era and give these new categories of 'social dirt' opportunities to find new, non-economic sites of social and political power and satisfaction?

## Notes

1 R.B.J. Walker, *Inside/Outside: International Relations as Political Theory* (Cambridge: Cambridge University Press, 1993), p. 3.
2 William J. Clinton, 'Remarks at the World Trade Organization in Geneva, Switzerland', in *Weekly Compilation of Presidential Documents*, 25 May 1998.
3 Ignacio Ramonet, 'The One Idea System' (21 February 1995). Online. Available HTTP: http://www.ctheory.com (accessed 28 March 2000). First published in *Le monde diplomatique* (January 1995).
4 Virginia Postrel, 'Seattle Suprise', in *Reason*, vol. 31, no. 9 (February 2000).

5  Benjamin R. Barber, *Jihad vs. McWorld* (New York: Times Books, 1995), and Samuel P. Huntington, *The Clash of Civilizations and the Remaking of World Order* (New York: Simon & Schuster, 1996).

6  Fredric Jameson, *Postmodernism: Or, The Cultural Logic of Late Capitalism* (Durham NC: Duke University Press, 1992).

7  Peter L. Berger, 'Four Faces of Global Culture', in *The National Interest*, no. 49 (Fall 1997), p. 23.

8  Fredric Jameson, *The Geopolitical Aesthetic: Cinema and Space in the World System* (Bloomington: Indiana University Press, 1995), p. 82.

9  J. Orstrom Moller, *The Future European Model. Economic Internationalization and Cultural Decentralization* (Westport CT: Praeger, 1995).

10  Michael Zürn, 'The Challenge of Globalization and Individualization: A View From Europe', in Hans-Henrik Holm and Georg Sorensen (eds), *Whose World Order? Uneven Globalization and the End of the Cold War* (Boulder CO: Westview Press, 1995), p. 141.

11  David Holmes, 'Virtual Identity: Communities of Broadcast, Communities of Interactivity', in David Holmes (ed.), *Virtual Politics: Identity and Community in Cyberspace* (London: Sage, 1997).

12  Raul Reis, 'The Impact of Television Viewing in the Brazilian Amazon', in *Human Organization*, vol. 57, no. 3 (Fall 1998).

13  David Goldblatt, David Held, Anthony McGrew and Jonathan Perraton, 'Economic Globalization and the Nation-State: Shifting Balances of Power', in *Alternatives*, vol. 22, no. 3 (July/September 1997).

14  Stephen J. Kobrin, 'The MAI and the Clash of Globalization', in *Foreign Policy*, no. 112 (Fall 1998).

15  Goldblatt *et al.*, 'Economic Globalization and the Nation-State', p. 271.

16  François Chesnais, *La Mondialisation Du Capital* (Paris: Syros, 1994).

17  Philip G. Cerny, 'Globalization and Other Stories: The Search for a New Paradigm for International Relations', in *International Journal*, vol. 51, no. 4 (Autumn 1996), p. 620.

18  Claire Turenne Sjolander, 'The Rhetoric of Globalization: What's in a Wor(l)d?', in *International Journal*, vol. 51, no. 4 (Autumn 1996), p. 613.

19  James Der Derian, *Antidiplomacy: Spies, Terror, Speed, and War* (Cambridge: Blackwell, 1992), especially Chapter 6.

20  Peter F. Drucker, 'The Post-Capitalist World: Toward a Knowledge-Based Society', in *The Public Interest*, no. 109 (Fall 1992).

21  Thomas Friedman, 'Turning Swords into Beef-Burgers', in *The Guardian*, 19 December 1996. With the NATO bombing of Serbia in the Spring of 1999, the Big Mac thesis has become defunct; Belgrade has a number of McDonald's, so the golden arches obviously don't deter NATO that much.

22  Thomas Friedman in the *New York Times*, 14 February 1996. Quoted in Peter Beinart, 'An Illusion For Our Time', in *The New Republic*, 20 October 1997.

23  Giovanni Agnelli, 'The Europe of 1992', in *Foreign Affairs*, vol. 68, no. 4 (July/August 1989), p. 62.

24  Karl Polanyi, *The Great Transformation: The Political and Economic Origins of Our Time* (Boston: Beacon Press, 1957), p. 70.

25  Figures quoted in Douglas Mattern, 'Democracy or Corporate Rule?', in *Humanist*, vol. 58, no. 4 (July/August 1998). See also Michel Chossudovsky, 'Global Poverty in the Late 20th Century', in *Journal of International Affairs*, vol. 52, no. 1 (Fall 1998).

26  R.F.M. Lubbers, 'Globalisation and Value Systems', in Roberto Papini, Antonio Pavan and Stefano Zamagni (eds), *Living in the Global Society* (Aldershot: Ashgate, 1997).

27  Ken Silverstein, 'Millions for Viagra, Pennies for Diseases of the Poor', in *The Nation*, vol. 269, no. 3 (19 July 1999).

28  Rajni Kothari, 'Globalization: A World Adrift', in *Alternatives*, vol. 22, no. 2 (April/June 1997).

29  Philip H. Gordon, ' "Rogue States" and Transatlantic Relations', in Frances G. Burwell and Ivo H. Daalder (eds), *The United States and Europe in the Global Arena* (London: Macmillan Press, 1999).

30  Barry Buzan, 'The Rise of "Lite" Powers: A Strategy for the Postmodern State', in *World Policy Journal*, vol. 13, no. 3 (Fall 1996).

31  Beinart, 'An Illusion For Our Time'.

32  Andrew Linklater, 'The Transformation of Political Community: E.H. Carr, Critical Theory and International Relations', in *Review of International Studies*, vol. 23, no. 3 (July 1997), p. 328.

33  Barbara Epstein, 'Why Poststructuralism is a Dead End for Progressive Thought', in *Socialist Review*, vol. 25, no. 2 (1995), pp. 83–5.

34  For an alternative approach, see Cynthia Kaufman, 'Postmodernism and Praxis: Weaving Radical Theory from Threads of Desire and Discourse', in *Socialist Review*, vol. 24, no. 3 (1994).

35  Dean C. Hammer, 'Vaclav Havel's Construction of a Democratic Discourse. Politics in a Postmodern Age', in *Philosophy Today*, vol. 39, no. 2 (Summer 1995).

36  Albert Borgmann, 'Society in the Postmodern Era', in *The Washington Quarterly*, vol. 23, no. 1 (Winter 2000).

37  Alan Swingewood, *Cultural Theory and the Problem of Modernity* (New York: St Martin's Press, 1998), especially Chapter 9 ('Postmodernity and Mass Culture').

38  Ien Ang (ed.), *Living Room Wars: Rethinking Media Audiences for a Postmodern World* (London: Routledge, 1995).

39  Geoffrey Hartman, 'Public Memory and Its Discontents', in *Raritan*, vol. 13, no. 4 (Spring 1994).

40  James H. Mittelman (ed.), *Globalization: Critical Reflections* (Boulder, CO: Lynne Rienner, 1996); Saskia Sassen and Kwame Anthony Appiah, *Globalization and its Discontents* (New York: New Press, 1998); and Zygmunt Bauman, *Globalization: The Human Consequences* (New York: Columbia University Press, 1998).

41  John Gray, 'Globalization – The Dark Side', in *New Statesman and Society*, 13 March 1998. See also Matthew Greenfield, 'What We Talk About When We Talk About Culture', in *Raritan*, vol. 19, no. 2 (Fall 1999).

42  Jerry Mander, 'The Dark Side of Globalization: What the Media are Missing', in *The Nation*, 15–22 July 1996.

43  Ronald Steel, 'The Bad News', in *The New Republic*, 10 February 1997.

44  It may therefore not be surprising that the General Secretary of the International Confederation of Free Trade Unions, Bill Jordan, has referred to the process of economic globalization as a 'third world war', arguing that, although 'there won't be mortal casualties, there will be economic casualties'. Jordan believes that the globalization of trade is changing the world as dramatically as the end of the Cold War, and that EU Member States must defend their workers from the outside pressures of cheap labor, adding that '[t]he privilege of free trade is a great one and not to be given away. [But] it should be given in return for a pledge of civilization'. See *European Voice*, 15–21 February 1996, p. 20.

45  Heikki Patomäki, *The Tobin Tax: How to Make it Real*, Project Report by The Network Institute for Global Democratisation (NIGD), February 1999.

46  Susan Strange, *The Retreat of the State: The Diffusion of Power in the World Economy* (Cambridge: Cambridge University Press, 1996).

47  *Ibid.*, p. 14.

48  Donald J. Johnston, 'A New Global Age', in *OECD Observer*, no. 207 (August/September 1997).

49  Daniel Drezner, 'Globalizers of the World, Unite!', in *The Washington Quarterly*, vol. 21, no. 1 (Winter 1998), p. 210.

50  *Ibid.*, p. 222.

51 Kenichi Ohmae, *The End of the Nation-State: The Rise of Regional Economies* (New York: Free Press, 1995).
52 Ulrich Beck, 'Capitalism Without Work', in *Dissent*, vol. 44, no. 1 (Winter 1997), p. 51.
53 Vivien A. Schmidt, 'The Impact of European Integration on Member-States' Economic and Industrial Policies: Assessing the Loss of National Autonomy and Control from Globalization vs. Europeanization', Paper presented at the 1998 APSA annual meeting, Boston (September 1998).
54 Louis Emmerij has argued that '[t]he formation or strengthening of regional groups may occur as an intermediate step towards globalization, to make the economies of these countries stronger in order for them to eke out a greater part of the global market ... Globalization and regionalization can either go hand in hand or be antagonistic, depending on the prevailing circumstances'. See Louis Emmerij, 'Globalization, Regionalization and World Trade', in *Columbia Journal of World Business*, vol. 27, no. 2 (Summer 1992).
55 Rüdiger Voigt, 'Ende der Innenpolitik? Politik und Recht im Zeichen der Globalisierung', in *Aus Politik und Zeitgeschichte*, nos 29–30 (10 July 1998).
56 Klaus Hänsch, 'Reasserting the Political Will to Move Europe Forward', the Robert Schuman Lecture at the European University Institute (Florence), 27 June 1996.
57 For a general comparison of regional and global trade agreements, see Beth V. Yarbrough and Robert M. Yarbrough, 'Regionalism and Layered Governance: The Choice of Trade Institutions', in *Journal of International Affairs*, vol. 48, no. 1 (Summer 1994).
58 Alan S. Milward (with the assistance of George Brennan and Frederico Romero), *The European Rescue of the Nation-State* (Berkeley/Los Angeles: University of California Press, 1992).
59 *Ibid.*, p. 3.
60 Robert Picht, 'European Cultural Policy After Maastricht', in Paul Michael Lützeler (ed.), *Europe After Maastricht: American and European Perspectives* (Providence/Oxford: Berghahn Books, 1994), p. 280.
61 Philip G. Cerny, 'Paradoxes of the Competition State: The Dynamics of Political Globalization', in *Government and Opposition*, vol. 32, no. 2 (Spring 1997).
62 *Ibid.*, p. 251.
63 Thomas Risse-Kappen (with Daniela Engelmann-Martin, Hans-Joachim Knopf and Klaus Roscher), 'To Euro or Not to Euro? The EMU and Identity Politics in the European Union', European University Institute, EUI Working Paper Series, nos 98–9 (Florence, March 1998).
64 *Foreign Broadcasting Information Service (FBIS–WEU–96–227)*, 22 November 1996.
65 For a general discussion, see John B. Goodman, *Monetary Sovereignty: The Politics of Central Banking in Western Europe* (Ithaca NY: Cornell University Press, 1992), especially Chapter 6.
66 Interview with Karel Van Miert in *Libre Belgique* (25 March 1998), translated in *FBIS–WEU–98–084*, 25 March 1998.
67 Online. Available HTTP: http://europa.eu.int/comm/eurostat/ (accessed 9 May 2000).
68 Daniel Bell, *The Cultural Contradictions of Capitalism* (New York: Basic Books, 1996).
69 Beck, 'Capitalism Without Work'.
70 Richard Sennett, 'The New Capitalism', in *Social Research*, vol. 64, no. 2 (Summer 1997), p. 168.
71 Zygmunt Bauman, *Postmodernity and Its Discontents* (New York: New York University Press, 1997), p. 14.
72 *Ibid.*, pp. 42–4.
73 *Ibid.*, pp. 28–9.
74 *Ibid.*, p. 65.

75 Slavoj Zizek, 'For a Leftist Appropriation of the European Legacy', in *Journal of Political Ideologies*, vol. 3, no. 1 (February 1998), p. 70.
76 Mathieu Deflem and Fred C. Pampel, 'The Myth of Postnational Identity: Popular Support For European Unification', in *Social Forces*, vol. 75, no. 1 (September 1996).
77 Edward Luttwak, 'Central Bankism', in Peter Gowan and Perry Anderson (eds), *The Question of Europe* (London: Verso, 1997), p. 221.
78 Quoted in the *Financial Times*, 24 July 1998.

# 3 European identity beyond the state

Reading the EU

## Europe between *Gesellschaft* and *Gemeinschaft*

'Europe' is a forest of ideas, symbols and myths. It is also in many ways a mirror that reflects the image of a multitude of concepts and meanings, rather than a prism that concentrates the minds and hearts of its peoples around a single central theme. The discourse on 'Europe' therefore needs to be examined against the background of a multifarious pattern that weaves together different strands of past, present and future.[1] The debate about 'European integration' reflects this ambivalence, since the phrase has a wide variety of meanings in the vocabulary of the European debate. It may refer to a process of long-term *socio-economic convergence* among European societies; a careful and premeditated *process of co-operation among European nation-states and regions* on a variety of levels; as well as a process of constructing (or 'growing') of a *European identity* that may parallel, or even come to supersede, national identities. These are different readings of the European concept that, although closely linked, do not necessarily have to develop in a harmonious fashion.

It should be recognized that on a European level the processes of state-formation and nation-formation have not run parallel. When we define state-formation as the creation of an infrastructure of governance based on law and a constitution, the EU has already made significant progress; if anything, the EU is a community based on the rule of law. When we define nation-formation as the development of a European culture and consciousness within a 'cognitive region', the EU remains rather backward. In the history of Europe the consolidation of state and nation has in many cases run parallel, but it has also often run out of sync. The Polish state, for example, did not exist for several centuries, but the Polish nation has always persisted. The Soviet Union, on the other hand, has survived seven decades without the development of a coherent and robust Soviet 'nation'. How flexible the concept of the nation-state is may be illustrated by the fact that the annual 'Six Nations Rugby Championship' involves not only established states like Ireland, Italy and France, but also England, Scotland and Wales. Although history therefore 'teaches' us many different things (and therefore teaches us little), it is generally questioned whether state-formation and nation-formation can actually diverge too much. Is it not necessary for all political entities to be based on a self-conscious and active body of citizens that is capable of directing its claims to, and through, central institutions? Should not all polities be based on a certain organized community and kept together by a 'sense of belonging'?

The debate about European identity can be brought back to the two ideal types of social organization distinguished by Ferdinand Tönnies as the typology of *Gemeinschaft* vs. *Gesellschaft*.[2] The crucial distinction between these two concepts is that *Gemeinschaft* ('community') relates to a certain sense of belonging based on shared loyalties, norms and values, kinship or ethnic ties; it is conditioned by the feeling that this is a 'natural' and organic association based on an *a priori* social unity, on the idea of 'one people', and hence a clearly cognizable *demos*. *Gesellschaft* ('society'), on the other hand, relates to the idea that people as individuals remain independent of each other, but may decide in a 'social contract', or a 'convention', to group together for the conduct of profit-making transactions; it remains an artificial construct which will only continue to exist as long as its citizens find the contractual arrangements of common value. Tönnies' sociological categories remain valuable for reading contemporary Europe and the development of the Euro-polity in particular. In many respects we could argue that EU Member States have over the decades built a European *Gesellschaft*, but that the EU still does not have the flesh-and-blood characteristics of an internal, living and organic entity. It is, in other words, not (yet?) a truly European *Gemeinschaft*.

These questions of a 'European identity' are not academic, but have a number of practical implications. In the political and scholarly discourse on European integration, the creation of a European *Gemeinschaft* of some kind is generally deemed to be a prerequisite for the further unfolding of the European proposition. Contemporary Europe shows a diversity of peoples and communities with only marginally overlapping points of reference regarding values, meaning and identities. Europe's cultural and social topography is fragmented, lacking clear unifying principles and shared experiences around which people could identify. This value-free multiformity, which now characterizes the western world in general, complicates notions of solidarity and democracy in a European context. The notion of 'Europe' has become one of the many images competing for allegiance in the marketplace of ideas.[3]

When we (conveniently) skip an examination of the exact content of Europe's identity, and conceive it as a certain level of societal cohesiveness and solidarity, it becomes apparent that, with the development of the Euro-polity, traditional political questions of the distribution of wealth will have to be addressed.[4] Europe's monetary union implies that within the EU significant sums of money are being transferred from wealthier parts to poorer regions. The prospective eastward enlargement of the EU will only add to the transfer of resources from rich(er) to poor(er) countries and regions. For Central European countries to compete in the EU's common market, productivity has to be enhanced and infrastructure improved. This can hardly be done without cost to the current EU Member States and without more modest support for the current beneficiaries of the Structural and Cohesion Funds (like Ireland, Spain, Portugal and Greece). This implies that there must be widespread, grass-roots political support for these transfers of resources: something like the 'natural' solidarity that we take for granted within nation-states.[5] It raises the question of how homogeneous we need to be in European terms? What level of solidarity and 'shared experience' is needed? How far the EU should become a *locus* of identity for European citizens? For the further development of the European project it will be especially relevant to examine whether it is possible to imagine a movement going beyond 'national' homogeneity, but toward some form of polycentric, civic form of Europeanism?

## National identity: Primordial, ephemeral?

Timothy Garton Ash has argued that the 'minimal trust and solidarity between citizens that is the fragile treasure of the democratic nation-state does not, alas, yet exist between the citizens of Europe. For there is no European *demos* – only a European *telos*'.[6] Although it is not even certain that the EU has such a clear notion of its future, it can hardly be disputed that a European *Gemeinschaft* remains the official political *desideratum* for further integration. A 'European people' will be difficult to imagine, although it should also not be excluded as an absurdity, or as a contradiction in terms.[7]

In the debate on the development of a European identity, we can distinguish proponents of two opposing conceptions:

1   those who see national identity and nationalism as *primordial* to human beings, in the sense that we all belong as if 'by nature' to some ethnic community, perhaps in the same way as we all by nature belong to a family;
2   those who consider these notions as *ephemeral*, as manifestations of a modern, state-centric era that is now drawing to a close (at least, as is often argued, in the West).

The first assumption is based on the doctrine of teleology, arguing that the nation-state serves a clear purpose of (human) self-realization. S.N. Eisenstadt and B. Giesen argue that collective identity based on primordiality stresses the differences from 'others', who are considered outsiders and cannot be converted or even adopted, cannot be educated, developed or even understood. The 'Other' is not guilty and has done no wrong, but is 'simply unalterably different'. This implies that such strangers are often perceived as a threat to the natural homogeneity of the collectivity.[8] The second postulate is based on a mechanical reading of history that assumes all phenomena can be explained by principles of causation and negates the existence of a final cause or purpose in history. This is a civic construction of collective identity which stresses historicity and tradition, as well as hierarchical distinctions between the 'bearers of tradition' and possible new members of the collectivity. But, since newcomers can become insiders by participating in (local) practices and institutions, the processes of inclusion and exclusion remain vague and open to change.

The view of national identity as an almost mystical notion, as a bond between 'the people' through culture, memory and fate, can be traced back to German Romantics like Herder, who speaks of *das Gefühl einer Nation*, and the *Seele, Herz und Tiefe* of a people and a nation. Herder clearly does not subscribe to the dictum that 'the past is another country' – on the contrary: without a clear sense of history, both the present and the future will remain unintelligible, and interest in the past is a clear reflection of concern for the future. But Herder's nationalism is inclusive, democratic and anti-imperialist. As Sir Isaiah Berlin has remarked, 'Herder optimistically believed that all the flowers in the human garden could grow harmoniously, the cultures could stimulate one another and contribute to a creative harmony'.[9] This is a far cry from the more aggressive nationalism which developed after the French Revolution and was most forcefully formulated in the Jacobin political program of fighting for the nation's life as well as for the ideals and institutions which have given the nation its 'political will'. The aggressive version of nationalism gained currency through the thoughts of Fichte, who argued that the superiority of the German 'character' and its culture form the very foundation of the German nation. Fichte was probably the first to argue that 'mankind is already divided into nations by nature, and the dissemination of nationalist doctrines will resemble calls to the faithful to prayer'.[10]

As a latter-day exponent of this Primordial School of nationalism, Anthony Smith argues that the nation-state continues to be the bedrock of world politics and that the nation and nationalism provide the only realistic socio-cultural framework in today's world order.[11] Smith flatly rejects the popular thesis that the nation-state as we know it has had its day, and that in a world of globalization other forms of political organization are better equipped and better positioned to deal with new challenges. His argument is built around the thesis that 'memory' is central to identity, and that 'we can discern no global identity-in-the-making, nor aspirations for one, nor any collective amnesia to replace existing "deep" cultures with a cosmopolitan "flat" culture. The latter remains a dream confined to some intellectuals'.[12] He goes on to explain that all members of a political community have a 'pre-history' which is based on shared experiences that, by definition, sets them apart from other people and endows them with a feeling of belonging.[13]

This clearly goes beyond a 'rational choice' by individual human beings about how to decide for themselves who they are, where they come from, and where they are going. Rather, as Smith argues,

> beneath the public version [of nationalism] there is often a deeper religious content to the sense of value and dignity of the national community, one which inevitably lends an air of exclusiveness to the core ethnic community of the nation. This is a sense of national dignity and chosenness.
>
> (Anthony D. Smith, *Nations and Nationalism in a Global Era* (Cambridge: Polity Press, 1995), p. 98)

This mythical, and more often than not also ethnic, nature and foundation of nationalism (which for many is a reason to argue that the Westphalian states system is war-prone and inherently unstable) is considered a key element of the contemporary nation-state. In present-day Europe, as in most other parts of the world, most identities are constructed as cognitive boundaries that are based on a sense of belonging. This, inevitably, assumes that 'identity' is an exclusive concept: you either 'belong', or you do not; you are either a 'citizen', or you are not. Without the Other, a regional or national sense of selfhood will be difficult to define and configure.[14]

Smith therefore finds it hard to imagine how a European federation could succeed in stamping out the deeply ingrained and historic identities and cultures of the many diverse peoples of Europe. He raises the interesting question of how the European project could advance without finding truly 'Pan-European' popular traditions and values, as well as their equivalent symbols and experiences. Since Smith's definition of identity focuses on a continuum of memory–situation–fate (which requires every robust identity to have a clear notion of its history, its present and its future), it will be difficult to construct a 'European memory' as well as notions of a 'European future'. Smith posits that there is no clear, popular notion of what 'Europe', 'European identity', or 'European culture', really stand for in terms of values, ideals and traditions. He also asks why anyone would want to choose a European identity/culture in preference to another, particularly in preference to his/her own national identity/culture?[15]

He goes on to argue that the European project constitutes neither a deep bond nor a real, vibrant community of fate, since without

> shared memories and meanings, without common symbols and myths, without shrines and ceremonies and monuments, except the bitter reminders of recent holocausts and wars, who will feel European in the depth of their being, and who will willingly sacrifice themselves for so abstract an idea? In short, who will die for Europe?
>
> (Anthony D. Smith, *Nations and Nationalism in a Global Era*
> (Cambridge: Polity Press, 1995), p. 139)

This leads him to conclude that in the current European political context, a truly united Europe, based on a European identity, could only emerge slowly through the formation of European memories and traditions, myths and symbols which would mirror the image of the contemporary nation-state. But it is clear that, for analysts like Smith, there is 'little prospect of a European "super-nation" until the majority of each European nation's population becomes infused with a genuinely European consciousness'.[16] Without a European *Gemeinschaft*-of-sorts, the way forward toward a 'political Europe' will remain troublesome.

At the other end of the conceptual spectrum we find those who argue that 'there are no natural links binding people to one another; people are therefore the authors of their own links, the artists of their own connections'.[17] This argument holds that national identity, nationalism and indeed the nation-state itself, are little more than political and cultural artifacts. Nation-states are read as social constructs that still look powerful and robust, but which are actually both ephemeral and open to modification. It acknowledges that Europe's nation-states are only a few centuries old, and have therefore lasted no longer than the Roman Empire. Indeed, the model of political authority for Europe has for centuries been the 'empire', rather than the nation-state.[18] From the Holy Roman Empire to the many European colonial empires (under French, Dutch, Belgian, Portuguese, Spanish or British dominance), the territorial, sovereign nation-state was either non-existent, or only one part of a diverse conglomerate of authority. As Alain de Benoist has argued, the empire is not primarily a territory, but 'an idea or a principle. The political order is determined by it – not by material factors or by possession of a geographical area. It is determined by a spiritual idea or juridical idea'.[19] In this historical context, the Herderian claim that individuals can only flourish within their own nation-state seems absurd. It also exposes nationalism as little more than a thinly veiled ideological exterior legitimizing the territorial sovereign state and its power apparatus.

This critique is part of a wider argument which claims that the nation-state and nationalism have been suitable and fitting for modern industrial society (which required mobile and literate citizens for effective performance). Nation-states have now lost much of their core purpose in a postmodern era, which requires new forms of political organization that go above and beyond the contemporary states system. The globalizing world, dominated by transnational firms, requires a totalizing *global* ideology and a more *global* and unified (and perhaps even homogeneous) culture of mass consumerism that responds to mass advertising. These ideas of postindustrialism are based on the assumption that new systems of mass communication and the use of computer-based technologies will put the nation-state under pressure by eroding and undermining established national identities. Rather than confined national entities, the era of globalization will call for continent-size markets regulated by one, clear set of economic and political rules and values.

This is the postmodern cosmopolitan culture that some consider the pinnacle, others the nadir, of human progress. It is a pastiche of cultures, rather than based on one, specific culture. It is eclectic in nature, disinterested in place and time, unconcerned about ethnic or national origins and blissfully ignorant of history. This follows the hegemonic 'logic' of the parallel processes of globalization and Europeanization which we examined earlier.

From this perspective, the Westphalian states system and its confined view of 'national interests' and 'national sovereignty' are (or, perhaps better, have been) functional during an era that is now drawing to a close, at least in most parts of the West (and in Western Europe in particular). This reading of the European integration process is based on a conception of material and historical determinism that works in a rather standardized and semi-automatic way, failing to make room for explanations that draw upon psychological and cultural factors, which analysts like Smith consider of such critical importance. Europe has been at a crossroads every other decade or so, and we should recognize that, over the course of its long history, a number of events have shaped the current structure of the continent which can hardly be explained by undiluted economic determinism. It is difficult to imagine how contemporary Europe would look if Charlemagne had *not* split up his heritage among his three sons – a decision that resulted in the separation of the west Franks from the east Franks, and subsequently led to the development of France and Germany. As Philip Allott has argued, 'there has been no natural and inevitable progression from the Athens of Solon to Economic and Monetary Union, there has never been a settled point of balance in the endless uniting and separating forces of European history'.[20]

This is a crucial point that needs to be emphasized. The European integration process is a unique consummation of political will and geopolitical circumstance. The European project has in many ways been a product of the Cold War, launched by the integrative stimulus of the Marshall Plan and hatched under the military wings of the US and NATO. But it has also been a voluntaristic project, based on the power of ideas and the forceful promotion of the concept of European unity and federalism. Participants of the Congress of the Hague, which founded the European Movement in May 1948, clearly agreed that the nation-state was the main source of the hatred and war among European peoples that had to be overcome. This anti-nationalist tenet, which has been a constant in the debate about Europe's future, was initially based on the geopolitical necessity of containing Germany within a strong institutionalized European framework, and later became a phlegmatic response to the pressures of globalization which continue to question the centrality of the nation-state.

In this sense, the basis for overcoming the hegemonic cult(ure) of the state is founded on the notion that European integration is a means to promote peace, rather than merely an economic program to guarantee prosperity. In many ways, the European Coal and Steel Community was not about coal and steel at all, but about the pacification of the continent, German–French reconciliation and building a security community. It has been a mechanical process, willed and consciously constructed by Western Europe's economic and political elite. And for committed European federalists, it has also been a teleological process, based on the argument that the peoples of Europe may finally liberate themselves from the unnatural bonds of their nation-states and find their cultural self-realization in a freer, more open European political framework. Former British European Commissioner Lord Cockfield has summed up this argument by noting that '[t]he gradual limitation of national sovereignty is part of a slow and painful forward march of humanity'.[21]

I do not want to argue here that the 'truth' can be found somewhere in the middle, in a compromise between the Primordial and the Ephemeral perspectives on the nation-state and nationalism. However, it does seem rather brazen to proclaim the singularity of the nation-state and its indispensability for all meaningful human political and cultural development in the light of the nation-state's rather short historical life. In this context, one is reminded of the story Baudrillard tells of a nineteenth-century English naturalist, Philip Henry Gosse, who was studying fossils. As a devout Christian, Gosse argued that Creation had taken place *ex nihilo* and that

God thus had created at once fossils, geological sediments, exactly as they were in the 19th century, and he had created them as simulacra, as a *trompe l'oeil* in order to provide humanity ... with a history, hence a past. Therefore, God would have provided human beings with a retrospective past by creating fossils and geological sediments.

(Caroline Bayard and Graham Knight, 'Vivisecting the 90s: An Interview with Jean Baudrillard' (8 March 1995). Online. Available HTTP: http://www.ctheory.com/a24-vivisecting90s.html, accessed 28 March 2000)

In many ways, nation-states continue to author and carefully cultivate their national heritages, their cultural memories, as the indispensable fossils and sedimental sentiments for future generations to admire and 'learn' from. These national fossils may no longer be politically relevant, but they do continue to serve as one of the few remaining unifying and legitimizing instruments of state authority and power.

Mike Featherstone has further reminded us that it is also possible to find counter-examples of conceptions of culture which lack a centralizing unifying impulse. Ancient Rome, for example, 'remained syncretic and open to multiplicity and was therefore able to resist the strong insider/outsider divisions which are often used to create social and cultural unity'.[22] On the other hand, we should also acknowledge that if the state-centric system does indeed whither away, it will no doubt do so slowly and at a rate at times imperceptible to the social scientist's academic eye. As long as socio-paleontologists have not discovered new, shiny and attractive examples of truly *European* fossils, the nation-state's historical heritage is bound to remain a central part of our memory and identity. Europe is therefore certainly not predestined to unite, and the 'forces of globalization' still allow national governments some room for maneuver to come up with a political response that may well be different from intensified Europeanization. Turning globalism into the *deus ex machina* for European integration would be too shallow and naive an analysis.

The presumption that an 'identity' constitutes the substructure for national development should be further problematized. Should we take it for granted that national selfhood is some kind of puzzle that has a hidden solution based on the assumption that to know the 'nation' is to know the hidden national Self that lies buried deep within it? But what if this national Self, this national identity, does not really exist, cannot be discovered, and is actually made and continuously remade? This would render national and European identity more complex and turn it into something much looser, as an aggregate of methods and policies, of clusters of rules and regulations that ceaselessly interact in a prosaic process with the uncountable other facts of everyday life. Identity must not necessarily be considered as a gift and an inborn and primordial quality, but as a dynamic process that requires enormous energy to maintain and that will never be fully 'complete'. This would be a conception of Self that assumes the absence of totality and unity as a static condition. Through this analytical prism, the imperfections and limitations of Europe's contemporary identity should almost be taken for granted. No teleology, economic and social determinism or other totalizing quest for generating 'identity' can explain the discontinuity of the development of a notion of European selfhood. Instead, Europe's fragments and fractures may well be construed as one of its main attractions, offering unique openings and opportunities in today's postmodern era. Europe should neither succumb to the vanities of victimhood nor to the temptations of Groupthink, but should make a serious attempt to challenge existing conceptions of identity and turn this notion into an idiosyncratic, anti-canonical, open and fertile ground for cultivation.

Perhaps, therefore, the most important question should not be 'does national identity matter?' Rather we should ask 'under what circumstances and to what extent does national identity matter' as a factor in the process of Europeanization?

## Civic and ethnic Europeanism

The classical distinction is made between nations that define themselves along civic or ethnic lines. *Civic nationalism*, which we can find in France and the United States, defines the 'nation' in terms of the willingness of its people to adhere to a certain set of civic values and rules with *jus soli* (or citizenship by birthplace) as the norm. The focus of allegiance is the state and its institutions, which also implies a high degree of cultural assimilation as the price to be paid by ethnic groups for their integration in society. *Ethnic nationalism*, which we can find in Germany and Poland, defines the 'nation' in terms of ethnic origin and birth; nationality is determined by *jus sanguinis*, that is by ancestry and blood-ties, rather than by residence, choice and commitment.[23] In a somewhat simplified way, we could say that civic nationalism stresses the importance of the individual's commitment to the *Gesellschaft*, whereas ethnic nationalism tends to emphasize the organic sense of belonging that is central to *Gemeinschaft*. A third alternative for nationality would be the multicultural model in which the nation allows scope for the maintenance of cultural and ethnic differences. This would make full citizenship relatively easy without the requirement of cultural assimilation. The clearest examples of this alternative are to be found outside Europe (i.e., in Australia and Canada).[24]

Although the examples of France and Germany show that both civic and ethnic nationalism can be based on the dual principles of individual rights and liberty, it has proved difficult to anchor society and culture on tolerance and inclusion when allegiance is invested in ethnicity. By definition, ethnicity is a permanent element of identity that is not subject to choice; it cannot be easily concealed. Ethnic nations are, almost by definition, rather closed societies in which bloodline or skin-color may continue to brand you as an 'outsider'. In sharp contrast, allegiance, the defining element of civic nationalism, is more flexible and more inclusive. In starker terms, it can be argued that collective identity can be conceptualized as secular, civic and inclusive-pluralist on the one hand, and in terms of consanguinity, religion, and ethno-nationalist exclusiveness on the other.

But this is not all. We should further recognize that a sense of home does not have to be based on written sources and unquestioned elements of collective memory. Rather, it depends to a large extent on enacted ceremonial performances, commemorative rituals, language and formalities that regularly charge our emotional batteries and renew our sense of belonging. Since the state has become the 'standard' unit for political authority in Europe, nationalist thought has constructed a collective identity within the specific boundaries of national territory. This is how nation-states have throughout the centuries developed and cultivated the strong bonds of community. Roland Robertson has argued that, during the intense phase of globalization that took place between 1880 and 1920, European states responded with an extreme form of nationalism and a 'wilful nostalgia' in an effort to shelter their societies and cultures from the 'outside'.[25] New national symbols were developed, new ceremonies introduced and traditions (re)invented. These were new rites celebrating a 'glorious past' and based on readings of traditions and culture that sought to integrate and standardize citizens' loyalty to the nation-state and the national idea(l). Scottish nationalism, for example, is a modern phenomenon, which celebrates its clan culture through kilts and bagpipes in an effort to distinguish itself from increasing convergence with England within the United Kingdom. The fear of becoming 'British' has set off an emphasis on Scottishness – real or imagined, based on history or modern fabrications. This 'invention of tradition', often going hand in hand with the 'monumentalization of the past', obfuscates that states are rather formal constitutional arrangements only occasionally based on a genuine collective heritage. More often than not, states are products of the imagination, rather than 'objectively' and 'empirically' verifiable communities of interest and identity.[26]

It is all too obvious that as the economic and social patterns of nations and states converge toward a 'European' level, and as cultural distinctiveness wanes, a search for identity and belonging may provoke an initial backlash of intolerance. The fear of being overwhelmed by a Europeanized culture which questions the legitimacy of national habits, mores and traditions often reinforces localism – regionalism as well as nationalism. This is clearly noticeable in contemporary Europe. Klaus Hänsch has argued that throughout Europe we can find a

renaissance of nationalism. It is a paradox. Where the nation state can less deliver than ever before in history, a growing part of our citizens focus their affections on the nation state. And that is not without logic: because man does not live by bread alone. In a time of growing alienation the abstract European institutions, remote as they seem, are unable to attract the imagination and affection of our people.

(Klaus Hänsch, President of the European Parliament, in his Robert Schuman Lecture at the European University Institute, Florence, 27 June 1996. Online. Available HTTP: http://www.iue.it/AEL/documents/ haensch.html, accessed 15 August 2000)

In this context we should, however, raise the question whether this 'spiritual need' for a sense of belonging can only be satisfied within the confines of the nation-state, or whether we can image other, perhaps even cozier and warmer, communities on a sub-national level. These alternative communities do not have to be organized on a territorial basis, but may well be within a religious community or a societal group. I see no reason why the nation-state should have the monopoly of 'home' or should be the single arbiter of 'belonging'.

But to return to the theme of ethnic conflict as a response to homogenizing European and global pressures, we may quote Sigmund Freud who observed in 1917 that 'it is precisely the minor differences in people who are otherwise alike that form the basis of feelings of strangeness and hostility between them'.[27] This 'narcissism of minor differences', as Freud labeled it, is certainly a key element in explaining and understanding the development of a contemporary European 'identity'. Although men and women are practically the same down to a few chromosomes, their sense of identity is derived from how they differ from one another, and is not based on a perception of the essential similarity among the genders. In this sense, all identity-formation has an intrinsic antipathetic, at times even aggressive, character. Michael Ignatieff has argued that these 'differences', be they between the sexes, religions, races or nations, are in themselves neutral, but that it is 'the narcissist who turns them into a judgement on himself. Narcissistic anxiety expresses itself chiefly in passive self-absorption and epistemological closure. A narcissist is incurious about others except to the extent that they reflect back on himself. What is different is rejected if it fails to confirm the narcissist in his or her self-opinion'.[28] This 'closure' from the outside world is the last line of defense of identity, and on this reading it is easy to see why nationalism can be thought of as a kind of narcissism.

## European identity/affinity politics

This still leaves unanswered the troublesome question what the alternative might be to visualizing Europe as a cultural entity with a shared sense of community and a measure of homogeneity?[29] Should we conceive the European project 'as a dynamic and often contradictory process, the final shape or *telos* of which is indeterminate rather than teleological'?[30]

At least part of the problem can be found in the complex and novel nature of decision-making and power in the (West) European context. Within the EU, the 'classical' economic notion of power no longer makes sense and only limits our understanding of the policy-formation process. Thinking in terms of power as something that can be 'traded away', as some sort of commodity, seems pointless. Instead we might want to pursue Foucault's notion that we should understand power as 'something which circulates, or rather as something which only functions in the form of a chain ... employed and exercised through a net-like organization'.[31] This notion of power is most visually formulated by Wendy Brown, who has argued that '[p]ostmodern power incessantly violates, transgresses, and resituates social boundaries; it flows on surfaces and irrigates through networks rather than consolidating in bosses and kings; it is ubiquitous, liminal, highly toxic in small and fluid doses'.[32] In this sense, postmodern power is all shades and no distinct boundaries.

This may illustrate the exasperation of many participants and observers of the policy-making process within the EU, which is equivocal, fragmented, protracted and involves an assortment of actors who have varied roles and functions. The EU is a complex, composite and hybridized political entity defined by betweenness and multicultural diversity. But how to read this novel political entity? How to influence the direction of this process and the policy outcomes of the decision-making body? Europeanization is often accompanied by a certain sense of dislocation, displacement and puzzlement. This is not to say that Europe is foreign to us – particularly since all European societies are in one way or other an integral part of this political community – but it certainly problematizes our national identity and forces us to think how Europe resonates in our political understanding of the Self.

This increasing political homelessness has given rise to what has been called 'identity politics', which refers to the notion of accepting and pursuing politics in terms of gender, sexuality, race, region, state or continent, or other spatial or non-spatial terms of reference. Identity politics is based on a demand for authenticity, insisting on the right of those previously invisible and unrecognized to receive opportunities for self-realization.[33] Brown has defined this as a reaction 'to an ensemble of distinctly postmodern assaults upon the integrity of communities producing identity'.[34] Although there is little doubt that identity politics has increased the awareness of marginalization, discrimination and the very notion of 'difference', it has failed to develop into a long-term tool of social and political change. Identity politics has in most cases been a strategy and a compensatory technique to draw attention to underprivileged groups, and it has often led to more fragmentation, divisiveness and a continuous lack of unity.[35] Identity politics has therefore been criticized because it 'creates and perpetuates an understanding of public identity composed in terms of the suffering self: the oppressed are innocent selves defined by the wrongs done to them'.[36]

Focusing on identity therefore tends to be a passive instrument of division, a search for the qualities and values that divide people, rather than a quest for a human essence that may unite people, or at least connect them. Postmodern scholars have further problematized the subjective construction of particular identities, arguing that such different factors as race, gender, class and sexual preference cannot be regarded separately, and that any attempt to prioritize such factors would simply be another dimension of a totalizing and dominating essentialism.[37] By 'essentialism' is meant the attribution of presumably defining characteristics to a person, a group, or even a concept, assuming that some attributes can be expected to shape their relations to other persons, other groups, or other ideologies. Essentialist politics therefore asserts that some relations are more important than others (i.e., the Marxist assumption of class as the defining social and economic category) and therefore have to be taken into account when constructing strategies for political change.[38] The process of European integration should therefore be understood as a massive European venture of *reversed* identity politics: it can be read as a search for what makes it possible to think in terms of a concept of 'Europe'. It is a sustained effort to invent an all-embracing 'imagined community' on a continental scale.[39]

In this context the argument is frequently made that changes in technology, economic relations and social institutions have led to a contradictory and almost dialectical process of simultaneous globalization and localization. Technology homogenizes times and space, creating global images that erode established categories of identity. As a result, people have begun to imagine 'new communities' apart from the traditional nation-state, new 'homes' based on new social epistemes (i.e., what people collectively know about themselves as well as others).[40] These new 'homes' are developed along the lines of cognitive regions, whose borders are inevitably fluid but which nevertheless are defined by a shared, intersubjective understanding of culture, common identity and a commensurate sense of solidarity.[41] These new 'homes' are not simply and solely based on the subjective emotions of a certain undefinable we-feeling, but perhaps most of all on the basis of shared knowledge and a shared notion that we all inhabit a (non-territorial) space in which we can feel 'at home'.[42] Since Europe's identity will be of a disembedded quality, characterized by unsteadiness and lacking the solidity and continuity that has been the trade-mark of the modern era and its institutions, European integration offers opportunities for new or oppressed identities to find a societal niche for themselves. It will also increasingly call for new, looser senses of political affiliation to manifest themselves on the supranational level. In this sense, Europe calls for an identity politics of affinity, rather than a parochialized, narrow sense of Self.[43]

But we should be careful in imagining this new 'European home'. Ignatieff has correctly noted that as a matter of historical fact, 'Europe does not stand for toleration any more than it stands for ethnic cleansing. The doctrine of toleration *is* a European invention, but so is the concentration camp'.[44] As Zizek has noted: 'When one says "European legacy", every self-respectful Leftist intellectual has the same reaction as Joseph Goebbels had to culture as such – he reaches for his guns and starts to shoot out accusations of proto-Fascist Eurocentrist cultural imperialism'.[45] Clearly, Europe can look back on a checkered past and the only way to develop a 'European consciousness' might well be to turn our backs to European history and develop as a community that is oriented toward the future. This raises the further question of whether Europe could provide its many and diverse peoples with a new sense of belonging, probably not based on Smith's notion of 'shared memory' but on a foundation of common sedimented experiences, cultural forms which are associated, however loosely, with a place called 'Europe'. Perhaps the only way of achieving this aim is not to stress collective memory but rather collective amnesia, in an effort to collectively forget the centuries of strife and conflict among European peoples and states?

This would call for what Bauman has labeled a 'palimpsest identity', which is 'the kind of identity which fits the world in which the art of forgetting is an asset no less, if no more, important than the art of memorizing'. It is the kind of identity 'in which forgetting rather than learning is the condition of continuous fitness, in which ever new things and people enter and exit without rhyme or reason'.[46] This again follows Nietzsche's call for 'active forgetfulness', a conscious and incessant effort to protect the human being from absolute historical memory and to burden it with all so-called 'historical truths'.[47] Only such a palimpsest identity may provide Europe with the freedom to generously accommodate its many cultures and multifarious senses of 'we'. This would follow the postmodern understanding of culture as a superficial decoration, as a capricious and calculated playing with European ethnic and folk-motifs to festoon and beautify what is in essence a scientific and technocratic culture. The question is, however, would it really be advisable for a country like Germany to practice such an 'active forgetfulness', and how would its neighbors react to such historical ignorance?[48] There remains a certain fear that such a palimpsest Germany, forgetful of its past, would be tempted to repeat its mistakes. As a former Dutch ambassador to Germany asserted, 'Germans should not get normal'.[49]

I have already noted that postmodernism criticizes the assumption that Europe is the cradle of civilization, and that it does not accept a linear process of unbroken development from barbarity to modern culture. The view that Europe is culturally superior is offensive, and the idea that European values and norms should be spread around the world for the benefit of other cultures is in itself imperialistic and misleading. During the Middle Ages, the very term 'Europe' was used mainly to strengthen a sense of solidarity *vis-à-vis* a common enemy, especially during the period of Crusades to recapture the 'Holy Land' from the 'barbarians'. This view of a culturally superior and economically supreme 'Europe' became dominant with the ideas of the Enlightenment, a period in which the consciousness of Europe reached new and unprecedented heights. The industrialization of European society, newly generated wealth, new technologies and commensurate military prowess put Europe in a position of global leadership, which nurtured a sense of cultural aloofness and feelings of European 'specialness', if not 'chosenness'. Since it was during exactly these centuries of European global preponderance that most European nation-states were formed and consolidated, sentiments of a presumed 'natural' pre-eminence have been established in the historical psyche of many European nations.

But such a reading of history obviously excludes other cultural centers of gravity from the equation (China and the Muslim world, for example), and ignores the valuable inputs of other cultures to what we now know as 'European civilization'. A teleological perspective on European culture, from Homer to the Amsterdam Treaty, also conveniently overlooks the nastier bits of European history (i.e., colonialism, fascism and communism). We should also question the political consequences of replicating the processes of identity-construction and 'organic community'-building in an EU framework. There is certainly a risk that such a European *Gemeinschaft* will merely legitimize exclusion based on clear-cut division between 'us' and 'them', especially since the social construction of identity is such an indivisible part of the discourse on security.[50] The concept of 'national values' is a component of a political discourse that specifies an internal community by juxtaposing it with an external threat. Occasionally, this 'threat' may be found in supposedly 'non-European' values and ethics (like racism and militarism), which may explain the strong reaction of EU Member States against the inclusion of Jörg Haider's FPÖ in the Austrian government in January 2000. The security discourse is also about the creation of a political identity in an 'imagined community', usually within the boundaries of the nation-state. Europe's identity is therefore an integral part of the wider discourse on Europe's *home* and *outer* security, inevitably implying a sense of alterity and, ultimately, enmity.

How may the discourse on Europe's identity be kept on a prosaic, rather than on a securitized, heroic level? Maintaining and nurturing Europe's local and regional cultures is one prerequisite for developing a Euro-polity which has grass-roots support, based on a European identity that develops in parallel with other identities and which does not threaten to turn the continent into a much-feared Esperanto culture. The ethno-national approach of Smith toward the construction of a European *Gemeinschaft*, with all the traditional paraphernalia of statehood ranging from shared myths and memories to an anthem and European flag, will not offer a genuine alternative. It may perhaps not hurt (although even that remains to be seen), but it will certainly not do the trick by itself. A civic, rather than an ethno-national approach to nationalism and citizenship, unquestionably offers a better opportunity for building an open, postmodern Euro-polity. This is exactly the reason why EU Member States have decided to set up a Europe of the Regions at the same time as further steps toward Europeanization were taken at Maastricht. It is this celebration of difference that has formed, and should continue to form, the basis for a nascent European political community. This Europe will remain a cultural potpourri, even if national allegiances may face fierce competition from calls for regional and overarching European loyalties. This would also be a sound basis for a nascent European citizenship.

We should therefore accept that 'the uniqueness of the European Union order in the making requires new conceptual tools and a fundamental rethinking of standard models'.[51] It also serves to indicate that we should make a serious effort to conceptualize 'ordered disorder and complex syncretisms in which wholes are seen as looser agglomerations and polymers of parts, which we find celebrated in postmodernism'.[52] In other words, Europe's identity should be based on its celebrated diversity, its openness and inclusiveness. Its identity cannot be realized by talking about it; it cannot be grasped theoretically; it can only be derived from practice. European identity is an act which can experience the continuous redefinition of itself only through relationships with others. This, rather than a narrow-minded and narrow conception of 'Europeanness', should form the platform for a new, civic European identity.[53] We might want to go as far as accepting Derrida's notions of 'undecidability' and 'unfinalizability' of the European project, based on the conviction that Europe's political space remains an open, plural and polycentric place.

Accepting this notion has, of course, significant political ramifications. Turning 'Europeanness' into a postmodern badge of privilege and superiority, a new marker of pride and dignity, would risk emulating the trappings of nationalism on a European level, rather than grasping the opportunity to develop something qualitatively new. Would it, for example, really make much difference whether we heard 'Europe for the Europeans' or 'Germany for the Germans' as slogans in the discourse of the extremist Right? But if 'Europe' is not for the 'Europeans', who is it for? And, what is more, who should be the prime movers in advocating the European identity in the increasingly competitive marketplace of ideas and symbols?

## Engineers of the European soul

With the Maastricht Treaty of 1992, EU nationals can now take pride in their new European citizenship. This clearly adds a certain civic element to the development of a new community of European peoples. However, as was to be expected, there have been few signs that European citizenship has touched an emotional chord with the ordinary wo/man in Europe's streets. In principle, there is little problem with acknowledging that there is not – and most likely will never be – *one* European people, but that the European continent will embrace a number of European *peoples*. One European culture, on a par with a single European currency, will not come into existence, and we will continue to see a plethora of European languages, traditions, historical experiences and ways of life.

As I have argued, a European identity will not have to be modeled on the national identities that we know now. Instead, it should be focused on a set of shared values that underpin all (or at least most) European cultures. It should be associated with the idea that there is a certain 'European way of life', analogous to the 'American way of life' that has become one of the instrumental myths of the United States' culture of capitalist individualism. Europe's identity would than be molded on the belief that Europe has found a unique balance between the 'market' and 'social protection'; a unique balance between 'commerce' and 'culture', between 'capitalism' and 'socialism'. This should then be regarded as an uneasy equilibrium between these different forces and concepts, since Europe is supposed also to be based on diversity, not homogeneity, and on a high level of tolerance, not a numbing and anti-creative uniformity.

Fortunately or unfortunately, depending on your perspective, such a 'European way of life' does not really exist. Europeanization may over decades generate a broader European cultural basis for all peoples of the continent, but this will remain an erratic process with an uncertain outcome. In many respects, the process of Europeanization remains an elite-driven project. The regular *Eurobarometer* opinion polls, conducted by the European Commission, invariably register steady and broad support among the European population for the European project in all its different facets. Although this popular support for Europeanization is an important political factor, as early as the 1970s James

Caporaso had already warned us that public opinion polls may deceive political elites, since the argument could be made that 'the concept of Europe is popular precisely because it is only dimly perceived and affects Europeans' everyday lives only peripherally'.[54] For now, we may argue (with Trevor Lloyd) that 'most people who think of themselves as "Europeans" [probably] have at least a Master of Arts degree'.[55] It is clear that most European citizens do not feel that they are 'Europeans' in the way that they are Danish, Roman Catholic, lesbian, or a supporter of Sheffield Wednesday.

This can be explained partly by the fact that until the mid-1980s European integration was perceived as first and foremost an *economic* project, not directly touching upon the core values of its constituent peoples. Over the decades Europe's collective identity has developed hand in hand with an institutionalized 'culture of co-operation'. Organizations like the EU, in tandem with the Council of Europe and NATO, and (in a smaller political space) the WEU and the Benelux countries, have developed a real 'security community' in the Deutschian sense.[56] This 'culture of co-operation' is also referred to as Europe's 'embedded liberalism', based on the routinized and widely accepted mechanism of collective policy-making through (institutionalized) networks of interorganizational linkages. But although this consociational culture is crucial to understanding contemporary Europe, and the European integration project in particular, it has *ipso facto* remained an elite affair.[57] (For example, in her 1999 survey of European Commission senior career officials, Liesbet Hooghe has found that the EU's policy elite is keenly pro-European, due to socialization and institutional learning.)[58] Occasionally, this 'culture of co-operation' will trickle down to ordinary citizens, but it does not involve most of them in a direct way. So, as Philip Schlesinger has summarized, if there is a plausible story of emergent Europeanness to be told, 'it will probably have to be rooted in a gradualist saga of growing together through institutional sedimentation, the patient outcome of the *longue durée* rather than the quick-fire product of technocratic rationalism'.[59]

Although an approach based on 'technocratic rationalism' is unlikely to be of any help in reconstructing the European *Gesellschaft* in an authenticated *Gemeinschaft*, European policy-makers have from the outset understood that further steps toward the ultimate goal of a Federal Europe would require more than incremental change. Merely keeping the Functionalist machinery of spill-over moving will be insufficient. Robert Schuman therefore argued (in 1964) that a

> true community requires at least some specific affinities. Countries do not combine when they do not feel among themselves something common, and what must above all be common is a minimum of confidence. There must also be a minimal identity of interests, without which one attains mere co-existence, not co-operation.
>
> (Robert Schuman, *Pour l'Europe* (Paris: Nagel, 1964), pp. 195–6)

From the very beginning of the European integration process it has therefore been recognized that something more exciting than coal and steel was needed to imbue Europe with a sense of *mystique*. Jacques Delors has famously noted that 'Europeans will not fall in love with a Common Market'. Especially since European integration increasingly touches directly on the boundaries of traditional state sovereignty, there is a growing need to strengthen the public's identification with 'Europe'. Hence the official goals of fostering a European 'we-feeling' and forging a 'European identity' of sorts.

In this context, Brigid Laffan has suggested three dimensions of the EU's top-down policies designed to embellish Europe's identity:

1   the development of rights and citizenship;
2   the politics of 'belonging' and symbols; and
3   the development of, and support for, cross-national networks and co-operation.[60]

The remainder of this chapter will deal with the symbolic development of Europe and will also peripherally touch upon the importance of societal networks across Europe. The key element of citizenship, its implications for democracy and its potential for exclusion will be discussed in Chapter 6.

From the early 1970s onward, the notion of the cultural underpinnings of the EC has been widely discussed, also within the Brussels bureaucracy.[61] In 1973 the EC Foreign Ministers adopted a 'Declaration Concerning European Identity', followed by a 'Report on European Union' (1976), which introduced the concept of a 'Citizen's Europe'. Numerous declarations to breathe life into these notions have been aired during the 1980s, which resulted in the introduction of a European Flag (bearing a circle of twelve five-pointed golden stars set against an azure background), as well as an anthem (Schiller's *Ode to Joy*, set to music in the final movement of Beethoven's Ninth Symphony), and other paraphernalia symbolizing Europe's 'identity'.[62] The European Flag has become a rather potent symbol of Europe. It is now visible everywhere on public buildings, and during festivities and official meetings it flies next to national and regional flags. It decorates the license-plates of most cars registered in the EU, and in many ways it has become a natural part of the European scenery; hardly to be overlooked. In itself, this flag means little, but as usual there is a deeper narrative behind even the most innocuous of symbols. In his famous work *Visual Thinking*, Rudolf Arnheim has pointed out that the 'image of the sphere has been used through the ages to depict physical, biological, and philosophical phenomena. Roundness is chosen spontaneously and universally to represent something that has no shape, no definite shape, or all shapes'.[63] I do not want to digress too much into semiotics, but in this sense one could argue that the European Flag does indeed reflect the indeterminate past, present and future of the continent. What is more, the twelve golden stars initially symbolized the then twelve EU Member States, which brings to mind the metaphor of Thomas Mann (in *Buddenbrooks*) that stars will shine brightest when their actual power has already subsided.

The basic *political* (and psychological) idea behind the introduction of these European symbols is to gradually modify the consciousness of the peoples of Europe of the political entity to which they belong.[64] But the strengthening of a European identity, which would not replace national identity but would be one of many identities held by individuals, is a process of both top-down voluntarist management and bottom-up attitudinal changes. Attempts to create a European identity through European symbols seem a dead-end. European citizens now have a standard (deep-red) passport, but anyone travelling inside the EU will discover that borders remain relevant (if only when moving out of the EU/Schengen area). What is more, although these passports (significantly, still referred to as *identity* papers) have a standardized cover, some Member States have given their interiors a notably national edge: the Dutch passport, for example, shows a brief pictorial history starting with the ancient Batavi and leading up to the present-day Netherlands.

The physical presentation of the Euro and the consolidation of a European foreign and security policy worthy of the name, might (just *might*) constitute the basis for a somewhat more robust European identity. 'Kosovo' has boosted the development of Europe's Security and Defence Identity (ESDI). At the EU's Helsinki summit of December 1999 European leaders took a decisive step toward the development of a new Common European Security and Defence Policy (CESDP) aimed at giving the Union a stronger role in international affairs backed up by credible military force. It is, however, difficult to see how the EU, as a civilian power, could change its spots and become a military one. For the moment 'Europe' still lacks *der Wille zur Macht* and will continue to lean on the United States for heroic, military support.

In the absence of such a military European identity, it is especially the introduction of the Euro that has been heralded as a potentially powerful source of unity among 'Europeans': 'The day the citizens of the European Union begin to pay with the [Euro], instead of pesetas, pounds, escudos or drachmas, this new dynamic society will be more European and more of a Union on several, not only economic, levels'.[65] The argument is often made that banknotes and coins reflect the national values and history that are central to people's consciousness: 'Each time a Spaniard pays with pesetas, images of distinguished figures of Spanish culture get registered in his brain. Spanish poets, writers, musicians, as well as beautiful Spanish landscapes and celebrated cultural achievements'.[66] This is naturally and surely an unconscious process in which currencies form part of the 'national currents' that continuously recharge the batteries of nationalism.

It is important to note that the EU has been well aware of the semiotics of the Euro. In a special communication the EU has described the design of the notes and coins as well as the Euro symbol:

> Every Euro coin will carry a common European face. On the obverse, each Member State will decorate the coins with their own motifs. *No matter which motif is on the coins they can be used anywhere inside the 11 Member States. For exam-*

*ple, a French citizen will be able to buy a hot dog in Berlin using a Euro coin carrying the imprint of the King of Spain.* The common European face of the coins represents a map of the European Union against a background of transverse lines to which are attached the stars of the European flag. The 1, 2 and 5 cent coins put emphasis on Europe's place in the world while the 10, 20 and 50 present the Union as a gathering of nations. The 1 and 2 Euro coins depict Europe without frontiers.

(EU's server 'Europa'. Online. Available HTTP:
http://europa.eu.int/euro/html/entry.html,
accessed 15 August 2000. Emphasis in the original)

The Euro-notes too, have their own narrative:

The designs are symbolic for Europe's architectural heritage. They do not represent any existing monuments. Windows and gateways dominate the front side of each banknote as symbols of the spirit of openness and co-operation in the EU. The reverse side of each banknote features a bridge from a particular age, a metaphor for communication among the people of Europe and between Europe and the rest of the world.

(EU's server 'Europa'. Online. Available HTTP:
http://europa.eu.int/euro/html/entry.html, accessed 15 August 2000)

As for the Euro-symbol, the EU argues that 'it was inspired by the Greek letter epsilon, in reference to the cradle of European civilization and to the first letter of the word "Europe". The parallel lines represent the stability of the Euro'.[67] Will these reflections of non-existent buildings, unknown Queens and Kings, windows and gateways, encourage the Europeanness of the countries that participate in the Euro-zone? It is difficult to answer such a question with any degree of confidence.

It is therefore doubtful that the introduction of a European anthem, a European Flag, European monuments for the 'glorious dead', European ceremonies, universities and museums for 'European heroes' or Europe's 'Founding Fathers', will generate the feeling of historicity, of common roots and belonging. Even in an era where the image has become the principal method of collective appeal and public address, the notion of Europe has so many competitors that it will be difficult to capture a market niche in the collective consciousness of European society. It is also manifestly evident that Member States have no ambitions whatsoever to produce a standardized 'European wo/man'. Politics as the art of engineering the human soul is clearly *passé*. Europe's postmodern polity has shed all illusions and ambitions to mold society and culture after some illusory ideological model, although some regrets and phantom pains in the amputated instruments of power are on occasion painfully noticeable.

Only a limited apparatus of statecraft remains available for Europe's political elite. Jean Monnet's famous remark that 'if we were beginning the European

Community all over again, we should begin with culture', has dawned upon the European Commission in the 1980s, resulting in a growing awareness that efforts should be made to turn 'Europe' (i.e., the EU area) into something like a 'common cultural/communicative space'. The forces of globalization have also encouraged European countries to take a further step toward Europeanization by promoting the study of foreign languages (especially English, German and French) at schools and universities. Educational exchange is only one element of a larger EU project to encourage the development of a 'European culture'. A dense web of youth programs now exists with special programs to increase student mobility across Europe with the explicit purpose of developing the 'European dimension' of higher education programs. The European Commission's biggest success is probably its all-European student exchange system (called the ERASMUS program). The Commission's aim has been to raise significantly the percentage of students who study abroad, from the current level of 4 per cent to 10 per cent in the not too distant future. The figures for 1998/99 indicate that more than 1,600 universities (or equivalent institutions) from 24 countries are benefiting from this program; the activities approved by the Commission comprise the exchange of more than 200,000 students and 35,000 teachers. It is telling that this program has as its motto 'Bringing students to Europe; Bringing Europe to all students'. ERASMUS also specifically encourages teaching staff exchanges and 'transnational curriculum development'.

The Maastricht Treaty now provides the EU with a clear-cut legal basis for dealing with a much wider range of cultural matters.[68] Article 128 (paragraph 4) stipulates that the 'Community shall take cultural aspects into account in its actions under the provisions of this Treaty, in particular in order to respect and *to promote* the diversity of its cultures'. I would like to emphasize that the explicit goal of promoting cultural diversity is crucial in understanding both the limits of cultural Europeanization and the very complex nature of this effort. The Union has adopted the UNESCO definition of culture, which is a rather comprehensive one: 'culture consists of all distinctive, spiritual and material, intellectual and emotional features which characterize a society or a social group.'[69] The EU therefore considers it as its role to (among other things) 'improve the knowledge and dissemination of the culture and history of the European peoples', and to 'conserve and safeguard cultural heritage of European significance'. This will be done (of course 'while respecting national and regional diversity') with the explicit aim of 'bringing the common cultural heritage to the fore'. One manifestation has been the launching of a yearly rotating 'European City of Culture'. Since 1985 the EU has sponsored this annual event with the explicit objective of 'bringing the peoples of Europe closer together'. It aims to promote 'the richness and diversity of Europe's cities, while highlighting their shared cultural heritage and the vitality of their artistic creation'.[70]

But the Union's cultural policies also have an important external function to play. Apart from the EU's new responsibilities actively to support the cultural co-operation among Member States, the Europeanization of culture can also be read as an explicitly protective mechanism, shielding Europe's culture from abroad. The Commission has argued that the globalization of trade and communications networks will inevitably impinge upon cultural issues. As a result, the EU will 'aim to protect the ability of the Member States to take any appropriate measure to promote the respect for cultural diversity and encourage creativity and cultural development in Europe'.[71]

The Europeanization of culture therefore serves two ambitious functions. Firstly, to encourage a feeling of Europeanness and spiritual, emotional and intellectual belonging, and secondly to protect Europe's culture(s) from the 'tidal waves' of globalization. It should be clear that these internal and external functions are complementary. It should also be clear that Europe's nation-states have obviously come to the conclusion that their own, national cultures may well be too weak separately to survive the onslaught of globalization. Here again, Europeanization is both a sanctuary for Europe's culture(s), as well as an inescapable mechanism that will promote some degree of harmonization within the European cultural sphere itself.

## Media, MAI and the cultural Maginot line

A central role will be played by the (news) media in shaping society's under-standing of what constitutes 'Europe' and determining what place the emerging Euro-polity will come to play in the political discourse. Since mass media are the dominant source of information on political matters in postmodern society, their news coverage and commentaries even *create* the symbolic environment in which politics is being conducted. Mass media not only produce the content of politics, they also help to determine the hierarchy of political issues. This is not to say that news media determine what political *opinions* people may come to hold, but they certainly play a role in deciding what *issues* people start thinking about in the first place.[72]

In the development of a Euro-polity, news media are bound to play a critical role. By providing an essential forum for public debate on political matters, media have an important legitimizing function in the evolution of a European civil society, and potentially in enhancing the feelings of community and solidarity. We should not forget that news media have played a similar role in the construction of the modern nation-state, and that the freedom of the press was perceived not only as a vital element of democracy but, first and foremost, as a symbol of the democratic *state*. Benedict Anderson has claimed that in the conceptualization of the nation-state, the printed press was essential in the development of nationalism, and that the newspaper was a 'technical means for "representing" the kind of imagined community that is the nation'.[73] This is still very much the case today: media are still for and of their own country, focusing on national issues for a national (or linguistically defined) audience. Even a cursory examination of Europe's mediascape testifies that its institutions are still very much nationally specific, dominated by national regulatory regimes and political determinants. But it is also clear that the link between the news media and 'their' nation-state is no longer exclusive.

Although still confined by linguistic borders, newspapers like the *Financial Times* and the *International Herald Tribune* are printed around the globe, reaching millions of readers with a 'global' message. CNN and Internet-based news bulletins and magazines have an equally global reach. A truly European mediascape is not yet in sight, but modern distribution systems (such as satellite and cable) are encouraging more intra-European co-operation between Europe's media enterprises and creating a subsequent demand for more European programs. Transfrontier satellite broadcasting, which started in the late 1970s, has from the outset represented a serious challenge to national media sovereignty.[74] Both the EU and the Council of Europe have animated the development of European TV programming by encouraging new productions and cross-boundary media co-operation. Apart from the pursuit of cultural objectives, a certain industrial logic has driven these initiatives, in an attempt to open up Europe's closed national markets and develop a wider European audiovisual space. Initial attempts by the European Broadcasting Union (EBU) to develop pan-European media channels have failed, as did short-lived experiments to launch Europa TV (which collapsed in 1986, after one year's operation). Other EBU-sponsored channels, such as Eurosport and Euronews, have been more successful. Euronews in particular (launched in 1993) clearly reflects the desire to air a 'European' perspective of European and global economic and political developments.[75] Euronews now broadcasts in five languages (English, French, German, Italian and Spanish) and reaches about 90 million households in 43 European and South Mediterranean countries.

The European Commission's Green Paper, *Television Without Frontiers*, published in 1984, was explicitly aimed at opening intra-Community frontiers for national television programs and contributing to the development of a single European broadcasting space. The paper argued that information

> is a decisive, perhaps the only decisive factor in European unification ... European unification will only be achieved if Europeans want it. Europeans will only want it if there is such a thing as European identity. A European identity will only develop if Europeans are adequately informed. At present, information via the mass media is controlled at [the] national level.
>
> (Commission of the European Communities, *Television Without Frontiers*, Green Paper (Brussels, 1984), quoted in Philip R. Schlesinger, 'Europe's Contradictory Communicative Space', *in Daedalus*, vol. 123, no. 2 (Spring 1994), pp. 29–30)

Philip Schlesinger has rightly pointed out that this perspective assumes a rather simplistic causal relationship between media consumption and the formation of a collective identity along European lines.[76] Using radio and TV as the cultural instruments of nation-building may be an outdated, obsolete 'modern' notion that has little chance of effectively forging a stronger European consciousness. Such a European audiovisual space should certainly not be confused with more reporting on European issues through the national media. It would, however, imply that newspapers, magazines, radio and TV channels would offer information, entertainment and other programs for a Europe-wide market, thereby trying to create a nation-state-transcending communicative context. This would, of course, imply that Europe's multiple language barriers can be overcome. Europe's linguistic Tower of Babel may not lend itself easily to a general, homogeneous approach.[77] Since communication is inevitably linked with language and linguistically mediated interpretations of the world, European opinion-forming will remain problematic, and European citizens continue to find it difficult to participate actively in the emerging Euro-polity.

But 'Europeanization' has also been considered as a possible last line of defense against what is perceived as the 'Americanization' of a supposedly specific European culture.[78] The concept of a specific European identity is a blurred and contested one, but as a political phrase in the discourse on European culture, identity and unity have formed a powerful and somewhat idealistic counterbalance to what might otherwise be considered as a parochial, hard-nosed protectionist argument for building, in economic and media terms, a Fortress Europe. One only has to recall the massive protests of several thousands of European intellectuals and artists in the mid-1980s, who called for the exclusion of 'cultural works' from the new GATT arrangement then under negotiation. The European position that films and TV programs are cultural artifacts which should not simply be regarded as other tradable commodities is clearly at odds with the free-trade approach of the United States. This initiative was led by French intellectuals, who were especially adamant about defending their culture against the purported threat of 'Hollywood'. France has called for measures to shield the European cultural market from trashy American series and movies, and asked for a 60-per-cent quota of 'European content' in films shown on TV, as well as a tax on cinema tickets to be used to subsidize innovative films, art-house cinema and independent distributors. Interestingly enough, the EU ultimately succeeded in excluding audiovisual services from the GATT accords (in October 1993), despite strong objections from Washington.[79]

The notion that Europe should defend its cultural autonomy against the assault of 'Hollywood' and the subsequent global dominance of US 'cultural products', has been a central driving force behind these policies. Europe has a US$7-billion deficit with America in the whole audiovisual industry, and 80 per cent of the export sales by the Hollywood film industry is now made in Europe; American made-for-TV movies now fill about 60 per cent of European screen time. European film-goers and TV-watchers obviously could not care less that their vision of 'reality' is fashioned by American imagery, but Europe's cultural elite clearly understands the far-ranging impact this may have on the development of the arts and politics of the continent. The president of the European Film Academy, Wim Wenders, has stridently noted that Europe will become a 'Third World continent' mainly because it will 'not have anything to say on the most important medium ... There is a war going on and the Americans have been planning it for a long time. The most powerful tools are images and sound'.[80]

This is therefore not a debate about the national origins of culture but rather about the future development of European cultural space and the disposition of much of Europe's political elite to resign itself to the emerging hyperreality of communication and its product: meaning. Baudrillard has argued that 'the media are producers not of socialization, but of exactly the opposite, of the implosion of the social in the masses'. Global media's pivotal mechanism – advertisement – simplifies all modes of communication, resulting in the 'superficial transparency of everything'. Advertisement is therefore (in Baudrillard's words) the 'destroyer of intensities, [the] accelerator of inertia'.[81] This is not a future that Europe's elite (or, for that matter, America's elite) is looking forward to. This projection of things to come not only undermines their role and place in society as the intellectual accumulators and propellers of cognitive and social change, it also challenges the overall cultural dynamics of society in general. This vision of the future further problematizes the development of a European public sphere, a location (or site) on which a European image addressing a European audience may be conceived that goes beyond the superficial transparency of entertainment, but may instead touch upon a wider range of emotional and aesthetic chords.

This debate again flared up with the negotiations (1995–9) among OECD countries to introduce the Multilateral Agreement on Investments (MAI). The MAI was designed to facilitate the movement of assets by individual and corporate investors across international borders. Negotiations started in 1995 and have been postponed a number of times. At the time of writing, MAI has not been concluded, but remains on the political agenda in a more low-key format. Countries that would join an MAI-like arrangement would (among other things) have to treat foreign investors no less favorably than domestic firms; remove restrictions on the movement of capital; and accept a dispute-resolution process that will allow investors to sue governments for damages before an international tribunal when they believe a country's law is in violation of the MAI. This would let transnational firms take national governments to court for any profits lost because of laws that discriminate against them. These firms could then take the offending national, or regional, government to this tribunal and claim compensation for past and potential future damages. Proponents argue that such an agreement would provide the protection against discrimination and expropriation that international investors need, and that it would therefore open up new markets and help to improve the efficiency of the global economy as a whole. It is argued that it would give international investors a 'level playing field' and spur economic growth. Opponents argue that countries would then have to compete for FDI by lowering wages and environmental safeguards (i.e., by social and ecological 'dumping'), and that it would undermine cultural diversity by treating culture as a mere 'commodity' and 'investment'. An MAI-like arrangement could also well put at risk international UN treaties on climate change, over-fishing and biological diversity (among others), as transnational firms demand equal access to the world's resources.

The French cultural 'trade union' SACD (*Société des Auteurs et Compositeurs Dramatiques*), one of the fiercest opponents of MAI, has referred to this proposed agreement as an 'economic war that American investors are waging on the European market, this time to win, and particularly to take its highly coveted plum: the audiovisual market'.[82] Beatrice Clerc of the SADC has argued that

> creative artists refuse to see their works reduced to the status of merchandise and to see cultural identities disappear, little by little, throughout the world. It is high time to draw aside the veil masking one of the most serious attacks ever orchestrated by the United States against creative activity in Europe.
> (Quoted in the *Guardian*, 12 February 1998)

It should, however, be acknowledged that part of Europe's current problems in developing a vibrant film and audiovisual industry is inherent in its fragmentary cultural landscape and the diversity of its languages. At least half the films that have recently won the European (Film) Academy Award (formerly known as the *Felix*) are known only in their country of origin.[83] It therefore seems that only the United States can generate the images and pictures that catch the attention and stimulate the imagination of *all* European people.

So, what we are seeing is the development of a postmodern battle between the US and Europe over images and sound. The US, employing its 'soft power' of commercialized culture, takes advantage of the forces of globalization by exploiting the global attractiveness of its language, its movies and music, its throw-away consumer ethics and its individualistic mentality. Joseph Nye had already argued in 1990, that America has more 'soft power' than other countries in the international system and that it can use its cultural and ideological resources to 'structure a situation so that other nations develop preferences or define their interests in ways consistent' with its own.[84]

Here, again, it is France that most vocally and passionately airs its discontent.[85] Jean-Gabriel Fredet, for example, has argued that 'Hollywood has become the flagship of the American empire, and its international domination the most evident symbol of the Americanization of the world, with Donald Duck as Foreign Minister'.[86] Former Minister of Foreign Affairs Hervé de Charette, further argued in 1997 that we now

> live in a world threatened by the standardization of cultures and modes of thought. A single language has a very destabilizing effect. We French are the first to become aware of this: The world cannot be based on images which are the same for everyone. If France wishes to take part in this contest, it will do so through its businesses and through the images it provides. *What is at stake here is vital for civilization.*
> (Interview with De Charette in *Le Monde*, 18 March 1997. Emphasis added)

This, we may assume, would refer not only to the vitality of French culture but to the cultural life of Europe as a whole. Globalization and technological progress have set in a trend toward cultural homogenization that may well choke off difference. The proliferation of images and sound may temporarily blind and deafen us to the reality that we now have more messengers, but significantly *fewer* messages. France's Minister of Education, Jack Lang, has therefore referred to the MAI as the 'creation of a kind of global economic soviet, one led by the leaders of large companies and beyond the control of the people'.[87] So, what is at stake with MAI (in its current or future guise), and the globalization of the world economy in general, is not 'merely' culture, but perhaps the democratic basis for Europe's societies in general. (See Chapter 6 for a more detailed discussion.)

Given the French inclination toward protectionism, it has been relatively easy to dismiss this French (and in a wider context European) resistance as a rearguard battle against the assumed logic and inevitability of globalization. But for Europe, the dominance of a pop culture – the notion that culture is first and foremost a 'product' designed to circulate freely as any ordinary merchandise in a global economy – remains unacceptable, since this would threaten to dilute its own cherished cultural distinction and diversity. Culture is not considered to fall within the realm of Fordist entertainment (i.e., mass-produced pleasure), and it is not considered a commodity devoid of political, social or historical content and message. In many ways, Europe is therefore opposing the postmodern notion of culture as cosmopolitan, universal and timeless, in essence superficial and devoid of any social or political 'message'. However, Europe's definition of a rooted, 'deep culture' does not travel, does not resonate even across the board *within* its very own continent, let alone around the globe, so there is little reason to assume that a European audiovisual sanctuary of some sort will be able to form a protective shield against ceaseless Disney-attacks.

What is more, Europe's cultural Maginot line will be trivialized by the digitalization of audiovisual 'products' which will be offered to a European audience via pay-per-view and digital TV. The dawning Information Society will make it possible to transmit any kind of service (voice, data, video) over any kind of network (fixed, wireless, satellite). This will soon make it impossible to separate 'traditional' telecoms from computer-based communications and broadcasting. A new regulatory framework for communications and media in Europe will be required to address the challenge of convergence between telecommunications, computer, audiovisual and publishing technologies, services and industries. These electronic networks will not respect national political boundaries – which will make it all the more important to develop a multicultural European (and preferably global) international charter aimed at preserving public interests and shaping the emerging Information Society so as to protect Europe's cultural uniqueness and diversity.

Here, again, Europeanization is a 'Beauty and the Beast' phenomenon: its 'beauty' lies in the united effort of EU Member States to provide a more-or-less united stance against the danger of cultural homogeneity by cherishing Europe's cultural pluralism; the 'beast' lies in the inherent futility of the whole attempt to turn the continent into a politico-cultural sanctuary in which Europe's fragile identity-of-sorts can be nurtured. European culture has a chance of strengthening the sense of belonging among its many and diverse peoples, and Europe's political elite realizes this all too well. But, since this European culture does not exist as a monolithic entity, but is instead composed of a multitude of *cultures*, over-emphasizing the necessity of a cultural underpinning for the European project may well undermine, rather than stimulate, the development of European integration. A voluntaristic approach to styling a European identity will no doubt be ineffectual. European society and culture seem inevitably destined to drift toward a commercialized, consumption-based notion of hedonism.

George Steiner already argued that only trees have roots, but that Man has legs. It is therefore first and foremost mobility and change that will offer opportunities for a European identity to develop. Europe's palimpsest and postmodern identity will not politically satisfy and aesthetically please those who still crave the solidity and robustness of modernity's ambitions. Europe is likely to become what Ernest Renan has called the 'daily plebiscite' that nations require and receive as a measure of their popular and voluntary support.[88] Like the nation-state, the European polity and community will have to make and daily remake its meaning in everyday, prosaic life. The nation-state may lose its central role as the territorial form of signification, as the central system of political meaning for 'its' citizens; Europe is well-placed to add another facet to the kaleidoscopic identity of its citizenry. This will be an overarching Europe – embracing both West and Central. Although amalgamating these two histories and narratives of Europe will be complex and troublesome, Zizek has rightly noted that 'what transpires in the gap that separates the two perspectives is a glimpse of a "Europe" worth fighting for'.[89]

It may seem somewhat puzzling that European unity may only be achieved by heterophylia, by emphasizing difference and sheltering the multifarious homeless Selves of Europe's postnational citizens. Postmodernity's discontents will certainly continue to call for a more comprehensive and totalizing model of European order and identity. But Europe's modest achievement is that it has now come to realize that there can be identity in non-identity: that is to say in a sense of belonging that continuously shifts and overlaps. Homesick Europeans who continue to dream of European purity are therefore bound to be disappointed.

## Notes

1 For a short introduction, see J.G.A. Pocock, 'What Do We Mean By Europe?', in *The Wilson Quarterly*, vol. 21, no. 1 (Winter 1997). For a longish one, see Norman Davies, *Europe: A History* (Oxford: Oxford University Press, 1996).

2 Ferdinand Tönnies, *Community and Association* (London: Routledge, 1974).

3 For an overview of questions related to European identity, see Frank R. Pfetsch, 'Die Problematik der europäischen Identität', in *Aus Politik und Zeitgeschichte*, no. 25–6 (12 June 1998), and Thomas Risse-Kappen, 'A European Identity? Europeanization and the Evolution of Nation-State Identities', in Maria Green Cowles, James Caporaso and Thomas Risse-Kappen (eds), *Europeanization and Domestic Change* (Ithaca NY: Cornell University Press, 2000).

4   Paul Howe, 'A Community of Europeans: The Requisite Underpinnings', in *Journal of Common Market Studies*, vol. 33, no. 1 (March 1995).

5   It is, however, noteworthy that the debate over the internal allocation of federal funds among the different *Länder* (states) within Germany is similar to the debate over the redistribution of EU funds among EU Member States. The German debate over the so-called *Finanzausgleich* ('financial compensation') is as fierce as can be and does not reflect the cosy national 'solidarity' which is often assumed to set nation-states apart from supranational polities like the EU. See Jürgen W. Hidien, *Der bundesstaatliche Finanzausgleich in Deutschland* (Baden-Baden: Nomos, 1999).

6   Timothy Garton Ash, 'Europe's Endangered Liberal Order', in *Foreign Affairs*, vol. 77, no. 2 (March/April 1998), p. 59.

7   For a general overview of the debate, see Menno Spiering, 'The Future of National Identity in the European Union', in *National Identities*, vol. 1, no. 2 (July 1999).

8   S.N. Eisenstadt and B. Giesen, 'The Construction of Collective Identity', in *Archives of European Sociology*, vol. 36 (1995), p. 78; S.N. Eisenstadt, 'Modernity and the Construction of Collective Identities', in *International Journal of Comparative Sociology*, vol. 39, no. 1 (February 1998); and Sasja Tempelman, 'Constructions of Cultural Identity: Multiculturalism and Exclusion', in *Political Studies*, vol. 47, no. 1 (March 1999).

9   Ramin Jahabegloo, *Conversations With Isaiah Berlin* (London: Peter Halban, 1992), p. 99.

10  J.S. McClelland, *A History of Western Political Thought* (London: Routledge, 1996), p. 634.

11  Anthony D. Smith, *Nations and Nationalism in a Global Era* (Cambridge: Polity Press, 1995). For an insightful conversation on the importance of nationalism in Central and Eastern Europe, see Anatol Lieven, 'Qu'est-ce qu'une Nation?', in *The National Interest*, no. 49 (Fall 1997), and the critique by Noel Malcolm of Lieven's account (entitled 'Qu'est-ce qu'une Refutation/Reply'), *ibid.*, no. 50 (Winter 1997/98). See also Godfrey Hodgson, 'Grand Illusion: The Failure of European Consciousness', in *World Policy Journal*, vol. 10, no. 2 (Summer 1993).

12  Smith, *Nations and Nationalism in a Global Era*, p. 24.

13  *Ibid.*, p. 98.

14  Iver B. Neumann, 'Self and Other in International Relations', in *European Journal of International Relations*, vol. 2, no. 2 (June 1996).

15  Smith, *Nations and Nationalism in a Global Era*, p. 128. It is therefore worth noting that Germany's Minister of Foreign Affairs, Joschka Fischer, has noted that 'History is Europe's identity. This is what makes its unification so exceedingly difficult'. See Joschka Fischer, 'Europe's Choice: Full Unity or Old Balance-of-power Wars', in *New Perspectives Quarterly*, vol. 14, no. 4 (Fall 1997).

16  Anthony D. Smith, *National Identity* (London: Penguin, 1991), p. 152.

17  Pierre Manent, 'On Modern Individualism', in *Journal of Democracy*, vol. 7, no. 1 (January 1996), p. 5.

18  Peter Calvocoressi, 'The European State in the Twentieth Century and Beyond', in *International Relations*, vol. 14, no. 1 (April 1998), p. 1.

19  Alain de Benoist, 'The Idea of Empire', in *Telos*, no. 98–9 (Winter 1993).

20  Philip Allott, 'The Crisis of European Constitutionalism: Reflections on the Revolution in Europe', in *Common Market Law Review*, vol. 34, no. 3 (June 1997), p. 472.

21  Quoted in Alan S. Milward (with the assistance of George Brennan and Frederico Romero), *The European Rescue of the Nation-State* (Berkeley/Los Angeles: University of California Press, 1992), p. 2.

22  Mike Featherstone, 'Globalizing the Postmodern', in Mike Featherstone (ed.), *Undoing Culture: Globalization, Postmodernism and Identity* (London: Sage, 1995), p. 81

23  In May 1999, the German Government adopted new citizenship laws allowing for exceptions to the established rule of *jus sanguinis*. Since January 2000 a limited version

of *jus soli* applies, granting German citizenship to almost anyone born on German soil to parents who have resided and worked in the country for at least eight years.

24 Mark Mitchell and Dave Russell, 'Immigration, Citizenship and the Nation-State in the New Europe', in Brian Jenkins and Spyros A. Sofos (eds), *Nation and Identity in Contemporary Europe* (London/New York: Routledge, 1996).

25 Roland Robertson, 'After Nostalgia? Wilful Nostalgia and the Phase of Globalization', in Bryan S. Turner (ed.), *Theories of Modernity and Postmodernity* (London: Sage, 1990).

26 Michael Wintle, 'Cultural Identity in Europe: Shared Experience', in Michael Wintle (ed.), *Culture and Identity in Europe: Perceptions of Divergence and Unity in Past and Present* (Aldershot: Avebury, 1996), p. 18.

27 Quoted in Michael Ignatieff, 'Nationalism and Toleration', in Richard Caplan and John Feffer (eds), *Europe's New Nationalism: States and Minorities in Conflict* (New York: Oxford University Press, 1996), p. 213.

28 *Ibid.*, p. 214.

29 Marco Bifulco, 'In Search of an Identity For Europe', Rheinische Friedrich Wilhelms-Universität Bonn, Zentrum für Europäische Integrationsforschung, Discussion Paper Series, no. 23 (1998); and Sven Papcke, 'Who Needs a European Identity and What Could it Be?', in Brian Nelson, David Roberts and Walter Veit (eds), *The Idea of Europe: Problems of National and Transitional Identity* (New York: Berg, 1992).

30 Theodora Kostakopoulou, 'Why a "Community of Europeans" Could Be a Community of Exclusion: A Reply to Howe', in *Journal of Common Market Studies*, vol. 35, no. 2 (June 1997), p. 305.

31 Michael Foucault, 'Two Lectures', in Colin Gordon (ed.), *Power/Knowledge: Selected Interviews and Other Writings* (New York: Pantheon, 1980). Quoted in David Campbell, 'Political Prosaics, Transversal Politics, and the Anarchical World', in Michael J. Shapiro and Hayward R. Alker (eds), *Challenging Boundaries: Global Flows, Territorial Identities* (Minneapolis: University of Minnesota Press, 1996), p. 18.

32 Wendy Brown, 'Feminist Hesitations, Postmodern Exposures', in *Differences: A Journal of Feminist Cultural Studies*, vol. 3, no. 1 (Spring 1991), p. 64.

33 For an overview, see Martha A. Ackelsberg, 'Identity Politics, Political Identities: Thoughts Toward a Multicultural Politics', in *Frontiers*, vol. 16, no. 1 (1996).

34 Brown, 'Feminist Hesitations, Postmodern Exposures', pp. 66–7. See also Katherine Kia Tehranian, 'Global Communication and Pluralization of Identities', in *Futures*, vol. 30, no. 2–3 (March/April 1998).

35 Kristin Severson and Victoria Stanhope, 'Identity Politics and Progress: Don't Fence Me In (Or Out)', in *Off Our Backs*, vol. 28, no. 4 (April 1998).

36 Susan Bickford, 'Anti-anti-identity Politics: Feminism, Democracy, and the Complexities of Citizenship', in *Hypatia*, vol. 12, no. 4 (Fall 1997).

37 Nicholas C. Burbules and Suzanne Rice, 'Dialogue Across Differences: Continuing the Conversation', in *Harvard Educational Review*, vol. 61, no. 4 (November 1991), p. 394.

38 Barbara Epstein, 'Why Poststructuralism is a Dead End for Progressive Thought', in *Socialist Review*, vol. 25, no. 2 (1995), p. 94

39 Benedict Anderson, *Imagined Communities: Reflections on the Origin and Spread of Nationalism* (London: Verso, 1995).

40 Zdravko Mlinar, 'Individuation and Globalization: The Transformation of Territorial Social Organization', in Zdravko Mlinar (ed.), *Globalization and Territorial Identities* (Aldershot: Avebury, 1992).

41 Emanuel Adler, 'Imagined (Security) Communities: Cognitive Regions in International Relations', in *Millennium: Journal of International Studies*, vol. 26, no. 2 (Summer 1997).

42 William Bloom, *Personal Identity, National Identity and International Relations* (Cambridge: Cambridge University Press, 1990).

43  Ross Posnock, 'Before and After Identity Politics', in *Raritan*, vol. 15, no. 1 (Summer 1995).

44  Ignatieff, 'Nationalism and Toleration', p. 221.

45  Slavoj Zizek, 'For a Leftist Appropriation of the European Legacy', in *Journal of Political Ideologies*, vol. 3, no. 1 (February 1998), p. 73.

46  Zygmunt Bauman, *Postmodernity and Its Discontents* (New York: New York University Press, 1997), p. 25.

47  Gayatri Chakravorty Spivak, 'Translator's Preface', in Jacques Derrida, *Of Grammatology* (Baltimore MD and London: Johns Hopkins University Press, 1998 – corrected edition), pp. xxx–xxxi.

48  W. James Booth, 'Communities of Memory: On Identity, Memory, and Debt', in *American Political Science Review*, vol. 93, no. 2 (June 1999); James E. Young, 'Germany's Memorial Question: Memory, Counter-Memory, and the End of the Monument', in *The South Atlantic Quarterly*, vol. 96, no. 4 (Fall 1997); and Paul Ricoeur, 'Gedächtnis-Vergessen-Geschichte', in Klaus E. Müller and Jörn Rüsen (eds), *Historische Sinnbildung: Problemstellungen, Zeitkonzepte, Wahrnehmungshorizonte, Darstellungsstrategien* (Hamburg: Rowohlt, 1997).

49  Quoted in Klaus von Beyme, 'Shifting National Identities: The Case of German History', in *National Identities*, vol. 1, no. 1 (March 1999), p. 51.

50  David Campbell, 'Apartheid Cartography: The Political Anthropology and Spatial Effects of International Diplomacy in Bosnia', in *Political Geography*, vol. 18, no. 4 (1999); Michael C. Williams, 'Identity and the Politics of Security', in *European Journal of International Relations*, vol. 4, no. 2 (June 1998); Neil Renwick, 'Re-reading Europe's Identities', in Jill Krause and Neil Renwick (eds), *Identities in International Relations* (London: Macmillan, 1996); Ole Wæver, 'Securitization and Desecuritization', in Ronnie D. Lipschutz (ed.), *On Security* (New York: Columbia University Press, 1995); Ole Wæver, 'Identity, Integration and Security', in *Journal of International Affairs*, vol. 48, no. 2 (Winter 1995); James Der Derian, 'The Value of Security: Hobbes, Marx, Nietzsche, and Baudrillard', in Lipschutz (ed.), *op. cit.*; and Simon Dalby, 'Security, Modernity, Ecology: The Dilemmas of Post-Cold War Security Dialogue', in *Alternatives*, vol. 17, no. 1 (Winter 1992).

51  Kostakopoulou, 'Why a "Community of Europeans" Could Be a Community of Exclusion', p. 302.

52  Featherstone, 'Globalizing the Postmodern', p. 81.

53  André Berten, 'Identité européenne, une ou multiple? Réflexion sur les processus de formation de l'identité', in Jacques Lenoble and Nicole Dewandre (eds), *L'Europe au Soir du Siècle. Identité et Démocratie* (Paris: Esprit, 1992), pp. 94–7.

54  James A. Caporaso, *The Structure and Function of European Integration* (Pacific Palisades CA: Goodyear, 1974), p. 20.

55  Trevor Lloyd, 'Union and Division in Europe', in *International Journal*, vol. 52, no. 4 (Autumn 1997), p. 548.

56  This was defined by Karl Deutsch in the 1950s as a region in which war is no longer contemplated as a possible way of resolving disputes between states, and a community 'in which there is real assurance that the members of that community will not fight each other physically, but will settle their disputes in some other way'. See Karl Deutsch, *Political Community and the North Atlantic Area* (Princeton NJ: Princeton University Press, 1957), p. 5.

57  Arend Lijphart, 'Consociational Democracy', in *World Politics*, vol. 21, no. 2 (January 1969).

58  Liesbet Hooghe, 'Supranational Activists or Intergovernmental Agents? Explaining the Orientations of Senior Commission Officials Toward European Integration', in *Comparative Political Studies*, vol. 32, no. 4 (June 1999), pp. 459–61.

59  Philip R. Schlesinger, 'Europe's Contradictory Communicative Space', in *Daedalus*, vol. 123, no. 2 (Spring 1994), p. 28.

60 Brigid Laffan, 'The Politics of Identity and Political Order in Europe', in *Journal of Common Market Studies*, vol. 34, no. 1 (August 1996).

61 Robin B. Hodess, 'The Role of News Media in European Integration: A Framework of Analysis for Political Science', in *Res Publica*, vol. 39, no. 2 (1997).

62 Chris Shore, 'Inventing the "People's Europe": Critical Approaches to European Community "Cultural Policy" ', in *Man* (London), vol. 28, no. 4 (December 1993); and P. Odermatt, 'The Use of Symbols in the Drive for European Integration', in J. Th. Leersen and M. Spiering (eds), *National Identity: Symbol and Representation (Yearbook of European Studies)*, vol. 4 (Amsterdam: Radopi Press, 1991).

63 Hugh Aldersey-Williams, 'Symbols and Lies', in *New Statesman*, 10 July 1998.

64 For an excellent introduction to the general topic, see M. Gottdiener, *Postmodern Semiotics: Material Culture and the Forms of Postmodern Life* (Oxford: Blackwell, 1995).

65 José Antonio Jauregui, 'The ECU as Vehicle of European Culture and Feelings', in Louis le Hardy de Beaulieu (ed.), *From Democratic Deficit to a Europe for Citizens* (Namur: Presses Universitaires de Namur, Collection 'Perspectives', 1995), p. 225.

66 *Ibid.*, p. 226.

67 These clarifications can be found on the EU's server 'Europa'. Online. Available HTTP: http://europa.eu.int/euro/html/entry.html (accessed 15 August 2000).

68 Robert Senelle, 'The New Cultural Policy of the European Union', in Leonce Bekemans (ed.), *Culture: Building Stone for Europe 2002* (Brussels: College of Europe/European Interuniversity Press, 1996).

69 European Commission, *First Report on the Consideration of Cultural Aspects in European Community Action* (Brussels, April 1996).

70 European Commission, DGX, *Information, Communication, Culture, Audiovisual Media*. Online; available HTTP: http://europa.eu.int/comm/culture/capeurculten.html (accessed 9 May 2000).

71 European Commission, *Explicit Integration of Cultural Aspects Into Community Action and Policy* (Brussels, 1998). Article F of the Maastricht Treaty also states that 'The Union shall respect the national identities of its member states'.

72 Here the seminal work remains Edward S. Herman and Noam Chomsky, *Manufacturing Consent: The Political Economy of the Mass Media* (New York: Pantheon, 1988).

73 Anderson, *Imagined Communities*, p. 25.

74 For a concise overview, see Peter J. Humphreys, *Mass Media and Media Policy in Western Europe* (Manchester: Manchester University Press, 1996), especially Chapter 8 ('The European Community and Pan-European Broadcasting').

75 Apart from Euronews, France and Germany are sponsoring the dual-language channel ARTE, which specifically aims at preventing commercial interests from coming to fully occupy Europe's cultural space. See Susan Emanuel, 'A Community of Culture? The European Television Channel', in *History of European Ideas*, vol. 21, no. 2 (1995).

76 Schlesinger, 'Europe's Contradictory Communicative Space'. For a critical assessment of the postmodernist approach to thinking about (European) identity, see Schlesinger, 'Wishful Thinking: Cultural Politics, Media, and Collective Identities in Europe', in *Journal of Communication*, vol. 43, no. 2 (Spring 1993).

77 On the issue of languages, see David D. Laitin, 'The Cultural Identities of a European State', in *Politics and Society*, vol. 25, no. 3 (September 1997).

78 David Puttnam, *Movies and Money: The Undeclared War Between Europe and America* (New York: David McKay, 1998).

79 Mel van Elteren, 'GATT and Beyond: World Trade, the Arts and American Popular Culture in Western Europe', in *Journal of American Culture*, vol. 19, no. 3 (Fall 1996).

80 Quoted Schlesinger, 'Europe's Contradictory Communicative Space', p. 33.

81 Jean Baudrillard, *Simulacra and Simulation* (Ann Arbor: University of Michigan Press, 1994), p. 92.

82 *L'AMI: l'Ennemi* (Paris: SACD, 1998).

83 Derek Malcolm, 'You Silly Santer: Pass the Popcorn', in *The Guardian*, 9 April 1998.

84 Joseph S. Nye, Jr., *Bound to Lead: The Changing Nature of American Power* (New York: Basic Books, 1990), p. 191.

85 For a concise French perspective of this problematic, see Alain Minc, *The Great European Illusion: Business in the Wider Community* (Oxford: Blackwell, 1992), especially Chapter 11.

86 Jean-Gabriel Fredet, 'France–US: The Cultural War is 50 Years Old', in *Le Nouvel Observateur*, 26 February – 4 March 1998; translated in *FBIS–WEU–98–061*.

87 Jack Lang, 'MAI is the Enemy', in *Le Monde*, 10 February 1998; translated in *FBIS–WEU–98–049*, 18 February 1998.

88 Ernest Renan, 'What is a Nation?', in H.K. Bhaba (ed.), *Nation and Narration* (London: Routledge, 1990), pp. 8–22.

89 Zizek, 'For a Leftist Appropriation of the European Legacy', p. 71. See also Andrei Plescu, 'Welchen Patriotismus braucht Europa? Die verlorenen Söhne und ihre Sünden', in *Süddeutsche Zeitung*, 5 June 1997.

# 4 Sovereignty, territoriality and the representation of political space

## Postmodern space and virginity

In academic literature, as well as in the popular media, the nation-state is often endowed with a sanctity that is mystifying, to say the least. Flags, monarchs and national soccer teams continue to arouse an unparalleled level of communal emotion that can probably best be read as an instance of nostalgic inertia, a craving after collective belonging and nest-warmth. But it should also be clear that reifying the holy triad of nation-state, sovereignty and territory as defining analytical concepts walls in the political discourse and excludes alternative options for governance within a European, or wider, global space. More often than not, sovereignty is treated as if it were equivalent to the nation's virginity, with the inevitable implication that losing 'it' would be decisive, perhaps only comparable to rape. This anthropomorphism inherent in the individual/state analogy is not only questionable, because it emotionalizes the political discourse, it also overlooks that pre-existing, material bodies may not be unproblematic in terms of identity and politics.[1] State power may also be read as a gendered problematic, insofar as it is 'a historical product and expression of male predominance in public life and male dominance generally'.[2] At the same time, the nationalist discourse often allegorically figures the nation-state as a 'mother', so that motherhood and 'the image of mother as a sanctuary to be defended is a primary vehicle for the symbolic representation of national identity'.[3]

Territory and territorial control as part of this holy triad usually come to the fore in the public debate on immigration controls, cross-border crime and transnational environmental concerns. In this context the dichotomy of Self/Other is often invoked to dramatize 'security' concerns and rationalize ignorance of the lives lived on the other side of the state 'boundary'. It is often overlooked that boundaries and borders are ambiguous concepts; they make it possible to protect communities and peoples against outside violence, but they also close off possibilities of being that might otherwise come to fruition.[4] Borders provide the possibility for identity formation and collective action, but they may also sustain internal violence and cruelty. States are therefore in many ways and many cases both a source of danger as well as agents of protection.[5]

Borders limit and codify sovereignty and at the same time endow the state with the power and legitimacy to silence 'domestic' differences and critiques that question the assumptions of its very sovereign identity.[6] It may be worth recalling that, etymologically, the word 'territory' is presumed to derive from *terra*, which means earth, land and sustenance. But the *Oxford English Dictionary* suggests that it may also derive from *terrere*, which means to frighten, or to terrorize. William E. Connolly has therefore suggested that these two meanings are still closely linked, since '[t]o occupy a territory is to receive sustenance and to exercise violence. Territory is land occupied by violence'.[7]

The territorial conception of politics is part of the Westphalian state-centric framework that is now gradually being eroded by globalization, Europeanization and politico-cultural fragmentation.[8] The command in Romans 13:1 – 'let every person be subject to the governing authorities, for there is no authority except from God, and those authorities that exist have been instituted by God' – has been in decay since Nietzsche declared God dead, and no other authority has yet taken its place. It is the intellectual inertia of coming to terms with this systemic change that leads to the somewhat schizophrenic situation in which the nation-state continues to be worshipped as the optimal cultural and democratic area, whereas most modern and postmodern states are selling the remains of their sovereignty to the highest bidder on a daily basis. Nation-states are clinging desperately to as much political authority, democratic legitimacy and problem-solving capacity as they possibly can, but seem prepared (and occasionally coerced) to relinquish their territorial sovereignty as a *quid pro quo* for remaining in the 'geopolitical business' in the first place. Within the global political space, nation-states are occasionally criminal rapists as well as defenseless victims.

All states now face a menu of political choices that has been constrained by a new international network of economics, politics and culture. Here, the key question is what is left of national sovereignty and how should they cope with the eroding territoriality of the postmodern political assemblage? More broadly, we may also ask how far territorial organization is being challenged by different, non-spatial political communities? Following the discussion of the previous chapter, we may ask how far the nation-state as the *locus* of political identification has been replaced by a certain level of dependence on other forms and methods of political association? These questions are difficult to assess and should be elaborated in several dimensions. Obviously, this interrogation cannot be compressed between the covers of a single book, let alone in one chapter; I will therefore examine a few central elements of this problematic and probe the territoriality/sovereignty dyad as well as the political puzzle that the development of European integration presents us with.

Derrida has noted that sovereignty 'is presence, and the delight in presence'.[9] In our efforts to make sense of the world (and our place in it), he claims that we formulate a series of hierarchical understandings by imagining dual principles, such as sovereignty/anarchy, inside/outside, Self/Other and domestic/foreign. Following this line of argument, 'sovereignty', like the other first principles (i.e., 'inside', 'domestic'), comes to be thought of as something that can be assimilated and that belongs to us, whereas the second principles (i.e., 'outside', 'foreign') are essentially *anarche*, which implies (following Greek etymology) that they are without first principles, without a foundation.[10] David Campbell has argued that this human desire for presence and fear of absence favors geopolitical analysis and the presumption of agency. The postmodern rendition of uncertainty and complexity – a condition which is both permanent and irreducible – almost automatically induces a dialectic desire for fixity and order, a longing for some conceptual and epistemic moorings and geopolitical perimeters. The dominant discourse of sovereignty, Campbell notes, is therefore based on three assumptions:

> [first] that there is a 'center stage' or pinnacle of power from which most if not all relationships can be governed; [second] that the site of power can only ever be occupied by one source of authority; and [third] that the presiding source of authority has to be an easily identifiable, unitary agent.
>
> (David Campbell, 'Political Prosaics, Transversal Politics, and the Anarchical World', in Michael J. Shapiro and Hayward R. Alker (eds), *Challenging Boundaries: Global Flows, Territorial Identities* (Minneapolis: University of Minnesota Press, 1996), pp. 18–19)

An argument can be made that the modern sense of Self corresponds closely with the emergence of the modern notion of the nation-state as a totalizing and independent, autonomous unit. The conceptual history of sovereignty parallels the invention of the nation-state in Europe, based on the monopolization of power over a territorially-delimited people. The personification of the state is the result of many centuries of idealizing the individual/state as sovereign, independent and self-contained, as a political entity which aims at preserving its autonomy and maximizing its self-interest in an anarchical world dominated by equally self-interested individuals/states.[11] In this context it should be noted that the Realist nomenclature and vocabulary engenders the state as a masculine entity.[12] The individual/state is associated with typical 'masculine' qualities and properties like strength, power, autonomy, independence and rationality, which all find their expression and ultimate value in competition and conflict as well as the individualization and atomization of society. Co-operation and interdependence are shunned as a potential source of insecurity and a possible intrusion of the autonomous Self. This is also the reason why many feminist reconstructions of politics emphasize citizenship as a *practice* (as opposed to an inherently woman-unfriendly and exclusionary conceptualization of citizenship as a *status*), which does not so much articulate participation in the official public sphere (for which few women can find the time) as invite the kinds of informal 'neighborhood politics' in which women tend to take the lead.[13]

The EU's Schengen arrangement may serve as an example of how the individual/state is defining itself as a closed and social order which employs an elaborate network of mechanisms to shield itself from 'foreign' bodies, just as the human body defends itself from outside intrusion.[14] The Schengen network of information flows on unwanted aliens, criminals and *louche* types protects Europe's social and political purity and economic health in a way comparable to the human body's own natural defense mechanisms, and probably for similar reasons. As Bauman has claimed, 'It is not the intrinsic quality of things which makes [polluting agents] into "dirt", but solely their location; more precisely, their location in the order of things envisaged by the purity-seekers'.[15] But the political prominence of border controls as one of the main points of the EU's new administrative role also says a lot about how Member States keep this dream of purity and fixity alive. This has led Zizek (with usual hyperbole) to note that Schengen is 'a clear indication that we are dealing with anti-politics, with the reduction of politics to social *Polizei*'.[16] Sovereignty is therefore a special mechanism for determining the limits of 'politics as usual', since it works as a mental and physical shield that keeps the violence 'outside' and permits peace and justice 'inside'; it wards off external threats by patrolling territorial borders, and it permits and fosters the development of both individual and state identity within them. It therefore constitutes the central plank of the Realist notion of a Great Divide between the 'international', representing the anarchic playground of nation-states, and the 'domestic', which offers ample opportunities for order and tranquility.[17]

It should be clear that such a commitment to sovereignty and geopolitical space becomes an oddity in our postmodern era, which is marked by feelings of dislocation and centrifugal notions of power. Identity and citizenship are increasingly circumscribed and patterned within a vortex of social, cultural and political relations that stretch beyond the geopolitical limits of the national space. In a sense, the master metaphor of territory, space and boundaries, which together constitute the 'language of the state', is not intrinsically innocent, but plays an active and central role in shaping and linguistically disciplining prosaical notions of identity and political community as well as theory and research.[18] But, given the ongoing trends of globalization and Europeanization, it is our challenge to represent political life and organization going beyond sovereignty. It is this feeling of homelessness, of a lack of tradition and history, that has encouraged the identity politics which we discussed in the previous chapter. We must thus be better prepared to accept segmentarity and to come to a further appreciation of the complex and varied social forces, often unseen, which constrain and shape our wor(l)d(s).

## Obsolescent territoriality, divided sovereignty

The concept of territoriality is central to our notion of national sovereignty. In the closing section of this chapter we will discuss at greater length how during the Middle Ages, the historical period prior to the contemporary Westphalian system, sovereignty did not exist, since every ruler endured limits on his authority within his own territory and enjoyed claims over other rulers and other territories. Sovereignty and territoriality are therefore modern notions;[19] they are the necessary ingredients of the contemporary system of international relations.

Without the notions of boundary and border, without discrete territorial spaces, it would be difficult to imagine alterity and to make a clear distinction between the Self and the Other. In many ways, 'being' (based on the notion of identity), implies contact and communication, which in turn implies the crossing of borders, real or imagined. Bakhtin has noted that

> Man has no internal sovereign territory; he is all and always on the boundary; looking within himself, he looks in the eyes of the other or through the eyes of the other ... I must find myself in the other, finding the other in me (in mutual reflection and perception).

(Quoted in Tzvetan Todorov, *Mikhail Bakhtin: The Dialogical Principle* (Minneapolis: University of Minnesota Press, 1984), p. 96; emphasis in the original)

Identity is therefore shaped by borders, just as sovereignty is shaped by territoriality.

European integration is increasingly challenging our notion of borders between Member States, as well as between the EU and 'third' countries. In their ongoing pursuit of further integration, West European countries are redefining and reinventing both sovereignty and territoriality and now seem to have reached a defining moment. In many ways, Europe is characterized by borders and boundaries that pass everywhere, making the concept of internal and sovereign territory increasingly irrelevant. Physical borders within Europe, as well as the very notion of spatial limits on national spheres of jurisdiction, are being challenged. Dominique Moïsi has therefore argued that Europe's geographical space is 'like a rapidly growing child. [It] does not know where its body ends'.[20] In a sense, this may explain Europe's current political clumsiness and its unwieldy character. But, with rather awkward candidate member countries like Turkey and Ukraine waiting in the wings, Europe's current geographical ambiguity seems politically convenient. At the same time, the fragmentation of European identity may well result in alternative forms of political rule that find their basis in non-spatial criteria. But for the moment, the nation-state continues to form the ultimate organizing principle for its citizens, based on the residence within a discrete *national* territory.

The existence of borders continues to clarify where national jurisdiction begins and ends. But this is subject to change. Loyalties may have multiple *foci*, shifting toward cultural, religious and other forms of sovereign as well as non-sovereign rule, undermining our current understanding of international relations. Communities, as well as community-building, are no longer constrained by space but can be virtual in nature, helping people across Europe (and beyond) to create social network capital, knowledge capital and a sense of communion.[21] The Internet is increasingly conceptualized as a new, decentered public sphere offering a new site for democratic and interactive political conversation. Although it may be too early to herald the birth of a new 'Digital Nation' of cosmopolitical netizens (instead of state-bound citizens),[22] it should be clear that the prospects for cyberpolitics introduce an unprecedented novelty for the nation-state as well as for political theory. The nature of political authority may well shift from territorial lineages and spatial authority-holders to an almost disembodied and potentially global community in which politics and the political are overlapping. This urge for a new self-definition is a consequence of the cultural desiccation of western society and the drying up of traditional sources of moral, ethic and religious authority.[23]

At the same time, the concept of sovereignty also limits our notion of democracy, in particular since the universalistic democratic idea(l) has only found a particularistic realization within the confined contours of the nation-state. As I will argue in more detail in a later chapter, the hegemony of state sovereignty in the political discourse puts strict limits on our understanding and imagination of potential alternative sites of democratic praxis. This will especially hinder democratic practices that are not of a spatio-temporal nature but built upon specific public and political interests and issues. The erosion of individual/state sovereignty is an expression of the fundamental uncertainties of postmodern life which can no longer be totalized and explained by grand philosophies of history and unified interpretations of events. Equating state sovereignty with democracy (analogous with individual sovereignty and 'self-control' as the foundation of western conceptions of maturity and adulthood), makes it not too difficult to take a further step toward understanding both 'international anarchy' and non-democratic regimes or actors as the ultimate Other, the 'primitive enemy'. It should also be recognized that the high level of internal pacification in western industrialized societies has been achieved within the Manichean, black/white context of the Cold War. This context – 'solidarity at home, clear-cut enemies abroad' – has now disappeared. As Giddens has argued, 'Where states have no enemies, but only face the diffuse threats of a potentially but not actually hostile environment, disintegrative tendencies internally might again become strong'.[24] What is more, by focusing our attention on these two abstract modern sovereignties – the state and the individual – the true nature of political community and prosaic life is often overlooked. Walker has noted in this context that the

> character of the community in which people actually live, work, love, and play together has seemed unproblematic and uninteresting, of peripheral importance to the serious business of capital and state. To engage with the local is to be sidetracked into the trivial ... Nor, of course, should one think seriously about constructing a meaningful democracy in such places either.
> (R.B.J. Walker, 'On the Spatiotemporal Conditions of Democratic Practice',
> in *Alternatives*, vol. 16, no. 2 (Spring 1991), p. 254)

Nevertheless, it should be acknowledged that territory seems to have lost its almost fetishist fascination for most West European countries. In this part of the world, the power reflex of territorial conquest has waned over the decades and has gradually been replaced by a quest for prosperity and well-being. The traditional dilemma of any victor ('what to do, having won?') is even more conspicuous today than in the past. Territory is less valuable in contemporary

Western Europe because its intrinsic economic value is debatable and controversial. The major factors of production in today's Europe are no longer land but knowledge and information, which are by their very nature evanescent and difficult to seize and hang on to. This has led Richard Rosecrance to suggest that we are now entering a world of the 'virtual state', a state that has deliberately limited its territorially-based production capability and has almost 'emancipated' itself from the land.[25] Since transnational firms locate their production facilities wherever it is most profitable, the competition state has to negotiate with foreign and domestic firms and labor organizations to entice them into its economic space in order to stimulate economic growth. In this new era of 'virtual states', geographical space and size no longer determine economic potential and 'power'. Even the endowment of natural resources is becoming a factor of less-than-strategic importance.

It should be axiomatic that this does not describe the *global* state of affairs, but mainly Western Europe and the limited OECD area. Iraq invaded Kuwait; the war in Bosnia has been a quest for self-determination and territory; China still does not recognize Taiwan; Russia and Japan have unresolved claims over the Kuril islands. But in the postmodern era countries will come to realize that their problems cannot be solved by launching an invasion of another state. The link between prosperity and fixed resources (i.e., industrial facilities) will continue to diminish, whereas intangible factors (i.e., capital, knowledge and services) will increasingly inform our notion of economic strength and political influence. But, since states have by definition only limited influence over the accumulation and distribution of these factors, the very notion of territoriality loses its political relevance. Other organizing principles may have to be conceived which make more sense in the context of postmodern (dis)order.

Like most ideas, the view that the territorial, sovereign state may be withering away is not new. We have already alluded to the Marxist notion that capitalist states would be overtaken by a 'proletarian brotherhood'. Idealists have insisted that only a world government would produce a 'warless world', an utopia stubbornly blocked by the refusal of territorial states to gracefully hand over their sovereignty; and liberal economists (one would now call them 'globalizers') have long argued that markets would increasingly become more important than nation-states in the international system. It is also clear that sovereignty may mean different things to different people in different geopolitical circumstances. Realists consider the sovereign state as the principal agent in world politics, which will be as robust as ever and ready to shrug off the slings and arrows of globalization and regionalization; in line with the Primordial face of nationalism, the territorial, sovereign state is considered the only practical organizing principle within the contemporary socio-cultural global framework. Others, in contrast, hail the demise of state sovereignty as a unique opportunity for achieving a peaceful, prosperous and more just post-territorial world order. Liberals may be expecting a borderless world dominated by free trade in goods, services, finance and people; environmentalists may hope the world is finally moving toward an ecologically sound and organic order based on the principles of sustainable development; and some postmodernists may look forward to the development of a global community based on the principles of cyberspace and multi-layered, overlapping identities.

Within this swirl of opinions and expectations, it will be important to recognize that the Westphalian system is only one particular historical form of social and political organization, initially Eurocentric in nature and certainly not a timeless 'reality'. It was only after decolonization halfway through the twentieth century that a truly *global* Westphalian system was instituted. The censure of 1648 only applied to Europe and excluded the Ottoman Empire and the colonial belongings of the main European powers. Only gradually has the Westphalian system become relevant to other peoples around the globe, substituting the state for other *foci* of identity, such as the tribe, clan, ethnic group, or religious community. But even this system has been volatile and dynamic: during the second half of the seventeenth century Germany consisted of some 234 countries, with 51 free cities and around 1,500 independent knightly manors; only in 1871 was German unification achieved. Similarly, it took France from the thirteenth century until the French Revolution to supplant the fragmented and at times overlapping local and regional identities (Alsatians, Basques, Bretons, Burgundians, Corsicans, etc.) with a single, centralized, national identity.[26] But the fact that this process took more than three centuries to consolidate might serve to indicate that paradigmatic change is not always unequivocal and manifest, but may be piecemeal and surreptitious. In Westphalian Europe, however, the idea of an autonomous, hierarchical political authority within a well-defined territorial space has been a very powerful one and continues to dominate our collective political imaginations. 'Sovereignty' informs us about our identity; it also tells us who is part of our political community and who should be regarded as an 'outsider'.

Modern conceptions of territorial sovereignty have been grounded on spatial exclusion, emphasizing political control, bureaucratic predictability and permanence. In this respect they continue to form the foundation for western democracy, and their claims to encapsulate our 'cardinal identity' have yet to find credible rivals. The nostalgic use of sovereignty is a manifestation of what Jameson has called 'the geopolitical aesthetic'.[27] As a conceptual device for understanding our position in a changing world, sovereignty is part of a nostalgic call for a return to a more 'transparent national space'. Jameson maintains that these concerns are part of a movement toward 'an aesthetic of cognitive mapping – a pedagogical political culture which seeks to endow the individual subject with some new heightened sense of its place in the global system'.[28] In today's postmodern era the persistence of, and hankering after, the aesthetics of territorial sovereignty seems little more than a rather dismal political anachronism. Political elites in Western Europe can still try to mobilize their electorates with the rhetoric of nationalism and sovereignty, resurrecting these antiquated notions as shields against globalization and/or Europeanization. But by doing so they lend emphasis to rather obsolete, even archaic, political questions, avoiding issues that are more pertinent to people's prosaic security and well-being. Backlashes against the dreaded erosion of territorial sovereignty not only include chauvinism and xenophobia but may well become perverted into religious extremism and ethnic cleansing, as the ultimate push to purge society from 'evil outside influences'.[29]

## Operational sovereignty

In order to structure this somewhat coarse-grained narrative, I will first of all assume that sovereignty is a *relative* notion.[30] The idea of an absolute sovereign state is an ahistorical and grotesque myth. Quite unlike virginity, sovereignty is usually lost gradually, and may well be reformulated on manifold levels and by ingenuous methods. It is also useful to realize that sovereignty is neither the equivalent of power nor the same as law. Sovereignty has first and foremost to do with *legitimate authority*, which, for a variety of reasons (usually an amalgam of law and tradition), is accepted by society. During the closing years of the Middle Ages, rulers used the concept of sovereignty for external and internal purposes. *Externally*, it justified freedom from influence of the Emperor and the Pope; *internally*, it was invoked to strengthen control over autonomous vassals and as a means to consolidate an exclusive territorial jurisdiction.[31] These two faces of sovereignty (internal and external) are still analytically valid and useful.

Sovereignty may have lost its absolute character, but the state is still the main subject of international law. National sovereignty still serves as a threshold for political and economic intrusion in the domestic affairs of a state-based political community. This even holds true for today's European Union.[32] Nation-states decide themselves whether they want to participate in the EMU, the Schengen agreement, the MAI, and to accept other limitations on their economic and political authority. But, as we will discuss at more length below, existing economic, political and treaty commitments have limited the European states' room for maneuver and locked them into dense networks of activities that have grown up around past institutional and political decisions. These are the 'sunk costs' of European integration that preclude 'sovereign' Member States from simply tearing up the Union's founding treaties, packing their bags and returning to a policy of national autarky. The constantly increasing costs of this exit option (which is *de jure* not an existing option at all, since EU treaties do not indicate how a Member State might possibly 'exit' from the Union), affects the perception of national sovereignty as well as the place and role which Member States see for themselves in the overall European project.

But the notion of external sovereignty is still a vibrant one. Connor Cruise O'Brien, for example, has clearly stated that the

> sovereignty of national parliaments is only an imperfect barrier against the intrusions of German hegemonic power, but it is the principal barrier we have, and we should take care to hold on to it ... A federal Europe would be dominated by the new, confident, united Germany.
>
> (Connor Cruise O'Brien, 'Toward European Disunion',
> in *Harper's*, July 1992)

In a similar vein, Barber has argued that the

> irony of our time is that just as the large multinational companies, above all
> the media conglomerates, have become globally powerful, we are disman-
> tling the only countervailing institutions we have ... Absent the emergence
> of some kind of a syndicalism of nations where states band together, what
> on earth can make a difference.
>
> (Nathan Gardels, 'The Making of McWorld (Interview with Benjamin Barber)',
>                   in *New Perspectives Quarterly*, vol. 12, no. 4 (Fall 1995), p. 12)

On this reading, sovereignty is a shield, protecting the national virgin grounds
from 'outside' intervention. It should be said that attachment to this sentiment is
dwindling or changing its character. Barber, for example, opens up a little
thinking space by emphasizing the urgent need to 'create international civic,
voluntary and non-state associations that have some chance on the global level to
challenge McWorld'.[33] This would be a world in which Greenpeace-type
organizations would vigorously resist the homogenization of cultural differences,
just as they currently struggle to protect endangered species. This would be a
truly new form of 'external sovereignty', defined not along territorial lines but as
a particular personal line of defense against the pressures of globalization.

Internal sovereignty is an altogether different matter. Most European states
have become accustomed to limitations on their domestic authority – for
example by accepting the compulsory jurisdiction of the European Court of
Human Rights, or signing up to arms control agreements like the Treaty on
Conventional Forces in Europe (CFE) or the Nuclear Non-Proliferation Treaty
(NPT). All EU Member States have ceded major chunks of their autonomy on
political, monetary, economic and social matters to 'Brussels'. Moreover, all
European states are increasingly subordinating their welfare states to the
perceived stipulations of the global marketplace. Sovereignty, like territoriality,
has now become 'unbundled':[34] the nation-state has come under attack by new
actors, varying from transnational firms to social movements to regional/local
entities. However, in most cases national and regional governments' sense of
sovereignty remains resistant, since sovereignty still evokes and absorbs the
allegiance and respect of a majority of people. This is clearly linked with the
Primordial face of nationalism, which assumes a certain natural and spontaneous trust and affection between the nation-state and its citizens. It is, of course,
questionable whether such a political system rooted in tradition and customary
faith in authority will continue to endure, especially if the nation-state can no
longer satisfy the material and moral needs and demands of its citizens. It
therefore seems inevitable that sovereignty will become a more fragmentary
concept, since the scope of affairs over which the state has direct authority (let
alone direct control) within its territorial space is perceptibly declining.
Globalization and Europeanization may not have turned the nation-state into a
passive bystander, but they have certainly deprived the state of its centrality as an
autonomous actor. They are eroding and reconstituting the powers of nation-

states, turning them into willing or reluctant brokers of the allegedly autonomous forces of globalizing processes.

Political and academic disagreement on these issues has produced not only varied research agendas among scholars, but also (and arguably more importantly) different policy choices by decision-makers. The lack of conceptual clarity can be explained by the conflicting tendencies of the simultaneous *de-* and *re-*territorialization of space in post-Cold-War Europe. The integration of political units within the EU is matched in different parts of Europe by a continuous devolution of state authority to units of marginal power and size, or even by a breakdown of authority altogether (as in Albania in the 1990s). Whereas the EU aims at a loose bundling of multifarious political identities, in other parts of Europe we witness widespread cultural differentiation and the return of atavistic ethnic strife and conflict (usually referred to as 'Balkanization' – see Chapter 7). With the end of the East–West divide, Central European countries have gone through a phase of nationalist celebration, 'rediscovering' their original identity after decades of Soviet domination. Public opinion in these new, and in some instances still rather delicate, states clings to attractive abstractions such as national sovereignty and independence. It should be clear that the popular revolutions of 1989 did not call for postmodern pragmatism and a celebration of difference and hybridity; instead they claimed space for notions like 'national identity' and 'culture'.[35] However, Barber has added that 'some of the recent revolutions in Eastern Europe had as their true goal not liberty and the right to vote but well-paying jobs and the right to shop'.[36]

At the same time, the Central European political elite has committed itself to joining Europe's key institutions (NATO and the EU), realizing all too well that this implies compromising and sharing their recently reclaimed national sovereignty. The institutionalized schizophrenia of the rhetoric of newly salvaged independence and the harsh conditions of globalization are as confusing for the general Central European public as they are conceptually intelligible. But the dissolution of Yugoslavia and the Bosnia/Kosovo wars have further reminded Europe and the world (insofar as they needed to be reminded), that claims to sovereignty and self-determination are still very much alive on a continent where the majority of nation-states are gradually transferring their autonomy upward as well as downward.

So how should we understand sovereignty in the contemporary European context?[37] It is clear that the Realist view of the state as a mere agglomeration of territorially organized power needs to be continued and extended. We should rather give up the idea that a single logic can be formulated, a comprehensive theoretical narrative of postmodern sovereignty which will be universally valid for all sites of global politics. Sovereignty – like anarchy – is what nation-states (are willing and able to) make of it.[38] Their role and place in the global environment restricts their political options, changing the political cost-benefit ratio of clinging to the myths and realities of *de facto* sovereignty. Sovereignty is therefore determined by praxis and through interaction. Like identity, the basis as well as praxis of sovereignty is *narrative* (the stories we tell and continue to believe in) as well as *performative* (the actions we undertake and compromises we are prepared to make).[39] In this context, Alexander Wendt has argued that sovereignty 'is not an intrinsic feature of state agency but one social identity a state may have'.[40] Wendt claims that some states' identities and interests are derived primarily from relations to domestic society (i.e., they are 'liberal', 'democratic', or at times 'authoritarian'), whereas other identities are based on their role and place in international society (i.e., they may see themselves as 'hegemonic', or as a 'balancer'). This would support the notion that sovereignty is a flexible and multifaceted notion whose very ambiguity forms an integral part of its definition.

But sovereignty can also be understood as an operational concept. Robert Keohane has suggested that, under the existing conditions of complex interdependence, the idea of sovereignty 'provides the state with a legal grip on an aspect of a transnational process … *Sovereignty is less a territorially defined barrier than a bargaining resource for a politics characterized by complex transnational networks*'.[41] This follows a famous remark by the British politician Geoffrey Howe, that sovereignty should be read as a 'resource to be traded rather than guarded'.[42] In this notion of sovereignty (which has also been called 'operational sovereignty')[43], states understand that their legal sovereignty either can be maintained and exercised at increasingly high cost, or can be bargained away in return for some measure of a formal 'extra-territorial' say in the political affairs of other (European) states. In this sense, sovereignty is a true 'resource' that can be traded off in exchange for partial authority over others' policies, usually within international organizations.[44] For this reason, Keohane makes the case that globalization and international institutionalization are mutually reinforcing. It should be stressed not only that it is globalization that encourages institutional change, but also that the development of these sovereignty-modifying institutions will be essential for the very continuation of globalization. Globalization and institutional change do not work in one direction, but they almost inevitably go hand in hand.

Keohane's analysis therefore bears out the claim that the global nature of trade and the development of European integration are parallel and reciprocal processes. His notion of national sovereignty as something that can be 'traded' may be too mechanical (ignoring that sovereignty is not a static, easily quantifiable abstraction, but is shaped and formed through interaction and communication with a large number of state and non-state actors). Nonetheless, it has become increasingly clear to all European nation-states, regions and non-state actors that the EU has turned into an essential interlocutor in a rather complex process of European governance. It is the EU which, through a piecemeal process of metamorphosis, has transformed itself from a coal-and-steel caterpillar into a somewhat more agreeable, comprehensive European political entity. The question remains, however, whether this new European 'butterfly' can embody a significant and novel form of geopolitical aesthetic for its constituent peoples. In short, will the EU be accepted as a new 'sovereign'?

## The EU as a new 'sovereign'

Somewhat less aesthetically, Norman Davies has likened the EU to 'a giant salami-machine' that is 'cutting off slice after slice the members' various functions or "spheres of activity" and handing over each in turn to supranational agencies'.[45] It is certainly true that the EU (to continue the metaphor) has many a supranational, subnational and transnational mouth to feed (ranging from other international institutions, regional and local authorities, to firms and NGOs). The narrative of European integration can indeed be read as an incessant process of piecemeal transfer of authority from the nation-state to the European level. But this is in itself not a very interesting observation; it is more relevant to ask what is happening to all these specific 'slices' of sovereignty that have been severed from the nation-state's carcass over the years? Do they add up to a new and independent political entity, or are we just witnessing the dwindling of authority, heralding the world of Pinocchian ungovernance that we discussed earlier? The only honest answer to these questions is that we do not know. But one of the objectives of this book is to provide at least the background of an analytical apparatus and to open up the thinking space for arriving at a preliminary assessment.

Since national sovereignty does not have to be absolute, the EU's salami tactics do not necessarily have to undermine the nation-state's supreme authority. Recent European history offers the clear example of the Federal Republic of Germany, which has only gradually regained its sovereignty through its participation in the European integration process, as well as through NATO. By projecting its national identity on the process of European integration, Germany has *de facto* externalized its sovereignty until national unity again allowed for a somewhat more national rhetoric. The Marshall Plan is another story of how Western European nations have recaptured their national powers and sovereignty through co-operation. Smaller countries also understand that they have more say and greater clout in European and global politics by pooling their sovereignty within the EU than by going it alone. They clearly recognize that, in terms of optimizing their economic and political interests, they have little choice but to offer their sovereign charms to the European suitor. This reinterpretation of state sovereignty forms the very foundation for the further development of the European project, since it rationalizes the Europeanization of society. In this respect, the EU has become a new 'sovereign' (in the etymological and medieval meaning of 'superior') for both the individual Member States and its citizens. As Daniel Philpott has aptly argued:

> For the first time since the demise of the Holy Roman Empire, a significant political authority other than the state, one with formal sovereign prerogatives, has become legitimate ... EU law is still sovereign only in a limited number of areas, but Member States are no longer sovereign in *all* areas; neither body enjoys absolute sovereignty.
>
> (Daniel Philpott, 'Sovereignty: An Introduction and Brief History', in *Journal of International Affairs*, vol. 48, no. 2 (Winter 1995), emphasis added)

Both *de facto* and *de jure*, the sovereignty of European nation-states has been subject to limitations: governments only have a limited actual exercise of power over their territory, as well as a limited right to do so.[46] We may not register these facts as clearly as we should, because it is often understood that sovereignty is only infringed if one *state* is placed under the control of another *state*. Such a return to territorial imperialism will clearly not occur in Western Europe. But Ruth Lapidoth has reminded us that sovereignty can be divided in several ways, most commonly along functional lines. The 1982 UN Convention on the Law of the Sea, for example, grants 'sovereign rights' to littoral states *vis-à-vis* their continental shelves and the seas adjacent to the coast 'for the purpose of exploring and exploiting, conserving and managing the natural resources', but it denies these same states the right to regulate shipping within this 200-mile zone. The signatories to the Antarctic Treaty have tried to avoid the legal conundrum of whether states have the right to assert sovereign claims over part of Antarctica, but by fudging the issue they have *de facto* agreed to share sovereignty.[47] This may indicate that nation-states are prepared to use international law to reconceptualize what states can and cannot do in the world's unsovereignized commons: Antarctica, the oceans and the atmosphere.[48] This brings Lapidoth to conclude that 'sovereignty is not indivisible and that two or more authorities may have limited, relative, differential, or functional sovereignty over certain areas, groups or resources'.[49] This is in line with recent developments in international law which sideline the principle of the sovereign equality of all states and instead take into account divergences in their levels of economic development and their unequal capacities to tackle a given problem.[50] This is also a fair outline of the political panorama of the current EU.

The defining moment which has established the EU as a new 'European sovereign' has been the introduction of the single European currency. The Euro implies nothing less than the pooling (and hence the direct 'loss'), of a crucial part of the traditional realm of national authority, and therefore of national sovereignty. Member States no longer have the chance of modifying the exchange rates of their currencies to gain some measure of competitive advantage. With little direct control over monetary policy and continued pressure to harmonize their fiscal and social policies, national governments will have only a few remaining policy instruments to deal with pressing issues such as unemployment. One of the few ways Member States can compete is to boost efficiency and productivity. But these are structural and long-term strategies, and not the politically expeditious quick fixes for new-sprung problems that the political elite is often looking for.

Joseph Weiler has suggested two dynamics of integration that have carried us to this European junction regarding sovereignty:

1   a judicial-normative dynamic which emphasizes the role of the European Court of Justice (ECJ); and
2   a political decisional dynamic which is characterized by incrementalism and bargaining as a policy-making framework.[51]

Within Weiler's conceptual outline we could argue that the process of Europeanization challenges national sovereignty in three ways:

1 through the superiority of EU law;
2 through recourse to (qualified) majority decision-making in EU institutional practice; and
3 through the strengthening of other supranational EU institutions, such as the European Commission and the ECB.

Of these three factors, the superiority of EU law is the most crucial and consequential.

Since the mid-1970s, the European Community has been responsible for negotiating and signing trade agreement with third parties, and most EU market regulations now directly apply as part of the domestic law of Member States, without requiring the endorsement of national authorities. EU legal practice clearly challenges national sovereignty, since it obliges national authorities to obey Community law even in cases where it conflicts with domestic law. National governments, and even the national judiciary, therefore do not have the final say over which laws apply within their own territory. This forms an important and unique departure from traditional practice. Over the decades, Community law has therefore acquired a quasi-constitutional quality which cannot be readily and easily compared with traditional international law (which is based on agreements between sovereign states), public international law (which leaves the unilateral definition and the defense of governmental interests to the individual state jurisdiction), or private international law (which may apply to foreign laws but bases them on national sources). The ECJ has even gone as far as referring to the Treaties as a 'Constitutional Charter', despite the fact that the Treaty of Rome was explicitly intended not to become a constitution for the European people.

The story of the development of this new legal order based on Constitutionalism is well known[52] but is worth recalling in some detail here, since it illustrates so well how the EU has acquired its new 'sovereign'-like qualities and traits.[53] Since the 1960s the ECJ has, through a process known as 'structural constitutionalism', tried to produce norms that guide the relationship between the EC/EU and its Member States. Four aspects of this process need to be recalled: 'direct effect'; supremacy of EC law; 'pre-emption'; and judicial review. Firstly, in its famous decision *Van Gend en Loos* (1963), the ECJ declared that Community law 'not only imposes obligations on individuals but also intended to confer upon them rights which become part of their legal heritage'. Under certain conditions, provisions of EC law therefore had a 'direct effect' in Member States, and so functioned as a quasi-constitution, rather than an ordinary piece of international law. Secondly, the ECJ decided (in 1964) that Community law is superior to national law, introducing the notion of an external 'hierarchy of norms' that is a central aspect of any federal political system.[54] Thirdly, the ECJ decided in a number of cases that, as a general rule, Community law 'pre-empts' national legislation; this has come to mean that, in cases where there is EC law, national law should be considered superfluous. Fourthly, the ECJ has developed a system of judicial review by reviewing national laws: checking them for their compatibility with EC Treaties as well as secondary European legislation. This, again, is an essential element in any federal structure.

The activism of the ECJ has neither resulted in a true European Constitution, nor in a straightforward federal judicial system within the EU.[55] The Court has, through its case law, mainly tried to clarify the unclear relationship between European and national law, and the rights and obligations that the peoples of Europe can draw from this system. By formulating its decisions in apolitical and technical terms and by avoiding political controversies, the ECJ has played an autonomous role in legal integration, and hence in the overall process of European integration. But it is doubtful whether the Court can maintain this low-profile strategy, since steps toward further integration will inevitably touch upon elements that concern even more sensitive domains of national sovereignty and will therefore raise commensurate political and media attention.

The German Constitutional Court has already 'drawn a line in the sand' in its famous October 1993 decision on the Maastricht Treaty, by declaring that the EU should be considered an 'association of democratic states', and that 'the majority principle (in EU decision-making) is limited – through the requirement for mutual respect – by the constitutional principles and fundamental interests of the Member States'.[56] Christian Joerges has correctly concluded that

> the Court questions the juridification of the relations between the Community and the Member States. Decisions as to which interests are of 'fundamental interest' for Germany can and should only be determined by Germany itself ... The *BVerfG* does not view itself as a lower tier in a European juridical hierarchy, but prefers to define its link to the ECJ as a 'cooperative relationship'.
>
> (Christian Joerges, 'States Without a Market? Comments on the German Constitutional Court's Maastricht Judgement and a Plea for Interdisciplinary Discourses', in *European Integration online Papers (EIoP)*, vol. 1, no. 20 (1997), p. 7. Online. Available HTTP: http://olymp.wu-wien.ac.at/eiop/, accessed 15 August 2000)

Before further steps toward a more federal Europe can be taken, the ECJ therefore not only requires the support of public opinion, first and foremost it needs the passing of time. European Constitutionalism will need time to take root in the national soil of Member States if it is to acquire the endorsement of ordinary 'European citizens' as a new, third tier of judicial authority.

It is not unlikely that popular demands for more democratic legitimacy and transparency will drive the process of European Constitutionalism. A European Constitution would neither regulate the input of the policy-formation process, nor define its outcome; it would mainly provide the 'organizational and procedural rules guaranteeing the handling of public power in conformity with the principles and intended to avert abuses'.[57] A clear, concise and inspired

European Constitution would kindle the development of a European identity and encourage the understanding of its citizens that the European political space is an integral and natural realm for democratic will-formation, albeit perhaps of a qualitatively new nature. This is one of the reasons why Vaclav Havel has called upon the EU to establish

> a Charter of its own that would define the ideas on which it is founded, its meaning and the values it intends to embody ... a single, crystal-clear and universally understandable political document that would make it obvious at once what the European Union really is ... If the citizens of Europe understand that this is not just an anonymous bureaucratic monster to limit or even deny their autonomy, but simply a new type of human community that actually broadens their freedom significantly, then the European Union need not fear for its future.
>
> (Vaclav Havel, 'Speech to the European Parliament in Strasbourg, France', 8 March 1994. Online. Available HTTP: http://www.hrad.cz/president/Havel/speeches/indexuk.html, accessed 15 August 2000)

This is exactly the reason why a committee of worthies chaired by German ex-President Roman Herzog began drafting an EU fundamental-rights charter in February 2000. Although the idea of the Charter has remained vague, its main aim is to provide Europe's citizens with a clear overview of their rights and thereby to gather political and emotional support for the 'European cause' in general.

In this context it might be worth considering the approach of 'new constitutionalism', suggested by Stephen L. Elkin and Karol E. Soltan.[58] They argue that constitutional thought has failed to consider the emergence of a wide-ranging, politically active *demos*. By emphasizing the extent to which political institutions shape individuals within their cognitive environment (and hence affect their political identity), 'new constitutionalism' is sensitive to the fact that the success of any constitutional order is based on how the 'governed' see their own political role and place. More demanding and participating citizens will therefore expect a more inclusive and open constitution-building process. 'New constitutionalism' also argues that political institutions shape individuals and their relationships with others. Although this may sound a truism, constitution-makers should reflect this new pluralistic political condition by accepting that 'their' institutions are formative in nature and are bound to affect not only the nature and quality of governance but also (to a limited and unknown extent) the 'nature and quality' of the governed.

There are therefore only a few *a priori* reasons why European Constitutionalism should stop short of introducing a full-fledged constitution setting out the legal background of European governance. European governance is certainly a problematic matter, and with the pending enlargement of the EU toward Central Europe the demand for the effective guidance and handling of

European institutions will certainly only grow. But European Constitutionalism may also inform us about the possibilities of introducing Habermasian notions of a more decentered European public sphere based on *formally* institutionalized procedures of identifying public opinion, as well as procedures for the *informal* interaction with(in) developed public opinion. Although this proceduralism has been subject to severe criticism (especially by postmodern political scholars), it should merit serious deliberation, since it may offer valuable elements for the development of an uninhibited European public sphere where citizens may freely debate and engage in collective democratic will-formation.

## Fuzzy logic and the intergovernmentalist fantasy

'The European Union is simply not punching its weight on the international stage in the foreign and security policy areas where uncoordinated intergovernmentalism is still too frequently the *modus vivendi*.'[59] This lamentation by (the former) European Commission President Jacques Santer of the lack of political will among Member States to deal effectively with the horrors of the wars of what used to be Yugoslavia, is likely to be valid and relevant as long as Europe is made up of *de jure* sovereign nation-states. As long as the ethos of intergovernmentalism endures in political practice, European governance will remain problematic.

Most scholars refer to 'intergovernmentalism' to describe the existing political mechanisms in which the voices of the Member States can be clearly heard on the European level. As suggested by the concept itself, inter*government*alism only refers to the exercise of control and influence on the EU decision-making process through *national governments*.[60] Non-statist political movements that aim to challenge state policies have no place in this decision-making model. Intergovernmentalism is therefore a system where national governments represent the entrenched territorial interests of their limited political space, trying to find solutions through European governance for their national problems in an era of globalization and increasing international political turbulence. In many ways, intergovernmentalism is one of the last bastions of the beleaguered and troubled nation-state in guarding and defending its territorial sovereignty. Intergovernmentalism is also a valuable bargaining chip for European nation-states allowing them to 'sell' their autonomy at a high economic and political 'price'. As a political idea and as political practice, intergovernmentalism is the antithesis of federalism, which inevitably turns intergovernmentalists into anti-federalists and *vice versa*.

It should be recognized that most international organizations continue to do their business on the basis of consensus decision-making: each participating state cherishes its veto power, both as a bargaining instrument to affect the ultimate outcome in its favor and a formal token of its very independence and sovereignty. For decades intergovernmentalism has prevailed as the ultimate instrument for combining national sovereignty and European integration, mainly because Member States at least maintain their power of veto over decisions that they consider contrary to their 'national interests'. The argument is put forward that, since important decision-making powers within the EU remain firmly controlled by the representatives of each Member State (within the European Council and the Council of Ministers – see below), national sovereignty will *ipso facto* not be diluted. Since national representatives remain accountable to the parliaments of their countries, they are therefore considered (at least indirectly) to be bound to the national electorates that endow them with democratic legitimacy. On this reading, the intergovernmentalist system would not only guarantee a certain democratic legitimacy, but it would also maintain the centrality of the nation-state as the primary political unit in the overall European integration process.[61]

But this myth of a splendid *Europe des patries* has become increasingly problematic. Intergovernmentalism, as one of the three dominant modes of decision-making in the EU-system (together with supranationalism and transversalism – see Chapter 5), is gradually losing its grip on the nature and character of policy-formation within the EU. Our conversation on the character of European governance will show that institutional responsibilities and power are becoming ever more complex, indeterminate and enigmatic. All Member States are involved in a continuous balancing act: ceding parts of their authority to the exclusive responsibility of the EU's supranational institutions, meanwhile shaping the constitutional rules in intergovernmentalist bodies such as the European Council so as to ensure that they retain a powerful hold over the main strategic components of policy-making.[62] Within the EU, Member States have created arrangements and institutional entities in order to allow for efficient decision-making and effective enforcement of policies, granting to institutional bodies like the European Commission, the ECJ and the European Parliament considerable authority, political resources and influence. In particular, the Commission's major role as process-manager of an increasingly complex mode of policy-making, has curtailed the authority of Member States and resulted in a continuing, intricate contest for influence among all the actors involved. But if one considers European integration as a temporal process embedded in institutions, it is unmistakable that strong settings of territorially-entrenched politics are giving way to federal structures firmly established in multi-level governance.

The European project initially offered Member States the choice between strengthening intergovernmental co-operation and constructing a federal European polity. Hence the different 'schools' (Idealist, Functionalist and Realist) of understanding the nature of European integration. Over several decades of experience, Member States have gradually come to see that existing intergovernmental decision-making regimes have numerous weaknesses (i.e., low compliance and deficits in achieving, implementing and controlling common decisions), and that other modes of governance may be preferable. But this has been a slow and painstaking process.

Some national governments have, with mixed results, tried to strengthen the grip of the nation-state on political developments, of which the creation of the

European Council in 1975 was the most notable (and successful) example. The European Council (which brings together the Heads of State or Government, the Ministers of Foreign Affairs and the President of the European Commission at least twice a year) has come to play a central role in setting out the main direction of the European project, producing road-maps and basic guidelines for policy.

The Council of the EU, which is an altogether different body, serves as another forum for the territorial representation of national politics. 'The Council' is in fact a conglomerate of some twenty different 'councils' that bring together the ministers of the EU's member governments according to the topic under discussion. The Rome Treaty has given the Council of Ministers the power to decide on Commission proposals and to determine the extent of the Union's collaborative policies and actions. The Council significantly enlarged its structure in the 1970s, with an evolving role of COREPER (the French abbreviation for the Committee of Permanent Representatives), the expansion of the General Secretariat of the Council, the upgrading of the Council Presidency as well as a number of technical measures to strengthen Council-control over EC legislation. With the SEA and the Maastricht and Amsterdam Treaties, the European Parliament has through the co-operation and assent procedure gained limited co-decisional powers in EU decision-making; the Commission's role has also been steadily increased.

The current academic discourse on how to interpret European integration is largely a dispute between intergovernmentalists (whose imagery is firmly rooted in the Realist tradition of world politics), and supranationalists (whose imagery is often of a federalist nature).[63] Only recently, the constructivist discourse on European integration has gained momentum and might in due course provide an alternative reading of what 'Europe' is all about.[64] Although this controversy remains scholarly in nature, it is basically a confrontation between different understandings of the qualitative nature of the European arrangement of collective governance. Intergovernmentalists claim that the EU is essentially a framework for interstate bargaining based on the 'national interests' of Member States, who all seek to maximize their own advantage while avoiding serious infringements on their sovereignty. In this view, the political preferences and interests of nation-states are considered as given and therefore unproblematic; the focus of attention is on how Member States pursue those given interests while preserving their sovereignty. As Moravcsik has argued, 'In the intergovernmentalist view, the unique institutional structure of the EC is acceptable to national governments only insofar as it strengthens, rather than weakens, their control over domestic affairs'.[65] Claims that non-state actors exert influence only through the domestic political structure, just confirms the hegemonic position of the nation-state. Leaps forward in the European integration process can only be achieved through 'preference convergence' among national leaders. Robert Keohane and Stanley Hoffmann have therefore argued that the Treaty of Rome as well as the SEA 'resulted less from a coherent burst of idealism than from a convergence of national interests around a pattern of economic policymaking'.[66]

Like most grand theories that aspire to offer a total explanation of political life, intergovernmentalism fails to hold water after a detailed investigation of day-to-day policy-making inside the EU. A more prosaic approach to European political life offers a completely different picture of a complex and pluralistic policy-making process on the European level that is only loosely disciplined by EU Member States.[67] Students of industrial, regional, social and environmental policy-making within the Union have found that in many cases the European Commission and the ECJ have assumed a central role in developing policies that Member States obviously did not desire (e.g., in furthering gender equality, or in improving workplace health and safety regulations).[68] It seems clear that the generalized and universalized schema of political behavior based on the notion of an anarchical struggle for power among nation-states is now untenable, at least for the West European part of the globe. Realist/intergovernmentalist modes of 'problem-solving' rituals have shown themselves problematic and incapable of handling the dynamics of European governance. By classifying 'grand events' like the SEA and the Maastricht and Amsterdam Treaties as defining moments, these 'grand theories' fail to incorporate the temporal dimension of the European project. Notions of national sovereignty, based on a strict separation of inside/outside and domestic/foreign, are no longer relevant in a highly fragmented but also increasingly integrated European polity.

In the light of this critique, it comes as little surprise that the orthodoxy of intergovernmentalism has come under serious academic attack from several sides as the ideological foundation for a state-centric approach to European governance. This is not the place to deconstruct these readings of European politics, but in order to point out the limitations and practical boundaries of EU intergovernmentalism, it may be useful to briefly resummarize the academic comment on this statist focus on Europe. This serves to prepare the way for a more profound and wide-ranging examination of EU governance in the following chapter.

To start with, it has become clear that the relationship between the different actors participating in the European integration process is *not* of a zero-sum character. On the contrary, decision-making competencies on the European level are shared, instead of being strictly divided between the European, national and regional level. The increasing role of experts and non-state actors in almost all phases of the policy-formation process only adds to the kaleidoscopic and complex nature of EU governance. More attention should also be paid to the multiform domestic political landscapes of the EU Member States. As we will discuss at length in the following chapter, the institutional entrenchment of the regions in domestic political systems, and their growing role as participants in European policy-making, are major factors in understanding the postmodern Euro-polity. A final critique is that by focusing on a snapshot-like single 'defining moment', the full and convoluted motion picture of the development of the European project has often gone unnoticed. The intergovernmentalist approach is unduly static, thereby failing to comprehend the dynamic interaction between European and domestic politics.[69]

Within the EU's system of governance, a gradual shift has become apparent from intergovernmentalism to a political practice that remains outside our limited range of traditional categories. Perhaps this movement can be best described by drawing upon a contemporary theory of mathematical sets called 'fuzzy logic'. We have all become used to thinking in terms of conventional, Boolean logic, which divides the world into sharply bounded categories (or 'sets'). For example, in decision-making on the European level we consider the national veto as part of 'intergovernmentalism'; qualified majority voting (QMV), on the other hand, is considered an element of 'federalism'. Although this may appear clear and simple, Member States have through practical experience come to realize that EU decision-making defies binary logic. Brussels is a much more 'fuzzy' political place, functioning according to a logic that does not define matters in terms of either/or prospects, but as matters of degree: items can belong to more than one 'fuzzy set' at the same time.[70] Some matters are 'more likely' to be dealt with in such and such a way, but in the end it may well be 'somewhat' different. Unexpected consequences, decision-makers' restricted time horizons, and the very issue-density of European politics all have profound implications for our way of thinking and of categorizing our knowledge. National actors striving for an optimal European policy outcome must grapple with a complex process which involves constantly changing variables that are characterized by vagueness and ambiguity, rather than by transparency and predictability. In this context, it is not always clear that intergovernmentalism is the best choice; in many cases, it is not even clear whether intergovernmentalism is a choice *at all*. Perhaps the very idea of intergovernmentalism has become a less than useful fantasy based on archaic notions of individual/state sovereignty.

The EU's fuzzy logic offers Member States an exit to this existentialist dilemma by creating wider room for maneuver. More often than not, decision-making at the European level is managed in a novel way, generally defying orthodox taxonomies.

## Neo-medievalism as a parable for postmodern Europe

But what taxonomy might be more helpful in understanding the extraordinary political experiment that we are now witnessing in Europe? Friedrich Kratochwil has reminded us that, while

> postmodernists have shown the 'mythical' nature of modern nations relying on the construction of a common ancestry, they seem largely to believe that by exposing the 'irrational' elements of such constructions, their job has been done. Implicit in this approach is then an argument that, since something is the work of imagination, *anything is possible*, because anything seems to be imaginable.
>
> (Friedrich Kratochwil, 'Citizenship: On the Border of Order', in *Alternatives*, vol. 19, no. 4 (Fall 1994), p. 502, emphasis in the original)

This is certainly true. But, despite this helpful caveat, I would nevertheless like to challenge the worn and somewhat tired classifications by likening the current state of European governance to scholarly insights on politics and power during the Middle Ages.

When we presuppose that the Westphalian states system is now giving way to a more complex system of governance (at least in Europe), the question is immediately raised of how we should conceptualize this emerging post-statal system. For understanding policy-creation at the European level the model of multi-level governance is helpful, but remains confined to what occurs in 'Brussels'; obviously European politics goes beyond Brussels and its institutions. In this context the medieval metaphor for postmodern Europe has been suggested by a number of authors.[71] The Westphalian state-centric system has made us familiar with entities that are based on linear and fixed boundaries that separate continuous and mutually exclusive spaces. This has not always been the case. However far-fetched it may seem, the reference to neo-medievalism is useful, since it reminds us that in the Middle Ages, Europe was characterized by a system of overlapping and often discontinuous territories. Only in modern Europe was the principle of hierarchical subordination gradually replaced by the canon of spatial exclusion.

The argument is now made that, *qua* governance structure, postmodern Europe might be as complex and ambiguous as medieval Europe. In this context, Lewis H. Lapham has argued that as yet

> nobody has drawn a map that reflects this new order, but if somebody were to do so, I suspect it would look more like medieval France than 19th century Europe ... The hierarchies of international capitalism resemble the feudal arrangements under which an Italian noble might swear fealty to a German prince, or a Norman duke declare himself the vassal of an English king. The lords and barons of the transnational corporation become lieges of larger fiefs and holding companies, owing their allegiances less to a government (any government) than to Sony or McDonnell Douglas or Citicorp. It is the company that pays their pensions, insures their lives, bestows on them their titles and badges of identity.
> (Lewis H. Lapham, 'Leviathan in Trouble', in *Harper's Magazine*, September 1988)

Thinking about alternatives to the modern states system is neither new, nor limited to the discourse about the future of Europe and European integration. In most texts touching upon neo-medievalism, a tribute is paid to the work of Hedley Bull who argued in his book *The Anarchical Society* (1977) that if

> modern states were to come to share their authority over their citizens, and their ability to command their loyalties, on the one hand with regional and world authorities, and on the other hand with sub-state or sub-national authorities, to such an extent that the concept of sovereignty ceased to be

applicable, then a neo-mediaeval form of universal political order might be
said to have emerged.

(Hedley Bull, *The Anarchical Society: A Study of Order in World Politics*
(London: Macmillan, 1977), pp. 254–5)

Since this argument is embedded in the overall discourse on the political
consequences of economic globalization, this analogy may well also eventually
be applied to world politics in general, and not only to Europe.

Taking the medieval metaphor seriously will offer a good starting point for
imagining a new, postmodern representation of political space.[72] It raises a
number of issues that merit serious discussion, since the economic and political
uncertainty that will inevitably accompany the transition toward a postmodern
system of governance remains difficult to interpret and comprehend. It touches
upon a wide range of social and political issues, from the impact of technology
on state sovereignty, to the individualization of society characterized by the
dissolution of traditional alignments and identities. Globalization – and on a
more modest scale Europeanization as well – is opening the door to a dis-
nationalist approach to political order and community.[73] Postmodernism
celebrates both pluralism and discontinuity, which makes it possible to overcome
the overcoded boundaries of existing nation-states and translate them into
numerous overlapping divisions. Emerging cross-national and non-statist political
movements are challenging statal priorities and policies on a wide range of
issues, which inevitably pluralizes the existing sites of collective political
identification. These identities are shaped without taking the state or any sense of
territoriality into account and thereby amplify the voices of new socio-political
communities.

Stephen Kobrin has identified six facets of the medieval organization of
society that might help us in imagining what such a future might look like:

1   complex notions of space, geography and borders;
2   the ambiguity of authority;
3   multiple loyalties;
4   transnational elites;
5   no clear distinction between public and private office; and
6   a unifying belief system and supranational centralization.[74]

Kobrin makes the case that territorial sovereignty is not historically privileged,
that there have been other bases for the organization of authority in the past,
and that there may well be others in the future. The argument is made that the
modern states system might be a 'detour', and that the nation-state might be an
ephemeral political form, a 'European peculiarity', if you wish. One could also
posit that the political development from premodern (i.e., medieval), to modern
to postmodern should be read as a 'movement from relative to absolute and then
back to (new) relative conceptions of space'.[75] But as an interim meaning of
neo-medievalism, we may argue that it entails a multiple and overlapping

framework of power and authority, where identity is shared among local, regional, international and global domains in the context of a system of multi-tiered allegiances.

In contemplating the neo-medieval metaphor, we should be warned that most 'analysis of precapitalist geopolitical systems suffers from projecting the familiar vocabulary of states and markets, the domestic and the international, into differently structured pasts'.[76] Borders in medieval Europe were diffuse, shifting and permeable. What is more, a singular relationship between authority and territory had not yet been established.[77] The notion of a 'legitimate political unit' did not exist, and one could therefore ask, when French kings were Kings of England and English kings were also Kings of France, 'what was England, what was France? British kings continued to bear the title "King of France" long after they had ceased to control any part of France'.[78] Not surprisingly, therefore, sovereignty as the legitimate authority within a certain discrete space, had little political relevance.[79] The Pauline metaphor of the 'Body of Christ' was frequently used by philosophers and theologians to describe political reality. Kings, the Pope, bishops, counts and peasants all had their proper place in a complex organic system of authority connected through a baroque labyrinth of privilege, prerogative and multiple lines of allegiance and identity. This *Res Publica Christiana* knew few clear rules of the game, and clear judicial procedures were adamantly lacking. No two authorities were similar;[80] all were linked through a dense and nebulous network of feudal and familial obligations, which made idiosyncrasy the norm, rather than the exception.

The feudal system of political organization was decentralized, non-hierarchical and non-territorial, and to a large extent based on personal bonds. Feudal property, for example, was conditional, since it carried with it explicit political and social obligations. Multiple titles to the same landed property were the norm, rather than the exception. In the medieval system of rule 'different juridical instances were geographically interwoven and stratified, and plural allegiances, asymmetrical suzerainties and anomalous enclaves abounded'.[81] The distinction between 'inside' (i.e., domestic politics) and 'outside' (i.e., international politics) did not make sense in the medieval political context, since many rulers wielded authority over different regions in their respective lands. The feudal ruling class was able to assume governance over regions all over the European continent, based on an impressive shared body of religion, law and customs. The widespread use of mercenaries and privateers (and the notable absence of national armies), only adds to the unique medieval political order. The political grammar of medieval segmented territorial rule therefore fails to relate to the modern concept of sovereignty which has clear connotations of exclusiveness based on unitary nationalism.

In this context, Tuomas Forsberg has argued that

> it is not necessary that power is organized territorially by the use of linear, exclusive boundaries, or that power is organized territorially at all. As we know, there have been territorial alternatives to the nation-state system and

there are many more possibilities that have often failed to manifest themselves historically.

(Tuomas Forsberg, 'Beyond Sovereignty, Within Territoriality: Mapping the Space of Late-Modern (Geo) Politics', in *Cooperation and Conflict*, vol. 31, no. 4 (December 1996), p. 364)

As known alternatives, Forsberg identifies the *functional* organization of power, confined to a particular domain of human activity or material, and a *personalized* relationship of power, which implies that power can only be exercised over a distinct group of people. In both cases the important difference from the accepted idea of political territoriality is that these power relationships have little to do with notions of geographical space. In the vast majority of political analysis the permanency of states is taken for granted; other forms of political authority and community are as a rule not even considered. What would security mean without the state, or without the state playing a dominant role? It seems that orthodox studies of IR are just about incapable of analyzing security without taking the state for granted. But by dehistoricizing the state, by ignoring the many domestic fault lines that are covered by state sovereignty, the state is rendered permanent, usually leading to spurious and highly conservative conclusions. This ignores the simple fact that, during nearly all of humanity's chronicle, the state as a territorially defined political entity did not exist.

Arguably, this makes contemporary state-centric IR concepts analytically antiquated, at least for a future-oriented study of postmodern politics. Ruggie has already argued that the Realist, statal paradigm fails to conceptualize 'the most important contextual change in international politics in this millennium: the shift from the medieval to the modern international system'.[82] For similar reasons, much of the body of orthodox IR texts falls short in helping us understand and explain the coming 'contextual change' that will materialize and mature in the new millennium – that is to say the change from our familiar modern to a more postmodern international system. It is therefore both discouraging and unfortunate that the debate about the future of European integration remains confined within the intellectual and ideational limits of a 'United States of Europe', conceptualizing the EU as a political community with all (or at least most) of the attributes of a sovereign state organized along the traditional lines of political territoriality, but only on a somewhat wider geographical scale. So, even if we accept that the European integration process is challenging the continued existence of sovereign state, we must be aware of the fact that the EU is bound to re-create a political community on a similar territorial basis. Similarly, sub-national entities such as regions are also territorial units *par excellence*. But, as Weiler has argued: 'It would be more than ironic if a policy set up as a means to counter the excesses of statism ended up coming round full circle and transforming itself into a (super) state'.[83]

The endeavor to develop a European identity as a complementary sense of belonging within a multi-layered cognitive environment fits well with the concept of neo-medievalism. As discussed in a previous chapter, an emerging European identity would not come to supersede or transcend other identities, but would offer existing identities alternative points of reference to read and interpret the world. Here the notion of 'cognitive region' may be useful, since it emphasizes that people may base their common identities on shared culture and principles other than traditional territorial sovereignty. Identities are almost by definition situational, and, depending on the circumstances, one of the multiple identities may come to dominate. Identity is also, by necessity if not by choice, dynamic. Although we cannot (easily) change our gender, we can switch religions (or, most commonly, forsake religion for atheism), and we inevitably change age groups. These 'systems of meaning' therefore need not be limited to a specific geographical space, but are likely to be spatially differentiated, involving peoples that might not necessarily be neighbors.

Thinking along these lines constitutes a re-imagining of political community, and perhaps leads in due course to a revisioning of world politics. Ruggie's notion of a 'multiperspectival polity' is especially useful in this conversation, since it emphasizes that political communities can comprise more than a single-point, state-centered, traditional Westphalian geographical perspective, but may hold national, supranational as well as transnational identities which share the same cognitive space.[84] This is especially relevant to our understanding of the EU as a polity which lacks a dominant center of political power. Within Europe the territorial state has become just *one* of the spaces that can make up such a 'cognitive region', but the institutionalization of the prosaics of European politics and society is developing a sense of 'we-ness' derived from a shared high level of constitutional loyalty, from a civic culture of respect for minorities and solidarity with fellow human beings within and outside European borders.[85] This may in due course turn 'Europe' (however defined), into an independent 'cognitive region' on a par with the current nation-state. Ruggie therefore appropriately refers to Europe's political elite as the 'entrepreneurs of alternative political identities'.[86] This would turn the EU into a postmodern empire of sorts, an empire established on the spiritual and juridical 'idea of Europe'. Almost by definition, such a European Empire would be incapable of hegemony and imperialism, since it would be based on a generous inclusion of a multitude of nations and peoples, all with their own mores, cultures and voices.[87]

In conclusion, it is worth noting that two rather different types of 'neo-medievalism' could be envisaged: one of an anarchic/capitalist nature, and another of an emancipatory/ecological nature. Whereas both would accept that the boundaries of the EU between 'inside' and 'outside' would be vague and the lines of authority blurred, the former would tend toward a preoccupation with law and order *within* the EU area and (perhaps even) conflict and discord outside, combined with a general feeling of powerlessness and a lack of a firmly rooted identity among the vast majority of the population. Quite in contrast, the latter would tend toward assuming a more inclusive system of participation which would be 'empowering' European citizens; this would be a new and innovative kind of political community developing within the EU, based on a myriad of overlapping centers of power and identities which would result in an inclusive and ecologically sound site for the development of a new style of 'cosmopolitan democracy'.[88] The erosion of national sovereignty would wear away the habit of seeing security mainly as a matter of defense against 'external' threats; it would encourage a different reading of who 'we' are and no longer deny the possibility of finding alternatives to parochial and ethno-centric emotions of community and communality.

Of course, the state remains a political category in a way unlike either Europe or the globe in general; we can comprehend statal security in political terms in a way that neither European nor global security can, at the moment, be understood. But with the increase of mobility and speed, with the ever-extending wiring of social life into a vast postmodern cyberspace, it becomes clear that space and territory are emptied of the traditional, local meanings.[89] One of the main challenges facing western society in the decades ahead will therefore be to grasp the opportunities offered by the postmodern moment and encourage developments that will offer opportunities for openness and diversity, rather than accepting the anesthetic political paralysis of globalization's McWorld.

## Notes

1  Jay Prosser, *The Body Narratives of Transsexuality* (New York: Columbia University Press, 1998); Judith Butler, *Bodies That Matter: On the Discursive Limits of Sex* (New York: Routledge, 1993); and Robert Hanke, 'Theorizing Masculinity: With/In the Media', in *Communication Theory*, vol. 8, no. 2 (May 1998).

2  Wendy Brown, 'Finding the Man in the State', in *Feminist Studies*, vol. 18, no. 1 (Spring 1992), p. 12.

3  Robin May Schott, 'Maternal Bodies and Nationalism', in *Philosophy Today*, vol. 41 (1997 – Supplement 'Remembrance and Responsibility'), p. 107; and Sandhya Shetty, '(Dis)figuring the Nation: Mother, Metaphor, Metonymy', in *Differences*, vol. 7, no. 3 (Fall 1995).

4  Heikki Eskelinen, Ilkka Liikanen and Jukka Oksa (eds), *Curtains of Iron and Gold: Reconstructing Borders and Scales of Interaction* (Aldershot: Ashgate, 1999); and John MacMillan and Andrew Linklater (eds), *Boundaries in Question: New Directions in International Relations* (New York: St Martin's Press, 1995).

5  R.B.J. Walker, 'Security, Sovereignty, and the Challenge of World Politics', in *Alternatives*, vol. 15, no. 1 (Winter 1990), p. 4.

6  Richard K. Ashley, 'Untying the Sovereign State: A Double Reading of the Anarchy Problematique', in *Millennium: Journal of International Studies*, vol. 17, no. 2 (Summer 1988).

7  William E. Connolly, 'Tocqueville, Territory, and Violence', in Michael J. Shapiro and Hayward R. Alker (eds), *Challenging Boundaries: Global Flows, Territorial Identities* (Minneapolis: University of Minnesota Press, 1996), p. 144. Like Gilles Deleuze and Felix Guattari, Connolly maintains that societies territorialize, fragment and limit space pretending that these boundaries are in some way both natural and true. Connolly refers to the production of a 'civi-territorial complex' as the location and creation of civilization by the consumption of land. See Gilles Deleuze and Felix Guattari, *Anti-Oedipus: Capitalism and Schizophrenia* (New York: Viking, 1977).

8  Timothy W. Luke, 'Governmentality and Contragovernmentality: Rethinking Sovereignty and Territoriality After the Cold War', in *Political Geography*, vol. 15, no. 6/7 (1996). Luke argues that: '[d]ifficult though it might be, we must more rightly write about how these new realities are wrighting societies and spaces today. Doing so

will require us to surrealize the realist political writs of stabilizing order inherently from the past in stories about sovereign governmentality by identifying the wrights of chaotic disorder among products of sovran contragovernmentalities in the present' (p. 494).

9 Jacques Derrida, *Of Grammatology* (Baltimore MD: Johns Hopkins University Press, 1998 – corrected edition), p. 296.

10 Richard K. Ashley, 'Living on Borderlines: Man, Poststructuralism, and War', in James Der Derian and Michael J. Shapiro (eds), *International/Intertextual Relations: Postmodern Readings of World Politics* (Lexington MA: Lexington Books, 1989), pp. 261–2.

11 Laura Neack and Roger M. Knudson, 'Re-Imagining the Sovereign State: Beginning an Interdisciplinary Dialogue', in *Alternatives*, vol. 21, no. 1 (January/March 1996).

12 J. Ann Tickner, *Gender in International Relations: Feminist Perspectives on Achieving Global Security* (New York: Columbia University Press, 1992).

13 Ruth Lister, 'Dialectics of Citizenship', in *Hypatia*, vol. 12, no. 4 (Fall 1997).

14 Bruno Carchedi and Guglielmo Carchedi, 'Contradictions of European Integration', in *Capital and Class*, no. 67 (Spring 1999), pp. 141–8.

15 Zygmunt Bauman, *Postmodernity and Its Discontents* (New York: New York University Press, 1997), p. 6.

16 Slavoj Zizek, 'For a Leftist Appropriation of the European Legacy', *Journal of Political Ideologies*, vol. 3, no. 1 (February 1998), p. 77. See also J.W.E. Sheptycki, 'Policing, Postmodernism and Transnationalization', in *British Journal of Criminology*, vol. 38, no. 3 (Summer 1998).

17 Ian Clark, 'Beyond the Great Divide: Globalization and the Theory of International Relations', in *Review of International Studies*, vol. 24, no. 4 (October 1998).

18 Ilana Friedrich-Silber, 'Space, Fields, Boundaries: The Rise of Spatial Metaphors in Contemporary Sociological Theory', in *Social Research*, vol. 62, no. 2 (Summer 1995).

19 Ronald Bogue, 'Art and Territory', in *South Atlantic Quarterly*, vol. 96, no. 3 (Summer 1997), for an examination of the philosophical-aesthetic concept of, among other things, territorialization.

20 Dominique Moïsi, 'The World Moves On', in *Financial Times*, 8 June 1998, p. 14.

21 Jerry Michalski, 'What is a Virtual Community?', in *New Perspectives Quarterly*, vol. 12, no. 2 (Spring 1992), pp. 44–5.

22 Jon Katz, 'Birth of a Digital Nation', *Wired*, issue 5.04 (April 1997). Online. Available HTTP: http://wired.com (accessed 28 March 2000).

23 Margaret Canovan, 'Crusaders, Sceptics and the Nation', in *Journal of Political Ideologies*, vol. 3, no. 3 (October 1998).

24 Anthony Giddens, 'Post-Traditional Civil Society and the Radical Center', in *New Perspectives Quarterly*, vol. 15, no. 2 (Spring 1998).

25 Richard Rosecrance, 'The Obsolescence of Territory', in *New Perspectives Quarterly*, vol. 12, no. 1 (Winter 1995); and Rosecrance, 'The Rise of the Virtual State', in *Foreign Affairs*, vol. 75, no. 4 (July/August 1996).

26 Simone Weil, *The Need For Roots: Prelude To a Declaration of Duties Toward Mankind* (London: Routledge, 1996 – reprint).

27 Fredric Jameson, *The Geopolitical Aesthetic: Cinema and Space in the World System* (Bloomington IN: Indiana University Press, 1995).

28 *Ibid.*, p. 4, and Fredric Jameson, *Postmodernism, or, the Cultural Logic of Late Capitalism* (Durham NC: Duke University Press, 1992), p. 54.

29 In this context, Louis Henkin has noted that '[s]overeignty is a bad word, not only because it has served terrible national mythologies; in international relations, and even in international law, it is often a catchword, a substitute for thinking and precision'. Quoted in Ruth Lapidoth, 'Redefining Authority', in *Harvard International Review*, vol. 17, no. 3 (Summer 1995), p. 8.

30  Cynthia Weber, *Simulating Sovereignty: Intervention, the State and Symbolic Exchange* (Cambridge: Cambridge University Press, 1995).
31  Martin Wight, *International Theory: The Three Traditions* (New York: Holmes & Meier, 1992), pp. 2–3. See also Alan James, *Sovereign Statehood* (London: Allen & Unwin, 1986).
32  See the special issue of *Political Studies*, vol. 47, no. 3 (1999), on the (ir)relevance of the concept of 'sovereignty' in contemporary global politics.
33  Interview with Benjamin Barber by Nathan Gardels, 'The Making of McWorld', in *New Perspectives Quarterly*, vol. 12, no. 4 (Fall 1995), p. 12.
34  John G. Ruggie, 'Territoriality and Beyond: Problematizing Modernity in International Relations', in *International Organization*, vol. 47, no. 1 (Winter 1993).
35  Jürgen Habermas, 'What Does Socialism Mean Today?', in *New Left Review*, no. 183 (September 1990), pp. 7–8.
36  Benjamin Barber, 'Democracy at Risk: American Culture in a Global Culture', in *World Policy Journal*, vol. 15, no. 2 (Summer 1998), p. 30.
37  John Hoffman, *Sovereignty* (Minneapolis: University of Minnesota Press, 1998); and Timothy W. Luke, 'Nationality and Sovereignty in the New World Order', in *AntePodium*, no. 3 (1996). Online. Available HTTP: http://www.vuw.ac.nz/atp (accessed 28 March 2000).
38  Alexander Wendt, 'Anarchy is What States Make of It: The Social Construction of Power Politics', in *International Organization*, vol. 46, no. 2 (Spring 1992).
39  Paul Ricoeur, 'Narrative Identity', in *Philosophy Today*, vol. 35, no. 1 (Spring 1991). For performativity, see Judith Butler, *Gender Trouble: Feminism and the Subversion of Identity* (New York: Routledge, 1990); and Butler, *Excitable Speech: A Politics of the Performative* (New York: Routledge, 1996).
40  Alexander Wendt, 'Collective Identity Formation and the International State', in *American Political Science Review*, vol. 88, no. 2 (June 1994), p. 393.
41  Robert O. Keohane, 'Hobbes's Dilemma and Institutional Change in World Politics: Sovereignty in International Society', in Hans-Henrik Holm and Georg Sorensen (eds), *Whose World Order? Uneven Globalization and the End of the Cold War* (Boulder CO: Westview Press, 1995), p. 177 (emphasis in the original).
42  Geoffrey Howe, 'Sovereignty and Interdependence: Britain's Place in the World', in *International Affairs*, vol. 66, no. 4 (October 1990), p. 678.
43  Hans-Henrik Holm and Georg Sorensen, 'International Relations Theory in a World of Variation', in Hans-Henrik Holm and Georg Sorensen (eds), *Whose World Order? Uneven Globalization and the End of the Cold War* (Boulder CO: Westview Press, 1995), p. 196.
44  Georg Sorensen introduces the label 'postmodern state' explicitly for states that use their sovereignty as a bargaining chip. See Georg Sorensen, 'An Analysis of Contemporary Statehood: Consequences For Conflict and Co-operation', in *Review of International Studies*, vol. 23, no. 3 (July 1997), p. 262.
45  Norman Davies, 'The Euro is the Last Thing Europe Needs', in *The Sunday Times*, 24 May 1998.
46  James Crawford, 'Negotiating Global Security Threats in a World of Nation States', in *American Behavioral Scientist*, vol. 38, no. 6 (May 1995).
47  Stephen D. Krasner, 'Sovereignty: An Institutional Perspective', in *Comparative Political Studies*, vol. 21, no. 1 (April 1988), pp. 86–90.
48  Ronald B. Mitchell, 'Discourse and Sovereignty: Interests, Science, and Morality in the Regulation of Whaling', in *Global Governance*, vol. 4, no. 3 (July/September 1998).
49  Lapidoth, 'Redefining Authority'. See also Georges Benko and Ulf Strohmayer (eds), *Space and Social Theory: Interpreting Modernity and Postmodernity* (Oxford: Blackwell, 1997).
50  Philippe Cullet, 'Differential Treatment in International Law: Towards a New Paradigm in Inter-State Relations', in *European Journal of International Law*, vol. 10, no. 3 (1999).

51  J.H.H. Weiler, 'Community, Member States and European Integration: Is the Law Relevant?', in *Journal of Common Market Studies*, vol. 21, no. 1–2 (September/December 1982).

52  This section draws upon Donna Starr-Deelen and Bart Deelen, 'The European Court of Justice as a Federator', in *Publius*, vol. 26, no. 4 (Fall 1996).

53  Alec Stone Sweet and Thomas L. Brunell, 'Constructing a Supranational Constitution: Dispute Resolution and Governance in the European Community', in *American Political Science Review*, vol. 92, no. 1 (March 1998); and Karen J. Alter, 'Who Are the "Masters of the Treaty"? European Governments and the European Court of Justice', in *International Organization*, vol. 52, no. 1 (Winter 1998). Alter especially emphasizes the importance of the different time horizons of the ECJ and politicians, as well as the crucial difference between the legal and political rules of the 'game'.

54  The external hierarchy of norms refers to the notion that Community norms should be considered supreme over conflicting Member State norms. This cornerstone of the EU's 'New Legal Order' has, however, been directly and indirectly challenged, among others by the German Constitutional Court.

55  J.H.H. Weiler, *The Constitution of Europe* (Cambridge: Cambridge University Press, 1999), especially Chapters 1, 5, 6 and 9.

56  Judgement of the German Constitutional Court on the Treaty on European Union (i.e., the Maastricht Treaty): *Bundesverfassungsgericht*, Judgement of 12 October 1993, 2 BvR 2134/92 and 2 BvR 2159/92 (1994) 89 *Entscheidungen des Bundesverfassungsgerichts* (para C II a).

57  Dieter Grimm, 'Does Europe Need a Constitution?', in Peter Gowan and Perry Anderson (eds), *The Question of Europe* (London: Verso), p. 245. It should be noted that Grimm, a Justice at the German Constitutional Court, is himself (not surprisingly) less than enthusiastic about introducing a European constitution of sorts.

58  Stephen L. Elkin and Karol Edward Soltan (eds), *A New Constitutionalism: Designing Political Institutions for a Good Society* (Chicago: University of Chicago Press, 1993).

59  European Commission President Jacques Santer, quoted in the *Wall Street Journal*, 31 January 1995.

60  Ulrich Haltern, 'Intergovernmentalism as a Way of Union Governance', annex to A. Ballmann and J.J.H. Weiler, *Certain Rectangular Problems of European Integration*, Project IV/95/02, Directorate General for Research of the European Parliament (1996). Online. Available HTTP: http//www.iue.it/AL/EP/index.html (accessed 15 August 2000).

61  Lisbeth Aggestam, 'The European Union at the Crossroads: Sovereignty and Integration', in Alice Landau and Richard G. Whitman (eds), *Rethinking the European Union: Institutions, Interests and Identities* (New York: St Martin's Press, 1997).

62  Simon J. Bulmer, 'The European Council and the Council of the European Union: Shapers of a European Confederation', in *Publius*, vol. 26, no. 4 (Fall 1996).

63  For the (liberal) intergovernmentalist approach, see Andrew Moravcsik, 'Negotiating the Single European Act: National Interests and Conventional Statecraft in the European Community', in *International Organization*, vol. 45, no. 1 (Winter 1991); and Moravcsik, 'Preferences and Power in the European Community: A Liberal Intergovernmentalist Approach', in *Journal of Common Market Studies*, vol. 31, no. 4 (December 1993). For a 'federalist' approach, see Wayne Sandholtz, 'Choosing Union: Monetary Politics and Maastricht', in *International Organization*, vol. 47, no. 1 (Winter 1993).

64  A good overview of the constructivist debate on 'Europe' and European integration is given in the special issue of the *Journal of European Public Policy*, vol. 6, no. 4 (December 1999).

65  Moravcsik, 'Preferences and Power in the European Community', p. 507.

66  Robert O. Keohane and Stanley Hoffmann, 'Institutional Change in Europe in the 1980s', in Robert O. Keohane and Stanley Hoffmann (eds), *The New European*

*Community: Decisionmaking and Institutional Change* (Boulder CO: Westview Press, 1991), pp. 23–4.

67  Geoffrey Garrett and George Tsebelis, 'An Institutional Critique of Intergovernmentalism', in *International Organization*, vol. 50, no. 2 (Spring 1996).

68  C. Hoskyns, 'Women, European Law, and Transnational Politics', in *International Journal of the Sociology of Law*, vol. 14 (1986); I. Ostner and J. Lewis, 'Gender and the Evolution of European Social Policies', in S. Leibfried and P. Pierson (eds), *European Social Policy: Between Fragmentation and Integration* (Washington DC: Brookings Institution, 1995); V. Eichener, 'Social Dumping or Innovative Regulation? Processes and Outcomes of European Decision-Making in the Sector of Health and Safety at Work Harmonization', EUI Working Paper Series, no. 92–28 (Florence: European University Institute, 1993); and Liesbet Hooghe and Michael Keating, 'The Politics of European Union Regional Policy', in *Journal of European Public Policy*, vol. 1, no. 3 (September 1994).

69  Paul Pierson, 'The Path to European Integration: A Historical Institutionalist Analysis', in *Comparative Political Studies*, vol. 29, no. 2 (April 1996); and Tor Egil Forland, 'Autonomy – Community – Suzerainty: Decision-Making Control and European Integration', in *Cooperation and Conflict*, vol. 32, no. 3 (September 1997).

70  Daniel McNeil and Paul Freiberger, *Fuzzy Logic: The Revolutionary Computer Technology that is Changing Our World* (New York: Simon & Schuster, 1993). See also Deborah Merritt, 'The Fuzzy Logic of Federalism', in *Case Western Reserve Law Review*, vol. 46, no. 3 (Spring 1996).

71  Among them, Knud Erik Jörgensen, 'Beyond European Leviathans: Differentiating Layers of International Tranformation', in Nils Arne Sorensen (ed.), *European Identities: Cultural Diversity and Integration in Europe Since 1700* (Odense: Odense University Press, 1995).

72  Ronald J. Deibert, ' "Exorcismus Theoriae": Pragmatism, Metaphors and the Return of the Medieval in IR', in *European Journal of International Relations*, vol. 3, no. 2 (June 1997).

73  E. Tassin, 'Europe: A Political Community', in Chantal Mouffe (ed.), *Dimensions of Radical Democracy: Pluralism, Citizenship, Community* (London: Verso, 1996).

74  Stephen J. Kobrin, 'Back to the Future: Neomedievalism and the Postmodern Digital World Economy', in *Journal of International Affairs*, vol. 51, no. 2 (Spring 1998).

75  James Anderson, 'The Shifting Stage of Politics: New Medieval and Postmodern Territorialities', in *Environment and Planning: Society and Space*, vol. 14 (1996), p. 143. Quoted in Kobrin, 'Back to the Future: Neomedievalism and the Postmodern Digital World Economy', p. 363.

76  Benno Teschke, 'Geopolitical Relations in the European Middle Ages: History and Theory', in *International Organization*, vol. 52, no. 2 (Spring 1998), p. 327.

77  Michael Wilks, *The Problem of Sovereignty in the Later Middle Ages* (Cambridge: Cambridge University Press, 1964).

78  Philip Allott, 'The Crisis of European Constitutionalism: Reflections on the Revolution in Europe', in *Common Market Law Review*, vol. 34, no. 3 (June 1997), p. 473.

79  Joseph A. Camilleri and Jim Falk, *The End of Sovereignty: The Politics of a Shrinking and Fragmenting World* (Aldershot: Edward Elgar, 1992).

80  Charles Tilly has argued that the Europe of the sixteenth century included some 500 'more or less independent political units'. See Charles Tilly, 'Reflections on the History of European State-Making', in Charles Tilly (ed.), *The Formation of National States in Western Europe* (Princeton NJ: Princeton University Press, 1975), p. 15.

81  Perry Anderson, *Lineages of the Absolutist State* (London: New Left Books, 1974), pp. 37–8.

82 John G. Ruggie, 'Continuity and Transformation in the World Polity: Toward a Neorealist Synthesis', in Robert O. Keohane (ed.), *Neorealism and Its Critics* (New York: Columbia University Press, 1986), p. 141.

83 J.H.H. Weiler, 'Europe After Maastricht – Do the New Clothes Have an Emperor?', Harvard Law School, Jean Monnet Chair Working Paper Series, no. 12 (1995).

84 Ruggie, 'Territoriality and Beyond', p. 172.

85 Seyla Benhabib, 'On European Citizenship', in *Dissent*, vol. 45, no. 4 (Fall 1998), p. 108; and James Tully, *Strange Multiplicity: Constitutionalism in an Age of Diversity* (Cambridge: Cambridge University Press, 1995).

86 Ruggie, 'Territoriality and Beyond', p. 172.

87 Alain de Benoist, 'The Idea of Empire', in *Telos*, no. 98–9 (Winter 1993).

88 Andrew Linklater, *The Transformation of Political Community* (Columbia SC: University of South California Press, 1998); and Richard W. Miller, 'Cosmopolitan Respect and Patriotic Concern', in *Philosophy and Public Affairs*, vol. 27, no. 3 (Summer 1998).

89 Derek Gregory, *Geographical Imaginations* (Oxford: Blackwell, 1993).

# 5 European governance and the pursuit of promiscuous policy-making

## The necessity of governance

The growing complexities of European political life, the additional administrative workloads flowing from the EU's new responsibilities for monetary policy, internal security, foreign policy and defense issues, call for a new European system of governance. The European Commission, headed by its President Romano Prodi, therefore argues that the 'challenge is to radically rethink the way we do Europe. To reshape Europe. To devise a completely new form of governance for the world of tomorrow'.[1] Although the EU has traditionally given policy management a high priority, it has tended to overlook the modernization of its institutions needed to ensure effective performance of its growing 'state-like' function as a central source of authoritative allocation of values and wealth for European society.[2] Reforms of the EU's institutional and decision-making framework have therefore been haphazard and necessarily incremental in nature. Such reforms have been 'path-dependent', in the sense that reform strategies have been shaped more by the existing institutional structure than by the desired model of public administration. The two Intergovernmental Conferences of the 1990s (culminating in the Maastricht and Amsterdam Treaties), have added new tasks to an already crowded EU agenda. But old ideological battles and disagreements over the design of Europe's institutional architecture have blocked a serious overhaul of the administration of EU policies.

We have already argued that the political authority of national governments has come under increasing strain during the past few decades as a result of globalization and the new role of the private sector and an amorphous body of non-state actors. This competition for influence has significantly curbed the ability of the nation-state to control its direct environment and has delegitimated state actors who are often perceived as sluggish, bureaucratic and inept at processing data and knowledge swiftly enough to play a forceful and meaningful role in today's information-based global society. The blending of public- and private-sector resources, partnerships and a multitude of hybrid organizational formats is further challenging traditional concepts of governance. This has obviously also affected policy formation on the European level. The EU now has to accommodate a wide variety of public interest groups, regional and national governments as well as 'outside' groups, who all try to influence the shape of European-level policy solutions. In short: there is a great demand for European governance. However, given the complex administrative process, the extreme permeability, openness and multicultural nature of the EU's decision-making environment, this has evolved into a qualitatively new kind of Euro-polity, probably best characterized in the notion of 'governance without government'.

The meaning of the concept of 'governance' is not always clear, although it is very frequently used in EU (and especially European Commission) documents. The body of academic literature that is based on 'governance without government' tends to emphasize the role of international markets, international institutions and regimes, as well as formal and informal networks of co-operation. But what does 'governance' imply, if not the traditional meaning of 'governing'? A substantial body of academic literature has developed on the issue of (especially multi-level) governance in the EU.[3] In this literature, which draws on a range of detailed case studies, one of the common emerging themes is that the complexity and ambiguity of the European policy-making process on multiple levels results in dispersed and disjointed decisions and incomplete implementation.[4] The development of the notion of 'governance' is not limited to Europe *per se*. James Rosenau, for one, claims that the rapid and extensive global change is undermining the power structures of the passing present by shifting the *loci* of authority, so that the functions of governance are now frequently being performed by agents that do not find their origin in traditional governments.[5] He argues that '[g]lobal governance is the sum of myriad – literally millions of – control mechanisms driven by different histories, goals, structures, and processes', which implies that any effort to trace a 'hierarchical structure of authority that loosely links disparate sources of governance to each other is bound to fail. In terms of governance, the world is too disaggregated for grand logics that postulate a measure of global governance'.[6]

Rosenau further argues that both governance and government refer to purposeful behavior, to goal-oriented activities and systems of rule. But, whereas government is normally backed by formal authority, governance refers to activities backed by shared goals which are not necessarily embedded in a system of compliance. He therefore claims that governance 'embraces governmental institutions, but it also subsumes informal, non-governmental mechanisms whereby those persons and organizations within its purview move ahead, satisfy their needs, and fulfil their wants'.[7] The crucial point to make and to emphasize is that governance is a regulatory system which functions (effectively) without being vested in a formal complex of authority. The capacity for direct control over factors and actors has now been replaced with a capacity to influence processes. We could also argue that governing is not based so much on rationality and efficiency as on reasonableness and eligibility.[8]

In the particular context of the EU, governance can be seen as a continual flow of political communities within a dynamic process of policy formation that involves a wide range of state and non-state actors constituting a system of networks.[9] This is also the metaphor used by Commission President Prodi, who argued in February 2000,

> I believe we have to stop thinking in terms of hierarchical layers of compe-
> tence separated by the subsidiarity principle and start thinking, instead, of a
> networking arrangement, with all levels of governance shaping, proposing,
> implementing and monitoring policy together.
> (Romano Prodi, '2000–2005: Shaping the New Europe', Speech to the Euro-
> pean Parliament in Strasbourg, 15 February 2000. Online. Available HTTP:
> http://europa.eu.int/comm/externalrelations/news/0200/speech0041.htm,
> accessed 15 August 2000)

This implies that European governments are no longer 'governing', but try to shape their societies by managing mutual dependencies among state agencies, the private sector, non-governmental organizations, the media and international institutions and bodies that are continuously interacting as relative equals. Governance therefore implies that the nation-state has lost much of its traditional power resources and even much of its legitimacy to exert direct control. European nation-states retain their capacity to influence policy outcomes and are involved in efforts to optimize their problem-solving ability. But this is always done in close partnership with other national and transversal non-state actors and institutions. Within this network of governance, the nation-state still has a powerful voice. But national governments now focus more on setting priorities and defining strategic goals rather than on the practical implementation of policies, which is increasingly left to non-state actors. Finding themselves afloat upon the tidal waves of globalization, Europe's states are therefore clearly more intent on steering than on rowing.[10]

Although it may still be too early to qualify the emerging multi-tiered frame-work of governance as the European policy style *par excellence*, it is fair to say that the European project is now following a pluralistic trajectory of integration – one that does not involve the amalgamation of administrative functions of EU Member States, but rather presumes the partial policy autonomy of participating states and their shared responsibility for managing interdependence within a complex and pluralistic governance structure.[11] The EU is a far cry from the classical Weberian, hierarchical system of political organization, but it is taking the West European model of democratic governance based on partnerships, public-private joint ventures and the inclusion of experts, epistemic communities and advocacy coalitions to the extreme.

The famous system of 'comitology' of the EU, based upon numerous com-mittees of interests and experts linking the Council of Ministers and the European Commission, with further links to the national bureaucracies, illustrates the network-like nature of European policy formation. The EU has moved away from the old-style centralized policy-making approach and has adopted more flexible, disconnected styles of work based on the management of (administrative) partnerships aimed at enabling constituent organizations, groups and political actors to work together. The EU's network seeks effective and flexible management of a great array of information and knowledge in order to pursue the interests and objectives of national, regional, local and transversal actors, and to limit the centrifugal tendencies inherent in policy-making in a multicultural environment. In his study on the relevance of comitology for EU policy formulation, Rhys Dogan has made the case that (contrary to what is generally assumed), the European Commission does *not* consistently seek to extend its authority, and that Member States do *not* necessarily seek to maintain control over policy outcomes. Instead, EU competence and national sovereignty seem to have become secondary considerations for the actors involved, and policy outcomes seem to be shaped by preferences based on specific circumstances in the context of specific issues.[12] Institutional interests are clearly issue-specific, with the result that policy networks are becoming systems through which complex sets of preferences are channeled. This may indicate that the actors involved in the European policy game do not cherish consistent preferences about the location of power within the EU's administrative system, but are prepared to accept different decision-making modes in different circumstances.

The link between the debate on governance and the relevance of a postmodern approach to global politics is an organic one. Governance assumes a transformation from a modern to a postmodern (indeed a post-sovereign) world in which traditional concepts such as nationalism, hegemony and democracy have become problematic and are no longer central to the political debate. The traditional approach to global politics (reflected in the Realist approach to IR) assumes that the world is strictly divided into national and international realms of politics. As discussed earlier, an alternative – postmodern – conception of politics and security refuses to juxtapose the 'national' and 'international', but instead accepts a non-hierarchical and highly complex system of political matters and events which might look entirely different from different angles. The conceptual ambiguity of the concept of governance assumes a modicum of rule embedded within a shared system of norms and values, routinized arrangements and patterned behavior based on a pluralistic image of order. In many ways, therefore, governance and notions of postmodern order are interactive phenomena. This implies that any approach to EU policy-making and governance should go beyond the analysis of separate issue-areas or regimes. Obviously, the EU can be dissected and sliced into manageable academic pieces for easy scholastic consumption. But it is more important to understand that European governance is not confined to single-issue areas within the EU policy-making process, but instead refers to the norms and arrangements that fill the many crevices between the multiplicity of regimes, as well as arrangements for disentangling the overlaps among those regimes.

The crucial challenge for Europe is to ensure that this polyphony of voices within the EU and beyond can find a common harmony through a flexible system of governance. But managing European policies involves the co-ordination of tens if not hundreds of different actors from across the fifteen

Member States and from well beyond the confined boundaries of the EU itself. Within this multi-level framework of governance, the EU's main task is to ensure that these organizations are able to work together effectively and formulate practical policy outcomes. For Europe's citizens and numerous societal organizations in Europe, the EU is a key player in creating the norms that are increasingly governing their daily reality. We have already argued that in order to grasp the unique quality of EU policy formulation, the intergovernmentalist prism sheds little light on the complex nature of the European project. It has become increasingly difficult to assess power and authority by focusing on the 'national interests' involved. Notions of power politics and hard-nosed bargaining in a competitive zero-sum environment may still be relevant to the limited (though far from unimportant) field of Europe's heroic politics,[13] but in the vast field of Europe's prosaic existence it will have few insights to offer.[14] This does also imply that a certain level of epistemological pluralism not only allows but also encourages us to use numerous tools, approaches and perspectives in the search for the *loci* of governance.

## Of postmodern masculinity, levels, networks

But what taxonomy, what metaphor or hermeneutic approach offers us the best possible understanding of contemporary European governance? To answer this question it may profit us to take a somewhat indirect route: to adopt a feminist approach to global politics. Although feminist readings of politics and the political are diverse and complex,[15] it may be fair to say that feminist, gendered political practice gravitates toward decentralized notions of power and authority, emphasizing the importance of nurturing, caring and co-operation, as well as the indispensability of building consensus and recognizing mutual vulnerabilities.[16] This is customarily connected with the application of 'ecological metaphors' in the political discourse, focused on sensing strength in diversity, on conservation and adaptation, rather than on control and the imposition of physical power.[17] Wendy Brown has argued that, whereas women preserve life, 'men risk it; women tend the mundane and the necessary while men and the state pursue larger-than-life concerns; ... men discount or with their activities threaten the realm of everyday life while women nurture and protect it'. This leads her to conclude that the distinction between 'daily existence preserved by women and the male pursuit of power and prestige through organized violence is both what gives such a predatory, rapacious, conquering ethos to prerogative power and what disenfranchises women from this kind of power'.[18]

This particular feminist perspective (and there are many more) is based on the argument that male values of abstract rationality, formal proceduralism and hierarchy are antipodal to female values of substantive rationality, relationality and responsibility.[19] It also assumes that, through its monopoly of political control and its dominance of the political discourse, the state/male has been the authoritative actor in changing and restricting women's political practices. Brown offers us an interesting and provoking comparison between the 'new man' and the postmodern state, both of which present themselves as quasi-impotent, weaker and softer, and no longer (fully) in charge of their own direct environment. She argues that the 'central paradox of the postmodern state thus resembles a central paradox of postmodern masculinity: its power and privilege operate increasingly through disavowal of potency, repudiation of responsibility, diffusion of sites and operations of control'.[20] The postmodern state has been largely emasculated, made less dominant and relevant as a political actor both domestically and on the international stage. The *macho* state is no longer; it now tends to hide its assumptions of continued authoritative superiority behind a somewhat cynical mask of modesty and brittleness.

Postmodern masculinity may therefore serve as a good point of departure for understanding European governance, since it stresses the reluctant change from hierarchy and power to relationality and pluralistic flexibility as the defining concepts for policy formulation and implementation. Like national political leaders who are unwilling to make difficult decisions, European policy-makers seem prepared to take measures to tie their own hands or develop political formulas that bind their future actions.[21] At the same time, the concept of postmodern masculinity also recognizes the continuing indiscriminate nature of the emerging European policy style: its very openness and drive toward incessant interchange between policy-makers and a wide range of interested actors (and actresses), has led the EU to abandon an orderly and predictable life for recidivist political promiscuity. It is this loose conduct that has confused and fascinated segments of academia, giving birth to sundry 'models' and perspectives on European governance. Here I will dwell upon two of the more influential analytical approaches: multi-level governance and network analysis. Since both overlap in their assumptions on the nature of contemporary policy-making, I will consider them as a mutually reinforcing aggregate of perspectives on the European policy environment and as one exploratory route toward understanding how the Euro-polity differs from other, somewhat better known political systems.[22]

The image of policy-making as an ordered and predictable operation is surely obsolete. Mechanical examinations of the stances of political parties and elected officials, their manifestos and parliamentary deliberations are only of the smallest importance for understanding European political life. Anyone with even a scant interest in European politics will at once recognize that policy-making on the European level involves national and regional actors, bureaucrats, interest groups and an unpredictable range of other participants engaged in structured and *ad hoc* interactions. Although the national political playing field remains meaningful, non-state actors are politically engaged in national as well as supranational arenas and are no longer nested exclusively within nation-states. The understanding that EU politics is no longer a clear-cut 'two-level' game played by European and national actors has therefore become widely accepted. The European context offers an intricate web of multi-level, multi-arena and nested games determined by uncertainty and ambiguity.

Only 'hard-core' intergovernmentalists persevere in arguing that the nation-state continues to function as the ultimate 'gatekeeper' of national interest by monopolizing links between domestic and European actors, and that EU policy-making remains firmly based on unproblematic national preferences. Against this rather conventional and over-simplified approach, notions of multi-level governance and policy networks stand out for their analytical sophistication in capturing the complex, blurred and differentiated nature of policy-making in the EU. These concepts not only offer different insights into the workings of the EU policy process; perhaps more importantly, they also suggest alternative constructions of the very nature of the European proposition. They support a more critical attitude toward the dominant organization of contemporary politics by incorporating the principles of respect for other voices and the diversity of societal interests as the basis of European public administration.[23]

Contrary to the unitary representation of Europe as a state-based model, the notion of multi-level networks awakens images of a dense grid of close co-operation between many different political units that can be defined functionally as well as territorially. It is based on the realization that political rule on the European level can only be competent, effective and legitimate if it allows for the participation of representatives of all groups that are affected by EU policies. Especially since the democratic foundation of the EU is problematic, the wide participation of sociopolitical groups in the discursive production of decisions is crucial. The key argument underpinning the model of multi-level governance is that the state no longer monopolizes policy-making at the European level, and that the *locus* of political control has changed. EU collective decision-making among national governments, as well as by the European Commission, the European Parliament and the ECJ, erodes the proud pillars of state sovereignty. The EU has become the focal point of a multitude of demands and interests represented by sub-national, national and international actors, be they states, firms, NGOs, or other public-interest groups. Within the EU 'public' authority is diffuse and embraces many public and private actors. This lack of a clear center of authority and the actuality of a complex of rather weak formal procedures working within so-called policy networks, helps to explain the bewilderment that affects ordinary citizens who try to grasp the nature of the European integration process. Seemingly lacking a governance epicenter, the Euro-polity opens up a political vista in which traditional boundaries between the 'state' and society, the public and the private, are difficult to disentangle.

As an alternative framework of analysis, multi-level governance does not attempt to formulate categorical and universal assumptions. Instead it is based on the premise that sweeping statements about EU policy formulation are increasingly untenable, since decision-making patterns differ depending on the policy sector under consideration. The patterns of governance within the EU are themselves subject to constant modification, and a complex variety of formal and informal procedures and actors have an impact on the ultimate policy outcome. The complex relationships among the many actors involved in this Euro-policy play have resulted in a polity where political authority and managerial control are diffuse and decentered. In many cases, there is no agreement among these actors on the nature of the problem ('problem definition'), and there are recurrent struggles over who is to decide which policy matters ('problem ownership'). The increasing interconnectedness and interrelatedness of policies make the clear division of policy areas and issues problematic. Although some generalizations about the character of EU policy-making can still be made, we should accept their restricted exegetic value depending on the time-frame and the policy issues under discussion.

In their research on the European policy-creating process, Liesbet Hooghe and Gary Marks have studied the impact of supranational bodies like the European Commission and the European Parliament, as well as intergovernmental actors like the European Council and the Council of Ministers, on policy initiation and decision-making at the European level and on the phases of implementation and adjudication.[24] Their conclusion is that in all four phases of the European policy-formation process the 'EU is shaped by multiple, intermeshing competencies, complementary policy functions, and variable lines of authority – features characteristic of multi-level governance'.[25] Theirs is a strong case. They do not argue that the state is on the verge of political impotence. Rather, they contend that EU decision-making is now increasingly shaped by many interlinked competencies and overlapping political functions that form interlaced networks of authority. Sonia Mazey and Jeremy Richardson have further argued (in their study on the influence of interest groups on the 1996 IGC), that a

> central feature of the lobbying strategies of member states and interest groups is that partners in the 'policy games' are all unreliable – in the sense that no single actor can control the game and deliver the desired payoff. We believe that this is one of the main causes of the erosion of state influence over domestic groups.
> (Sonia Mazey and Jeremy Richardson, 'Policy Framing: Interest Groups and the Lead Up to 1996 Inter-Governmental Conference', in *West European Politics*, vol. 20, no. 3 (July 1997), p. 114)

A key element in the multi-level governance approach therefore is that a wide variety of groups and political entities is vying for power and influence within the EU, which often results in compromise solutions that were not intended by any one of the individual actors involved.

It would not be fully correct to assume that the EU, as a supranational and transversal polity, is the *unique* embodiment of postmodern uncertainty and ambiguity. We should keep in mind, for example, that the American system of governance, with its intricate web of checks and balances, has been purposely designed to be 'incoherent' and to a certain degree also 'inefficient'. While this may have occasionally magnified public skepticism about the managerial capacity of the US Government, it has presumably added to the diversity and democratic legitimacy of the American political system as a whole. The same may apply to the complex administrative and decision-making structure of the EU. It should also be acknowledged that the fashionable wish to 'reinvent government' by decentralizing decision-making and empowering managers and front-line administrators has promoted greater policy incoherence. The tendency to use more private-sector organizations and NGOs to provide public services has added to the existing co-ordination difficulties. Since the EU is slowly developing into a corporate actor in its own right,[26] the spirit of public sector entrepreneurship is making central co-ordination and control even more difficult. Reinventing itself as a European competition state, the EU has become a global competitor looking for clients and customers. In this new context, EU entrepreneurs are encouraged to develop creative and innovative capacities and to take responsibility for their own decisions. This consumer-oriented approach promotes policy incoherence, especially since the existing mechanisms that could create greater co-ordination are now increasingly delegitimated by ideological preferences for both subsidiarity and an emphasis on efficiency and competitiveness.[27]

Two additional factors affecting the Euro-polity are the growing *complexity* of the flow of policy problems that ceaselessly reaches the European Council's agenda, and the sheer *number* of facts, events and issues under discussion. Both dynamics have led the Council (i.e., the EU Member States), to broaden its reliance on the European Commission and the system of comitology for setting the policy agenda, fostering compromise and supervising the implementation of laws, regulations and policies. This has altered the Council/Commission nexus from a principal–agent relationship to a more complex one 'characterized by mutual dependence, complementary functions, and overlapping competencies'.[28] The assumption that national governments remain the indispensable link between the 'inside' and the 'outside' of EU Member States therefore clearly no longer fits the much more complex reality of European political life. The nation-state's traditional role of gatekeeper and exclusive channel of communication and influence is now almost routinely dishonored and sidestepped. In this context, Mazey and Richardson have pointed to two additional factors which have reduced the state's role as the cardinal aggregator of domestic interests:

1   the pressure of transnational firms on the European Union for standardization, harmonization, and the establishment of a so-called 'level playing field' within Europe; and
2   the campaigns of 'outsider groups' (i.e., traditionally politically weaker coalitions of environmentalists, consumers, disabled, women, minorities, etc.) who have often tried to press for satisfactory policies at the national level and failed.[29]

This has resulted in the development of novel patterns of multi-level governance for managing the participation of a melange of new policy actors.

This advocacy 'explosion' is therefore one of the principal causes for, as well as one of the principal responses to, the complexity of European policy-making.

Studies of lobbying on the European level have indicated that an increasing number of organized economic interest groups and sociopolitical organizations have opened regional offices in Brussels.[30] As the EU's policy competence has expanded (as it did dramatically with the passage of the SEA), so has lobbying at the European level.[31] This is a central element of the novel character of European policy formulation, which is not so much teleocratic but concerned with problem-solving via continuous debate, persuasion and consensus-building. It has become clear that national governments are in many cases the 'prisoners' of domestic and international circumstances. Interest groups play a central role in the new policy game by offering decision-makers an opportunity to test the degree of 'popular' support for certain policy proposals. In the absence of other democratic means of testing the waters before decisions are finally made, a wide range of interest groups may be able to represent a slice of European society reflecting (inevitably in a rugged way) their wants and choices.

As I have argued earlier, with the increasing globalization of society most policy sectors have come to recognize that the Europeanization of governance is both inevitable and necessary to maintain some political grip on key developments determining Europe's trajectory. Industrial groups have been instrumental in the development of the EU's internal market, which has reduced or eliminated many national barriers to trade and commerce, offering European firms opportunities to reduce transaction costs and achieve economies of scale to improve profitability and to sharpen their competitive edge. Wayne Sandholtz and John Zysman, in their study of the 1992 project, have claimed that 'European business and the [European] Commission may be said to have together bypassed national governmental processes and shaped the agenda that compelled attention'.[32] It is clear that business lobbies have been able to frame the EU discourse by calling for more Europeanization for the sake of maintaining and improving 'European competitiveness'. Although it cannot be said that the European policy agenda is determined by business interests, the power of this economic argument has been substantial and marked.

The axial role of non-state policy actors in transcending national boundaries and building transnational coalitions, irrespective of state policies, should therefore not be underestimated.[33] This group activity in the complex process of agenda setting and policy articulation not only enlarges our notion of democratic, grass-roots participation and political influence on the European level, it also erodes the possibility of constructing a Euro-polity in terms of a closed identity. It adds to the understanding of the essential 'undecidability' and 'unfinalizability' of the European project, framed within an open and polycentric political space. It thereby offers scope for 'outsiders' to raise their voices and supports the development of a European identity based on an unrobed politics of affinity, rather than a closed and parochial sense of Self. NGOs are exactly what the abbreviation stands for: *non-governmental* organizations, and as such assist in the emergence of a European civic culture based on the multiplicity of transversal contacts. New technologies (especially the Internet) have facilitated the work of environmental, human-rights and other social movements that can now swiftly and readily mobilize interests and shape cross-national coalitions to air their ideas, opinions and political message. International co-operation and the diffusion of understandings from country to country have resulted in a thickening of social relations and the development of a (still rather embryonic) regional/cosmopolitan civil society. This is all an integral part of the evolution toward a cognitive region that not only comprises Europe, but clearly extends beyond it.

The institutional and political complexity of the EU offers many opportunities for lobbies and issue groups to exert influence by pressing for policy innovation, most notably by framing the level of political controversy surrounding certain issues.[34] The 'new' global problems that have become more critical on the international agenda illustrate that the linkage between cultural and political globalization goes far beyond limited questions of EU policy-making. Environmental movements with transnational concerns have initiated new institutions and global conventions (such as the Earth Summit in Rio de Janeiro in 1992, the Beijing Conference on Women in 1995, the Environmental Summit in Kyoto in 1997, as well as the organized Seattle anti-WTO demonstrations in 1999) to address security issues with planetary implications. Environmental interest groups, such as Friends of the Earth, the World Wide Fund for Nature and Greenpeace, cannot rely on any kind of political firepower (like money or votes), but instead base their influence on their membership, the hold they have on people's imaginations and civic awareness. One of the most striking developments in international politics is the proliferation, professionalization and enhanced networking of international NGOs, as well as their consequent success in injecting their views in global decision-making processes.[35] One of the noteworthy consequences has been that the focus of politics has partially (though also gradually) shifted away from narrow state and inter-state concerns and activities and is gaining 'global' resonance. Most people have by now come to realize that many economic, political and environmental problems can no longer be defined exclusively in national or territorial terms, and that a wider, perhaps even global, focus may be required. Globalization and Europeanization clearly indicate that there is no escape from thinking through the possibilities for regional and even global forms of democracy. As Beck has warned us, 'Without a decisive step towards cosmopolitan democratisation, we are heading for a post-political technocratic world society'.[36] This clearly calls for a postnational understanding of politics, responsibility, justice and public interchange.

In many ways, the continued pressure for Europeanization mirrors this attention to global issues, albeit on a regional scale. At the same time, it also calls for a Europe that avoids a siege mentality and makes conscious efforts not to build a formidable, but soulless, Fortress Europe.

## Power/knowledge, civil association and transversalism

Asking the classical questions of political science – Who governs?, Who gets what, when, how? – remains relevant to the study of European policy-making, even though the answers to these questions are becoming ever more unsatisfactory.[37] Obviously, where financial matters are at stake, European states are keen to pay less into the EU budget and get out more. The near-impossibility of radically overhauling the Common Agricultural Policy (CAP) testifies to the rigidity of this egoistic streak among EU Member States.

However, the continued import of this classic fight for slices of the EU pie is only the surface of a more complex picture of European reality. Classical notions of political power are problematic in the European context, since there is no 'A' who has such power over any 'B' that s/he can get this 'B' to do something that 'B' would not otherwise do. Within the EU system, 'power' seems to work (as Talcott Parsons suggested long ago) as a 'circulating medium, analogous to money, within what is called the political system'. Following this metaphor, Foucault has added that power

> must be analyzed as something which circulates, or rather as something which only functions in the form of a chain. It is never localized here or there, never in anybody's hands, never appropriated as a commodity or piece of wealth. Power is employed and exercised through a net-like organization. And not only do individuals circulate between its threads; they are always in the position of simultaneously undergoing and exercising this power. They are not only its inert or consenting target; they are always also the elements of its articulation. In other words, individuals are the vehicles of power, not its points of application.
>
> (Michel Foucault, 'Disciplinary Power and Subjection', reprinted in Steven Lukes (ed.), *Power* (New York: New York University Press, 1986), p. 234)

These are especially valuable analytical points of departure, since the EU cannot be imagined as a simple multilateral political instrument. Instead, it has become a supranational entity with extensive bureaucratic competencies, a measure of judicial control and the authority to initiate, develop and implement policies. Although, like all complex organizations, the EU can be portrayed and translated into an organigram showing clear and unambiguous 'lines of authority', political practice is (as always) entirely different. In many ways the EU resembles a humming bazaar of policies and ideas which has more impact on the day-to-day lives of Europeans than they can imagine. Located at the interface of assiduous territorial, state-centric politics and the sphere of international politics, the EU relentlessly uses its authority to think up collective solutions to a wide range of problems which its Member States no longer can, or want, to address independently.[38] We should acknowledge that more legislation originates within the EU system than ever before. By use of so-called 'directives', the EU's dominant legal instrument, a joint European decision has to be transposed into national law with a certain flexibility and before a specific deadline. European law therefore often cross-dresses as national law, disguising its supranational origins and often deceiving citizens by presenting itself as home-made. In 1998, more than 60 per cent of German legislation had its origin in Brussels, which makes unclear both 'who governs' and what the means and methods of government and governance are. Moreover, through the ECJ's case law, the treaty system has been transformed and gained the semblance of a European Constitution. This has in turn made the EU far more responsive to the daily demands of a more transversal society. Within the EU, the legal system has reduced the capacity of national governments to control policy outcomes, and individuals no longer have to rely on 'their' state as intermediary to press their claims and pursue their interests.[39]

The tertiarization of European society – which refers to 'the partial displacement of conflict from issues of production and distribution to issues of quality of life, questions of personal identity, and forms of participation in all social spheres' – raises a whole new array of challenges and dilemmas for EU policy formation.[40] The traditional entrepreneurial approach to public administration has often justified policy outcomes by reference to criteria of effectiveness, efficiency, and occasionally also fairness. The EU's Single Market program has been a classic case of mechanical administration and policy engineering: establishing economic goals and strict deadlines for lifting national barriers to a free flow of matter, bodies and ideas. But at Maastricht European nation-states set out new and ambitious goals that can no longer be achieved through teleocratic and rule-driven government that relies on policy tools which have served them well over the past few decades.

This has only partially to do with the management deficit I mentioned earlier – although it should be clear that the EU now faces a more complex and crowded policy agenda than ever before. But it is not only complexity and crowdedness that challenges European governance; first and foremost it is the EU's new role and place within (West) European society. In his book *Modernization and Postmodernization* (1997), Ronald Inglehart claims that economic development, cultural change, and political change go hand in hand, following a rather predictable pattern.[41] Inglehart argues that premodern societies are characterized by sustained underdevelopment and a focus on physical survival, and are based upon traditional social values and non-democratic government. Modernization, on the other hand, calls for rational-legal authority structures, centralized and hierarchical institutions, democratic political forms, all embedded in a culture that emphasizes instrumental rationality, economic efficiency and material well-being. Inglehart has made a case that modern nations become postmodern when diminished returns from economic growth, bureaucratization and state-intervention, and welfare state programs give rise to a new set of postmaterialist societal values. These postmodern values emphasize the importance of self-expression, self-actualization, participation and subjective well-being. Or, as Inglehart formulates it, 'a modern worldview that was once firmly established has gradually given way to postmodern values that emphasize human autonomy and diversity instead of the hierarchy and conformity that are central to modernity'.[42]

His argument that advanced industrial (or postindustrial) society embraces such a set of postmodern values, de-emphasizing the instrumental rationality that characterized industrial society and thereby encouraging societal change, is on the whole convincing. Inglehart's suppositions help us understand how postmodernity has contributed to a decline of social class voting as well as to the rise of new social movements. The traditional left–right cleavage of political meaning has now been replaced by a much more diversified political arena which offers more meaningful choice to voters.[43] It further helps us visualize how modernity's instrumental and bureaucratic rationality, hierarchy and conforming authority gradually give way to postmodernity's emphasis on autonomy, self-expression and a call for a more active, radical democratic participation of individuals. Inglehart has further noticed that the 'feeling that the nation-state incarnated a supreme value, as the haven and the sole defense of a unique way of life, has largely vanished in contemporary Western Europe'.[44] This again suggests that the postmodern moment decenters not only the individual and his/her role in society but the nation-state and its new position in global politics as well.

The EU's novel place and role in European policy formulation, as well as its somewhat Byzantine but permeable governance structure, merely testify to this changing economic and political environment. The EU's tertiary concerns are therefore not a sign of policy overstretch but primarily a response to and reflection of the changed needs of postmodern European society. The classical vision of the 'state' as the teleocratic management of purposeful concerns speaking with one voice, has become problematic. This notion of government presupposes a high level of agreement about the goals of public policy and a uniformity in political discourse that one can hardly take for granted in contemporary Europe. What, for example, are the substantive ends of the EU? The very betweenness of the European polity reflects the ambiguity and multifaceted nature of the European integration process, and there is no broad acceptance of some sort of grand narrative or story that all European citizens would want to adhere to in understanding the EU.

The enigmatic nature of EU policy-making is therefore not inexplicable and puzzling, but it in many ways mirrors the complexity and fragmented nature of Europe's social and political postmodern condition. This has also been reflected in the heated academic debate on the role of reason and rationality as central considerations in contemporary theories of public administration.[45] Some postmodern students of organization have argued that the combination of rationalizing processes and control have resulted in authority-based organizations, and have recommended the dismantling of these oppressive structures.[46] They refer to the power/knowledge framework suggested by Foucault, which argues that disciplinary knowledge transforms knowledge into a mechanism of domination by creating totalizing definitions of 'reality' and inevitably constrains the possibilities for individual reflection and action. In this context, knowledge is seen as a sub-category of power, since it can be used as a means for social and psychological control.[47] The power/knowledge framework suggests that 'knowledge' inevitably delineates an analytical space and thereby engenders power, since that 'space' becomes a means of intervention that may control the actions (as well as limit the perceptions) of individuals. This is especially the case since every form of power tends to 'produce' its own reality through so-called 'rituals of truth'. In combination with Steven Lukes' definition of 'power' as the institutional authority to include and exclude,[48] the new quality of shaping EU policy may be grasped.[49] Especially since political life is now less dominated by reason and cultural authority than by turbulence and cultural fragmentation, the need for individual/group empowerment and organizational openness becomes apparent and understandable.

The crucial advantage of the EU's multi-level network of governance is that it does not confine political identities within a rigid institutional framework but encourages the continuous participation of individuals and societal groups in the policy-formation process. As Thomas Diez has argued, the EU thereby blurs the boundaries between different territories, 'between the social and the political, between inside and outside. The borders, once thought to be stable and given, can no longer be invoked (and thereby redrawn) to stabilize unitary identities and uncontested *wes*'.[50] The Euro-polity does not have one center of power but is defined by a plurality of centers of powers which itself is subject to change. It is generally difficult to identify the participants involved in the European political game, mainly since in different policy arenas they play for different teams. We should therefore visualize the EU not so much as the uncontested federal pinnacle of a European hierarchy of political power, but rather as one of the principal circles of political representation within a wider context of different sites and tropes of policy-making. Reading the European project in this way may open our eyes to the idea that the very ambiguity of EU policy-making is a fundamental quality of a process that is markedly different from the top-down management of (most) modern states.

It may be useful to revisit 'transversalism' as the concept that best captures the complex qualities of EU politics and decision-making.[51] Following Foucault's notion of the 'transversal', it refers to the dense web of relations that is not limited to one country, avoids references to national boundaries and does not invoke immediate associations with state-centered political problems. Notions of transversal politics do not accept the usual dichotomy between intergovernmentalism and supranationalism, but instead assume the relative unimportance of the state–EU dichotomy by advancing a qualitatively new meso-level of politics within the European context. The transversal paradigm takes into account the full picture of actors in a European decision-making network that relies heavily on informal processes and complex structures of policy formulation. It assumes that what shapes the administrative operation of the EU is technical expertise and a multitude of economic, social, political and cultural interests, rather than abstract notions of 'national' or even 'European interests'. Within the EU, the most notable elements of transversalism are comitology and the practice of lobbying. Both epitomize the interactions between *sub*national actors in a wider arena of nation-states and European and other international players. By emphasizing the role of advocacy coalitions, transversalism is interested in the development of new subsystems assigned to groups based on shared sets of normative and/or functional beliefs concerning specific policy areas. It thereby sheds the traditional focus on hierarchical notions of policy formulation and can therefore be considered the antithesis of classical agency theory. It further abandons the rigid dichotomy of politics *vs.* administration, but aims to develop a more flexible and contextual notion of how economic and political interests are mediated on the European level.[52]

The very laxity and betweenness of the Euro-polity encourages individuals and groups to construct their identity according to the policy context, rather than based on the unitary identity of territorial politics. Boundaries between nation-states become increasingly irrelevant as political factors, since individuals and groups are located on overlapping policy lines within this network of decisions. An important element of the network approach to European policy formation is therefore that it appreciates the fuzzy logic of EU political practice. In this context, Michael Spicer has aptly noted that 'the postmodern condition and its plethora of incommensurable language games call into question the very meaningfulness of any talk about the substantive ends or purpose of a community'.[53] The defining quality of postmodern Europe is the absence of a shared grand narrative that can give common meaning to our present-day world. We have, instead, a multiplicity of conflicting political stories about what 'Europe' is, was, should be and should do. Since these stories are also framed in many different and often dissimilar language games (all based on their own ideas of what is good and what is true), it has become impossible to devise a single generally accepted meta-language that speaks to the manifold identities in their own epistemic tongue.

The EU's abundance of issue networks and policy communities is by definition more diffuse in its membership than the well-structured 'iron triangles' that we know from the corporatist past. In many ways these networks and communities resemble in their structure and purpose the so-called 'civil association' (as identified by Michael Oakeshott), which is a form of political organization in which individuals consider themselves free to seek their own interests and determine their own values. This would be a framework in which the political system only offers a general outline for behavior, more like the rules of a game 'which are directions, not about how to win but about how to play, or the rules of public debate, which do not tell a speaker what to say and are wholly indifferent to any particular conclusion'.[54] Reading the EU as a civil association is especially appropriate, since no individual or sociopolitical group will be forced to participate in a monopolized political discourse based on one, hegemonic narrative on the nature and objective of the European integration project. Since the EU does not have, and should not have, a clearly defined substantive purpose of its own, it will be inherently more accommodating to the different images that the innumerable strands of European society will continue to project on the EU's empty screen. One of the main objectives of the EU should be to broaden the 'zone of possible agreement' by encouraging participation and debate.[55] The continued fuzziness of the boundaries of the EU's policy communities reflects the openness of policy-making at the European level; access to these networks can never be rigidly denied. This interconnectedness makes it difficult to distinguish between 'friend' and 'foe' and redefines those boundaries as spaces of identity and allowing for the development of a European identity that is truly decentered.

But this notion of the Euro-polity as a hospitable and generous framework of policy formulation is not widely accepted, mainly because it runs counter to the common belief that organizations are only justified insofar as they can, one way or another, demonstrate that the world would be poorer, less interesting, less attractive and/or more dangerous without them. Justifying their right to exist, complex organizations therefore tend to manipulate language in order to 'shape beliefs about their work and their impact on society'.[56] Since words shape our mental pictures and beliefs, we should accept that the capacity to manipulate symbols (including words) is just as important as the manipulation of things. It is in this semiotic arena that the EU has proved itself to be a lousy gladiator, since as a postmodern entity it often lacks *der Wille zur Macht*, the prestige and leadership, the sagacity and totalizing visionary genius to project a 'European' content on daily events and prosaic speech.[57] As we have discussed in Chapter 3, the European manipulation of symbols occurs in a diffuse communicative space and via a process of governance that goes beyond the mere administration of matter and events. EU policy formulation is not simply the aggregation of the individual preferences of the participants; it should rather be understood as the ultimate result of cognitive and organizational procedures that generate decisions *despite* incertitude and confusion.

## Garbage cans and bureaucratic politics

In 1972 Michael P. Cohen, James G. March and Johan P. Olsen published a study suggesting that decision-making at universities was a form of 'organized anarchy', and that such organizations could be understood as collections of problems looking for choice opportunities, solutions looking for problems, and participants looking for work.[58] From these insights they developed the so-called 'garbage can-model', in which decision-making is viewed as a garbage can where various kinds of garbage – that is, problems, solutions as well as human energy – are dumped at will by the participants in the process. When the full garbage can is collected, they argue, a decision is made. Their main argument is that decisions are only rarely made by clear-cut rational resolution; more often they result from 'decision-making by flight' (the problem 'goes away' and is withdrawn from the policy-making process), or 'decision-making by oversight' (decisions will be 'made' with a minimal investment of energy). In both cases, they argue, we should assume not a causal link between problems and their eventual solutions, but that somewhere in the metaphorical full garbage can they meet in a rather random way.

There is merit in visualizing policy formulation on the European level as a garbage can, embedded in a context of information overload, bounded rationality and a wide variety of goals and ambitions all 'dumped' at will by the many participants in the process.[59] The EU's institutional network, one could argue, is nothing less than the 'hospitable and generous framework' we mentioned earlier, and this forms the empty dumpster or skip for Member States and other participants to use. Without the periodic and routine collection of the garbage, political life in Europe's nation-states would become unbearable and rather smelly.[60] This image also underlines the service provided by the EU as a platform on which a shared understanding of values and practices can be developed within a European context. The European continent harbors a multiplicity of social, cultural, political and religious communities, all with their own stories to tell and their own distinct perspectives on the question of 'Europe'. In many cases, these communities have over time developed their own sets of consolidated understandings framed in their own language (i.e., the means by which their ideas and beliefs are communicated).[61] The European garbage can provides a prosaic common ground in which these different traditions can interact with each other in fruitful discourse. Through regular communication, Europe's policy communities offer places for exchanges of views, a framework for the evaluation of arguments and an opportunity to listen to other voices. The EU, therefore, provides the atmosphere and practical environment for overcoming the incommensurability of Europe's many sociopolitical and cultural communities through continued discourse.

Policy-making and governance in the EU also resembles the 'organized anarchy' which Cohen *et al.* refer to. This makes it difficult to come to reliable generalizations about EU governance, since the inside/outside dichotomy on which most models of policy-making (which look at either domestic politics or international policy-making and diplomacy) are based is clearly absent. The EU system is both unpredictable and relatively unstable, replete with multi-level and multi-arena 'games' played by a multitude of actors who may exhibit different characteristics at different times. This implies that it will be important to use different models of analysis for different levels of EU governance at different phases of the policy-making process (i.e., during agenda-setting, policy formulation, policy decision and policy implementation). Jeremy Richardson has therefore argued that the

> complexity of the EU policy process means that we must learn to live with multiple models and learn to utilize concepts from a range of models in order to at least accurately describe the policy process ... Similarly, our intellectual process may also need to be somewhat garbage can-like in these early years, before we can really explain the 'why' as well as the 'how' of the EU policy process.
>
> (Jeremy J. Richardson, 'Policy-Making in the EU: Interests, Ideas and Garbage Cans of Primeval Soup', in Jeremy J. Richardson (ed.), *European Union: Power and Policy-Making* (London: Routledge, 1996), p. 20)

It is, of course, not surprising that in this context an argument can also be made that the politics of the EU may be understood as a lucid case study in 'bureaucratic politics'. In many ways, offices and agencies are like metaphorical garbage cans, collecting problems, solutions and human energy, intermittently generating policy outcomes through circumvention and expenditure of the smallest amount of labor. B. Guy Peters, for example, claims that policy-making at the European level is characterized by the 'gradual accretion of common policies and standards through the European bureaucracy', which increasingly occurs in policy communities aimed at cajoling the European project along.[62] A glance at the structure of the European Commission suggests an organization firmly embedded in the classical hierarchical distribution of power and authority, a division of tasks based on technical competencies and a spirit of impersonal rule that minimizes personal discretion. But, as we have already argued, this neat organigram functions as a veil superimposed upon the more complex and obscure reality sketched out earlier. Although the European Commission is of course only one actor among several in Europe's spacious governance network, a bureaucratic politics approach would suggest that the promiscuous nature of EU policy formulation is instrumental to understanding the unique quality of the European integration project.

It should be clear that the traditional principal–agent model of policy-making has rather limited value for understanding contemporary Europe. The argument that politicians ('principals') wield full and direct political control over the bureaucracy ('agents') may apply to the exceptional sector of heroic politics, but becomes extremely problematic at the prosaic level of European political life.[63] Proponents of the agency model seem willing to sacrifice the accurate description of the complex reality of EU politics to the assumption that agents are rational actors with complete information seeking to maximize their bureaucratic needs. Realist scholars further assume that bureaucratic actions closely follow and reflect the 'political will' of elected officials and imagine the bureaucracy as basically a reactive policy instrument with a limited capacity for autonomous action. But in all complex organizations the necessity of delegation raises classical problems of management, since the bureaucracy has to fill vague and often ambiguous mandates with substantive content. This grants to 'agents' discretionary authority that inevitably detracts from the ideal type of democratic accountability and political representation. Since technical and political complexity results in an asymmetry of knowledge and information in the principal–agent dyad, principals only have limited capacities to supervise, assess and control ultimate policy outcomes. Inherent limits on cognition (human, artificial and organizational), inevitably preclude optimal and rational decision-making and give rise to individual and structured 'coping devices' and reliance on standard operating procedures that allow decisions finally to be made. Especially on technical and prosaic policy issues, principals therefore have at most 'latent political control' over the overall policy-formulation process, which further undermines the verisimilitude of the intergovernmentalist approach to European politics and reinforces the essentiality of reading the EU as a network polity.

With the expansion of the EU's policy agenda, these policy networks are filled with a wide range of so-called 'subgovernments': best defined as 'small groups of political actors, both governmental and non-governmental, that specialize in specific issue areas. [They] are created by the complexity of the policy agenda, and they help sustain that complexity'.[64] The internal dynamics of these policy communities tends toward microspecialization, carving out their 'own' policy niche and their ample catalogue of regular and reliable contributors to the process of policy formulation and decision-making. Since these policy communities tend to be based on broad alliances that cut across a large number of countries, the input of these interest groups tends to be more 'European' than the often restricted territorial interests of Europe's nation-states.

Indeed, within these subgovernments, bureaucrats and particularized interests often share a normative disposition or 'house style', which tends to define which issues are 'relevant' and 'important', and hence what sort of policy outcomes are likely to emerge. This may illustrate the common ground among the different discourses of participating sociopolitical groups within the EU's policy network. These emerging patterns of co-operation can be rather different among the EU's varied flock of policy communities, but they are all based on an impaired symbiotic relationship between European civil servants and other participants. Within the EU's complex policy environment, control and co-ordination becomes more difficult and the boundaries between 'government' and the 'public sphere' increasingly harder to define. Officials often rely on external advice from regular, dependable and knowledgeable sources among 'partners'. These policy communities are basically exchange-based relationships which provide the institutional mechanisms for resolving differences of interest between the actors involved in the process. In the face of the complexity of many real-world problems, they provide the Euro-policy system with a wide range of information, data and knowledge that would otherwise not be available.

The EU's dense web of institutions has had a powerful socializing effect on state actors that have for decades participated in the complex play of joint decision-making. The long-range process of negotiations, bargaining and exchange of views has remolded not only the perception of 'national interests' but, perhaps even more importantly, the identities of the actors involved. It should be accepted that policy actors are rarely as autonomous as they are at times presumed to be. Rather, individual agents are 'embedded', and their values are modified by the institutions with which they come in contact, just as those institutions are shaped and modified by the behavior of the individuals who work in and with them.[65] This emphasis on the role of identity and values is, of course, part of the constructivist reading of the EU.[66] It implies that although in a narrow definition the concept of national interests may still be valid (especially in the area of heroic politics), the pursuit of national and collective interests has become blurred by the realization that core 'national' interests can most effectively be realized at the European level. The EU's system of governance has therefore in a sense acquired a 'prismatic' character, in that a multitude of lines of authority and many different activities are either focused or scattered around through the Union's institutions. But, in the end, choices must be made among competing demands, which inevitably requires some political judgment about which interests should be disappointed and which indulged. In the end, the garbage cans have to be collected.

Orstrom Moller has claimed that 'economic internationalization and cultural decentralization do not contradict each other', but go hand in hand, noting that the 'European Union is the battering ram for cultural decentralization'.[67] Clearly, in a network-based organization like the EU, access to the international economy is no longer solely or even mainly guaranteed through the nation-state, but through 'Brussels'. Regional and local cultures are again flourishing because state-based industrial society is now, through the gradual process of tertiariza-tion, being replaced by a new, information-based postindustrial society. This new epoch, Moller assures us, will be an 'immaterial society' based on culture, knowledge and information. This leads him to conclude that 'with the fading away of the industrial age we see the withering away of the artificial national state ... The broad political center is gradually endorsing the evolution toward a European Union'.[68]

## Regions and Europe's decentered core

Like federalism, regionalism comes in many forms and shapes. Both concepts are intimately related to each other. As Manfred Dammeyer, President of the EU's Committee of the Regions argued in 1998, 'A European Union organized along federal lines will have to take into account the regional dimension. It will move away from the traditional concept of a Europe of the nations where only two levels counted – Europe and the Member States'.[69]

During World War II, European federalists developed the concept of 'integral federalism' which advocated a future Europe based on strong regions. As John Loughlin has noted:

> The link between federalism and regionalism in 'integral federalism' lies in the so-called 'federalist dialectic': the notion that the federal unity of Europe will come about through a 'return to the sources', that is, to the family, the commune, the religious or ethnic community, and the region. By 'returning to the sources', the nation-state will be bypassed and the unity of Europe will be built on a federation of these subnational entities.
> (John Loughlin, ' "Europe of the Regions" and the Federalization of Europe',
> in *Publius*, vol. 26, no. 4 (Fall 1996), p. 105)

This would be a *Europe des ethnies*, a Europe in which powerful ethnic groups currently submerged and semi-captive within the state were 'liberated'. This would, it was argued, offer opportunities to ancient ethnic groups and nations to reclaim their *de facto* independence and freedom within a federal European political framework. This spirit of regional independence has survived the modern era and has now become (as John Newhouse has claimed)

Europe's current and future dynamics. Its sources vary, but it is judged on many sides to be partly a protest against the authority of national capitals by people who see themselves as belonging, historically and otherwise, more to 'Europe' than to a nation-state of clouded origins and dubious boundaries.

(John Newhouse, 'Europe's Rising Regionalism', in *Foreign Affairs*, vol. 76, no. 1 (January/February 1997), pp. 67–8)

In many ways, therefore, regionalism can be seen as the dialectical counterpart of a federalist vision of Europe, as a political tool to undermine the monopoly of territorial identity and political authority of the nation-state. By working within state boundaries, regionalism has during the process of European integration developed into a serious challenge to the centralized nation-state as the principal unit of identity and as the uncontested political actor within European society.[70] This is a reflection of the increasingly popular notion that the nation-state is too large for the quotidian problems of its citizens, yet too small for the planetary problems that haunt us. The EU and regionalization/localization are closing this policy void by addressing both sides: the process of Europeanization offers a sanctuary based on the notion that a stalwart and sturdy EU will offer European society some safeguards for overcoming the drawbacks and challenges of the globalizing world economy; regionalization/localization offer greater opportunities for self-governance to small (territorial) communities who should have greater flexibility in responding quickly and decisively to the fast-paced and competitive economic environment they are facing today. Europe's regions have gained their power in the context of *de*centralization within the Member States, and a certain measure of *re*centralization at the European level.

It should be emphasized that territorial minority politics, with a few notable and highly visible exceptions, hardly plays a role in the trend toward regionalism. Europe's ethno-nationalisms (for example, the Basque, Breton, Catalan, Flemish, Scots and Welsh movements) obviously still exist, but in present-day Europe the role of the regions has shifted markedly toward the formulation and implementation of policy within a European context. Radical separatist regionalism, like the Basque ETA movement or the Northern League in Italy, who seek separation from the dominant culture of the state in which they find themselves, is clearly an anomaly. Regionalism today is primarily concerned with maneuvering for governance space and less with any illusory quest for regional autonomy or even possible secession from the nation-state itself. The argument is made that, due to the process of economic globalization (with its information revolution and low-cost, high-speed travel), local entities – be they regions, provinces or big cities – feel themselves better placed and better equipped to manage their own affairs than a distant bureaucracy, whether that bureaucracy operates from a national capital or from Brussels. On matters such as unemployment, immigration, the fight against drugs and crime, and other issues that affect people directly, it has become clear that a more comprehensive and effective political framework can only be devised on a European level, and that it is the regions that are better placed to manage these problems on a day-to-day basis.

Most regions are therefore actively engaged in networking with each other within Europe (and beyond), not so much to search for their ostensible cultural roots or identity as to devise practical and flexible ways of creating effective economic and political solutions to shared problems. The internationalization of the global economy and the dawn of the post-Fordist model of industrial production has put a premium on flexibility and differentiation. Europe's regional and metropolitan elite increasingly links itself directly to the global economy, instead of working through national capitals. Many regional and local authorities have developed experience in securing EU funding, have set up departments to co-ordinate their policies *vis-à-vis* the EU and established lobbying offices in Brussels. The German *Länder* and the Belgian regions are particularly active, even at the formative stages of EU policy-making. In 1986 (with the ratification of the SEA) the *Länder* legally formalized their co-determination rights in the German federal government's decisions regarding European affairs, and simultaneously tried to return more areas of policy-making to subnational levels by pushing the principle of subsidiarity. The 1992 Maastricht Treaty was further accompanied by a number of modifications in Germany's Basic Law (i.e., constitution) which have codified and further extended the rights of the *Länder* in the European integration process; changes in the European treaties now require approval of the *Länder* (via the Bundesrat). This revision has obviously strengthened regional policy autonomy within Germany.[71] We are therefore now seeing a parallel process of vertical and horizontal *Politikverflechtung*, a concept also known as 'co-operative federalism' and 'network politics'.[72] The German *Länder* have been the driving force of emulating this German notion at the European level by (1) strengthening codetermination rights of the regions on European affairs within their domestic political systems; and (2) strengthening horizontal co-operation among Europe's regions within the EU's Committee of the Regions and other subnational co-operative bodies.

The same applies to other federally structured states like Belgium, where numerous areas and competencies have been delegated to the regions, among others ecology, energy and traffic, as well as several important economic functions. In all these domains, the Belgian regions have direct ties with EU institutions. Luc Van den Brande, former Christian Democratic Premier of Flanders, has argued that Flanders should no longer work toward greater autonomy within Belgium only, but should try to establish a wider economic association to encompass parts of northern France, Flanders and the Dutch province of Zeeuws Vlaanderen. The Belgian state itself, Van den Brande has argued, has been a mere 'accident of history'.[73] The regional economic zones that are emerging in Europe should therefore be read as a means of creating wealth and prosperity, rather than as a deliberate plot to undermine the political authority of the nation-state. For some European nations this may offer a unique opportunity to develop their identity without immediately and necessarily claiming their own state. Interregional co-operation between the Basque Autonomous Community (in Spain) and the Aquitaine Region (in France), for example, has been actively encouraged by the EU (financially as well as politically).[74]

This means that regionalization is a counterpart of Europeanization as well as globalization. The SEA (of 1986) and the introduction of the Euro have increased competitive pressures on all EU Member States and have removed many traditional national instruments for regional development and regional protectionism. The gradual dissolution of Europe's internal frontiers called for by the SEA already required a financial package deal to assist relatively underdeveloped regions to catch up and confront the sometimes cold wind of quasi-unchecked intra-European economic competition. With the introduction of the EMU the issue of regionalization has acquired an even higher priority. With the transfer of monetary authority toward the European level a rather rigid, inflexible one-size-fits-all European monetary system has been put in place; a system which in many ways fails to respond to the diversity of national and regional exigencies. Since the EU is no so-called 'optimal currency area' (due to its limited labor mobility, its rigidity in wages and prices, and cultural, linguistic and legal differences), nations and regions will be affected differently by external shocks, but will, however, no longer have recourse to traditional monetary instruments like loosening monetary policy or the devaluation of its currency.[75] This explains the emphasis of the SEA as well as the Maastricht Treaty (which established the EMU project) to deal with these national and regional disparities through special compensatory funds: the Structural Funds and the Cohesion Fund.[76]

With the establishment at Maastricht of a new Committee of the Regions (CoR), for the first time territorial entities below the level of the nation-state were recognized within the Treaties of the EU. One could therefore argue that the CoR is another institutional element of a congruent process of Europeanization and regionalization. It also illustrates that the EU is an active player in the rearrangement of governance within Europe by encouraging cities and local authorities, regions as well as community groups, to become engaged in the European policy process in an effort to transform the practice and mentality of 'top-down' government into a more flexible and efficient system of 'bottom-up' governance. The CoR has encouraged the establishment of networks which allow local authorities to share experiences, information and expertise. These policy networks may be organized along territorial or functional lines; they can also be built around a particular project. The European Council now also has to consult the CoR in areas like education, culture, public health and regional policy.[77] But in the meantime, the CoR's role in the process of European integration is bound to remain modest and marginal – important though not crucial. As the CoR's Secretary-General, Dietrich Pause, noted in 1994, the Committee of the Regions will remain 'more of a feeling than a fact – a metaphysical idea arising from people's intuitive fear of losing their roots and being overcome by centralization'.[78]

Despite this caveat, the EU's active involvement in and political support for regionalization has resulted in a growing regional awareness of the opportunities offered by European integration, as well as of the crumbling of national borders, both physical and cultural. The impetus toward regionalization continues to have a functional and normative component. Strengthening regional governments is part of the overall process of more decentralized delivery of public goods; the normative element is clearly grounded in democratic theory aimed at reducing the distance between citizens and the nation-state and to increasing the opportunities for participatory democracy.[79] The EU's ambition to shed its image as a detached and bureaucratic entity and to come 'closer to European citizens', should be read in this context. The dual notions of flexibility and subsidiarity, which are emerging as the central planks of the further development of the Euro-polity, further illustrate the strength of Europe's regional identity. Subsidiarity, which stands for the idea that 'action to accomplish a legitimate government objective should in principle be taken at the lowest level of government capable of effectively addressing the problem',[80] codifies the understanding that decision-making authority should be localized if at all possible. It celebrates the virtues of self-determination and recognizes that Europe's peoples should benefit from a substantial measure of local and regional autonomy. Flexibility offers another opportunity to modify general rules so as to take into account the special characteristics and requirements of different communities, and hence to preserve their local identities. These are valuable strands within the EU's administrative fabric which recognize and value the diversity of Europe's communities and cultures, but which also acknowledge that the widening of the EU's sphere of policy competence has turned broad-based public support from a political luxury into an absolute prerequisite for the European integration process to succeed and proceed.

With territorial boundaries losing, or at least changing, their meaning across Europe, deeply rooted patterns of cultural, linguistic and commercial interaction are again re-emerging and filling the crevices of authority and identity which the nation-state has opened in its retreat. But the crucial point to make here is not that we are seeing an illusory 'balance of power' within Europe's nation-states changing in favor of the periphery and to the detriment of the economic and political centers of decision-making. The key shift in the 1990s has been toward decentering Europe's cores – so dramatically and thoroughly that the drive toward regionalism has already run out of steam due to its very success. The central state authority on which regionalism has focused most of its opposition has lost the bulk of its all-encompassing power and authority, and, since the presumed center of greed and exploitation of the past no longer exists the reasons for waving the flag of regional peculiarity and exceptionalism have gradually disappeared. The dual processes of globalization and Europeanization have turned many strong regions into their very own individual centers of culture, commerce and political identification, allowing for a renewal of many zones of intensive infrastructural concentration and prosperity.[81] Super-regions which stretch from south-eastern England through northern France and parts of the Benelux countries and then down to the Rhine Valley into Switzerland, and from Veneto in Italy through Lombardy and Piedmont into the Rhone-Alpes and on through the French Mediterranean coast into Catalonia, are becoming economic and political forces in their own right. In many ways, they have become the new, but smaller and more decentralized, centers of authority within postmodern Europe.[82] It used to be self-evident that firms should locate their headquarters in, say, Paris, since from there all of France could be covered. Now that the nation-state has lost its grip on the economic and financial life of the state, though, this logic has changed. It is now much better to establish smaller regional headquarters to benefit from regional presence and local knowledge. Following the medieval metaphor, Newhouse has argued that if

> the nation-state is modernism and the EU postmodernism, regions consti-tute the premodern. They are also the most direct link to postmodern Brus-sels; first, because they weaken the nation-states, and second, because their aversion to unnatural borders has led them, with some exceptions, to sup-port an integrated EU more strongly than its membership has.
>
> (John Newhouse, *Europe Adrift* (New York: Pantheon Books, 1997), p. 28)

It remains unclear whether these regions might in the long term supersede the nation-state as the main sources of political authority. Regions and cities are gradually grasping many of the economic and political tools of authority that used to be in the hands of central national government. Quite a number of Europe's stronger regions have a well-documented independent ('national') history (and, in the case of Catalonia, even its own language), and have run their own affairs in the past. There are no reasons why they could not do so again in a not too distant future. As Trevor Lloyd has argued: 'If Estonia or Slovenia is to join the Union ..., it would be hard to say that there are too few Bavarians or Walloons or they have too little cultural identity to be accepted as new states'.[83] It is clear that regions will form a significant new layer in the multi-level structure of governance that is developing in Europe – though, as with any form of territorial organization, regionalism's territoriality inevitably carries with it the seeds of 'terrorism'. Redrawing Europe's borders is a valuable exercise in disturbing and problematizing many established notions of territorial organiza-tion. By drawing upon local narratives of culture, politics and economic practice, regionalism opens space for the development of multiple sites of authority in a more responsive and fragmented European society. Regional boundaries will not be guarded and shut off, but will, almost by definition, remain fluid and unable to silence differences and critiques that question the assumptions of its own identity.

Borders, boundaries and political systems have changed often in the twentieth century, and there is little reason to assume that Europe's present political system will not be subject to change in the decades to come.

**Notes**

1 Romano Prodi, '2000–2005: Shaping the New Europe', Speech to the European Parliament in Strasbourg, France, 15 February 2000. Online. Available HTTP: http://europa.eu.int/comm/externalrelations/news/0200/speech0041.htm (accessed 15 August 2000).

2 David Easton, *The Political System: An Inquiry Into the State of Political Science* (New York: Knopf, 1953).

3 For an early overview of the relevant literature, see the review essay by Jan-Erik Lane, 'Governance in the European Union', in *West European Politics*, vol. 20, no. 4 (October 1997).

4 William Wallace, 'Government Without Statehood: The Unstable Equilibrium', in Helen Wallace and William Wallace (eds), *Policy-Making in the European Union* (Oxford: Oxford University Press, 1996), p. 445.

5 James N. Rosenau, 'Governance, Order, and Change in World Politics', in James N. Rosenau and Ernst-Otto Czempiel (eds), *Governance Without Government: Order and Change in World Politics* (Cambridge: Cambridge University Press, 1992), p. 3.

6 James N. Rosenau, 'Governance in the Twenty-first Century', in *Global Governance*, vol. 1, no. 1 (Winter 1995), p. 16.

7 Rosenau, 'Governance, Order, and Change in World Politics', p. 4.

8 On the importance of 'reasonable' principles and standards of behavior and governance, see John Rawls, *Political Liberalism* (New York: Columbia University Press, 1993).

9 Tanja A. Börzel, 'Organizing Babylon – On the Different Conceptions of Policy Networks', in *Public Administration*, vol. 76, no. 2 (Summer 1998).

10 B. Guy Peters and John Pierre, 'Governance Without Government? Rethinking Public Administration', in *Journal of Public Administration Research and Theory*, vol. 8, no. 2 (April 1998).

11 Les Metcalfe, 'The European Commission as a Network Organization', in *Publius*, vol. 26, no. 4 (Fall 1996).

12 Rhys Dogan, 'Comitology: Little Procedures With Big Implications', in *West European Politics*, vol. 20, no. 3 (July 1997).

13 Peter van Ham, 'Europe's New Defense Ambitions: Implications for NATO, the US, and Russia', Marshall Center Paper Series, no. 1 (Garmisch-Partenkirchen, June 2000).

14 Although it should also be clear that the division between (what Stanley Hoffmann has famously labeled) 'high' and 'low' politics is contested. All actors involved in the European policy-formulation process are aware of the importance of 'framing' the issues on the policy agenda as either 'high' or 'low' politics.

15 Remember Catherine MacKinnon's famous remark: 'I am not saying that viewpoints have genitals'. Quoted in Richard Rorty, *Truth and Progress: Philosophical Papers, Volume 3* (Cambridge: Cambridge University Press, 1998), p. 202.

16 D. Lynn O'Brien Hallstein, 'A Postmodern Caring: Feminist Standpoint Theories, Revisioning Caring, and Communication Ethics', in *Western Journal of Communication*, vol. 63, no. 1 (Winter 1999).

17 For an overview, see J. Ann Tickner, 'Introducing Feminist Perspectives into Peace and World Security Courses', in *Women's Studies Quarterly*, vol. 23, no. 3–4 (Fall 1995); and Tickner, *Gender in International Relations: Feminist Perspectives on Achieving Global Security* (New York: Columbia University Press, 1992).

18 Wendy Brown, 'Finding the Man in the State', in *Feminist Studies*, vol. 18, no. 1 (Spring 1992), p. 25.

19 Kathy E. Ferguson, *The Feminist Case Against Bureaucracy* (Philadelphia: Temple University Press, 1985), pp. 158–69.

20 Brown, 'Finding the Man in the State', p. 29.

21  Robert Pahre, 'Endogenous Domestic Institutions in Two-level Games and Parliamentary Oversight of the European Union', in *Journal of Conflict Resolution*, vol. 41, no. 1 (February 1997).

22  R.A.W. Rhodes, *Understanding Governance: Policy Networks, Governance, Reflexivity and Accountability* (Buckingham: Open University Press, 1997), especially Chapter 9 ('Towards a Post-Modern Public Administration: Epoch, Epistemology or Narrative?').

23  Thomas Diez, 'International Ethics and European Integration: Federal State or Network Horizon?', in *Alternatives*, vol. 22, no. 3 (Summer 1997).

24  For a summary of the main arguments, see Liesbet Hooghe and Gary Marks, 'Contending Models of Governance in the European Union', in Alan W. Cafruny and Carl Lankowski (eds), *Europe's Ambiguous Unity: Conflict and Consensus in the Post-Maastricht Era* (Boulder CO: Lynne Rienner, 1997); and Gary Marks, Fritz Scharpf, Philippe C. Schmitter and Wolfgang Streeck, *Governance in the European Union* (London: Sage, 1996).

25  Hooghe and Marks, 'Contending Models of Governance in the European Union', p. 33.

26  Gerhard Fuchs, 'The European Commission as Corporate Actor? European Telecommunications Policy After Maastricht', in Carolyn Rhodes and Sonia Mazey (eds), *The State of the European Union: Building a European Polity?* (Boulder CO: Lynne Rienner, 1995).

27  B. Guy Peters and Donald J. Savoie, 'Managing Incoherence: The Coordination and Empowerment Conundrum', in *Public Administration Review*, vol. 56, no. 3 (May/June 1996), pp. 282–5.

28  Hooghe and Marks, 'Contending Models of Governance in the European Union', p. 38.

29  Sonia Mazey and Jeremy Richardson, 'Promiscuous Policymaking: The European Policy Style?', in Carolyn Rhodes and Sonia Mazey (eds), *The State of the European Union: Building a European Polity?* (Boulder CO: Lynne Rienner, 1995), p. 340. The title of this chapter obviously echoes the Mazey/Richardson contribution.

30  Audrey McLaughlin and Justin Greenwood, 'The Management of Interest Representation in the European Union', in *Journal of Common Market Studies*, vol. 33, no. 1 (March 1995).

31  Sonia Mazey and Jeremy Richardson (eds), *Lobbying in the European Community* (Oxford: Oxford University Press, 1993); and R.H. Pedler and M.P.C.M. van Schendelen (eds), *Lobbying in the European Union: Companies, Trade Associations and Issue Groups* (Aldershot: Dartmouth, 1994).

32  Wayne Sandholtz and John Zysman, '1992: Recasting the European Bargain', *World Politics*, vol. 42, no. 1 (October 1989), p. 116.

33  Peter J. Spiro, 'New Global Communities: Nongovernmental Organizations in International Decision-Making Institutions', in *The Washington Quarterly*, vol. 18, no. 1 (Winter 1995).

34  John Peterson, 'States, Societies and the European Union', in *West European Politics*, vol. 20, no. 4 (October 1997).

35  Tom Farer, 'New Players in the Old Game', in *American Behavioral Scientist*, vol. 38, no. 6 (May 1995).

36  Ulrich Beck, 'The Cosmopolitan Manifesto', in *New Statesman*, 30 March 1998, p. 30.

37  Robert A. Dahl, *Who Governs? Democracy and Power in an American City* (New Haven CT and London: Yale University Press, 1961); and Harold Laswell, *Politics: Who Gets What, When, How?* (New York: Meridian, 1958).

38  Simon J. Bulmer, 'The European Council and the Council of the European Union: Shapers of a European Confederation', in *Publius*, vol. 26, no. 4 (Fall 1996).

39  Alec Stone Sweet and Thomas L. Brunell, 'Constructing a Supranational Constitution: Dispute Resolution and Governance in the European Community', in *American Political Science Review*, vol. 92, no. 1 (March 1998).

40  Alan W. Cafruny and Carl Lankowski, 'Europe's Ambiguous Unity', in Alan W. Cafruny and Carl Lankowski (eds), *Europe's Ambiguous Unity: Conflict and Consensus in the Post-Maastricht Era* (Boulder CO: Lynne Rienner, 1997), pp. 11–12.

41  Ronald Inglehart, *Modernization and Postmodernization: Cultural, Economic, and Political Change in 43 Societies* (Princeton NJ: Princeton University Press, 1997). For a summary of his argument, see Ronald Inglehart, 'Globalization and Postmodern Values', in *The Washington Quarterly*, vol. 23, no. 1 (Winter 2000).

42  Inglehart, *Modernization and Postmodernization*, p. 27.

43  Ronald Inglehart and Paul R. Abramson, 'Economic Security and Value Change', in *American Political Science Review*, vol. 88, no. 2 (June 1994).

44  Ronald Inglehart, *Cultural Shift in Advanced Industrial Society* (Princeton NJ: Princeton University Press, 1990), p. 412. See also Mattei Dogan, 'Comparing the Decline of Nationalisms in Western Europe: The Generational Dynamic', in *International Social Science Journal*, vol. 45, no. 2 (May 1993).

45  John Hassard and Martin Parker (eds), *Postmodernism and Organizations* (London: Sage, 1993); David John Farmer, *The Language of Public Administration: Bureaucracy, Modernity, and Postmodernity* (Tuscaloosa: University of Alabama Press, 1995); and Charles J. Fox and Hugh T. Miller, *Postmodern Public Administration: Toward Discourse* (London: Sage, 1995). For a debate on 'old' and 'new' institutionalism, see Philip Selznick, 'Institutionalism "Old" and "New" ', in *Administrative Science Quarterly*, vol. 41, no. 2 (June 1996); and Ellen M. Immergut, 'The Theoretical Core of the New Institutionalism', in *Politics and Society*, vol. 26, no. 1 (March 1998).

46  Stephen Linstead and Robert Grafton-Small, 'On Reading Organizational Culture', in *Organization Studies*, vol. 13, no. 3 (1992).

47  Steven P. Feldman, 'The Revolt Against Cultural Authority: Power/Knowledge as an Assumption in Organization Theory', in *Human Relations*, vol. 50, no. 8 (August 1997).

48  Steven Lukes, *Power: A Radical View* (London: Macmillan, 1974).

49  Lyotard's notion of the 'differend' is also useful for understanding the mechanisms of exclusion from a political community. See Jean-François Lyotard, *The Differend: Phases in Dispute* (Minneapolis: University of Minnesota Press, 1988).

50  Diez, 'International Ethics and European Integration', p. 298 (emphasis in the original).

51  Joseph Weiler has suggested the term 'infranationalism' to describe the same set of phenomena. See A. Ballmann and J.H.H. Weiler, *Certain Rectangular Problems of European Integration*, Project IV/95/02, Directorate General for Research of the European Parliament (1996), especially the annex on 'Infranationalism and the Community Governing Process'. Online. Available HTTP: http://www.iue.it/AEL/EP/index.html (accessed 15 August 2000).

52  Jeff Worsham, Marc Allen Eisner and Evan J. Ringquist, 'Assessing the Assumptions: A Critical Analysis of Agency Theory', in *Administration and Society*, vol. 28, no. 4 (February 1997).

53  Michael W. Spicer, 'Public Administration, the State, and the Postmodern Condition', in *American Behavioral Scientist*, vol. 41, no. 1 (September 1997).

54  Michael Oakeshott, quoted in Spicer, 'Public Administration, the State, and the Postmodern Condition'.

55  James K. Sebinius, 'Challenging Conventional Explanations of International Co-operation: Negotiation Analysis and the Case of Epistemic Communities', in *International Organization*, vol. 46, no. 1 (Winter 1992).

56  Murray Edelman, quoted in David Dery, ' "Papereality" and Learning in Bureaucratic Organizations', in *Administration and Society*, vol. 29, no. 6 (January 1998).

57 Jan Zielonka, *Explaining Euro-Paralysis: Why Europe is Unable to Act in International Politics* (New York: St Martin's Press, 1998).

58 Michael P. Cohen, James G. March and Johan P. Olsen, 'A Garbage Can Model Of Organizational Choice', in *Administrative Science Quarterly*, vol. 17, no. 1 (March 1972). This section draws on Jeremy Richardson's work on European public policy, especially his 'Policy-Making in the EU: Interests, Ideas and Garbage Cans of Primeval Soup', in Jeremy J. Richardson (ed.), *European Union: Power and Policy-Making* (London: Routledge, 1996).

59 For such an approach to the EU's IGC leading up to the Amsterdam Summit of June 1997, see Mazey and Richardson, 'Policy Framing'.

60 For an interesting essay on the 'constitutive hybridity', the 'chronotopic multiplicity' and the 'motif of redemption' related to garbage, see Robert Stam, 'From Hybridity to the Aesthetics of Garbage', in *Social Identities*, vol. 3, no. 2 (June 1997).

61 Richard J. Bernstein, *Beyond Objectivism and Relativism: Science, Hermeneutics, and Praxis* (Philadelphia: University of Pennsylvania Press, 1983).

62 For an introduction to this argument, see B. Guy Peters, 'Bureaucratic Politics and the Institutions of the European Community', in Alberta M. Sbragia (ed.), *Euro-Politics: Institutions and Policymaking in the "New" European Community* (Washington DC: Brookings Institution, 1992), pp. 76–7.

63 For a critical analysis of the principal–agent model, see Kenneth J. Meier and Richard W. Waterman, 'Principal–Agent Models: An Expansion?', in *Journal of Public Administration Research and Theory*, vol. 8, no. 2 (April 1998).

64 Randall B. Ripley and Grace A. Franklin, *Congress, the Bureaucracy and Public Policy* (Homewood IL.: Dorsey Press, 1984), quoted in Grant Jordan and William A. Maloney, 'Accounting for Subgovernments: Explaining the Persistence of Policy Communities', in *Administration and Society*, vol. 29, no. 5 (November 1997).

65 B. Guy Peters and John Pierre, 'Institutions and Time: Problems of Conceptualization and Explanation', in *Journal of Public Administration Research and Theory*, vol. 8, no. 4 (October 1998), p. 566.

66 Rey Koslowski, 'A Constructivist Approach to Understanding the European Union as a Federal Policy', in *Journal of European Public Policy*, vol. 6, no. 4 (December 1999).

67 J. Orstrom Moller, *The Future European Model: Economic Internationalization and Cultural Decentralization* (Westport CT: Praeger, 1995), p. 38.

68 *Ibid.*, p. 40.

69 Manfred Dammeyer (President of the Committee of the Regions of the European Union), 'Speech at the Europe Conference of the European Movement in the Hague, the Netherlands', 10 May 1998.

70 Karlheinz Reif, 'Cultural Convergence and Cultural Diversity as Factors in European Identity', in Soledad Garcia (ed.), *European Identity and the Search for Legitimacy* (London: Pinter, 1993).

71 Richard E. Deeg, 'Germany's "Länder" and the Federalization of the European Union', in Carolyn Rhodes and Sonia Mazey (eds), *The State of the European Union: Building a European Polity?* (Boulder CO: Lynne Rienner, 1995); and Tanja A. Börzel, 'Does European Integration Really Strengthen the State? The Case of the Federal Republic of Germany', in *Regional and Federal Studies*, vol. 7, no. 3 (Autumn 1997).

72 Gerhard Lehmbruch, 'Institutional Linkages and Policy Networks in the Federal System of West Germany', in *Publius*, vol. 19, no. 4 (Fall 1989).

73 Luc Van den Brande, quoted in 'Could Flanders Be Reinvented?', in *The Economist*, 20 September 1997.

74 Francisco Letamendia, 'Basque Nationalism and Cross-Border Co-operation Between the Southern and Northern Basque Countries', in *Regional and Federal Studies*, vol. 7, no. 2 (Summer 1997), especially pp. 35–9. For a general picture of Spanish regionalism, see Crispin Coates, 'Spanish Regionalism and the European Union', in *Parliamentary Affairs*, vol. 51, no. 2 (April 1998).

75　For a political analysis of EMU, see *The Economist*, 'A Survey of EMU: An Awfully Big Adventure', 11 April 1998.

76　For a good overview, see Nicholas Rees, 'Inter-Regional Co-operation in the EU and Beyond', in *European Planning Studies*, vol. 5, no. 3 (June 1997).

77　Bruce Millan, 'The Committee of the Regions: In at the Birth', in *Regional and Federal Studies*, vol. 7, no. 1 (Spring 1997).

78　Quoted in John Newhouse, *Europe Adrift* (New York: Pantheon, 1997), p. 28.

79　Brigid Laffan, 'Nations and Regions in Western Europe', Paper presented at the 2nd ECSA-World Conference, Brussels (May 1994).

80　George A. Berman, 'Subsidiarity in the European Community', in Paul Michael Lützeler (ed.), *Europe After Maastricht: American and European Perspectives* (Providence RI/Oxford: Berghahn Books, 1994), p. 140.

81　Lothar Baier, 'Farewell to Regionalism', in *Telos*, no. 90 (Winter 1991).

82　Karl-Johan Lundquist and Lars-Olof Olanter, 'Regional Economies: A Threat to the Nation-State?', Paper presented to the Conference 'The Survival of the Nation State', Lund University, Sweden (30 March 1998).

83　Trevor Lloyd, 'Union and Division in Europe', in *International Journal*, vol. 52, no. 4 (Autumn 1997), p. 551.

# 6   Europe's essential vacuum

## Democracy and citizenship as political derivatives

### What we talk about when we talk about democracy

While democracy is many things (involving popular sovereignty, accountability, participation and solidarity), the crucial element is that it offers people an 'open society': that is, a society without closure which enables critical reflection and activism.[1] Democracy therefore denotes not merely the organizational structure of government but a way of life, a set of attitudes and a culture of individual independence based on a general willingness to co-operate. As Barber has argued, 'Democracy is government without heroes; ordinary women and men doing extraordinary things on a regular and continuing basis'.[2] Democracy as a method of governance and as a mentality opens up new opportunities and positions of speech, continuously enabling novel elements of social life to become part of the political process. Democracy is therefore characterized by ambiguity, the possibility of variation and change, the absence of fixity. The uncertain and indeterminate nature of democracy offers opportunities to articulate alternative conceptions of democratic practice and experimentation. This makes democracy surely preferable to other political alternatives – especially since it acknowledges its own lack of clear and fixed criteria for judgement and is firmly embedded within the postmodern condition which advocates a sustained attention to difference and heterogeneity. Since the reins of power are no longer in the hands of an arbitrary authority, it is fair to say that in a democracy 'power belongs to no one. There is no determinate representation of authority, no foundation to any particular form of society. It is [a] space of contradictions and ambiguity'.[3]

This may be the postmodern daydream of democracy. But democracy as the current dominant political norm and ideal, is also a modern category, rooted within the project of the Enlightenment, focused on rules, procedures and legitimations of the existing social order. Democracy's myths are manifold and multifarious, but they center around the dual notion that it is the most effective way to *advance and defend* individual/group identities and that it offers an open system in which identities are best *discovered and transformed* through free discussion and interaction. But perhaps the most valuable element of democratic organization is that its freedoms of speech, association and regular voting present the individual with opportunities for independent self-development and moral growth, continuously making choices and opening up roads toward self-knowledge and intellectual and spiritual maturity. On this reading, democracy and freedom are valuable in their own right, regardless of any utilitarian assertion based on the Benthamian notion of the 'greatest happiness of the greatest number'. These arguments for a vibrant participatory democracy are all the more important since they offer individuals and communities more chance to make their own choices, increasing their awareness of and empathy with other voices through discourse, while helping to reclaim both moral and practical judgement.

However, despite its many valued traits, democracy, both as a political abstraction and as a political practice, has become even more problematic than it has always been, mainly due to the challenges posed for it by the advance of postmodern society. Although democracy comes in all shapes and forms, its modern translation centers on the representation of the individual's interests and values through continuous delegation. Traditional democratic theory is based on the notion that democracy organizes and transforms the will of an abstract and illusory 'people' (*demos*) into a continuous flow of normative acts. But, as we shall discuss at some length below, in the European context this mythical 'will of the people' is a copy of a copy, making the quasi-supreme *vox populi* expressly vague and easily adaptable to the political requirements and exigencies of the day. It is also not the only voice – or, more precisely, not the only *voices* – calling for attention and political space. In European democracy His Master's Voice is in many ways as invisible and illusory, as ephemeral and fleeting, as the voice emerging from the famed Gramophone which catches the attention of man's best friend.

Democracy, nationalism, modern science and capitalism not only share a similar genealogy, they have all developed in parallel phases. The idea of the nation-state has (especially in England) reflected the value of rationality as the faculty which entitles each individual the right to liberty and democratic participation. The critical mind and the preference for empirical knowledge has informed modern science and contributed to the development of industrialization. It has made economic activity respectable and redefined social stratification by justifying occupational mobility.[4] In (and through) this process, democracy has evolved into the political aesthetics of state power. It has turned into a cardinal national founding myth; it has become the soul and spirit without which the state can hardly function. With the exception of a few dozen 'rogue states' and other outcasts, most states now at least formally subscribe to the democratic creed. As John Dunn has argued:

> Democratic theory is the moral Esperanto of the present nation-state system, the language in which all Nations are truly United, the public cant of the modern world, a dubious currency indeed – and one which only a complete imbecile would be likely to take quite at face value, quite literally.
> (Quoted in R.B.J. Walker, *Inside/Outside: International Relations as Political Theory* (Cambridge: Cambridge University Press, 1993), p. 141)

We are now witnessing the true globalization of democracy. This is not an altogether pretty sight, since democracy, like nationalism, continues to reify sovereignty and territoriality as the ultimate treasures of state-centric political association, and often (willingly or unwillingly) (re)fuels the batteries of national identity. Liberal democracy has come to be linked to both popular sovereignty and national self-determination, where nationality and citizenship have gradually been fused. In a sense, liberal democracy is based on the fiction that the vestiges of political order are traceable to an act or form of political consent or authorship. As a result, it is now the general perception that democratic rights can only be fully consumed within the context of the nation-state; democracy and nation-state have conceptually merged. In order to function smoothly and properly, democracy must assume a homogeneous political space in which social categories and values are stable and predictable, based upon a foundation of common-sense meanings to which 'all' citizens would be able to subscribe.

It is here that contemporary democracy's political puzzle starts. Democracy's 'rules of the game' differ substantially across the extensive landscape of western political practice. With the increasing diversity of identities, communities and meanings circulating within Europe, it should be clear that people now confront these democratic rules as arbitrary political routines that work to discipline their ambiguity and limit their identity by erecting exclusionary boundaries. Democratic governance still follows the mechanical notions of representation and delegation of political authority which reflects a rather archaic, nineteenth-century political reality, rather than the fragmented eclecticism of postmodern practice. Unreconstructed representative democracy in a sense helps to 'create' our modern sovereign state by endowing 'him' with the right to represent 'us', the non-present people(s). It thereby produces effects of (national) presence and (national) identity, reconfirming the fictitious rootedness of society in a world dominated by transitory foliage of individualism.

The dominant narrative of democracy also offers us the enticing promise of a process of shared transcendence, of moving from individual impotence to communal strength. Through popular discourse and teleocratic reason, man/society 'may subdue history, quiet all uncertainty, clarify all ambiguity, and achieve total knowledge, total autonomy, and total power'.[5] The democratic myth incorporates the same universal elements as nationalism and supports the same dual transcendental ends of sovereignty and territoriality. More often than not, the *demos* is not freely floating, but is closely linked with the alleged *telos* of the nation-state, the furtherance of which ultimately legitimates the polity as well as its policies. The question of *demos* informs both our subjective understanding of the origins of authority and legitimacy of state power, and our awareness of the state's operational rules for inclusion and exclusion. Citizenship, as the entry ticket to the political arena, defines the *demos*, and in doing so constitutes sovereign wo/man as well as the sovereign state. A case can be made that until the end of the eighteenth century representation was clear, authentic and straightforward. Foucault, for example, has argued that representation has become problematic since the object and subject of representation have become (too) closely linked, rather than separate and autonomous, making natural representation no longer feasible.[6] This would imply that in the postmodern world genuine, neutral and natural representation has died.

Few tears should be shed for this loss, since representational democracy's problematical condition may also open up opportunities and offer new challenges. It illustrates that the modernist social contract with an illusory uniform body of 'citizens' is an incomplete and over-stringent framework for radical democratic governance. From a Foucauldian perspective, we should acknowledge that any political order constructs its own practices of collective identity, compatible with the existing practices of disciplinary society. This means that subsequent fictions of 'democratic consensus' emerge just to rationalize and authorize the arbitrariness of the new political order.[7] In this context postmodernism may not necessarily offer a clear-cut prescriptive approach to resolving this social problematic, but it does offer a temporal means by which a new framework of governance may ultimately develop.

Behind representative democracy's mask of death, a variety of political, economic and cultural elites have long administered society for better or for worse. European governance has been no exception. As Jacques Delors commented in 1993: 'Europe began as an elitist project [in which it was believed] that all that was required was to convince the decision-makers. That phase of benign despotism is now over'.[8] Consensus can no longer be forged within a limited network of relatively like-minded actors; now a kaleidoscopic European audience has to be captured through an interactive mode of communication in a focused prism of policy. It is here that the main problems arise, since Europe's turbulent and fragmented society now has more crevices and interstices than hitherto. Beyond the 'inside' of the *demos*, the 'order' of citizenship and the sovereign voice of the individual/state Self, there is increasingly an 'outside' voice of exile which represents the uncertainty, darkness and 'anarchy' of immigration and (semi-)illegality. These exiles do not necessarily speak the language of democracy; they do not necessarily occupy the same democratic space; they certainly are not frequently heard.

Such exiles do not necessarily come to us from burnt villages, physically and psychologically mutilated, poor and dirty, although these may be the most forcible and visible flows of refugees washed upon Europe's shores. The point to make here is that most Europeans will in a certain phase of their lives find themselves in marginal sites, moving from mainstream thought, morality and/or practice to dissidence, interrogating and testing the limitations and exploring previously excluded possibilities. By thinking *other*-wise and by continuously questioning the individual Self, ambiguity and interdeterminacy are accepted as valid and genuine. Identity does not become static and stagnant, but is constantly 'on the move', recrafted and reshaped through communication and as the conscious, artistic work of life. People change their job, profession, village, religion, partner, life-style, hair color, party affiliation, supermarket, TV channel and the shape of their nose and/or breasts more easily and more often than before. In Europe, an increasing commitment to postmaterial values now draws upon questions dealing with the quality of life, rather than a quest for material survival. To some degree, this identity-surfing reflects a crisis of confidence, the injury of all kinds of faith, as well as a loss of belief in a universal 'truth'.[9] But, for all their diversity, these developments do not in themselves compose a coherent and powerful challenge to the established democratic paradigm. Democracy's challenger is not a radically new, wild-eyed nihilistic ideology ready to fight for the minds of its citizens. Rather, democracy is being eaten away by indifference, apathy and wide-spread incredulity toward ossified metanarratives based on notions like the 'nation', 'people', 'government'.

In this context, democratic representation is becoming problematic as the cultural fluidity of society becomes enhanced. Metanarratives and logocentric discourse are no longer accredited and affirmed by common consent. Co-opting representation from the private sphere into the public sphere and proclaiming what others mean and want, inevitably does violence to the emotions, feelings and interests of the individual. Western democracy continues to organize government by assuming a homogeneous society that no longer exists, and so its method of representation takes for granted the validity of a delegation process that is nothing but a simulacrum, a copy of a copy, for which, in the end, there is no longer an uncontested original.[10] As Baudrillard has noted:

> Abstraction today is no longer that of the map, the double, the mirror or the concept. Simulation is no longer that of a territory, a referential being or a substance. It is the generation by models of a real without origin or reality: a hyperreal.
>
> (Quoted in James Der Derian, 'The (S)pace of International Relations: Simulation, Surveillance, and Speed', in *International Studies Quarterly*, vol. 34, no. 3 (September 1990), p. 299)

Postmodernity is the condition where the label 'as shown on TV' serves as the ultimate certificate of reality, as the contemporary definition of the 'really real'. In this societal context, Europe's current political map of territorially carved up democracies assumes that these different but separate peoples are worthy enough to be represented by their respective nation-states. But could it also not be the other way around – that these representative democracies are themselves ultimately creating the 'truth' and political 'realities' that they are supposedly reflecting?

In the postmodern condition European democracy has become hyperreal. It has become a functioning, legitimate and moderately effective way of governance now looking for 'its' *Volk*, 'its' *demos*, which is slowly crumbling under its searching hands. Democracy as construed by Abraham Lincoln at Gettysburg is all about 'government of the people, by the people, for the people'. But, in a European context, who are *the* people? And what does 'government' mean? In the end, our conversation therefore pauses with the somewhat despondent summation that democracy is historically a Siamese twin of nationalism, a dyad which may seem somewhat unfortunate but which should be accepted as a political eventuality. As Anthony Barnett has noted, 'it is the mass feeling of shared identity that makes it possible for *a* people to want to choose *their* government. Nationalism lays the basis for democracy'.[11] This inevitably makes the concept of European democracy problematic, since a European identity and strong feelings of European belongingness are adamantly absent.

So how do we approach democracy in the context of the emerging Europolity? Efforts to analyze and 'answer' this basic question have by now become a bantam academic discipline probing the nature and depth of Europe's proverbial 'democratic deficit'.[12] Rather than rehearse this debate or take sides in it, it may be useful to try to tread this academic minefield, watching out for scholarly detonations and the metaphysical booby-traps. But it is not so much the alleged deficits in democratic theory and practice that are of interest here. The central concern should be why both scholars and politicians are making such a fuss about the 'democratic deficit' in the first place? Perhaps the fundamental question should be not 'whether the EU is democratic or not, but to what extent the EU can handle the *traditional concerns of the democratic process* while at the same time solving the effectiveness problems of the Member States'.[13] This is an altogether different examination, since it shifts the discussion from classic concerns about the 'democratic deficit' to the more general notion of concerns for the democratic *process* of European policy formation and the capacity of the EU to assist all participants in the process to come to terms with an increasingly complex European society.

## Europe and democracy: Please mind the gap(s)!

European policy formation follows rules which defy the categories of classical state-based democratic systems. As discussed in the previous chapter, the EU is mainly a complex network that lacks a single authority clearly responsible for the policy outcomes with which ordinary people are ultimately confronted. Europe's multi-level network of governance does not have a clear 'government'; it lacks a clear 'opposition' that can provide an alternative within the democratic system; it fails the standard democratic tests of transparency and accountability of decision-making; and it has no structured majority, personalized by identifiable leaders.[14] The EU's peculiar system of sharing responsibilities among the European Commission, the European Council and the European Parliament, all embedded in the network of comitology, makes for a collegial-executive system with interlocking arrangements, and this produces little clarity regarding the preparation of decisions, timing, scope and the consultation of external interests, experts and other interested actors.[15]

As a democratic citizen, how can I enter into a dialogue with 'the EU' on the merits of its particular policies? And, as a member of a European electorate, how can one 'throw the scoundrels out'?[16] These are simple questions which both have a (from a democratic perspective) rather embarrassing answer: it is just not possible. One could therefore justifiably contend that 'the EU is more like an anonymous calculating machine, adding one decision to another, often incoherently, and then calling the resulting pile *acquis communautaire*.[17] But as calculating machines go, they can hardly be classified as 'democratic mechanisms'; trying to throw them out may occasionally be tempting, but will usually not help either.

It is now 'received knowledge' among scholars and practitioners that there is no simple remedy for the EU's democratic predicament. The debate on European democracy now tends to focus on a set of four closely related puzzles: the *demos* in 'democracy'; the elusive nature of European citizenship; the shift in the *locus* of decision-making from the nation-state to the European level; and the democratic nature and quality of policy formation within the EU. It should be clear that each puzzle contains pieces of the other, and that conceptual gaps are bound to remain regardless of how well these puzzles are laid out. This is to be expected, if only because the democratic process is by nature 'unfinished business'. But it is these gaps that provide the tension in the debate on European democracy and offer to those whom any unanimity on this matter may marginalize the opportunity to voice their beliefs and wants. Since these puzzles form part of one text, I will address them together and pay specific attention to what is left unspoken.

Central to the debate on Europe's problematic democratic properties are the notions of 'citizenship' and 'legitimacy' – portmanteau categories that wear academic and political coats of many colors.[18] It should be emphasized here that doubts about the relevance of classic representative democracy are raised in what is all but a societal vacuum. On the contrary, grievances concerning the erosion of the nation-state and calls to redress a perceived 'democratic deficit' (on the national as well as the European level), go hand in hand with the individual crisis of identity so characteristic of postmodern life. Individual rootlessness and statal inadequacy and destitution are synchronous processes which may play and grow on each other in a number of ways.

Bauman has made a clear case that in our postmodern era individuals carry more moral responsibility for their lives than before.[19] He argues that during modernism, institutions like the state and the church have taken over moral responsibility from individuals not only by telling them what (not) to do, but also by a process of 'adiaphorization' – by which he means that a number of important human actions were declared morally adiaphoric: i.e., neutral from the moral viewpoint.[20] Bauman claims that both forms of moral regulation are now in crisis and that people no longer trust large institutions to tell them what to do. Most orders of 'truth' are now no longer part of the common domain, no longer the subject of public commandments, but have instead become a *Privatsache* (a personal matter). The authority of the church, the state, politics in general, academia, is on the decline:

> The responsibility which was taken away from the individual [during modernism] is coming back – you and I are very much left alone with our decisions. We do not have a moral code which has all the visibility of being absolute and universal ... [T]his brings us back to the question of moral

choice and responsibility – it makes you responsible and many people do not like it.

('Modernity, Postmodernity and Ethics – An Interview With Zygmunt<br>Bauman', in Telos, no. 93 (Fall 1992), pp. 137–8)

Postmodern ambivalence offers the individual more freedom than before to mould his/her life. As Bryan Appleyard has argued:

> Certainly there is no cultural core, no body of virtue to be transmitted. Our souls become enfeebled. Knowing nothing and thinking nothing, we wander through life as through a bewildered undifferentiated freak show. Why is this saint more important than this bearded lady? What does this philosopher know that this clown does not?

(Bryan Appleyard, 'Post-Scientific Society', in New Perspectives Quarterly,<br>vol. 10, no. 3 (Summer 1993), p. 53)

Adam Przeworski has gone as far as calling democracy the 'institutionalization of uncertainty'.[21] Democracy's doubts are therefore closely linked with the renewed relationship between the individual and society's traditional centers of authority, including, of course, the state. This relationship is embedded in a political sphere which is increasingly becoming postmodernized. Western society is becoming more and more *decentered*, since the state no longer serves as the sole or even the primary *locus* of political authority; it has become *fragmented* as a result of the growing number of distinct political visions, movements and fashions; and political life has become *eclectic*, as individuals and movements develop political strategies from all sorts of possible political styles. All this has blurred the boundaries between the political, the personal, the cultural and the economic sphere.[22] Such symptoms should not be read as a list of negative postmodern phenomena, but rather as the manifestation of a search for new approaches and intellectual and spiritual horizons. The loss of social cohesion, shared meanings and an externalized Self do not (necessarily) prompt the total breakdown of modern society.[23] The postmodern condition produces ambivalence and pluralism, and those willing to accept this now know that the sense of ambivalence and contingency is here to stay; their challenge is to learn how to live under this new condition. Postmodernism therefore serves as a vehicle for change and renewal, rather than as an antagonistic alternative to modernist practice.

In this context, the question frequently asked is whether we can still argue that citizenship remains unchallenged as the centerpiece of postmodern political life. The concept of citizenship – and its corollary notion of the public sphere as the market place for the formation of political ideas, opinions and preferences – are truly modernist abstractions, the political heritage of the Enlightenment which we still drag along with us.[24] The state has historically been contingent upon the separation of sovereignty from the person of the Sovereign (or Prince) by becoming an attribute of the 'people'. This 'people', as the supreme object of loyalty and bearer of sovereignty, has always been read as fundamentally homogeneous and in principle only superficially divided by status, class, locality or ethnicity.[25] Citizenship therefore rests on the rational abstraction that the *demos* can be read as a universal category that can transcend all the differences and particularities of the backgrounds and beliefs of the individual 'citizens'. In many ways representative democracy requires and presupposes exactly what it was supposed to achieve, namely an enlightened and rather homogeneous citizenry. This concept is interwoven with the modernist, essentialist interpretation of citizenship as based on the 'free individual' whose identity is not necessarily shaped by membership of other, particularistic, communities. The 'individual citizen', placed outside of and prior to history, is therefore the creation of modernity.

Like democracy, citizenship upholds the nation-state as the hegemonic center of individual identity, and thereby functions as a stifling, bland blanket covering the variety of micro-public spheres, all of which have their own discourses and claims on the loyalty of their participants. Classic notions of citizenship therefore overlook the shifts in the nature and quality of postmodern public life which have undermined the centrality and unity of the traditional public sphere. The public sphere is no unitary concept, and limiting the *legitimate* public stage to existing democratic institutions is an ideological myth of liberal democracy. Instead we see diverse and fragmented, even atomized, *publics*.

Norbert Birnbaum has correctly noted that this has bred a systemic cynicism in most western democracies, which in turn has led to the renunciation of political responsibility, especially for development in the national realm. This has led him to argue that

> substantial numbers of citizens of the western democracies (not only in the United States) live without inner or outer involvement in politics. Still, large numbers of citizens do need at least a simulacrum of connection to their nation, a minimal sense that its leaders are not total usurpers.
>
> (Norman Birnbaum, 'Democracy is as Democracy Does: An Inquiry', in *Salmagundi*, no. 116/117 (Fall 1997), pp. 168–9)

Consequently, it is even rather insolent to use the term 'public' in relation to politics, since the sphere of common deliberation has now been enlarged to include a wide range of groups and individuals that were previously simply ignored. Fragmentation and eclecticism have turned the political category of state-centered citizenship into a chaotic hotchpotch of values and accounts of civic life. This may not have made the notion of citizenship trivial, but it is certainly making it more problematic.

We should therefore acknowledge that reconceptualizing democracy involves rethinking the issue of the public sphere, focusing on the question whether democracy and social complexity are compatible. As Jürgen Habermas has argued: 'how can disenchanted, internally differentiated and pluralized lifeworlds be socially integrated ... if the risk of dissension is growing?'[26] Indeed, western society has become normatively heterogeneous, and this has caused the suspension of its search for a transcendental, overarching claim for political legitimacy. Habermas therefore envisages a decentered justification of political authority by means of *formally* institutionalized procedures of identifying public opinion and creating citizens' resolve, combined with *informally* organized networks in the public sphere to which political authorities have no direct access. This is a central part of the discourse ethics that plays such an important role in Habermas's argument of argumentative speech.[27] But this Habermasian vision of a free public of private citizens, exchanging views and opinions with each other and reaching a common understanding about the public interest, has become questionable.

Dana Villa has formulated two basic objections to the normative notion of the public sphere as a site of free political debate.[28] First, it naively relies upon the conditions of non-hierarchy and reciprocity as the assumedly adequate guarantees of a coercion-free political space, neglecting the disciplinary mechanisms that are inherent in the operation of power in modern society. Second, the Habermasian ideal of public discourse feeds on the Enlightenment metanarrative of emancipation and, through its focus on proceduralism, threatens to limit the plurality of language games and voices that might want to participate in this public debate. It should be clear that there is no easy way out of this predicament; there is no single and universal solution to be found to overcome the incompatibilities among discourses and so achieve what Lyotard has called the 'terror' of consensus.[29]

This has become especially problematic since the traditional Cartesian political space, determined by face-to-face interaction, no longer serves as the arena of exchange. This applies not only to the imaginary European public sphere, but to all imagined communities. Since the media have now *become* the public sphere, citizens are increasingly isolated from the more traditional 'real' spaces of politics.[30] To all intents and purposes, the public (and the public sphere) has not so much disappeared as become fragmented and threatened in its freedom by finance and institutionalized power. Mass media have abolished the distinction between debate and diversion, between politics and entertainment (hence the phenomenon of 'infotainment'); they are providing legitimating rituals for the contemporary structures of power rather than a coercion-free forum for public debate.[31] As Peter Dahlgren has argued, 'while television is the dominant medium of the public sphere, "public sphering" is clearly not television's dominant purpose'.[32] Western media superficially embrace the paradigm of the 'public sphere' and occasionally parade the symbols of multiculturalism, but this tends to involve little more than displaying the bland and shallow logos of consumerism without in any way touching upon the differences among people that really make a *political* difference.[33]

Insofar as there remains something like a public within the 'public sphere', its most visible characteristic is its passivity – hardly surprising, since we should not expect activity from a public when the political sphere is both elsewhere and nowhere. For many, the terms 'political' and 'politics' have all but mutated into a stigmatizing epithet, and politics is considered at best a rather unwelcome intrusion in prosaic life, an intrusion that should be avoided as much as possible and at all costs. The exclusion of interests that are considered as private, domestic or otherwise not suitable for public discussion has given rise to (what Nancy Fraser calls) subaltern counterpublics, or 'parallel discursive arenas where members of subordinated social groups invent and circulate counterdiscourses to formulate oppositional interpretations of their identities, interests and needs'.[34] These manifestations of postmodern identity politics show that the self-formation of groups and cultures is not necessarily achieved at the price of surrendering particularity to this 'terror' of consensus and the 'general interest'. Rather, they indicate that different cultures and alternative lifestyles are in themselves a sufficient site for the self-articulation of needs and desires, as well as, potentially, for the formulation and articulation of political positions.

Scholars like Seyla Benhabib and Dean C. Hammer suggest following Hannah Arendt's thoughts on narrative politics and identity, based on the notion that the 'unchangeable identity of the person, though disclosing itself intangibly in act and speech, becomes tangible only in the story of the actor's and speaker's life'.[35] The underlying premise of this approach is that institutions – political and other – may provide us with the procedures and operational settings by and in which we live, but that it is stories, narratives (in the sense of *petits récits*), that serve as the prosaic expressions of human experience.[36] The crux of postmodern democracy therefore lies in recognizing difference and conflict by legitimating and continuing the wide variety of antagonism inherent in all human society. Postmodern politics is therefore not necessarily called upon to do what traditional modern politics is supposed to do, namely to create 'practices, discourses, and institutions that seek to establish a certain order and to organize human coexistence'.[37]

L.A. Kauffman could therefore claim that the proliferation of multiple publics and the breakdown of the rigid barriers between political and private life has dramatically weakened the hegemony of the state. Since '[p]ractitioners of identity politics attribute great importance to the exploration and articulation of individual and collective identities', he argues, they 'tend to focus more heavily on individual and group self-transformation than on engaging with the state'.[38] For many people, the collective base and universalizing tendencies of citizenship are taken for granted, and it is the particularities, the things that set them apart from others, that have become the crucial *locus* of power relations. The myth of a harmonious public sphere has therefore collapsed, which has dire consequences for the notion of the universality of citizenship and the claims it can make on individual loyalty and the structure and *telos* of civil society. With the departure of universalizing claims of a citizenship-based politics and the proliferation of multiple publics, as well as the breakdown of the barriers between political and private life, it remains an open question whether it will be viable to somehow forge a common political identity and a common public sphere.

It is here that an important gap in democratic theory and practice becomes increasingly conspicuous. As Ulf Hedetoft has formulated it, 'The space of democracy, the space of sovereignty and the space of identity must correlate, otherwise "deficits" will show up, in one form or another'.[39] With state sovereignty eroding and national identity fragmenting, state-centered democracy has become problematic. Clearly, the contemporary spaces of democracy, sovereignty and identity no longer overlap flawlessly. The dominant myth of a unitary public sphere based on citizenship has evaporated. Democratic theory has concerned itself mainly with the domestic, statal definitions and challenges to democracy, but it has yet to come to grips with the question of whether one can envisage a functional democratic structure in which the state is no longer at the center. When scholars like Robert Dahl are questioning whether international organizations (including the EU) can be governed in ways consistent with democratic goals, one can only conclude that the problematic of democratic governance is politically pertinent as well as acute.[40] Many social movements and feminist scholars have always rejected the notion that politics, state and citizenship should be coterminous, and have claimed a more radical reading based on democratic praxis rather than official/legal status. But still, when the *locus* of effective political power is no longer found within the boundaries of the state, and when more and more people cherish multi-layered identities in which national identity is no longer necessarily dominant, we must ask how these new forms of geo-governance can be structured along democratic lines?[41]

This central problem remains unresolved as long as there is no agreement on whose consent is required to produce democratically legitimated decisions. It has frequently been suggested that a relevant democratic community should include all those who are directly affected by a certain decision or policy.[42] In a globalizing world based on an almost organic interconnectedness of economic and financial systems, it becomes obvious that in most cases the state is too small and modest a political entity. The lives of many people are affected by decisions taken outside the framework of the state, on which they have little or no influence. The spatial disintegration of territorial sovereignty has therefore problematized the electoral and accountability base of society. This dislocation of political practice and popular mentality is consistently unsettling our image of the democratic myth.[43]

Although the nation-state continues to be looked upon with a kind of retrospective nostalgia, it becomes increasingly clear that its internal homogeneity is crumbling, and conflicting communal and regional allegiances and identities are (re)emerging. This has led some scholars to call for a 'new vocabulary of citizenship' that 'will be shaped by concepts of liberal moral ideals that emphasize their cultural particularism and their partial nature'.[44] As Veit Bader has aptly formulated it, 'Historical states are not such warm, horizontal *Vergemeinschaftungen* or free and democratic associations, based on consent, but rather cold vertical institutions, based not on free entry but on enforced membership and physical violence'.[45] Citizenship in western liberal democracies (according to Joseph H. Carens) can therefore be read as the 'modern equivalent of feudal privileges – an inherited status that greatly enhances one's life chances. Like feudal birthright privileges, restrictive citizenship is hard to justify when one thinks about it closely'.[46] We could therefore call for the 'unfastening of the semantic link between citizenship and national identity',[47] arguing that the notion of 'the citizen' finds its disposition not in ethnic-cultural commonalties, but instead in a wide array of democratic procedures, involving discourse and decision-making. This would be a new sort of citizenship, based on what Habermas has called 'constitutional patriotism', which would be anchored within a common political culture and praxis. On this reading, it is prosaical interaction that moulds citizens. Individuals invent themselves repeatedly and differently through the course of communication practices. It is through critical discourse that democratic action can be undertaken, be it necessarily without any guarantor and without any definite 'end'.

## The commodification of democracy

We have already argued that the role of the nation-state as the general regulator of the national economy and as a staunch and effective promoter of its 'national interests' (in economic, social and political terms) shows visible signs of erosion. Globalization has called into question the appropriateness of old-style state structures which are no longer capable of playing a powerful role in the complex global system of local, regional, national and transversal fields. Clearly, the new discourse of globalization has become dominant in the idiom of politics and business, framing the language games of other debates, including our conversation on the nature and future of European democracy. The debate on how globalization (and Europeanization) affects the nature of democracy has yet to start. Besides the optimistic calls for a vibrant and radical form of cyberdemocracy, we can also hear gloomy predictions that globalization 'is not so much hostile as indifferent to democracy'.[48] Apart from perhaps still somewhat naive notions of a new global digital village, it has become clear that, since the welfare state is gradually being overtaken by the competition state, liberal democracy is no longer capable of embodying the kind of communal solidarity which has given the modern nation-state both its deeper legitimacy and its institutionalized power.[49]

Cerny has argued that, whereas the welfare state has tried to take certain economic activities out of the market (in an effort to 'decommodify' society), the competition state actively pursues the increased marketization of society in order to make the nation-state more competitive in international and transnational terms.[50] He has made the case that we see an increasing 'commodification of the state', in which the nation-state loses its ability to act as a strategic or developmental actor. In its place we see the emergence of so-called 'splintered states', with 'state actors and different agencies increasingly intertwined with "transgovernmental networks" – systematic linkages between state actors and agencies within particular jurisdictions and sectors, cutting across different countries and including a heterogeneous collection of private actors and groups in interlocking policy communities'.[51] This does not necessarily herald the end of politics, the nation-state and democracy *per se*, but it certainly heralds the end of politics, the nation-state and democracy as we have hitherto known them.

The post-national proposition involves two central elements. The first is the notion that the emerging competition state will erode the posited underlying bonds on which the nation-state is allegedly based. The primordial face of nationalism assumes a qualitative sense of communion and communal goals that forms the *raison d'être* of the modern state. But, with the ongoing commodification of the state, the national *Gemeinschaft* may well become a 'mere' pragmatic association for common ends: a 'mere' *Gesellschaft*. The second element proposes that, since the welfare state has not been able to protect the national economy from the violence of globalization, the emerging competition state is increasingly seen as the enforcer of decisions and outcomes emerging from the interplay of global markets, transnational firms and national/regional actors. Under the conditions of late capitalism, globalization has restricted national options for redistributing resources among its citizens, thus undermining social-democratic readings of 'democracy' which are rooted in the aspiration to modify by public action the resource inequalities generated by capitalism.[52] This has made the notion of democracy as a 'just society' problematic. Globalization therefore limits people's expectations of the state as the source for the authoritative allocation of values and wealth. Even the best-run state can no longer offer its citizens the kind of public services and the redistributive arrangements that have long been central to the western welfare state. This will make the nation-state a deliberate, 'willed' political community which can no longer provide for 'its' citizens' content, and therefore can no longer arrogantly assume their consent.

But will the commodification of the state not ultimately engender a similar commodification of democracy? This central question relates to our earlier inquiry into how Europeanization may help to avoid a Pinocchian world of ungovernance, as well as an unaccountable world based on the understanding that the market economy should replace our current practice of democratic governance. A vision of Europe where people would 'vote' (or express their con(s/t)ent) with their credit cards and wallets, would distort the notion of democracy, turning it into a banal hyperreality. As Barber has noted, 'The freedom to buy a coke or a video of the Lion King is not yet the freedom to determine how we will live and under what kind of regime'.[53] This mode of consumer-oriented freedom would move the market to the center of individual self-constitution, replacing and dominating moral and political deliberations and reflections. It would lend sovereignty to consumers, rather than citizens and individuals *qua* human beings. Consumerism would turn consumption and purchasing power into the defining essence of the society's political geography, thereby annihilating the very idea of commonality and the 'public' that is central to social relationships.[54] Especially since markets do not lend social and moral significance to any specific choice, it will be difficult to continue cherishing the promises of salvation, virtue and justice connected to the notion of liberal civil society.[55] Instead, it would mould citizens into consumers, urging us to consider ourselves to be the 'customers', or 'clients' of regional, national and European bureaucracies.

These dilemmas are bound to become more painful and profound over time, since, although the nation-state continues to be an important focal point of loyalty and a mechanism for societal consensus-building, its new role as competition state forces it to turn itself into a quasi-market actor. It will be difficult, on the one hand, to provide public goods or other communal services as a political agent, and, on the other, to act as a commercial agent focused on efficiency and profit. The commodification of politics and society therefore not only affects national governments, but the authority and legitimacy of other state institutions as well. Globalization and the postmodern condition do not merely scratch the surface of the democratic arrangement of politics but affect its nuts and bolts; they corrode the skeletal frame of political life.

At the same time, the level of cognitive inertia in accepting this radical change is striking. Mainstream political parties frequently find themselves barking up the wrong tree by calling for national action or holding their own government responsible for matters that are, or have already been, decided at a European or other supranational level. These political parties continue to spend much time trying to resuscitate the already decaying welfare state they themselves conceived with so much dedication after World War II. But most political actors now finally seem to have discovered that the beloved nation-state has lost its unique role in economic management, political authority and cultural hegemony. In this hallucinatory process of discovery, national political actors have metamorphosed into 'actors': a cast of characters playing the play of politics on the national stage, roughly representing different strands of society, but only marginally affecting the 'real world', which still remains 'out there'.

This has contributed to the emergence of what Klaus von Beyme has called 'postmodern political parties'. Von Beyme argues that

> party-membership in postmodern society is – just like membership in a church, in an association, or even in a marriage – no longer an attachment for life. 'Omnibus parties' have developed. People enter the vehicle, are carried for a while and drop out when they do not see any reason to go further.
>
> (Klaus von Beyme, 'Party Leadership and Change in Party Systems: Towards a Postmodern Party System?', in *Government and Opposition*, vol. 31, no. 2 (Spring 1996), p. 147)

For the rank-and-file member as well as for your average party leader, political parties have become instrumental, and robust ideological affiliation is clearly declining. The central dilemma here is that recognizing the substantiality of the competition state would further undermine the status of national political 'actors', calling into question the very foundation of state-based representative democracy. Ian Budge has rightly argued that political parties 'enable citizens to sift through the mass of facts and to narrow down alternatives'.[56] But, whereas

Budge takes this as a practical and laudable role for political parties, it may well be that limiting the options for an increasingly heterogeneous 'public' to choose from will no longer serve postmodern society's needs. At the same time, it should be clear that the trend toward a 'hollow state' only adds to societal frustration. It further undermines popular confidence in the national parliamentary system and other democratic institutions, which in turn helps to legitimate right-wing and anti-democratic extremist groups and political parties.[57]

In this context, Svein Andersen and Tom Burns have argued that the EU is developing in the direction of what they have labeled 'post-parliamentary governance'.[58] They claim that national parliaments are no longer the centers of enlightened public debate, but are instead on the verge of degenerating into mere decorative elements in the multi-level, pluralist game of governance. Andersen and Burns assert that individual citizens do not expect to influence the composition of political authority at the European level, much less vote 'them' out of office; the EU is not a political system in which decision-makers are held personally accountable for their policies and actions. Instead, it is characterized by the principles of national representation, interest presentation and the contribution of information and expertise. This limits the political relevance of traditional notions of representative democracy through parliamentary institutions, but inaugurates novel governance arrangements based on policy networks and social movements. This also bears out the conclusions of studies indicating that

> citizens may have confidence in their Parliaments for reasons largely unre-
> lated to its capacity to determine public policy ... The processes – the way
> in which a Parliament operates as part of a political process – may be far
> more important than the actual immediate outcome (in policy terms) of
> those processes.
> (Philip Norton, 'Legislatures in Perspective', in Norton (ed.), *Parliaments in
> Western Europe* (London: Frank Cass, 1990), p. 147)

It is important to be aware that these arguments are not phrased as a complaint, or a lament for the demise of traditional democratic notions. Instead, the principal ground for the erosion of the parliamentary system is 'that Western societies have become highly differentiated and far too complex for a parliament or its government to monitor, acquire sufficient knowledge and competence, and to deliberate on'. From this perspective, the 'complex differentiation of society is reflected in the differentiation and complexity of governance, the differentiation of representation, the differentiation of systems of knowledge and expertise, and the spectrum of values and lifestyles of ordinary citizens'.[59]

This inquisitive attitude seems to capture much of the uniqueness of the democratic nature of Europe's contemporary structure of governance. The notion that, in today's economic environment, markets are highly differentiated, that administration and public services are complex and require continuous adaptation to societies that are culturally diverse, both in values and lifestyles, clearly directly affects governance at the national as well as at the European level. The gradual evaporation of a specific center of territorial 'government' based on representative democratic legitimacy is also noticeable on the national level. But, since the Euro-polity is still in *statu nascendi* and not firmly rooted in traditional modern state-structures, postmodern governance is more obvious and more visible on the European level than anywhere else. The EU's elaborate decision-making structure, based to a large extent on comitology, not only undermines classical notions of governance, but classical notions of democracy as well.

The precise meaning of democracy on the European level refers to notions such as openness and mutual respect, recognition and equal treatment, knowledge-based and interest-based representation, as well as comprehensive representation. This is not the classical definition of democracy that European peoples have become used to over decades and centuries. Perhaps we should acknowledge that the EU has taken a *saut qualitatif* toward a new, postmodern democratic system, a quantum leap toward a new kind of democracy that may be more applicable for addressing today's challenges and for managing the demands of a larger and more diverse political space.

## Legitimacy and the calculus of con(s/t)ent

Globalization has made democratic governance the norm; democracy is *comme il faut*. Globalization has been a major force driving the transition from centrally-planned, authoritarian regimes, toward a market-based system in which democratic rights are supposed to be safeguarded. New technologies and global media inform people directly from international sources that are increasingly difficult for governments to censor; the continuous stream of information and news has become unruly and relentless. Modern mass media show people around the world what is 'really real', what they can have and be. This has practically eliminated the option for governments to isolate themselves – and more importantly their citizens – from the rest of the world. Bauman has therefore claimed that

> the fatal blow to communism was delivered by postmodernity. Communism could live happily ever after with the modern world, which was all about increasing production – more steel, more coal, building irrigation systems and so on. But it could not live with the world based on enjoyment, freedom, game, playfulness, variety, etc. That is what communists could not produce.
>
> ('Modernity, Postmodernity and Ethics – An Interview With Zygmunt Bauman', in *Telos*, no. 93 (Fall 1992), p. 144)

At the same time, the discourse of globalization suggests that the 'forces' of marketization are supposed to be uncontrollable, making the shift from the welfare to the competition state an incontestable and irrefutable necessity. The commodification of politics and culture is now sold to postmodern society as its fate and nemesis. But by accepting this language game, we would also acknowledge that globalization is the economic manifestation of a real or imagined 'invisible hand', wresting formal political power away from the nation-state and its citizens and throwing it in the lap of the global economy and its agents. It also asks us to acknowledge that during this power-shift globalization has (in the words of Strange), 'left a yawning hole of non-authority, ungovernance'. This reading of today's political trends clearly overlooks the circumstance that nation-states are not merely passively responding to quasi-autonomous exogenous pressures, but have themselves consciously *created* (or at least have actively contributed to) the emerging global economy. Moreover, it raises a number of rather complex and troublesome questions relating to our traditional understanding of democratic governance and how it could be salvaged. As is well known, the process of Europeanization initially concentrated its efforts on coal and steel, but has now acquired a qualitatively new, postmaterialist character. Europeanization has been credited with the rescue of the nation-state (which I doubt). May we not now also rely upon the EU to rescue democratic governance (which I hope for)?

Although the EU touches directly upon the innumerable prosaic concerns of all Europeans, for the general public 'Brussels' still remains remote and emotionally distant. Europe's citizens have for decades offered their 'permissive consensus' by accepting EU policies without asking too many difficult questions about democratic legitimacy and accountability. But since the Maastricht Treaty, the elite-driven approach to European integration no longer seems justifiable or practical. The EU has now moved away from a preoccupation with policy (e.g. the Single Market, EMU) toward a genuine concern for institutional management and reform. The main reason why legitimacy has now become a matter of concern is that the EU's system of governance functions without a *formal* source of authority. Michael Shackleton has therefore argued that 'the [legitimacy] crisis is a product of the realization that we do not yet have the means to move from a system essentially concerned with the *administration of things* to one concerned with the *governance of people*'.[60] This has become especially pertinent since the 'people' is now seriously questioning the authoritative basis on which both the nation-state and the EU allocate contentious values and limited resources. The Amsterdam Treaty and the Union's enlargement toward Central Europe have further broadened the thematic of the legitimacy of EU policy formulation.

This has raised the political question of why European citizens (do not) support the European 'project'? Although there are numerous narratives relative to Europe's integration, three rather cohesive 'explanations' stand out in the scholarly literature.[61] The first argument centers on the notion of cognitive mobilization, which assumes a relationship between the cognitive skills of European citizens and their attitudes toward European integration. Inglehart has made the case that a high level of political awareness enables citizens to identify with a supranational polity like the EU; this will also make him/her feel less threatened by the prospect of European integration. In particular, the level of education may be positively related to support for European integration, mainly because education offers citizens economic and social opportunities in a more liberalized EU labor market. 'Human capital' enables citizens to adapt to the occupational competition within a more integrated market. The second statement focuses on political values. As we have discussed in a previous chapter, Inglehart has argued that the EU represents a political vehicle for those citizens who cherish postmaterialist values and are aiming toward a less nationalistic and more egalitarian society. The third argument provides a more utilitarian appraisal of integrative policy, claiming that European citizens base their consent for European integration on the measure of their individual content, their satisfaction with their socio-economic situation and the welfare gains they perceive themselves as realizing via the EU.[62]

This is not the place to evaluate these competing claims about the genesis of grass-roots legitimacy for the European proposition. But it is clear that all these elements touch upon the normative foundations of European integration, as well as the foundations of EU and state authority. But what does legitimacy suggest and announce? Daniela Obradovic has argued that legitimacy refers to a 'sense of obligation', which 'embraces the expectation that the decisions generated by a system will be right in terms of some moral or ethical standard'. As such, she claims, 'legitimacy is a concept founded on the premise of the doctrine of popular sovereignty, that the people may be the only legitimate source of power since they represent ultimate authority'.[63] Legitimacy therefore requires not just a uniform body of citizens, but also a logocentric narrative, a (national) myth which places society's beliefs on a metaphysical pedestal. This renders the legitimacy of EU politics especially problematic, since such a European metanarrative is absent, as is the European *demos*. It is difficult to find an unproblematic repository of legitimacy for the authority now circulating within the EU domain, mainly because the European Parliament, as well as national governments and parliaments, only has a limited impact on the policy outcomes of the Union.[64] What is more, since national governments frequently use the EU as a scapegoat for implementing unpopular domestic policies, 'Brussels' is regularly depicted as an 'outside' actor, rather than as an integral part of the national constituting Self.

Pierre Manent has argued along similar lines, claiming that the 'democratic principle of legitimacy is the principle of *consent*'.[65] This follows the classical argument made by John Locke that human beings are rational actors evaluating their own interests and binding their future actions through commitments and law.[66] Manent contends that, since the Enlightenment, democracy and the nation-state have found a common existence, which explains why the *political* problem of democracy has remained largely unrecognized. In short, the democratic principle does not define the framework within which it operates. Manent therefore claims that, with the weakening of the nation-state as the traditional framework of community, democracy is consequently undermined. This is especially worrying because 'the democratic principle, after having used the nation as an instrument or vehicle, abandons it by the wayside' without having found a credible new political form. He argues that

> as democracy today grows more and more self-aware and self-confident it tranquilly bids farewell to the nation, the framework that seemed so natural to it for two centuries. Democracy punishes the nation for the follies it caused her to commit, but also, one fears, for the services it has rendered her.
>
> (Pierre Manent, 'Democracy Without Nations', in *Journal of Democracy*, vol. 8, no. 2 (April 1997), pp. 98–9)

But, he claims, democracy 'cannot be without a body ... What is a democracy without a body, a democracy deprived of what psychologists call the sentiment of one's own body?'[67] Obviously, Manent does not feel that this abstract notion of 'Europe' offers opportunities for the new democratic body to become real and able to produce an awareness of its new-sprung Self.

The democratic problematic therefore centers around the alleged need for a body or a stable platform of the political where competition and discourse can be staged. Claude Lefort has therefore argued that

> democracy is instituted and sustained by the dissolution of the markers of certainty. It inaugurates a history in which people experience a fundamental indeterminacy as to the basis of power, law, and knowledge, and as to the basis of relations between self and other, at every level of social life ... [In a democracy,] no one has the answers to the questions that arise.
>
> (Claude Lefort, *Democracy and Political Theory* (Minneapolis: University of Minnesota Press, 1988), p. 19)

This reading of democracy inevitably negates the notion of identity as a fixed essence. It also questions the political need for a 'sentiment of the body' in the Manentian sense. Instead it encourages the constitution of the Self through continual discourse, not necessarily oriented toward a pragmatic political accord (as Habermas presumes)[68] but by decentralizing and multiplying the public sphere. The challenge will be to encourage the sense of community in an environment where sovereignty is dispersed and citizenship formed across multiple sites of civic engagement.[69] As Mark Poster has rightly reminded us, 'the age of the public sphere as face-to-face talk is clearly over: the question of democracy must henceforth take into account new forms of electronically mediated discourse'. This raises the question what 'complexes of subjects, bodies and machines are required for democratic exchange and emancipatory action?'[70]

But, quite apart from the 'mechanics' and dynamics of democracy, it seems clear that the exercise of political authority will continue to change dramatically. Poster therefore assumes that 'a new term will be required to indicate a relation of leaders and followers that is mediated by cyberspace and constituted in relation to the mobile identities found therein'.[71]

## Citizenship and the embrace of democratic complexity

'Citizenship of the Union is hereby established. Every person holding the nationality of a Member State shall be a citizen of the Union'. This is how Article 8 of the Maastricht Treaty on European Union reads.[72]

The concept of European citizenship has raised more questions than it has answered, which is probably as it should be at this stage of the European integration process.[73] Central to this concept are the dimensions of identity; economic, social and political rights; and political participation. But, like national citizenship, European citizenship is not merely a neutral, legal formula, but rather a mechanism of social closure.[74] The notion of citizenship has not been dreamt up solely (or even primarily) as a status allowing active participation in the political arena, but as a device to keep the Other outside and absent. Since citizenship has frequently been based on racial and ethnic criteria, to rationalize exemptions from national rights and duties, the dangers of a particularistic approach should be clear.[75] Citizenship asks 'who belongs' to 'us'? Who is a refugee, a migrant, marginal and forgettable? It asks about the structures of political membership, civic obligations and participation. It is also one of the mechanisms for distributing the responsibilities, benefits and burdens of membership in a polity. These are central elements of the Roman notion of citizenship, as primarily a legal status which reads the citizen as a subject. But the classical Athenian conception of citizenship as a *participatory ideal* may be more valuable for our conversation. It is this active citizenship based on participation, rather than passive membership based on subjecthood, that may provide options for an inventive approach to a new, democratic conception of governance. It is based on the valuable notion that only through engagement, communication and discourse can individuals cultivate the practical judgement and sensitivity to others that effective civic participation in governance requires.[76]

Be that as it may, the nation-state continues to monopolize the notion of citizenship, fixing the territorial boundaries of identity and community.[77] Every time concepts such as 'citizenship' and 'democracy' are raised in the discourse on the EU, a knee-jerk association is made with other abstractions, like 'the state' and 'its people'. We have become so used to the dyads citizen/state and democracy/state that it is hard to examine the idea of 'European citizenship' outside the conceptual statal realm. This may be understandable, but it is also unfortunate. As Joseph Weiler has argued, 'the introduction of European Citizenship to the discourse of European integration could mean not that the *telos* of European integration has changed, but that our understanding of citizenship has changed, is changing, or ought to change'.[78] Weiler therefore calls for a reconceptualization of this new notion of European citizenship around the fragmented sovereignty of the postmodern state, as well as around the fractured Self of the human beings who comprise these states. This can only be accomplished by rejecting European citizenship as a new type of emotional attachment on a par with nationality-based citizenship. Weiler therefore argues that 'the decoupling of nationality and citizenship opens the possibility, instead, of thinking of co-existing multiple *demoi*'.[79] On this reading, the absence of a cohesive European people on which a homogeneous *demos* could be based, should be considered an advantage, since it precludes the option of building a European 'Superstate', with all the flaws of fatuous Euro-nationalism.

In practice, however, citizenship is a violent criterion for determining who should be allowed to cross the drawbridge of Fortress Europe, and who should remain outside. The debate on European citizenship is a prism for analyzing the history and practice of inclusion and exclusion, the nature and aesthetics of Europe's political community, its real or imagined bonds of solidarity in a real or imagined 'community of fate'.[80] It also determines who may be trusted to participate within the official public sphere. In this sense, the question is asked how effective is the concept of citizenship as a 'gatekeeper' between humanity in general and a smaller political unit (be it the nation-state or the EU).[81] This is no trivial matter, since Europe now contains an increasing number of 'outsiders' in the form of asylum-seekers and permanent residents. There are more than nine million people now living and working in the EU who are not granted the status of 'European citizen'. These nine million aliens and denizens are consistently marginalized, and strict measures are now in place to limit further immigration.[82] In this sense it is quite ironic that the Schengen Agreement (which seeks to abolish all border controls among the Benelux countries, France, Germany, Italy, Spain and Portugal) has spurred national governments to strengthen their external borders and their competence and ability to carry out checks and controls, as well to store and exchange information, on 'unwanted individuals'. The Schengen Implementation Agreement includes detailed measures on illegal immigration, the status of refugees, asylum and cross-border surveillance, as well as a common computerized system for the exchange of personal data in the so-called Schengen Information Service (SIS).[83] The very notion of citizenship therefore makes it clear that all political communities are by definition of a 'limited solidarity'. Europe is no exception to that.

In an earlier chapter we have already discussed the ethnic and civic faces of Europeanization, arguing that the celebration of plurality should continue to form the basis for Europe's political community. An ethereal European identity would be the unmarked base for a nascent European citizenship. This would be a postmodern identity, without a 'big code', but instead based on shifting interests, shifting *loci* of interaction and/or identification. It would be an identity in flux, an identity which could only be retained on the condition of not clinging too tightly to it. This is reflected in the situation of contemporary Europe, where many groups now take identity politics as their point of departure, rather than an abstract citizenship which only offers them political agency through the umbilical chord with 'their' state. Elizabeth Meehan has therefore argued that a new kind of citizenship is emerging that is neither national nor cosmopolitan but that is multiple in the sense that the identities, rights and obligations associated ... with citizenship, are expressed through an increasingly complex configuration of common [EU] institutions, states, national and transnational voluntary associations, regions and alliances of regions.

(Elizabeth Meehan, *Citizenship and the European Community*
(London: Sage, 1993), p. 1)

This raises the question of whether the basic concept of a territorially-based democracy has not become an anachronism in the postmodern European context? Might we want to make efforts to extend the territorial and functional scope of democratic practice and try to imagine how this novel sphere of responsibility and accountability could go *beyond* current state borders? Is it possible to discuss and think about state-less forms of democracy?

Perhaps this is not even so much a political or philosophical question, as a matter of encouraging effective, democratic governance on the European level. The network horizon on European governance offers at least the beginnings of an opportunity for Europe's fragmented society to reflect the diversity of values we associate with democracy (equality, participation and individuality) toward the organization of the European public sphere. It is the complexity of contemporary society that necessitates the input of specialized technical and/or scientific expertise, as well as the feedback of interests and concerns of the multiple societal sectors and groups in all the phases of the European policy-making process. Since both lobbies and experts are often transversal, rather than organized along national lines, Europe's emerging democracy is not bound within a confined geographical space. Representatives of non-EU countries are actively trying to influence decisions made in Brussels, opening up the European policy-making process to extra-European interests and concerns. On this reading, post-parliamentarian and post-territorial democracy is also of a pronounced postmodern nature.

We should therefore expect that the unique institutional setting of European governance calls for a new approach and a new model of democracy within the Euro-polity. Since notions of sovereignty and democracy have become closely linked in the course of the twentieth century, the evaporation of the national political space problematizes traditional democratic practices. It should therefore be no surprise that state-centric models of democracy cannot be reciprocated on a European level. Multi-level governance involves a wide range of actors, creating a complex melange of lines of authority trying to find pragmatic solutions to the complex problems facing the EU and its Member States. Within the EU's community-wide sphere of work, networking has now replaced the traditional vertical hierarchy as the main characteristic of the decision-making process. This has created the strong impression that the EU's institutions are intangible as well as unintelligible to ordinary people. Lobbying and the input of expert knowledge have become central elements in the direct representation of interests at the EU level.

However, we should concede that 'knowledge' can never be truly value-neutral, but is always part of a certain social order that inevitably benefits some more than others. The role of 'experts' in the structure of EU governance can therefore not be accepted as unproblematic and a quasi-substitute for representative forms of democracy. Giandomenico Majone has claimed that, for the EU, the legitimacy of its policies could be found at the 'output'-side, in the provision of solutions that are widely considered to be in the 'public interest'. He therefore argues that, since the EU has serious shortcomings in its institutional system, it should not try to turn itself into a traditional parliamentary system on a supranational level, but rather limit the perspectives of majoritarian institutions.[84] This is an interesting, if also somewhat lackadaisical and defeatist, attitude to the democratic challenge facing the EU and European integration in general. It is also a far cry from the ultimate of direct, radical democracy. As C. Douglas Lummis has reminded us:

> we must not start thinking of the cave, which we originally entered to get out of the wind, as if it were the whole world, or confuse the stove with the sun. This is the error we fall into when we define democracy as identical to the institutions of the 'actually existing democracies'.
>
> (C. Douglas Lummis, *Radical Democracy* (Ithaca NY: Cornell
> University Press, 1996), p. 163)

European governance is little more (but also not less) than this supranational cave, a cave which reflects a principle that, according to E.M. Forster, deserves two cheers, but never three.

To enlarge the scale of democratic decision-making and bring it into line with the swelling dimensions of globalization, this will be Europe's direct democratic challenge. It will ultimately imply developing a European – ultimately even a global – political community on the basis of a 'cosmopolitan' notion of democracy. A primary condition for revitalizing western democracy, at local, national and European level would be society's reconquest of the economy.[85] It should be clear that globalization and Europeanization are not autonomous processes, and that the choice between a centralized, hegemonic state and a completely free and privatized market is a simplified and distorted reading of reality. But unless communal needs and wishes are brought into play in central decisions on the allocation of wealth and norms, the essential fabric of society is bound to disintegrate, bringing democracy down in its wake. The philosophy of 'everyone should take care of themselves, and too bad if people can't cope' undermines and erodes the soil in which every imaginable form of democracy can flourish.[86] Clearly, postmodern uncertainty creates its discontents, its inequality and alienation, and even despair for many. The 'Third Way' between unfettered capitalism and outmoded state-controlled socialism must take the authentic increase in the number of autonomous centers of decision as its starting point.[87]

But what will be a really crucial element for the democratization of the economy will be a democratic public and citizenry using the available (public) spaces which are continuously being (re)created. These are spaces that are not limited to the official public sphere but also involve the often forgotten and overlooked political valuations that are part of the prosaic and private lives of every individual. This will certainly not become a reality without creating a new sense of possibility, a new sense of imagining a more radical and never-finished picture of democratic praxis. It has become painfully evident that the liberal democratic model devised by eighteenth-century French and British thinkers no longer accommodates complex twenty-first-century societies that embody sophisticated and diverse electorates with highly differentiated interests. But, although the cogwheels of the Newtonian clockwork of democracy are clearly out of sync with the contemporary world of digitalization and global integration, we have yet to develop the necessary software – the rules of interaction, knowledge, values, ethics and morals – which could help us facilitate responsible use of the available high-tech computerized machinery that may allow us to organize a new, grass-roots democratic movement. The anachronistic model of representative democracy can no longer manage the dynamic postindustrial society; this requires new systems (most likely cybernetic models) which are self-regulated and contain feedback loops at all levels. It has to be recognized that there is nothing sacrosanct about the system of representative democracy, just as there was nothing 'divine' about the notions of empire and monarchy. Given the limits posed by time and space, representative democracy was devised because it was the only system that could work for a sizeable nation-state during the eighteenth century. But today the basic conditions for democracy have changed dramatically, and a digital democracy could be envisaged, also – and perhaps in particular – for imagining a future European democratic system of governance.

It is this continuous flow of feedback loops – the interaction between people and decision-makers – that feeds the complex process of policy formulation. Voting every other year or so is simply too unrefined and crude. Europe may be in need of a redesigned and more instantaneous form of democracy, using high-speed data-processing, new communication technology used for electronic 'town hall'-meetings and polling. These ideas are, of course, hardly new, but they are (surprisingly enough) also hardly used.[88] It was in February 2000, that the European Commission initiated a public debate and dialogue on institutional reform which for the first time included the use of new technologies (Internet as well as videoconferencing).[89] European Commissioners committed themselves to debate the future of integration, peace and stability, as well as the enlargement of the Union with European citizens and with a wider public. Questions could be forwarded electronically via an Internet mailbox and some of the debates have been broadcast on EBS television (the televised information service of the EU) and by satellite (on 'Europe-by-Satellite').

Another interesting example of how the European public sphere might be envisaged and reinvigorated has been the simulation site 'Lexcalibur – The European Public Square', prepared under the direction of Weiler. This website has been officially set up to further 'democratization and transparency in European governance. It opens legislative processes and regulatory measures to all interested citizens and interest groups'.[90] The central idea behind this project (which was sponsored by the European Parliament), is to encourage the diffusion of information on EU policies and offer European citizens and other individuals and groups the opportunity to participate in online conversations on issues that touch their concerns and daily lives. By proposing the Lexcalibur project, Weiler (and his colleagues) have tried to offer an alternative to the basic limits of representative democracy, and have suggested experimentation with legislative ballots on specific issues to be voted for by European citizens. The Lexcalibur project has not so far been realized, but the idea certainly has a lot going for it. Weiler *et al.* suggest that the opportunity of a direct, more radical form of democracy would enhance, symbolically as well as tangibly, the voice of individuals *qua* citizens, through praxis rather than status. The proposal is also seen as a means of encouraging the formation of European parties and coalitions, as well as the transversal mobilization of political forces in general. Lexcalibur would be a virtual site that would make visible the entire decision-making process of the EU, especially (but not only) the process of comitology. It would therefore not mirror the official websites of the EU, but would rather offer interested individuals and groups a more in-depth insight into the scope and purpose of European legislation or regulatory measures, the persons and administrative departments who are responsible for the process and the timetables of the decision-making process, as well as all non-confidential documents which are part of that process. Weiler *et al.* make clear that one of the central aims would be to enhance the potential of all actors involved for playing a more informed critical role in Europe's official public sphere. Although Lexcalibur has remained a simulation site and has not been operationalized, it opens an exciting new perspective on how democratic legitimacy as well as practical and responsible European citizenship could be envisaged.

Although Tip O'Neal has famously argued that 'all politics is local', the Internet and also the problems which ordinary people face are anything but local.[91] Globalization and the communications revolution have made us aware that we can communicate perhaps with people in different continents more easily than with our grumpy old neighbor. Problems, opportunities and human contact are now no longer bound by place or time. An argument can therefore be made that there are opportunities for establishing effective democracy and citizenship on a supranational level, and conceivably even on a global level. These questions have now forced themselves on the academic agenda, although not (yet) on the political agenda. We can now see an historical trend toward expanding economic and technological change from a regional, national to a global level, which may well require a commensurate fragmentation-cum-broadening of democratic political institutions. David Held has suggested that this new configuration of democratic governance would

involve the development of administrative capacity and independent political resources at regional and global levels as a necessary complement to
those in local and national polities ... A cosmopolitan democracy would not
call for the diminution *per se* of state power and capacity across the globe.
Rather, it would seek to entrench and develop democratic institutions at
regional and global levels as a necessary complement to those at the level of
the nation-state.

> (David Held, 'Democracy and Globalization', in *Global Governance*,
> vol. 3, no. 3 (September/December 1997), p. 263)

This notion of a democratic internationalism clearly clashes with the Realist
vision of a causally decisive international sphere isolated from domestic
politics.[92] However, in many ways, the Cartesian inside/outside boundary still
dominates the discourse on democracy. Walker has correctly argued that the

> claims of people as people came to be subordinated to the claims of people
> as citizens, as the subjects of specific sovereign powers. In short, the possi-
> bility of reason, progress and justice within states has depended on the
> presumption that differences between states must be settled, at least in the
> last resort, by force.

> (R.B.J. Walker, 'Genealogy, Geopolitics and Political Community: Richard K.
> Ashley and the Critical Social Theory of International Politics', in
> *Alternatives*, vol. 13, no. 1 (January 1988), p. 85)

By relinquishing the postulate that there can ever be a rational solution, a
truly coercion-free consensus on the central questions of justice in a democratic
society, postmodern democracy must give up the dream of a place called home.
If democratic theory is to take difference, as well as the multiplicity of identity,
seriously, it should accept that domestic politics is a far cry from womb-like peace
and tranquility, but is as full of power, conflict and the struggle for value and
meaning as is the 'outside'. By accepting the permanence of antagonism and
incommensurability, all notions of the political are in principle and praxis
undecidable. As Chantal Mouffe has argued, '[w]e have therefore to abandon
the very idea of a complete reabsorption of alterity into oneness and harmony'.[93]

Ronald Beiner has defined postmodernism as the notion that 'all social reality
is untranscendably local, plural, fragmentary, episodic, and infinitely rearrange-
able'.[94] The EU clearly fits this profile. But this profile will be empty, void, unless
it imbues the European integration process with two important gifts: patience
and generosity. Havel has argued that many politicians want 'to nudge history
forward in the way a child would when wishing to make a flower grow more
quickly: by tugging it'. But, he has noted, the

> postmodern politician must learn, in the deepest and best sense of the word,
> the importance of waiting ... His waiting must be the expression of respect

for the inner dynamics and tempo of Being, for the nature of things, for their integrity and their independent dynamics, which resist coercive manipulation ... [O]ne must also listen to the polyphony of often-contradictory messages the world sends out and try to penetrate their meaning. It is not enough to describe, in scientific terms, the mechanics of things and events; their spirit must be personally perceived and experienced.

(Vaclav Havel, 'Speech to the Academy of Humanities and Political Science in Paris, France', 27 October 1992. Online. Available HTTP: http://www.hrad.cz/president/Havel/speeches/1992/2710uk.html, accessed 2 August 2000)

Clearly, this articulates the notion that the modern social contract is a rather incomplete and unsatisfactory framework for democratic government and practice. It must therefore keep an ear open to the dynamics of society itself and try to adjust to accommodate difference. This postmodern disposition would conceive democracy not as a prescriptive theory for addressing and ultimately resolving social chaos, but rather as an opportunity for constructing social relationships to adjust to (and accommodate) the collapse of antiquated ontological meanings. The classic homeostasis model of government, where political elites manipulate social behavior to bring society back into a preconceived equilibrium, is clearly antithetical to the postmodern vision of self-organization, multiplicity and diversity of meaning. It offers at least the potential for changing the nature and quality of democratic politics, from a battle of extremes based on futile polemics to the collaboration of multiple perspectives. Postmodern democracy is therefore not a *new* order, but perhaps a more self-aware quest for a more inclusive and mercurial means of governance.

But the most essential element of the emerging European democracy will be what Connolly has called the 'cultural ethos of generosity'. This ethos will have to form the foundation of an open, vibrant and diverse EU, since

the most fragile and indispensable element in a pluralizing democracy is an ethos of responsiveness in relations between identities, an ethos that opens up cultural space through which new possibilities of being can be enacted. A pluralizing ethos is one that risks the production of new challenges to established cultural constellations in a variety of domains.

(William E. Connolly, 'Tocqueville, Territory, and Violence', in Michael J. Shapiro and Hayward R. Alker (eds), *Challenging Boundaries: Global Flows, Territorial Identities* (Minneapolis: University of Minnesota Press, 1996), p. 155)

## Notes

1 Claude Lefort, *Democracy and Political Theory* (Minneapolis: University of Minnesota Press, 1988); and Benjamin R. Barber, 'Three Challenges to Reinventing Democracy', in Paul Hirst and Sunil Khilnani (eds), *Reinventing Democracy* (Oxford: Blackwell, 1996).
2 Barber, 'Three Challenges to Reinventing Democracy', p. 155.

3  Patrick F. McKinlay, 'Postmodernism and Democracy: Learning From Lyotard and Lefort', in *Journal of Politics*, vol. 60, no. 2 (May 1988), p. 491.

4  Liah Greenfeld, 'Nationalism and Modernity', in *Social Research*, vol. 63, no. 1 (Spring 1996).

5  Richard K. Ashley and R.B.J. Walker, 'Speaking the Language of Exile: Dissidence in International Studies', in *International Studies Quarterly*, vol. 34, no. 3 (September 1990), p. 262.

6  Michel Foucault, *The Order of Things: An Archeology of the Human Sciences* (New York: Vintage, 1994), especially Chapter 7 ('The Limits of Representation').

7  Michel Foucault, 'Governmentality', in Graham Burchell, Colin Gordon and Peter Miller (eds), *The Foucault Effect* (Chicago: University of Chicago Press, 1991).

8  Quoted in Daniela Obradovic, 'Policy Legitimacy and the European Union', in *Journal of Common Market Studies*, vol. 34, no. 2 (June 1996), p. 193.

9  It is best to read here Douglas Coupland, *Life After God* (New York: Pocket Books, 1997).

10  Jean Baudrillard, *Simulacra and Simulation* (Ann Arbor: University of Michigan Press, 1994).

11  Anthony Barnett, 'The Creation of Democracy', in Paul Hirst and Sunil Khilnani (eds), *Reinventing Democracy* (Oxford: Blackwell, 1996), p. 161.

12  Alfred Pijpers, *De Mythe van het Democratisch Tekort. Een Discussiebijdrage over de Europese Politiek* (The Hague: Instituut Clingendael, October 1999); Svein S. Andersen and Kjell A. Eliassen (eds), *The European Union: How Democratic Is It?* (London: Sage, 1996); Brigitte Boyce, 'The Democratic Deficit of the European Community', in *Parliamentary Affairs*, vol. 46, no. 4 (October 1993); Dimitris N. Chryssochoou, *Democracy in the European Union* (London/New York: Tauris Academic Studies, 1998); Paul Close, *Citizenship, Europe and Change* (London: Macmillan, 1995); Soledad Garcia (ed.), *European Identity and the Search for Legitimacy* (London: Pinter, 1993); Juliet Lodge, 'Transparency and Democratic Legitimacy', in *Journal of Common Market Studies*, vol. 32, no. 3 (September 1994); Michael Newman, *Democracy, Sovereignty and the European Union* (New York: St Martin's Press, 1996); and J.H.H. Weiler, 'Legitimacy and Democracy of Union Governance', in Geoffrey Edwards and Alfred Pijpers (eds), *The Politics of European Treaty Reform* (London: Pinter, 1997).

13  Svein S. Andersen and Kjell A. Eliassen, 'Democracy: Traditional Concerns in New Institutional Settings', in Svein S. Andersen and Kjell A. Eliassen (eds), *The European Union: How Democratic Is It?* (London: Sage, 1995), p. 253 (emphasis added).

14  Marcus Höreth, 'The Trilemma of Legitimacy: Multilevel Governance in the EU and the Problem of Democracy', Discussion Paper Series, no. 11 (Bonn: Rheinische Friedrich Wilhelms-Universität, Zentrum für Europäische Integrationsforschung, 1998); Knud Erik Jörgensen (ed.), *Reflective Approaches to European Governance* (London: Macmillan, 1997); and Gary Marks, Fritz W. Scharpf, Philippe C. Schmitter and Wolfgang Streeck, *Governance in the European Union* (London: Sage, 1996). On the problem of transparency, see Lodge, 'Transparency and Democratic Legitimacy'.

15  Simon Hix, 'Elections, Parties and Institutional Design: A Comparative Perspective on European Union Democracy', in *West European Politics*, vol. 21, no. 3 (July 1998), pp. 23–7.

16  J.H.H. Weiler, Ulrich R. Haltern and Franz C. Mayer, 'European Democracy and its Critique', in Jack Hayward (ed.), *The Crisis of Representation in Europe* (London: Frank Cass, 1995).

17  Karlheinz Neunreither, 'Governance without Opposition: The Case of the European Union', in *Government and Opposition*, vol. 33, no. 4 (Autumn 1998), p. 435.

18  Gary Marks, Liesbet Hooghe and Kermit Blank, 'Integration Theory, Subsidiarity and the Internationalisation of Issues: The Implications for Legitimacy', EUI Robert Schuman Centre Working Paper Series, no. 95–7 (Florence: European University Institute, 1995).

19  Zygmunt Bauman, *Modernity and Ambivalence* (Cambridge: Polity Press, 1991); and Bauman, *Intimations of Postmodernity* (London: Routledge, 1992).

20  Zygmunt Bauman, 'The Social Manipulation of Morality: Moralizing Actors, Adiaphorizing Action', in *Theory, Culture and Society*, vol. 8, no. 1 (1991).

21  Quoted in McKinlay, 'Postmodernism and Democracy', p. 493.

22  L.A. Kauffman, 'Democracy in a Postmodern World?', in *Social Policy*, vol. 21, no. 2 (Fall 1990), p. 8.

23  Linda F. Dennard, 'The Democratic Potential in the Transition of Postmodernism', in *American Behavioral Scientist*, vol. 41, no. 1 (September 1997).

24  Thomas Bridges, *The Culture of Citizenship: Inventing Postmodern Civic Culture* (Albany: State University of New York Press, 1994); Aryeh Botwinick, *Postmodernism and Democratic Theory* (Philadelphia: Temple University Press, 1993); Chantal Mouffe, *The Return of the Political* (London: Verso, 1993); and Anne Phillips, *Democracy and Difference* (University Park: Pennsylvania State University Press, 1993).

25  Greenfeld, 'Nationalism and Modernity', p. 11.

26  Jürgen Habermas, *Between Facts and Norms: Contributions to a Discourse Theory of Law and Democracy* (Cambridge MA: MIT Press, 1996), p. 26.

27  Simone Chambers, *Reasonable Democracy: Jürgen Habermas and the Politics of Discourse* (Ithaca NY: Cornell University Press, 1996), especially Chapter 7 ('Jürgen Habermas and Practical Discourse').

28  Dana Villa, 'Postmodernism and the Public Sphere', in *American Political Science Review*, vol. 86, no. 3 (September 1992). Villa actually identifies three objections, but his third problem (an ontological one) is less relevant to the conversation here.

29  Jean-François Lyotard, *The Postmodern Condition: A Report on Knowledge* (Minneapolis: University of Minnesota Press, 1984), p. 63. Lyotard further argues that '[c]onsensus has become an outmoded and suspect value' (p. 66).

30  John Hartley, *The Politics of Pictures: The Creation of the Public in the Age of Popular Media* (London: Routledge, 1992); and David Buckingham, 'News Media, Political Socialization and Popular Citizenship: Towards a New Agenda', in *Critical Studies in Mass Communication*, vol. 14, no. 4 (December 1997). Buckingham argues that the western world is living through a process of fundamental qualitative change in which traditional notions of citizenship are effectively being surpassed, and therefore defines citizenship as a continuous struggle over the means and substance of cultural expression, particularly over those which are made available by the electronic media.

31  Douglas Kellner, 'Techno-Politics, New Technologies, and the New Public Spheres', in *Illuminations: The Critical Theory Website* (no date). Online. Available HTTP: http://www.uta.edu/huma/illuminations (accessed 28 March 2000).

32  Peter Dahlgren, *Television and the Public Sphere: Citizenship, Democracy and the Media* (London: Sage, 1995), p. 148.

33  James Bohman, 'Citizenship and Norms of Publicity: Wide Public Reason in Cosmopolitan Societies', in *Political Theory*, vol. 27, no. 2 (April 1999).

34  Nancy Fraser, 'Rethinking the Public Sphere: A Contribution to the Critique of Actually Existing Democracy', in Craig J. Calhoun (ed.), *Habermas and the Public Sphere* (Cambridge MA: MIT Press, 1993).

35  Seyla Benhabib, *The Reluctant Modernism of Hannah Arendt* (London: Sage, 1996); and Dean C. Hammer, 'Incommensurable Phrases and Narrative Discourse: Lyotard and Arendt on the Possibility of Politics', in *Philosophy Today*, vol. 41, no. 4 (Winter 1997). The quote from Arendt is from Hammer, p. 481.

36  Lyotard, *The Postmodern Condition*, Chapter 6.

37  Chantal Mouffe, 'Decision, Deliberation, and Democratic Ethos', in *Philosophy Today*, vol. 41, no. 1 (Spring 1997), p. 26.

38  Kauffman, 'Democracy in a Postmodern World?', p. 10

39  Ulf Hedetoft, 'The State of Sovereignty in Europe: Political Concept or Cultural Self-Image', in Staffan Zetterholm (ed.), *National Cultures and European Integration:*

*Exploratory Essays on Cultural Diversity and Common Policies* (Providence RI/ Oxford: Berg, 1994), p. 34.

40 Robert A. Dahl, 'The Shifting Boundaries of Democratic Governments', in *Social Research*, vol. 66, no. 3 (Fall 1999).

41 For a good summary account of this debate, see Andrew Linklater, 'Transforming Political Community: A Response to the Critics', in *Review of International Studies*, vol. 25, no. 1 (January 1999).

42 Richard Simeon, 'Citizens and Democracy in the Emerging Global Order', in Thomas J. Courchene (ed.), 'The Nation State in a Global/Information Era: Policy Challenges', John Deutsch Institute for the Study of Economic Policy, The Bell Canada Papers on Economic and Public Policy no. 5 (Kingston, Ontario, 1997).

43 Ulrich Beck, 'Das Demokratie-Dilemma im Zeitalter der Globalisierung', in *Aus Politik und Zeitgeschichte*, no. 38 (11 September 1998).

44 Bridges, *The Culture of Citizenship*, p. 114.

45 Veit Bader, 'Citizenship and Exclusion', in *Political Theory*, vol. 23, no. 2 (May 1995). Eric Hobsbawm has noted that '[a]t the time of the French Revolution, only half of the inhabitants of France could speak French, and only 12–13 percent spoke it "correctly"; and the extreme case is Italy, where at the moment it became a state only 2 or 3 Italians out of a hundred actually used the Italian language at home'. See Eric Hobsbawm, 'Language, Culture, and National Identity', in *Social Research*, vol. 63, no. 4 (Winter 1996), p. 1068.

46 Joseph H. Carens, quoted in Bader, 'Citizenship and Exclusion'.

47 Jürgen Habermas, *Faktizität und Geltung* (Frankfurt a/M: Suhrkamp, 1992), p. 634.

48 Benjamin R. Barber, 'Democracy at Risk: American Culture in a Global Culture', in *World Policy Today*, vol. 15, no. 2 (Summer 1998), p. 30.

49 Philip G. Cerny, 'Paradoxes of the Competition State: The Dynamics of Political Globalization', in *Government and Opposition*, vol. 32, no. 2 (Spring 1997), pp. 258–63.

50 Philip G. Cerny, 'Globalization and Other Stories: The Search for a New Paradigm for International Relations', in *International Journal*, vol. 51, no. 4 (Autumn 1996).

51 *Ibid.*, pp. 635–6.

52 David Miller, 'The Left, the Nation-State, and European Citizenship', in *Dissent*, vol. 45, no. 3 (Summer 1998).

53 Barber, 'Three Challenges to Reinventing Democracy', p. 152.

54 Jocelyn Pixley makes the argument that there can be no genuine citizenship unless all adults are employed. See Pixley, *Citizenship and Employment: Investigating Post-Industrial Options* (Cambridge: Cambridge University Press, 1993).

55 John D. Aram, 'Challenges to the Social Foundations of Capitalism in an Age of Global Economics', in *Human Relations*, vol. 50, no. 8 (August 1997).

56 Ian Budge, *The New Challenge of Direct Democracy* (Cambridge: Polity Press, 1996), p. 176.

57 Christianne Hardy, 'European Political Parties and the European Union: Some Disintegrating Trends of Integration', in *World Affairs*, vol. 157, no. 1 (Summer 1994).

58 Svein S. Andersen and Tom R. Burns, 'The European Union and the Erosion of Parliamentary Democracy: A Study of Post-Parliamentary Governance', in Svein S. Andersen and Kjell A. Eliassen (eds), *The European Union: How Democratic Is It?* (London: Sage, 1995).

59 *Ibid.*, pp. 228–9.

60 Michael Shackleton, 'The Internal Legitimacy Crisis of the European Union', Europa Institute, University of Edinburgh, Occasional Paper Series, no. 1 (1994), p. 5.

61 Matthew Gabel, 'Public Support For European Integration: An Empirical Test of Five Theories', in *Journal of Politics*, vol. 60, no. 2 (May 1998).

62 Matthew Gabel, *Interests and Integration: Market Liberalization, Public Opinion, and European Union* (Ann Arbor: University of Michigan Press, 1998).

63  Obradovic, 'Policy Legitimacy and the European Union', pp. 194–5.

64  Juliet Lodge, 'Federalism and the European Parliament', in *Publius*, vol. 26, no. 4 (Fall 1996); and Mark Shephard, 'The European Parliament: Laying the Foundations for Awareness and Support', in *Parliamentary Affairs*, vol. 50, no. 3 (July 1997).

65  Pierre Manent, 'Democracy Without Nations', in *Journal of Democracy*, vol. 8, no. 2 (April 1997), p. 92 (emphasis in the original).

66  John Locke, *Two Treatises of Government* [1690] (Cambridge: Cambridge University Press, 1988).

67  Manent, 'Democracy Without Nations', pp. 98–9.

68  Jürgen Habermas, *The Structural Transformation of the Public Sphere* (Cambridge MA: MIT Press, 1989).

69  Michael J. Sandel, *Democracy's Discontent: America in Search of a Public Philosophy* (Cambridge MA: Harvard University Press, 1996), especially Chapter 7 ('Community, Self-Government and Progressive Reform').

70  Mark Poster, 'Cyberdemocracy: The Internet and the Public Sphere', in David Holmes (ed.), *Virtual Politics: Identity and Community in Cyberspace* (London: Sage, 1997), p. 225.

71  *Ibid.*, p. 220.

72  Josephine Shaw's overview of European citizenship provides a good introduction to this multi-faceted problem. See Josephine Shaw, 'Citizenship of the Union: Towards Post-National Membership?', Harvard Law School, Jean Monnet Working Papers Series, no. 6 (1997).

73  Seyla Benhabib, 'On European Citizenship', in *Dissent*, vol. 45, no. 4 (Fall 1998).

74  Rogers Brubaker, *Citizenship and Nationhood in France and Germany* (Cambridge MA: Harvard University Press, 1994).

75  Douglas B. Klusmeyer, *Between Consent and Descent: Conceptions of Democratic Citizenship* (Washington DC: Carnegie Endowment for International Peace, 1996), especially Chapter 13.

76  For a feminist reading of this notion of citizenship, see Ruth Lister, 'Dialectices of Citizenship', in *Hypatia*, vol. 12, no. 4 (Fall 1997). Lister argues that 'a feminist reconstruction of citizenship, as both a status and a practice, has to adopt an internationalist and multilayered perspective … [Such a] multilayered conceptualization of citizenship loosens its bonds with the nation-state, so that citizenship is defined over a spectrum which extends from the local to the global, reflecting local and regional pressures for greater political autonomy on the one hand and globalizing tendencies on the other' (p. 10).

77  Rainer Bauböck, 'Citizenship and National Identities in the European Union', Harvard Law School, Jean Monnet Chair Working Paper Series, no. 4 (1997).

78  J.H.H. Weiler, 'The Selling of Europe: The Discourse of European Citizenship in the IGC 1996', Harvard Law School, Jean Monnet Working Paper Series, no. 3 (1996), p. 1. See also J.H.H. Weiler, *The Constitution of Europe* (Cambridge: Cambridge University Press, 1999).

79  Weiler, 'The Selling of Europe', p. 18.

80  Friedrich Kratochwil, 'Citizenship: On the Border of Order', in *Alternatives*, vol. 19, no. 4 (Fall 1994).

81  Andrew Linklater, *The Transformation of Political Community* (Columbia SC: University of South Carolina Press, 1998).

82  For a formal account of marginality, see Sam C. Nolutshungu, 'Introduction', in Sam C. Nolutshungu (ed.), *Margins of Insecurity: Minorities and International Security* (Rochester NY: University of Rochester Press, 1996).

83  Monica den Boer, 'Justice and Home Affairs: Co-operation Without Integration', in Helen Wallace and William Wallace (eds), *Policy-Making in the European Union* (Oxford: Oxford University Press, 1996).

84 Giandomenico Majone, 'Independence and Accountability: Non-majoritarian Institutions and Democratic Government in Europe', EUI Working Paper Series, no. 94–3 (Florence: European University Institute, 1994).

85 Linda K. Kerber, 'The Meanings of Citizenship', in *Dissent*, vol. 44, no. 1 (Fall 1997).

86 Charles K. Wilber, 'Globalization and Democracy', in *Journal of Economic Issues*, vol. 32, no. 2 (June 1998).

87 Anthony Giddens, *Beyond Left and Right: The Future of Radical Politics* (Stanford CA: Stanford University Press, 1995).

88 Philippe C. Schmitter, 'The Future of Democracy: Could it Be a Matter of Scale?', in *Social Research*, vol. 66, no. 3 (Fall 1999), offers a number of possible innovations to improve the political salience of the EU. See also Hazel Henderson, *Paradigms in Progress: Life Beyond Economics* (San Francisco CA: Berrett-Koehler, 1995).

89 'Commission Encourages Public Debate on Institutional Reform', Press Release IP/00/163, 15 February 2000 (Brussels). The European Commission continued its public information and dialogue during the 2000 Intergovernmental Conference (IGC) through its 'Europa' website.

90 The site can be found at http://www.iue.it/AEL/EP/Lex/index.html (accessed 15 March 2000).

91 Jerry Berman and Daniel J. Weitzner, 'Technology and Democracy', in *Social Research*, vol. 64, no. 3 (Fall 1997); and Poster, 'Cyberdemocracy'.

92 For a debate on the democratic internationalist paradigm, see Alan Gilbert, 'Must Global Politics Constrain Democracy?', in *Political Theory*, vol. 20, no. 1 (February 1992).

93 Chantal Mouffe, 'Democracy, Power, and the "Political" ', in Seyla Benhabib (ed.), *Democracy and Difference* (Princeton NJ: Princeton University Press, 1996), p. 254.

94 Ronald Beiner (ed.), *Theorizing Citizenship* (Albany: State University of New York Press, 1995), p. 9.

# 7   Europe and/as the Other

## Alterity, enmity and cultural hybridness

### Europe, alterity and fear

The Cold War and its concomitant Realist discourse has bequeathed Europe an identity/difference dichotomy construed along the dyads Self/Other and order/anarchy. This discursive system of classification has juxtaposed 'the West' as the contemporary guardian of stability and democracy in opposition to 'the rest', which is regarded as potentially threatening and not occupying an identical (or even overlapping) moral/virtuous space.[1] The East–West divide has also offered western states a unique opportunity to accentuate and reinforce the political, economic, social and cultural qualities that they supposedly have in common. The Cold War has focused our attention on the vertical division of the world into sovereign states and has tended to overlook the horizontal forces that cut across borders and boundaries.[2] It has emphasized the role of national territorial power and has given little attention to culture, religion and the frontier-defeating energy of technological change.

Still, the *culture* of the Cold War has dramatically affected the identity of western states, and it can therefore be argued that the anarchy problematic has provided modern states with a solid foundation of meaning and *raison d'être*.[3] As Jim George has noted, the sovereign United States

> can be understood to have construed its global identity in terms of the discourse of anarchy and danger 'external' to it. Its foreign policy, consequently, is accorded an irreducible logic that privileges the theory and practice of power politics in its efforts to respond to the anarchical world it must control for the sake of systemic order.
>
> (Jim George, 'Understanding International Relations After the Cold War', in Michael J. Shapiro and Hayward R. Alker (eds), *Challenging Boundaries: Global Flows, Territorial Identities* (Minneapolis: University of Minnesota Press, 1996), p. 65)

Through the Cold War, western liberal states have constructed their identity as the heroes and saviors of 'freedom' and 'democracy', as the ultimate voice of the 'international community', based on the assumption that capitalism and democracy are universal circumstances superior to all others. This cosmopolitan provincialism has dichotomized a particularistic representation of western selfhood and legitimized the economic and political *status quo* of western society. As a result of the Cold War, the West has acquired a position of leadership and global hegemony whose power resources and dynamic are now being questioned. Not only has this contributed to the development of a specific capitalist world order, it has also had an important effect on the *domestic* arrangements of the western polity and its understanding of the political. Clearly, political discipline and order can more easily be maintained and exercised by stressing the clear and present danger of nuclear war and Soviet infiltration and/or invasion. Domestic cohesion can be better realized and more easily assumed within the classical framework of the Cold War. But, as Ronald Steel has pointed out with reference to the US, 'The "melting pot" was, to some extent, a myth, and it had a lot of lumps'.[4] With the Cold War's centripetal dynamic now depleted, these societal lumps are becoming more obvious and sticky. The demise of the traditional Soviet threat has caused this foundational presence to crumble, and with its departure the western Self has tumbled into a rather traditional crisis of identity.

But this identity crisis goes deeper than the disorienting absence of immediate alterity. Since communism has emerged as a narrative built on the utopian assumptions of the Enlightenment, the same forces that have undermined central planning and bureaucracy have begun to erode the foundations of capitalism. It can be argued that neither socialism nor communism are fundamental alternatives to capitalism, since all three models are simple refractions of modernity. Stjepan Mestrovic has therefore noted that 'all narratives spun from the Enlightenment are now in serious jeopardy in the postmodern era', making him wonder why 'so-called Western nations gloat at the collapse of communism without realizing that the infrastructure of capitalism might be collapsing alongside communism'.[5] Although communism has for decades served faithfully as the reliable Other of western liberal democracy, the sudden disintegration of the dream of rationality and rational state planning has made the West uneasy. By externalizing the critique of liberal democracy and capitalism for more than four decades, the West may have bought time to come to terms with its old internal conflicts, but these conflicts have certainly not been resolved. One could therefore say that the definitive obliteration of communism has plunged liberal democracy into a crisis of identity precisely when it should have been most self-confident and secure. Perhaps the West's victory has been too sudden and too complete, and therefore ultimately Pyrrhic.

The collapse of Big (Br)Other comes at a time when contemporary political practice has eradicated many other systems of exclusion. The cumulative effect of multiculturalism, immigration, global communication and globalization in general has been the erosion of pivotal pillars of national cohesion and the traditional structures of occidental identity. Western society has gradually humanized and accepted the physical presence of formerly subordinate societal categories/groups – women, gays and lesbians, as well as ethnic minorities, indigenous peoples and gypsies. All these groups have been exposed to unjustified practices of exclusion and discrimination which have triggered the closure of communities, encouraged national parochialism and strengthened the state's disciplinary powers. With the *de*demonization of these marginal groups, western society has lost many of its internal and external points of reference, since the notion of a single national culture, however complex, has now become untenable. By emphasizing the multitude of (often transversal) subcultures, the idea of a national culture, 'the notion that members of a group can claim a common history or origin and a specific cultural heritage',[6] is by implication denigrated. Local, regional and transversal group loyalties are built at the obvious expense of a larger, holistic national identity, making the very understanding of a national identity problematic and perhaps even anachronistic.

Globalization and the advance of mass communication have also affected the outlook of ordinary people, who have come to reconsider how others (both as individuals and groups) re-embed and reread themselves in a new global social context. By annihilating distance and borders, the revolutions in travel and telecommunications now make it possible to occupy more than just one site in the national, physical world. Cyberspace is beginning to supplant the existence of Cartesian space, stimulating the 'virtual imagination' of those who surf in it, and encouraging human communication to defy traditional notions of space/time.[7] The Internet offers the dubious privilege of escaping from 'real life' without moving, of communication and existence within multiple temporalities and social sites. In this process of change modern media have become broad and powerful forces in shaping civil society, acting as modeling agents of 'real life', actively intruding into the collective psyche of groups and nations, rearranging the categories of knowledge and experience which form the basis of politics and the political. Media reshape cultural identity by remolding notions of the here/there, now/then, as well as public/private and good/evil. Television viewing plays an especially important role in citizenship formation, determining cultural and political identity by blurring the distinction between them.[8] One certainly does not have to be a disciple of Adorno to accept that media culture now keeps individuals gratified, atomized and subservient to the practices of late capitalism by absorbing and deflecting oppositional cultures (including *national* ones).[9]

The ongoing detraditionalization of western society raises further questions about the centrality of the nation-state as the prime focus of territorial identity.[10] Especially since national sovereignty has been so closely linked to the ultimate right to exclude unwanted bodies, the reconfiguration of Europe's territorial police is disturbing the national founding myth that claims about freedom, democracy, justice and the 'good society' can only be made within strictly demarcated spatial boundaries. The blurring of the inside/outside distinction requires a review of the mental schemes that have for so long determined the political agendas of nation-states. Modern identity is typically conferred by establishing boundaries, by drawing lines to distinguish and separate one community from the other. But this practice of delineation is always also a fundamental act of social and political violence, since an identity forged *vis-à-vis* the Other calls for the continuous policing of these fragile, porous and always temporary borders. Since the Other, by its very existence, is always challenging established borders, always threatening and trying to get in, all identity politics is principally based on forms of aggression. Instead of 'flexible response' and the defense of the Fulda Gap, the strategic discourse is now determined by a dual-track policy of keeping unwanted outsiders out by means of a new definition and delineation of borders and perimeters.

Psychologically, the stereotypified and dehumanized images of the outgroup – the Other – constitutes the basis of the Self: the identity which makes difference 'define' the often hostile relationship between 'us' and 'them'. This may indicate that identity is not simply something to be had; rather it is something achieved and maintained through praxis, formed and reformed in discourse. Alterity implies that the social Self is neither natural nor necessary, but is always evolutionary, developed and constructed. Ever since modernity separated the Self from larger cosmological structures and hierarchies of identity, 'alterity' has become a permanent and inevitable condition of social existence. But this does not imply that the Other has to be the Enemy; alterity does not have to be enmity – at least not always.

For 'Europe' to know its Self, it must look into the rather shadowy mirror of all that does *not* belong to Europe. This is a systemic effort, since one could certainly argue that 'making an Order is making an Other'.[11] The Other therefore plays a central role in fostering the senses of cultural homogeneity and collective identity that forms the somewhat crude building blocs of international society.[12] Since identity is inconceivable without alterity, contrasting the sense of community with difference is unavoidable and therefore rather unremarkable. Foucault has indicated that the Other is usually perceived as an abnormal, often delinquent, person. He has argued that social consensus is produced by mechanisms of exclusion, by stigmatizing as outcasts those who fail to comply to the dominant image of rationality, normality and modern responsibility.[13] The Other is therefore not merely someone else; but its very existence implies disorder, and his/her presence in our midst represents an anomaly and a latent pathology for the healthy social organism. Frequently, the Other objectifies the evil of our own society by attributing and projecting it on the empty screen of alterity. These psychological mechanisms are especially relevant for understanding Europe's postmodern anguish, now that traditional moorings like the nation-state, the national currency and cradle-to-grave welfare security have given way to Europeanization, the Euro and greater individualization. It is clear that, with the end of the East–West divide and its Manichean clarity of good/evil, postmodern anxiety and the nostalgia for closed and stable communities has grown. As Pierre Hassner has argued, 'Individual, social and national insecurity, the preoccupation with law and order, jobs and the nation are thus combined into one complex syndrome in which external threats and internal doubts are hard to disentangle'.[14]

But alterity does not have to manifest itself in present-day; it may also have a clear historical character. Ole Wæver, for example, has made a case that the rhetoric of the European project has always emphasized the need for co-operation as the only way to avoid revisiting Europe's conflictual past.[15] Russell Berman has aptly noted that '[p]erhaps Germans are so pro-European less because they are, like Nietzsche, "good Europeans", but because trading their national identity for a regional one, they think they can escape the burden of being German'.[16] Along similar lines, Thomas Risse-Kappen *et al.* have argued that 'Europe's "Other" in the German political discourse is constructed as the continent's and – more important – Germany's own past of wars and nationalist excesses'.[17] For Germany, the notion of the Other, the non-European, can be found in the authoritarianism, militarism, anti-Semitism and nationalism of its own national past. For German policy-makers, the option of a renewed Teutonic hegemony over Europe has to be foreclosed by tying down the German Gulliver with the many small strings of a law-based organization like the EU. One of the principal goals of EMU and the CFSP has been to bring German economic and political power under the EU's multilateral umbrella. Former German Bundeskanzler Helmut Kohl illustrated this sentiment in a controversial and much debated speech, when he remarked that, '[T]he policy of European integration is really a question of war and peace in the 21st century', and added that 'if we suffer a setback now on the road to Europe it will take considerably longer than one generation before we are given such an opportunity again ... this will not only lead to standstill but also retrogression'.[18]

In many respects this may be considered a continuation of what has been the traditional role of the European integration process since the 1950s: to accommodate Germany's economic resources and political weight inside a European framework. In contemporary Germany, to question the course and pace of European integration automatically raises suspicions of an innate desire for a German *Sonderweg*, a German unilateralism that may ultimately provoke a renaissance of nationalism and everything that stands for Germany's own bloody past.

But Germany also projects its own national past on the future of Europe. Its aversion to blunt power-political rivalry and its postnationalist rhetoric continues to set the tone for debate in European circles, emphasizing the need for democracy and human rights (in contrast to Germany's – and Europe's – own conflict-ridden history), as well as for a social market economy (in contrast to Soviet-style communism and Anglo-Saxon *laissez-faire* capitalism).[19] In his study of German security policy after unification, John Duffield has pointed out that these cultural factors play an important, if not decisive role, in shaping state behavior.[20] German history is an integral element of its postwar identity, which therefore calls for a constructivist reading of German politics, rather than a confined Realist conception limited to narrow 'national interests'. This indicates that the German notion of Self is not based on a liberating amnesia (although questions are now beginning to be asked about whether Germany should not finally put an end to its somewhat masochistic routine of memory and remembrance of the Holocaust).[21] It also helps to explain why many German politicians (especially those on the 'left' of the political spectrum) have reacted so violently against the challenge of European values by Haider's FPÖ in Austria. By excluding this populist party from the legitimate public debate, Germany again tries to exorcise its own past and future fascist bias. Both the concept of Europe and the idea of 'the Other' therefore remain at the core of contemporary Germany's postnational identity.[22] These notions are neither pure invented communities or traditions, nor pure fabrications, but they are elements of a flexi-identity that responds to the requirements of the day.

## Europe's narrative identity and the resident Other

The German reading of identity illustrates that Paul Ricoeur's ontology of the Self, which is not based on homogeneity and permanence but on the narrative, is central to understanding European reality.[23] Clearly, in a world where Others seem to proliferate in their particularity, it is necessary to explain and contextualize identity and to conduct a subversive reading of fixed concepts of identity and essence. This is the role played by the narrative, which has one foot in history and one in fiction and treats the Self as a character in a plot that can be reread and changed, if possible or if needed.[24] Events can be rearranged and reinterpreted to provide a different background for the plot that provides the character its identity and relationship to the Other(s). The narrative transforms daily occurrences into necessary episodes by providing the context and reading the links with other events. It leaves room for the reinvention of the past, based on the notion that identity is open-ended and derived from practice through mobile and fluid social relationship. Narrative identity therefore offers the challenge of creating a dynamic sense of Self which defies the incompatible categories of identity/diversity that underpin our place and role in society.[25]

Julia Kristeva has further argued that we are not only confronted with alterity, but that Otherness is always within ourselves; the alien is the hidden face of our own identity. Kristeva therefore claims that keeping this 'alienness' at a safe distance will prevent us from keeping *ourselves* together.[26] By confusing the multiple, mobile and metamorphic reality that is ours with the unchanging representations that we distil from it, we impose arbitrary divisions and turn them into metaphysical entities. This is what Marc Fumaroli has referred to as the 'grave of identity', arguing that the 'hardening of living singularities into a barren "identity" spiked with defenses is always the final stage of their withering away, of their drying out'.[27] Kristeva's position is closely related to Ricoeur's notion of the Self as an Other, to the idea that remaining reliable to others is a central element of the Self. Otherness does not have external origins, but should be seen as part of the meaning and the ontological constitution of selfhood. The Self should not pretend to occupy a foundational center, but Otherness and selfhood blend like the skin and flesh of a living body. In this sense, '[s]elfhood implies a "lived" otherness, of which the flesh is the foundation'.[28] Ricoeur therefore suggests that only by remaining open and reliable to the Otherness of the Self, egotism and ethnocentrism may be avoided because it implies a readiness for discourse and offers an horizon of equality.

Iris Marion Young has therefore argued that the '[n]arrative fosters understanding across differences without making those who are different symmetrical'.[29] Young describes three ways in which the narrative does justice to the postmodern circumstance of difference. First, 'the narrative reveals the particular experiences of those in social locations, experiences that cannot be shared by those situated differently but that they must understand in order to do justice to the others'. Storytelling plays this crucial role by fostering understanding for those who cannot share these particular experiences. Second, the narrative 'reveals a source of values, culture, and meaning'. Young implies that conflicts often arise due to differences in value premises, cultural practices and meaning, and that only the narrative may explain to outsiders what these practices, places and symbols actually mean to the people involved. Finally, the narrative is often also able to reveal more comprehensive forms of social knowledge, offering others insight into how 'their own position, actions, and values appear to others from the stories they tell'. The narrative is therefore not only a central means of communication, digging deeper than the simple exchange of opinions, but it is also the mirror that individuals, groups and nations show each other: a mirror that reflects the Other as well as singular parts of the Self.

Although in the identity game the Self is both an actor and a vector, driven both by choice and by fatal circumstance, an argument can be made that to be free is to a large extent to be free to identify and to read one's own identity independent of the Other.[30] This would be the ultimate unencumbered Self which rests on a voluntarist and disembodied conception of identity, the notion that self-understanding and values are *not* shaped through community-mediated, communicative processes of socialization but are instead the product of personal choice and preference. Although a case can be made that certain sites of identity are individual, private and based on decisional autonomy, national identity seems almost by definition socially and historically embedded.[31] No group or imagined community is a solipsistic presocietal entity which constructs its identity in isolation from others. Derrida's work clearly indicates that there is nothing outside the (con)text, and that any particular meaning or identity also carries with it the structural and necessary possibility of its own sabotage by alternative recontextualizations or re-inscriptions. Denis-Constant Martin has therefore pointed out that narrative identity is never produced only from inside the Self, but that it 'is formed as much because others believe it exists'. This would imply that imagined communities are formed not only – or even primarily – because their members, or supposed members, believe in them or identify with them, but that 'being ascribed to a group may force people who would not have considered themselves members to join the organizations set up to defend it'.[32] Clearly, Europe's narrative identity is not authored by 'Europe' alone, but is written and continuously rewritten and reread by ordinary people and political elites both 'inside' and 'outside' Europe's fuzzy boundaries. Since (as Judith Butler has argued) identity is to a large extent 'performative' and contextual, 'the rules governing signification not only restrict, but enable the assertion of alternative domains of cultural intelligibility'.[33] Politics therefore resembles a market place for identity narratives, all vying for influence and support and calling for (often blind) faith. The important thing to note is that in this competition for allegiance there are always a number of identity narratives available, which makes the signification of the Self at least in part a matter of discretion.

For contemporary postmodern Europe, this is a very relevant debate. Especially since we are not simply talking about a clearly identifiable external Other (as during the Cold War), but also about inner alterity: the 'resident Other'.[34] With its millions of (illegal) immigrants and denizens, Europe has many minority groups within its boundaries that are perceived to injure its cultural and social cohesion. The resident Other is not comfortably spatially distant, but often lives across the street and confronts us with different mores, values and practices that challenge hegemonic cultural patterns. Immigrants, refugees, asylum-seekers are the new 'peripheral peoples'; they are ex-colonials, usually second-class citizens that add to the cultural hybridness of western nation-states.[35] They are immigrants now settling in post-imperial countries who often have dual citizenship; they are permanent residents or naturalized citizens whose experience of citizenship often remains ambiguous and who have mixed the liberal democratic narrative of political and civil society with their own often confused and confusing experiences and cultural backgrounds. These marginal populations that reside in European host societies are raising serious questions about pluralism and representation; they are instilling doubt about the validity of established frameworks of civil society and the rules of the emerging Euro-polity.[36]

Clearly, few European countries can continue the fiction of the rational and hierarchical culture of modernity, since the totalizing impulse of the ideal of (national) community is now denied by the intrusion of visible, touchable and increasingly vocal and active resident Others. In the not too distant past, immigrants and refugees were coerced to become 'like us', to accommodate and conform to hegemonic societal norms and cultural mores, with the melting pot as the ultimate centripetal mechanism producing the 'good citizen'. Although the minimum loyalty demanded of new peripheral peoples remains based on the Habermasian foundation of 'constitutional patriotism', postmodern European society has become less uneasy with the new kinds of cultural and political localities, the new neighborhoods, churches and schools that visualize the oppositional differentiation along (among others) racial, religious and class lines.[37] These new peripheral identities have become permanent fixtures of the societies in which they reside, without the requirement of conforming to all dominant moral principles. Since postmodern society is fragmented along multiple lines and contains many alternative lifestyles, peripheral peoples are 'just' one marginal grouping among many.

These resident Others are making a major contribution to the development of western society into what Foucault has called a heterotopia, a place where things are different (rather than good or bad).[38] European society no longer cherishes the dream of utopia, but its multifarious lines of fracture and (un)veiled lineages makes it clear that these 'other places' silently question the social and political space in which we live. In many ways, European society has come to resemble the postmodern airport, this ultimate 'bubble of discontinuity in the social and geographical landscape', where travelers from all over the world touch each other without absorbing each other's cultural assumptions.[39] European society no longer aims at integrating the resident Other, but instead accepts that the difference of those who are different does not really (or no longer) make much difference. This postmodern condition, where thesis (normality) and antithesis (the Other) do not provoke synthesis (which may take forms as diverse as the Holocaust or affirmative action), has added to the collapse of the grand narratives of national sovereignty and progress through politics.

## Security, Kosovo and the balkanization/integration nexus

This is most evident in the area of heroic politics, a site where the nation-state still considers itself to be most conspicuously glorious. Western nation-states have clearly shifted their tone and rhetorical maneuvers in their security discourse, exchanging the grand narrative of ideological and nuclear threats for a more diverse debate about security challenges derived from multiple guerrilla tactics aimed at national purity and sovereignty. As Walker has argued, security policy 'is not just a matter of defense against external threat. It is also the site at which particular political communities become aware of the limits to their own claim to pursue universalizing standards of conduct'. By pooling their national sovereignty within the EU, European nation-states have shifted 'the point at which democracy, openness, and legitimate authority must dissolve into claims about *Realpolitik, raison d'état*, and the necessity of violence'.[40] Lene Hansen has further noted that, rather than simply viewing security policies as strategies for defending a state (or alliances of states), 'it should be analyzed as one of the most important practices through which states construct their identity'.[41] Any debate about 'national security', or the formulation of a 'national security strategy', ultimately becomes an exercise in constructing (national) identity – the (national) Self – by examining outside threats and challenges and by focusing on the differences between the 'inside' (the state) and the 'outside'.

Like sovereignty, security is not so much an ontological given, with a stable meaning, as the site of a continuous political struggle in which the nature of statehood may be inferred from practice and experience. All efforts to define, redefine and reconstruct security therefore engage in a wider political practice to stabilize the concept's definition and purpose. Wæver has argued that 'security' lacks a generic concept, but that it has a clear temporal dimension derived from an established set of practices. The label of 'security', says Wæver, 'has become the indicator of a specific problematique, a specific field of practice',[42] in which the state determines the rules of the (language) game. In terms of semiotics, 'security' is therefore not a signifier (indicator) which refers back to a referent (which it is supposed to represent), but the

> utterance *itself* is the act. By saying it, something is done (as in betting, giving a promise, naming a ship). By uttering 'security,' a state-representative moves a particular development into a specific area, and thereby claims a special right to use whatever means are necessary to block it.
>
> (Ole Wæver, 'Securitization and Desecuritization', in Ronnie D. Lipschutz (ed.), *On Security* (New York: Columbia University Press, 1995), pp. 54–5)

Security has thereby become an act; the word and concept itself has become its primary reality, providing the state with special rights and privileges. By fixing the meaning of security (always in spatial and temporal dimensions), security thereby *de facto* writes the state.

Wæver identifies three major problems with this statal hegemony over the security discourse. First, it tends to imply that any response to a security problem, risk or perceived threat is to be expected first and foremost from the state. Second, the concept of security tends to reinforce the logic of nationalism and Manichean 'us/them' thinking grounded in the tradition of viewing threats as coming from the 'outside' (i.e., outside the state's own borders). This also tends to encourage a militarization of our thinking. Finally, since the concept of security is basically defensive, it tends to defend the *status quo* and thereby precludes alternative realities that may be preferable to that which *is*. Wæver summarizes his arguments in his claim that '[w]hen a problem is "securitized," the act tends to lead to specific ways of addressing it: Threat, defense, and often state-centered solutions'.[43] The discourse of security is therefore not a neutral, academic terrain, but a continuous struggle for political power, access to resources and the authority to articulate new definitions and priorities of security. 'Security' is therefore a socially constructed concept which emerges from its discourse (Wæver's 'speech act') and from the discursive practices that constitute the ever-shifting boundaries and capacities of sovereign states and the interpretive communities in which they are embedded.

It is through this discursive practice that state-based sovereignty has denied thinking space for alternative options of regional and global order. These arguments clearly illustrate that the demands for different notions of security call for a radically different understanding of political identity. Since the familiar pattern of identification has been along the rigidly policed lines of national sovereignty, alternative resolutions between national particularity and transversal universality are problematic and confusing. The natural reaction to calls for such a different approach, as Walker argues, is usually the riposte that these alternative models of political community are all very well, 'but what about the … … (fill in the name of your favorite enemy of the moment)?'[44] 'Security' therefore now mainly has (following Baudrillard's nomenclature) an 'alibi function': it tries to assert the 'realness' of the state and its components; it tries to reaffirm and discursively frame and read that which it is supposed to signify in the first place. But, given the continued hollowing out of the territorial state, this has become increasingly difficult. Especially in Europe, the idea of 'national security' fails to pass most serious reality checks, which may explain why the anemic notion of 'European security' is now being reinscribed with new meanings and given a new lease of life in the invigorated context of post-Cold-War European integration.

In the context of the process of European integration this concept has become extremely relevant. For decades, EU Member States have been reluctant to develop a common European foreign, security and defense policy recognizing that sharing responsibility on security and defense would undermine their cherished national identity and limit their options for defining their national Self *vis-à-vis* their favorite Other. But, with the signing of the Maastricht and Amsterdam treaties, EU Member States have delegated major chunks of their national sovereignty to the European level, most notably monetary policy and (increasingly) competence over matters like internal justice (policing) and immigration. The Europeanization of security is now bound to follow the well-trodden path of economic, social and political integration in the EU context. For the time being, the EU has hardly been able to assert itself in the field of heroic politics and is competing with potent statal claims to 'security'. But, like organizations such as NATO, the EU's emerging 'desire for security is manifested as a collective resentment of difference – that which is not us, not certain, not predictable'.[45] The 'enemy' of Europe's volatile identity is thereby defined as the 'unknown', the 'unpredictable' and the 'unstable'. By reading Europe's Other in this way, the meaning of 'European security' is stabilized as an effort to limit the plurality of the continent's centers, to limit its multiple meanings to a strict canon and a fixed site, and to solidify the current fluidity of Europe's identity.

The process of European security integration is therefore likely to be advanced through the construction of a European Self (instead of a more narrowly defined national Self), which would in turn outline itself through a debate focused on European security (rather than a more narrowly based debate on national security) and *ipso facto* by contrasting itself with the non-European (resident and outside) Other. Nowhere have these margins of modernity been more clearly marked than in Kosovo during the war of the self-proclaimed 'international community' against Yugoslavia in the Spring of 1999 (they were also apparent, earlier and less distinctly, in Bosnia).[46] After the dissolution of the Federal Republic of Yugoslavia, rump Yugoslavia (nicknamed 'Serbia') became identified as the strange and alien entity that threatens European security by its ethnic and sectarian essentialism, its barbarian methods of 'ethnic cleansing' and its altogether premodern values, attitude and practices. In short, Serbia does not stick to the carefully crafted script of 'European' conduct. By falling out of line, by not accepting the rationales of European integration and European security, Serbia has come to pose the main challenge to the emerging New European Order (NEO). By ignoring the logic of NEO-realism, Serbia has brought to the fore the question that European policy-makers and theorists have tried to ignore: On which stable foundations can 'European security' be constructed?

From a Foucauldian perspective, it is here that the story of NATO's military intervention against Serbia (as well as its Montenegrin appendix) may tell us how the West's disciplinary power has been involved in the actual production of 'European security'. This is a story of the discursive production of an operational meaning along the lines laid out by Cynthia Weber, who has argued that 'intervention is understood as the flip side of sovereignty ... And what it means to violate sovereignty is decided by theorists when they operationalize the meaning of intervention'.[47] In Europe's security discourse, 'Kosovo' therefore tends to allegorize the balkanization of Europe: the ultimate metaphor of chaos and disintegration, the supposed antithesis of the 'real' Europe of peace and stability. As Wæver argued in this context, 'Balkanization is a tool for legitimizing an international order *without* a named enemy ... "Security" thus becomes shorthand for the argument: We have to do everything to ensure that integration, and not fragmentation, is the outcome'.[48] To speak of Serbia as the ultimate threat to 'European security' is to imply the very existence and strategic relevance of the concept of security through integration. Kosovo therefore serves as a useful alibi for the stabilization of what 'European security' actually means by operationalizing it through military intervention. Thanks to these acts of stabilization, Kosovo has written (and continues to write) European security.

The story of Kosovo tells us that those political actors who do not accept NEO-realism, who defy the logic of integration and co-operation, *de facto* deny their Europeanness, their family resemblances to other European (Family) Member States, and should expect to face the serious consequences.[49] Serbia's irruption into premodern savagery in the 'heart of Europe' has offered the rest of Europe a not-to-be-missed chance to manifest and constitute itself as the pinnacle of modern, rational civilization. Serbia's killing of Kosovo sets the parameters of the balkanization/integration nexus, offering 'Europe' (and the West in general) a unique opportunity to suggest itself as the strong center that keeps the margins from running away.

The discourse of 'European security' therefore produces a parallel paradigm of *European* sovereignty – a paradigm that faces serious challenges of local resistance (of the still-resilient state) – and external opposition (which questions the notion of 'Europe' as a privileged space of peace and stability).[50] It is on these unruly frontiers and borders that the concept of 'European security' is being challenged and problematized. Balkanization testifies to the recalcitrant domain of anarchy within Europe, a domain that must be subdued by the sovereign figure of the 'international community'. Whereas 'Europe' should stand for the sovereign center of domesticated territory and originary presence, Kosovo stands for the continuity of 'international politics', the inside/outside divide that privileges and legitimizes the domestic space of identity and continuity over the anarchic space of difference and discontinuity. It is this residual Balkan space that still seems to escape the rational truth of 'integration' and 'reasonable humanity', and must therefore be silenced and disciplined.

It is also in these locations where the new mode of NEO-realism, of order, is being produced, and occasionally imposed. Without the clear signs of 'War' and 'Security' as the inscription of international dangers, 'there would be no notion of a well-bounded domestic social identity – a population of sovereign men who know themselves to be at one with a social totality that is imperiled'.[51] Kosovo therefore illustrates Shapiro's argument that enmity and war are essential for the maintenance of a coherent society and body politic.[52] Since security is what takes politics beyond the ordinary, beyond the established rules of the game,[53] it allows (and even calls for) extraordinary measures to be taken to address the existential threat. The novelty with Kosovo is that this mode of statecraft is not being practised in a statal context; it is in the name of 'Europe' that a new narrative of modernity is constructed to fabricate and rationalize *European* domestic society *vis-à-vis* the unruliness and backwardness of the Balkan fringe. It is in the name of 'European security' that boundaries are drawn to discipline the behavior of those within and to distinguish 'Europe' from the Other. By altering the referent of security as speech act, 'Europe' is *de facto* finding and constructing itself.

It is therefore all the more fitting that the writing of 'European security' is being done in the only true hyperreal country in the world, since the Federal Republic of Yugoslavia does not really exist (and has never existed *de jure* as a sovereign state).[54] Perhaps this is exactly the sort of anomaly that can find no place in the NEO-realism of the twenty-first century, the sort of (what Weber calls) 'formless feminine fluids' that must provoke 'Europe' to use its 'stabilizing influence ... so [it] may heterosexually serve masculine purposes'.[55] Kosovo stands for an understanding of 'European security' that legitimates the use of military force in order to *de*legitimate the use of military force. It is the site where people are being killed and bombs being dropped for the sake of stability, peace and human rights. It is the domain where the forces of integration and balkanization do battle, since 'the multiculturalist doctrine that is fragmenting our universities as well as our intellectual life, and the "ethnic cleansing" of the Serbs, belong to the same troubling cultural and historical moment'.[56] In Kosovo, Europe is fighting itself in a narcissist attempt to get rid of the undesirable, of chaos and anarchy.

Kosovo is therefore both the *pre*text and the ultimate *con*text in which the contemporary reading of 'European security' is taking place. But it remains problematic to accept the Other as a legitimate ontology, mainly because doing so raises the possibility 'of accepting the Other's characteristics as a legitimate alternative and, consequently, of being taken over by the Other'.[57] The Milosevic regime has never been the opposite of the New European Order, but rather its ultimate symptom, its hyperreal foundation from which a new mode of order now seems to be emerging.[58] In this sense, therefore, Baudrillard was correct when he argued that the real story is that the Serbs, 'as vehicles of ethnic cleaning, are at the forefront of the construction of Europe. For it is being constructed, the real Europe, the white Europe, a Europe whitewashed, integrated and purified, morally as much as economically or ethnically'.[59]

Obviously, this would be a high price for Europe to pay. By delineating its identity in terms of security, Europe would inevitably reinforce the exclusionary logic of Us/Them, which will encourage a psychological drawbridge mentality that will inhibit the heterogeneity and tolerance, openness and universality which Europe is said to treasure. Defining 'Europe' through security will therefore be a risky enterprise, since it would endanger the very basis of the social and cultural elements of its identity. The securitization of the debate on Europe's identity and its role as an economic and political actor on the world stage might therefore prove to be a double-edged sword: while it might provide impetus for a more cohesive European approach to security matters by mirroring traditional patriotism and nationalism on a European level, it will simultaneously foreclose alternative and more generous readings of the new European polity. The EU's new defense ambitions (initiated at the EU's Helsinki summit of December 1999) are therefore a risky enterprise, not only because they may undermine NATO's hegemony in Europe (which should not be the main concern) but also because they testify to the EU's shift from a civilian power to a Euro-polity which takes on the attributes of a classic, full-fledged nation-state, including the desire to control its domestic and neighboring space by military means.

How, then, is this Europe to situate itself? I would like to suggest that Europe (however defined) has three central points of reference, three Others that have a bearing on its self-understanding and its place and role in global politics. The United States seems to be read as Europe's postmodern future; Russia as Europe's anarchic past; and Islam as the ultimate Other, undermining the remaining ethical/ethnic foundations of European society. These are simplified stereotypes that may reveal much more about the understanding of Europe of itself than of the Others which it takes as its subject.

## America as Europe's postmodern coming

Why is it that most Europeans both loath and love the United States? This ambivalence, clearly reciprocal, crystallizes in the love/hate relationships between Americans and France as well as between 'Washington' and 'Paris'. The simplest and most straightforward answer would be that Europeans both dread and adore American culture because they consider it to be their own future; Americans long for (as well as despise) European culture out of a nostalgic hankering after communal belonging and historical rootedness. These are the powerful clichés that color (and often fog) the lenses of transatlantic perception.

Most relevant for our conversation here is that the occasional rhetoric of 'cultural war' between the (alleged) unique diversity of Europe and the homogeneity of 'Hollywood' provides a basis for conceiving American culture, and the American way of life, as a threat to a still imaginary and embryonic European identity. The dichotomy between European and American culture is problematic and certainly cannot be simplified as the opposition of cultural refinement, on the one hand, and vulgar superficial 'mass culture' on the other. However, it should be clear that the stubborn individuality and variety of

Europe, of European tastes, mores and cultures, hardly lends itself to the 'economies of scale' that can be achieved through global TV programming, addressing a global audience with similar images and cultural icons. At the same time, the fact remains that, somewhat paradoxically, the 'United States produces – and has long produced – the moving images that most easily traverse European national barriers',[60] although these are the easy-traveling, vacuum-sealed and deep-frozen commercialized images that are usually not rooted in Europe's biography and not (yet) embedded in Europe's multiple narratives. However, with late capitalism embracing ephemerality as the ultimate quality of cultural production, cultural rootedness and the very idea of the geographical *location* of identity seem to have become archaisms. What we have for centuries considered to be the holy expression of national identity, 'culture' has become the main commodity for entrepreneurial and capitalistic activity.[61] Aesthetics has become commercialized to the bone and caters to the most marginalized cultural niche markets imaginable, mobilizing and manipulating human emotions and desires to continue uninterrupted production and consumption. Modern media manipulate meaning and give expression to the seemingly irreconcilable extremes of an unstable social habitat without offering shared points of reference regarding values, meaning and identity (apart from the postmodern cogito: 'I consume, therefore I am'). How can small European nation-states (and *all* European nation-states are small) even hope to continue putting their gloss on the national narrative, maintain the hegemonic fiction of national uniqueness, chosenness and particularity?

Since it is the US that is driving the dynamics of globalization, European nation-states are reluctant to give in to the postmodern temptation of not only accepting, but actually celebrating cultural shallowness as a marker of equality and the transitory meaning of moral categories. Can Europe maintain its assumed organic societal structure based on solidarity and cohesion in the face of global competition and the demise of the welfare state? Are Europeans prepared to go with the market as the new center of self-constitution, accepting that market standards derived from globalized practices will dominate, and perhaps even completely replace, the political and moral responsibilities of (national) governments? Americans seem perfectly willing to accept consumer-oriented freedom, mainly because it reflects the central assumption upon which the American Dream is based: fortune is a matter of personal commitment and hard work. But where Americans may envision a dream, most Europeans tend to see little more than the fetishism of superficiality and the empty embrace of value-free multiformity. For Europe, the United States seems to embody what Stuart Ewen has called 'pragmatism's postmodern poltergeist':[62] the deep peril of a society in which democracy can be found on supermarket shelves, the realm of imagination is dominated by economic exploitation and the citizen is considered a consumer of decisions.

This cultural chasm between America and Europe is not confined to the realm of aesthetics and personal taste. As we discussed in an earlier chapter, the political-economic logic of globalization also relates to how nation-states define their identity and defend their claim to authority within their territorial space. The prevailing view in the US is that culture is (and should be) devoted to entertainment, and should therefore be part of the global arrangements that guarantee free trade. Although opinions in Europe vary considerably, the general European concept of culture assumes a distinct relation between national culture and identity, between cultural difference and the *raison d'état* of Europe's statal patchwork. Mel van Elteren has summarized this discourse under three headings: Europe vs. America, culture vs. commerce and culture vs. national identity.[63] Van Elteren makes a clear case for a more nuanced and less rigid binary division between America and Europe, and for recognition of the intricate interplay between both cultures. Europe only borrows selectively from what America has to offer and often forgets about the other, more complex face(s) of American culture which do(es) not make it across the Atlantic.

Van Elteren further argues that the culture/commerce dyad should be problematized, since no rules can be designed to distinguish between cultural products available to the free market and works preserved for the benefit of the public of a particular country. A final element in the America/Europe conversation is that for all European states national culture produces national identity through a complex and selective process of memory, readings of the present and projections of the future. Just as American icons like Mickey Mouse are thinly disguised forms of the national self-image of incorruptible innocence,[64] European culture tells and reads its own stories, (re)inventing its traditions and (re)formulating and (re)capturing its desires and fears. Clearly, one of its fears is that the American Other, crystallized in the Hollywood film studios, will now do the storytelling for Europe and the rest of the world, offering synthesized versions of such essential elements of human history as colonialism and the Holocaust, as well as determining the limits of humor and drama.[65] Especially since European identity is narrative and performative, it is a widely held view that it should be Europe that does the talking and acting.

Although it is clear that America is just one rung higher on the current ladder of the market and the commodification of culture than Europe, the step that still separates minds across the Atlantic is an important one. In looking at the US, Europeans have the impression that they are – again – looking at their own future, and they clearly have mixed feelings about it. Europeans may sense that what little rootedness in the texture of nature and life they may still have left, will be washed away by globalization and what is still pejoratively called 'Americanization': a growing gap between rich and poor, crime and violence and increasing family breakdown. Former President of the European Commission Jacques Delors has phrased Europe's ambivalence aptly by arguing that '[o]ne cannot help but admire the resilience, adaptability and competitiveness of American society but be horror struck at the crime, violence and growing income inequality'. For Delors, Europe's lesson from American experience is this: While we say yes to a market economy, we must say no to 'market society'. A 'market economy for prosperity, yes. But only the rule of democracy can ensure social cohesion and the quality of life'.[66] Europe continues to cling to its post-World-

War-II social model based on high living standards and egalitarianism embedded in a social welfare state. It knows that, whereas the American labor market is more flexible and its workforce more mobile, the consequent low level of unemployment comes with low wages and without generous social benefits. The American hire-and-fire mentality comes at too high a price for most Europeans – but there is a gut feeling that this price may be forced upon them by the dynamics of globalization.

The bundling of traditional economic and postmodern cultural forces therefore offers an awesome arsenal of soft and 'hard' instruments of power to America's political elite. The process of cultural synchronization is grounded in the logic of late capitalism, which is preparing the ground for an American dominance of money and minds, of commerce and culture. American culture serves not only to prompt its consumers to 'think American' but, perhaps more importantly, to induce its audiences to *buy* American goods and to promote the American way of life. The Greek-born filmmaker Constantin Costa-Gavras has therefore called for strict limits on the 'American occupation' of global culture, arguing that people all over the world 'will have lost their souls completely in fifteen years' time if there is no protection. It is not that they will become Americans. They will become nothing, not even themselves. They will be tourists in their own country'.[67] Since Europeans are gradually losing their traditional roots, their particularistic moorings and mores, 'America' has become the ultimate cultural Other on which most of the accumulated postmodern *Angst* is projected. The social Darwinism of late capitalism is on display across the United States for all European tourists and (M)TV audiences to see, and for Europe's youth to decipher from gangsta rap lyrics.

This mixed bag of culturally discomforting and disquieting feelings *vis-à-vis* America filters through into the discomfort and disquiet that Europeans experience when they appraise their own integration process. The Europeanization of commerce and culture offers Europe's peoples and nation-states a kind of refuge, a semi-safe sanctuary from the forces of globalization. But by strengthening their communal lines of defense, Europeans are becoming increasingly aware that they are emulating the American federalist, single-currency, free-trading experience. The reluctance of at least part of Europe's political elite to embrace further steps toward European unification can be explained by its trepidation of becoming more and more like Them, of accepting Their standards of behavior and morals. The fact that the US has become the world's single superpower has not really helped to make Europe more comfortable and at ease with its current condition of inadequacy. NATO and the traditionally strong transatlantic link sustain the idea that Europe and America occupy the same moral site, that they form the nucleus and pinnacle of the 'international community' which is now called upon to judge and police global misdeeds and wrongs. But post-Cold-War experience has indicated that Europe has become little more than an at times hopeless and helpless sidekick of American hegemony. Nowhere has this become more disturbingly obvious than with the series of Balkan wars (and the Kosovo experience in particular), where it continues to be the US that sets both the tone and the pace of western policy and response.

Students of Gramsci will be aware that the exercise of hegemony not simply depends on raw physical power but also on shared norms and perceptions of what is legitimate action. Europe is at times called upon to provide Washington with the moral support and political weight to ensure that its military interventions in Iraq, its occasional bombings of 'terrorists' and its unilateralism in Bosnia/Kosovo are not based on naked power but have a wider, multilateral basis of support. But these intermittent outbreaks of European canned applause should not fool anyone. As Martin Walker has argued, '[f]or some $250 billion a year, the United States enjoys a global military dominance that combines the transoceanic reach of the Pax Britannica with the military power of Imperial Rome at the height of its powers'.[68] For Europe, it is both comfortable and highly disturbing to have the US as its best friend and to realize that for the moment and the foreseeable future there is little that may fundamentally spoil this long-standing association. The twentieth century has seen America twice saving Europe from itself, which makes Europeans both keen to maintain the momentum of continental integration as well as rightfully reluctant to undermine their live-saving transatlantic partnership. The hope of most participants in this delicate process is that, although further EU integration is bound to undermine the existing precarious arrangement of European political servitude, 'the West' will continue to remain a viable notion, comprising a less presumptuous and overconfident US and a more radiant and sanguine 'Europe'.

## Russia and the terror of anarchy

Europe has been subject to the continuous deconstruction of its own meaning and identity, involving competing allegiances, values and involvements. A major element of this incessant challenging of its own image and meaning has been its eastward open-endedness, the geographical fact that Europe is an unenclosed subcontinent sitting on the end of a vast land mass that stretches away to the Bering Strait. It has neither natural frontiers with neighboring Asia (apart from the Hellespont) nor clearly marked cultural borders; Christian Armenia and Georgia lie a thousand miles east of (partially) Muslim Albania and Bosnia.[69] Perhaps Europe is still worried by Nikolay Danilevsky's nineteenth-century analysis that Europe is not a separate continent at all, but should be considered as little more than a negligible peninsula of the Asian continent?[70] Russia's dazzling geographical space and cultural diversity have always worried Europe's elite and undermined its indulgent cultural vanity and political self-importance. Looking into the Russian mirror, Europeans see themselves reflected in a distorted way, perhaps more primitive and cruel, more communal and rooted, less 'globalized' and somewhat premodern. Unlike the United States, Russia does not hold out to Europe the postmodern offerings of culture and sophisticated high-tech gadgets, but the fundamental raw materials we have almost forgotten we cannot do without. Where America offers Europe a glimpse of its inconclusive future, Russia reminds it of its not-too-distant past. Both are too close for comfort, which may explain why alterity occasionally shifts into enmity.

Russia's Slavophiles were inclined to emphasize the 'native' and romantically primitive character of Russian civilization. Like German Romantic philosophers of nationalism, Slavophiles were critical of the need to modernize the Russian economy, fearing the destructive impact of capitalism on the organic, patriarchal traditions and archaic social structures of Russian society.[71] This Russian critique of capitalist civilization from a Romantic, conservative point of view is still offered today, somewhat uncomfortably reminding Europe that there may be more than one reading of the 'good society'. Slavophiles of the past argued that Europe was decadent and rotten, and that 'Russia should turn its back [on Europe] and hold its nose while the cadaver that was Europe slowly putrefied'.[72] A similar isolationist arrogance is now all too common among Russian Eurasianists, who argue that 'Russia cannot return to Europe because it never belonged to it. Russia cannot join it because it is part of another type of civilization'.[73] This idea of Russian exceptionalism is widely shared among Russia's strategic elite and has deep roots in Russian history and culture. The Russian historian Yuri Afanasyev has claimed that Russia is still a 'premodern society', a society that has not yet reached the stage of development where 'the emphasis [is] on the individual rather than the collective, the spirit of rational debate prevail[s] over emotion and myth, there [is] a legal contract between authority and the citizens, and a balance between private and the state economic spheres'.[74] Gennady Zyuganov, leader of Russia's Communist Party, has argued that 'Russia is a special world, a special type of civilization. [It is] hostile in its soul to the West [because of the West's] extreme individualism, militant soullessness, religious indifference [and] adherence to mass culture'.[75]

But Europe is not only worried by Russia's hostility toward *laissez-faire* and globalization. To a varying extent, this critique of cultural commodification and societal individualization is shared by many in Europe who doubt the virtues and morality of postmodern ambivalence and public rupture, of flagrant difference and ceaseless skepticism. What causes much more alarm for Europeans is that Russia's reluctance and inadequacy to enter the postmodern era is accompanied by economic destitution, political anarchy and outright conflict and civil war. The Russian case seems to illustrate – rightly or wrongly – that Europe has to go down the road of postmodernity and globalization briskly and without hesitation. The traditional good/evil dyad of the Cold War now seems to have been replaced by (what Ola Tunander has labeled) a cosmos/chaos divide which is 'separating the cosmos of the EU or NATO from the chaotic Eastern Europe and Russia'.[76] Russia, as Europe's new Other, therefore harks back to a medieval West Rome vs. East Rome divide – and this cleavage supposedly separates a democratic 'Europe', based on modern (or postmodern) principles, from Eastern Orthodoxy, which may oscillate between chaos and autocracy but will never commit itself to European normalcy and its democratic practice.

What is especially relevant for our discussion here is that since the collapse of communism and the end of the ideological divide in Europe, a new Other has emerged in the east, an Other embodied not so much in Russia itself as in the nebulous and therefore even more menacing constructs of chaos and instability. In the new definitions of 'security' that have emerged after the end of the Cold War we see how this specter of instability has conveniently replaced the Soviet threat. The civil wars in Bosnia, Kosovo and Chechnya have raised Europe's awareness that new, fuzzy dangers are again coming from the east. This is the source of nuclear suitcases and leaking submarines,[77] violent Mafia gangs, loony radical politicians with wild expansionist designs, as well as the manifest crumbling of a sense of law and order. For West European policy-makers, their eastern neighbors seem to cling to antiquated notions of ethnicity, territorial fetishism and geopolitics. It is the place where they can see Europe's past being replayed on a daily basis – a violent, wounded past in which international law and institutionalized rules of behavior seem to be practically irrelevant. It is therefore also quite common to see the order/chaos dichotomy invoked in a rather parochial manner by almost all Central European countries. Slovenia likes to emphasize its own European credentials and the ineluctable Balkanness of neighboring Croatia; Serbs will stress the traditional Orthodox Christian nature of their society while Bosnia represents the Muslim Other;[78] Romanians point to the non-Europeanness of Ukraine, while in the Ukrainian discourse Russia signifies the ultimate Asian Other.[79]

In this exclusionary process belonging to Europe has become a badge of honor and a means of excluding neighboring Others. After the end of the Cold War, Central European countries had to reinvent their history, rewrite their history books and answer the basic question: 'Who are we?' These countries now construct their national narrative on the basis of a selective memory, emphasizing their indisputable European roots and credentials. In particular, 'new' countries like the Baltic states, who for decades dwelled in the cold isolation of the Soviet Union, have recreated a national past which stresses their organic historical ties with Europe, Scandinavia and the medieval Hanseatic League.[80] In these new national narratives, Europe's institutional framework plays a central role as their new-found place of belonging, their future and destiny. Central European consciousness has been closely linked to the problematic geographical space it occupies between Russia and Germany. This is the *Mitteleuropa* of both German and Russian spheres of influence, the territories that through the centuries European Great Powers have used as pawns in the geopolitical chess game.[81] 'Joining Europe', the favorite banner of the velvet revolutions of 1989, still seems the only way out of this historical predicament.

Clearly, the Central European debate on Europe focuses on everything that is *not* Russia. Its inhabitants' experience with 'real socialism' has aroused an understandable aversion for things Russian. Since historical narrative provides the framework for locating the Central European Self within a particular interpretation of the larger story of Europe, the decades of oppression and Soviet occupation has meant that ordinary people have passed a negative Russian image on to the present generation. Despite Mikhail Gorbachev's claim that '[t]he history of Russia is an organic part of the great European history',[82] most Central Europeans would rather like to do without this organicism, preferring a Russia that no longer threatens them with imperialist plans, loose nukes or leaking nuclear facilities. Nowhere has Russia's alterity become as obvious as in the debate on the (re)arrangement of Europe's security architecture, and NATO enlargement in particular.[83] Moscow has done its utmost to antagonize its Central European neighbors by denying them their legitimate desire to shape their national and regional security. Instead, it has become clear that, as far as European security is concerned, Russia marches to a totally different drummer than the United States and most European countries; in doing its geostrategic bookkeeping, the Russian calculation of pluses and minuses differs significantly from that of all its neighbors.

In their Wilsonian naïveté, western analysts had initially simply assumed that the formidable pressures of globalization would also apply to Europe's 'Wild East', and that a continent-size power like Russia would be content with the role of sidekick to the West, transforming itself instantaneously and pulling itself up by the bootstraps as a late twentieth-century Baron von Munchausen. This has been utterly unrealistic. Instead, Russia has become the variable factor in Europe's security equation, since this vast country could fragment or expand, with equally disastrous consequences for its neighbors either way. In either scenario, Russia is bound to play the rather dubious role of the ultimate place of chaos and potential havoc. Despite its relative ethnic homogeneity, Russia (or, better, the Russian Federation) faces numerous fissiparous pressures: demands for autonomy, full-fledged sovereignty and in some cases (like Chechnya) even secession. Immediately after the dissolution of the Soviet Union, it became clear that neither the administrative borders between Russia's republics nor the ethnic divisions within Russia's federal structure were beyond dispute. Since the early 1990s the center/periphery and ethnic problems inside Russia have become aggravated, resulting in wide-ranging economic and political autonomy in the republics and regions, the break-down of the federal tax system, and disputes between the federal and local/regional governments over subsidies, prices for fuel, electricity and practically all other physical assets. Resource-rich regions in Siberia or Russia's Far East may find it difficult to resist the temptation to challenge Russia's obviously fragile statehood, although Gail W. Lapidus and Edward W. Walker argue that

> much more likely, and ultimately more catastrophic, is a fascist-like reaction that seeks to unify the country by mobilizing Russians against some imagined internal or external enemy – indeed, Russian expansionism, not fragmentation, is the greater threat to international order and Russian prosperity.
>
> (Gail W. Lapidus and Edward W. Walker, 'Nationalism, Regionalism, and Federalism: Center-Periphery Relations in Post-Communist Russia', in Gail W. Lapidus (ed.), *The New Russia: Troubled Transformation* (Boulder CO: Westview Press, 1995), pp. 108–9)

The violence of this scenario has been most graphically and tellingly illustrated by Russia's civil war in the self-proclaimed 'Islamic Republic of Chechnya', where the Russian military has been responsible for some 40,000–100,000 dead during the 1994–6 war, causing enormous destruction and suffering.[84] Although the 'first' war in Chechnya was finally brought to an end by General (ret.) Aleksandr Lebed, his eccentricity and capricious *persona* only seemed to corroborate the Khrushchev-like stereotype of the shoe-thumping, atavistic, perhaps even somewhat brutish representative of Eternal Russia. The 'second' Chechnya war, which started in 1999 and is still continuing in guerrilla mode, has seen the complete destruction of Chechnya's capital Grozny by Russian bombardment, again killing tens of thousands of civilians, under the guise of Moscow's 'fight against Islamic terrorism'. In February 2000 the European Parliament expressed its 'concern' over Russia's actions,

> deploring the thousands of war victims among the civilian population of Chechnya killed during the totally indiscriminate and disproportionate military attacks by the Russian Federal Forces, and [is] deeply concerned about the catastrophic humanitarian situation of hundreds of thousands of displaced persons in and outside Chechnya.
>
> (European Parliament, Resolution on 'The Case of Andrei Babitsky, Freedom of the Media and Violations of Human Rights in Chechnya', 17 February 2000)

But, all in all, little has been done beyond empty words to condemn the slaughter of the Chechnyan people and the destruction of their country and culture.

Clearly, Europe has had much experience with both chaotic fragmentation and violent expansion, and it can be argued that the process of European integration has been devised exactly to avoid and prevent the occurrence of either. It goes without saying that contemporary Russia is now daily reminding Western and Central European policy-makers what could happen if the ratchet of European integration is not continuously pushed one tooth further. Russia shows the rest of Europe its own hoary face, which, because it is so inherently a part of Europe's own history, causes not postmodern anxiety but old-fashioned premodern anguish.

## Islam as Europe's post-Cold-War Other

Where America figures as Europe's postmodern future and Russia as Europe's anarchical past, Islam performs the role of Europe's ultimate Other. Islam, which is a religion, a civilization as well as a culture, has come to be viewed as everything that Europe is not. The first 'foreign' culture one comes across when travelling south or east from Europe is Islam, which may explain why the Muslim world has always been Europe's first choice Other, and occasionally its preferred enemy.[85] For centuries, Islam has been the mirror of western culture and Christendom, reinforcing the perception that the boundaries of civilization needed to be guarded and defended against infiltration and perversion. As Norman Davies has argued, 'Islam's conquests [in the eighth century] turned Europe into Christianity's main base … The barrier of militant Islam turned the Peninsula in on itself, severing or transforming many of the earlier lines of commercial, intellectual, and political intercourse'.[86] A central plank of Europe's collective consciousness is therefore determined by the long, violent struggle between Christendom and the Muslim world, stretching from the defeat of the Arabs at Tours and Poitiers in 732, via the Crusades which extended from 1096 to 1291, to what is now perceived as the somewhat primitive, pre-industrial Islamic rebellion against western modernity and globalization.

It can be argued that the demise of the Cold War and the communist threat left a perceived 'threat vacuum' – now conveniently filled by an abstraction called 'Islam'.[87] A number of events and developments have brought the question of Islam into focus: the Iranian revolution, the Iran–Iraq war, the 1991 Persian Gulf War, terrorist attacks in France by Muslim fundamentalists in 1994–5, as well as the millions of Islamic resident Others now residing in European societies. In this conversation, one must inevitably refer to Samuel Huntington's study of the role of civilizations in the post-Cold-War era.[88] Huntington has pointed out that the Russian Orthodox and Muslim worlds have only been slightly touched by the key events that have ultimately shaped European history and civilization: the Renaissance, the Reformation, the Enlightenment, the French Revolution and the Industrial Revolution. This, Huntington suggests, not only affects the Orthodox and Muslim worlds negatively in economic terms, but they are (therefore) also less likely to develop stable democratic political systems. The result would be that a new 'Velvet Curtain' of culture has replaced the Iron Curtain of ideology as the dividing line between the West and the rest of the world. The simple facts that Islamic countries today are poverty-stricken, hopelessly inept militarily as well as scientifically backward, and therefore a threat to their own citizens rather than anyone else, seems not to disprove this popular 'Devil Theory of Islam'.[89] The discourse on the alleged Europe/Islam nexus is therefore a major instrument in subordinating and dehumanizing a whole culture, practically eliminating the possibility of a fair and balanced dialogue between Europe (and the West in general) and Islam.

The main reason for Europe's antagonism toward Islam must be sought elsewhere, not in a 'real-life', ominous threat to the nature and fabric of western society. Most likely, this reason can be found in Islamic fundamentalism's vocal rebuttal of the very foundations of western modernity. By rejecting all forms of sovereignty (individual and national) as well as the secularization of politics and public space, fundamentalism undermines the key pillars of modernism's rationalist epistemology. Roxanne L. Euben therefore claims that the different strands of Islam offer both a premodern and postmodern critique of western modernity, and these have to be considered as the most comprehensive indictment of globalization and late capitalism.[90] Although Euben recognizes that designations of premodern and postmodern society have taken shape within the framework of quintessentially western experiences, she argues that colonialism, imperialism and globalization have imposed these processes and ideas on the rest of the world, thereby delineating normative orientations toward such initially western ideas and commitments. The fundamentalist 'rage against reason' is embedded in the belief that rationality erodes revealed Truth, which only undermines and fractures organic communities and an innocent sense of Self. Fundamentalist Islam's critique of modern values such as secularism, rationality and scientific knowledge is often depicted as a rather archaic resistance to the global and objective forces of progress, incompatible with western readings of human rights, democratic governance and economic prosperity.[91] Since these are exactly the core elements of the western canon of politics, fundamentalist Islam has inevitably turned itself into the West's central opponent, its main epistemological antagonist.

The reasons for the absence of a serious political and cultural dialogue between Europe and Islam are diverse and complex. Part of the problem is that the West's notion of a global 'one-idea system' is based on the essential elements of democracy and capitalism, without realizing that (as Mohamed Sid-Ahmed has argued), by regarding its values 'as the only frame of reference, [it] inevitably breeds in non-western societies feelings that these societies are, to one extent or the other, victims of aggression. This is what is happening today in the confrontation with Islam'.[92] George Joffé has further argued that '[r]epresentative democracy is seen as alien to Islam; consultation (*shura*) and consensus (*ijma*) are sought instead'.[93] Joffé also claims that the holistic nature of normative Islamic society does not accept the premise of the socio-political atomism that is implicit in the democratic and capitalist projects. Islam therefore offers a powerful critique of the premises of modernity, since it does not subscribe to the mechanical, 'scientific' nature of western society based on expediency and rationality, but instead calls for moral imperatives based on divine revelation. By rejecting the modern foundation of the 'good society', Islam also sets limits to the logic of globalization by repudiating the undisturbed flow of scientific information and the flexible knowledge-based education systems that develop the dynamic human skills (such as spontaneity and originality) that are required to prosper in a postmodern world.

The key point in this necessarily abbreviated conversation is not that fundamentalist Islam is correct in questioning all aspects of western society. Rather, by attacking modernity from both premodern and postmodern sites of critique, fundamentalism taps in the existing sources of discontent and concern that are latent in the West as well. This fundamentalist yearning for absolute, divine truths is not unique to Islam but has deep roots in western Christendom. The postmodern anxiety which is becoming evident in western society feeds on this yearning for meaning, which explains why Islamic fundamentalism is so widely considered as a critique that must be externalized and ridiculed; it must not be taken seriously, for this would question the imperatives of modernity as well as the postmodern paradigm parasitic upon it. In a sense, the values and perspectives of Ayatollah Khomeini, Pope John Paul II and the Russian Orthodox zealotry of Aleksandr Solzhenitsyn are on the same side in a conflict with the postmodern cultural powers of Madonna, Mickey Mouse and the other foot soldiers of McWorld.

But externalizing this fundamentalist critique is becoming all the more difficult since West European countries today are generally subscribing to the canons of multiculturalism and multiperspectivity. Clearly, it is not only fundamentalist Islam that offers these critiques, but its physical proximity and vocal authority has turned it into a voice that resonates across Europe. How can a country like France, which has about four or five million Muslim inhabitants (half of whom have French citizenship), or Germany and Great Britain, each with a community of about 1.5 million Muslims, invalidate Islam as an alternative reading of politics and the political?[94] How can a Europe that aspires to be tolerant, inclusive and open, a Europe that cherishes dialogue and difference (in short, a postmodern Europe) relate to its ultimate Other? Islam just adds to the normatively heterogeneous qualities of European society, further undermining any claims for a single overarching reading of the polity's transcendental legitimacy. For the process of European integration, the challenge posed by Islam offers both opportunities for change and complicating problems of accommodation.

Europe's Islamic puzzle crystallizes in its troublesome relationship with Turkey.[95] Turkey applied to the Community for membership as long ago as in 1959, and this led to the Ankara Agreement (1963), which aimed at making it a full member. Turkey made a formal bid for full integration in 1987, but was again politely rejected by the European Commission two years later. The EU did officially endorse Turkey's wish to integrate into Europe and confirmed her eligibility for full membership, but it failed to set concrete dates for the commencement of membership talks. Since then, Europe's relationship with Turkey has turned sour, especially since in December 1997 no less than nine applicant countries (including Cyprus) were invited to start accession negotiations with the EU, and a rather perplexed Ankara government found itself humiliatingly queue-jumped. Understandably, this decision provoked a great outcry across Turkish society. Two years later, at the EU's December 1999 Helsinki summit, the Union finally changed its mind and agreed to start discussions on Turkish membership which might, ultimately, evolve into official accession negotiations. By opening these prospects of membership, the EU has proved that it does not want to define itself as a bulwark of Christianity and that it is willing to accommodate countries with different religions. Although Turkey has reacted with enthusiasm to these new EU moves, there remains frustration that it has had to wait so long and is still at the end of a queue which includes no less than twelve Central European countries.

In a 1991 interview with the German magazine *Der Spiegel*, former Turkish President Turgut Ozal was rather straightforward: 'Why are we not yet in the European Community? The answer is simple. You are Christians and we are Muslims'.[96] For most Turks, belonging to Europe and 'the West' is an integral part of the legacy of Kemal Ataturk and a necessary element of Turkey's declared goal of strengthening its relationship with the 'civilized world'. However, although in secular Turkey references to Islam as the official religion have been dropped from the constitution, the country is widely recognized as a Muslim society and state. With the disintegration of the Soviet Union, Turkey has also reoriented itself strongly toward the larger Turkic world in Central Asia, which has shifted its strategic and cultural attention eastward, potentially to the detriment of its ties with Europe. To some extent, this has made good links with Turkey an even more vital interest of Europe and the EU. As a country on the periphery of Europe, Turkey plays a central role between the unstable Balkans, the energy wealth of Central Asia and such key global and regional players as Russia, Iran and Iraq. Turkey's full participation in the European integration process would therefore be valuable and highly valued as a bridge toward the Islamic Other. It is likely that these factors have encouraged the EU to offer Turkey the prospect of joining the integration process. But, at the same time, fear of Islam will continue to play an important role in the geopolitical evolution of the EU.

Not that Turkey would fulfil the EU's criteria for accession, which, apart from the *acquis communautaire*, include respect for human rights and international law.[97] The continued 'dirty war' between Turkey's politically militant military and the Kurdish minority continues to pose a major obstacle to joining mainstream Europe. Nor do the complicated relationship between Turkey and Greece and the presence of Turkish troops in the northern part of Cyprus help to overcome European suspicions that Ankara is not committed to the dogma of co-operative security. But these 'objective' reasons for excluding Turkey from Europe's integration process are generally read as expressions of an anti-Islamic European fundamentalism. The EU's refusal to consider Turkish membership in 1997 was met with a wave of protest from Ankara and Turkish media newspaper reports, headlined 'The Truth at Last', asking why 'Brussels' had decided 'to prepare Europe for the twenty-first century within the framework of "civilization", forgetting that Turkey is one of the countries known as the "cradle of civilization". Is Turkey a country of savages with no culture or civilization?'[98] This sentiment is not unique to Turkey, but is shared on Europe's Islamic periphery in general. From across the Mediterranean, European integration does not look like an innocent and beneficial process, but as a potentially aggressive, fortress-building exercise, keeping the Islamic Other at bay. As Graham Fuller and Ian Lesser have argued, '[i]t is common for observers in North Africa, for example, to view the evolution of new European defense arrangements as a vehicle for intervention in the Muslim world by former colonial powers'.[99]

Europe's relationship with Islam will remain as problematic as it has always been. But Europe's postmodern moment makes it more difficult to neglect Islam and simply overlook its existence as a living critique of western modernity. It also makes it more difficult for Europe simply to take sides in a future 'clash of civilizations', fighting for allegedly unique Christian or western values that no longer underpin an increasingly variegated and morally mixed European society. Europe now feels obliged to show its generous and tolerant face to its multiple

Others, with visibly mixed eagerness and success. The tragedy of Sarajevo may stand for everything that Europe has to lose if it does not more convincingly defend pluralism and the basic right to differ. The mourners for Sarajevo have told Europe the now well-known story of the city's many cultures, its diverse faiths, a Balkan city created by Islam, Rome and Byzantium. As Fouad Ajami has argued, 'The Sarajevan way, we now know, was one of the few and finest moments of cosmopolitanism'.[100] By letting this moment slip by, just watching and hesitating, Europe has not only lost credibility in its relations with the Muslim world, it has also harmed itself. But since the Islamic Other is no longer the hidden face of Europe's own identity and is a vocal critic of the circumstances of late capitalism, Europe cannot simply acquire a whole sense of Self by keeping this 'alienness' at a safe distance. In a sense, therefore, Europe requires its American postmodern fate, its Russian premodern beyond and its Islamic face of alterity just to maintain the dynamic momentum of its narrative identity, to feed it with the stories of its past, present and future.

## Implications/premonitions (or, Why all these things matter)

The end of the Cold War has exposed the exhaustion of the liberal democratic political agenda in the West. The triumph of the market and the logic of globalization have awakened a painful and more vocal chorus of moral and political discontent, frustration and alienation caused by a sense of loss of community and self-government which has much to do with the growing obsolescence of the nation-state. Now that the nation-state is no longer able to perform many of its historical duties, the erosion of the primary political unit upon which liberal democracy is premised inevitably problematizes the future of democratic governance. Schumpeter's concept of 'creative destruction' – the constant process of renewal of economic structures that ensures their vigor and vitality – has now become the accepted hallmark of global capitalism and has therefore constituted itself as the new practical and moral foundation of western society. The new role and place of the nation-state in the process of European integration testifies to the powers of creative destruction in the institutional sphere of social organization, a process on a par with the swirling change now taking place in global society as a whole.

This book has obviously only offered a small contribution to the more general task of making some of these questions more pertinent, opening an academic conversation on the quality and nature of European integration from a postmodern perspective. It has pointed out that the Europeanization of many traditionally jealously guarded national policy areas has highlighted the need to reassess the necessity of a more robust European identity. The feeling of common purpose and of sharing common causes may be conducive to practical feelings of a European notion of solidarity. In turn, the transcendence of national identities may help to foster a more solid European identity alongside a plethora of other identities. It has argued that a European version of narcissism, a closure from the outside world and a passive self-absorption, would not make it any more worthy and commendable. A Europe that closed itself and constructed its identity in isolation from the Other would become unresponsive to critical voices, leading to intolerance and exclusion. Such a narcissistic Europe would reflect all the drawbacks of western modernity, only on a European rather than a national level. It would turn ethnic, cultural, territorial and perhaps even religious characteristics and virtues into unquestioned (and unquestionable) glorious qualities. Europeanness would be the magic word that opened the door to citizenship, community and potential prosperity. It is not argued here that the solution will lie in excessive self-criticism, or even self-abasement; European culture – however one wants to define it – has much to be proud of. But, just as nationalism is a distorting mirror that gives us a twisted picture of ourselves and the outside world, a narcissistic Europeanism would delude us in the same way but on a different scale.

As I have admitted from the outset, this study of Europe's postmodern moment will not arrive at fixed and explicit conclusions. Rather, I have tried to open a debate on how the European integration process can be read from a different point of view, making an effort to elucidate some new and relevant aspects within a rather restricted discourse on the development of European federalism and its maimed nation-states. Some academic observers of the EU have already argued that we

> need to abandon the notion that the EU is something and to consider it as always *becoming*. Moreover, we need to abandon the notion that the Union is evolving toward traditional state or nationhood. The Union is crafted onto existing forms of political order but in turn contributes to the transformation of such forms.
>
> (Brigid Laffan, 'The European Union: A Distinctive Model of Internationalisation', in *European Integration online Papers (EIoP)*, vol. 1, no. 18 (1997). Online. Available HTTP: http://olymp.wu-wien.ac.at/eiop/, accessed 15 August 2000)

Others claim that a 'new approach towards the system of the European Union is more necessary than ever ... New categories are required not only for scientific research, but also of perception by the average citizen and the political public'.[101] This book has tried to develop the beginnings of a postmodern narrative of European integration by proposing different categories of thought and by advancing many nuances of the European problematic.

For those who believe that humankind cannot live well without fixed and stable categories of natural and social life, the collapse of national authority will be a major source of concern. From a positivist perspective, the betweenness and ambiguity of European governance, democracy and identity implies a collapse of existing power structures without offering a clear and present alternative that satisfies a modern desire for order and predictability. These are clear and understandable concerns. But it should also be noted that in Europe's contemporary, culturally diverse societies public support of a gradual shift toward European federalism is growing. Those groups that hold the current nation-state to be unviable and unjust, who feel alienated from 'their' nation-state, may more easily shift allegiance toward 'Europe', their region or other, non-territorial cognitive categories of belonging. Here, too, Walker's classical question, 'whose security?', is relevant, since it effectively questions the uncontested assumption that states really provide their citizens with protection and safety.[102] Security for the state, based on sovereignty and territoriality, may not be the most effective and/or efficient way of optimizing the security of its people(s). Asking 'whose security?' decenters the discourse away from the state, claiming attention for the wishes and concerns of (transversal) groups that do not see themselves reflected in the political 'national interests' mediated by the nation-state.

It is, of course, premature to dismiss the value and application of modern notions such as sovereignty, territoriality and representative democracy. A global civil society that will no longer be built around the nation-state remains highly conjectural. What is more, the sentimental loyalty directed toward the nation-state remains. Kenneth Minogue, for example, has clearly acknowledged that the 'state is a monster, but it is our monster, in the sense that it must endure some sort of accountability, in democracies, to us'.[103] As one American policy-maker argued:

> The state is not disappearing, it is disaggregating into its separate, function-ally distinct parts. These parts – courts, regulatory agencies, executives, and even legislatures – are networking with their counterparts abroad, creating a dense web of relations that constitutes a new, transgovernmental order that is more effective and potentially more accountable than either of the cur-rent alternatives.
>
> (Roy Maclaren, 'Government and National Parliaments: How Relevant is Economic Globalization and Regionalization in the Next Millennium', in *Vital Speeches of the Day*, 1 May 1998)

Since Western Europe has taken the most courageous steps toward such a new postnational political system, the advantages and drawbacks of the emerging postmodern polity are most obvious and visible there. For most parts of the world this 'era of posts' (postmodern, post-industrial, post-ideological) is certainly still far away, and the bulk of humanity has still to reap the mixed benefits of a modern industrialized society based on capitalism, liberal democracy and scientific progress. The experiences of modernization are markedly different in Central and Latin America, Asia and Africa, continents that for the most part still have to reach their own postmodern moment.

In one of his uniquely personal academic works, Heinz Eulau has argued that

> social scientists have used and continue to use the notion of process freely and easily, and we sometimes claim that we are observing *the* political proc-

ess. Nobody has of course ever observed a process, unless we think of having done so when we 'see' a tablet of Alka Seltzer dissolve in a glass of water. But, then, we usually have a hangover when we do this and think we are observing a process of dissolution when, in fact, it is a process of combination or composition.

(Heinz Eulau, *Micro-Macro Dilemmas in Political Science: Personal Pathways Through Complexity* (Norman OK and London: University of Oklahoma Press, 1996), pp. 290–1; emphasis in the original)

This may also apply to ambitious political scientists who have made serious efforts to describe, explain and understand Europe's integration process. But we must understand that all these equally serious accounts are little more (and little less) than the scientific findings proffered by a wide range of epistemic communities situated in their particular places and times.[104] All these social and political theories on the EU and European integration remain radically 'underdetermined', only valid within the set of theoretical assumptions to which they subscribe. By offering a postmodern account of European integration, this book suggests another horizon of circumstances, events and developments described and analyzed in many other places. Although I do not want to reject this body of literature, I would certainly like to ask for more recognition that the European reality pictured in other places is by definition a social construction, and that the attempt to arrive at value-neutral generalizations and explanations of European integration will be illusory. The research focus in the field of European Studies may be more fruitfully shifted toward the nature of the situational context and the discursive processes that have shaped and still shape the construction of the EU and its multifarious social and political reality. This is the continuing challenge facing postmodern Europe, and Europe's academic community in particular.

## Notes

1 David Gress, *From Plato to NATO: The Idea of the West and its Opponents* (New York: Free Press, 1998).
2 Iver B. Neumann and Jennifer M. Welsh, 'The Other in European Self-Definition', in *Review of International Studies*, vol. 17, no. 4 (1991).
3 Stephen J. Whitfield, *The Culture of the Cold War* (Baltimore MD: Johns Hopkins University Press, 1991).
4 Ronald Steel, 'Who Is Us?', in *New Republic*, 14–21 September 1998, p. 13.
5 Stjepan G. Mestrovic, *The Balkanization of the West: The Confluence of Postmodernism and Postcommunism* (London/New York: Routledge, 1994), p. 5.
6 Selim Abou, 'The Metamorphoses of Cultural Identity', in *Diogenes*, vol. 45, no. 1 (Spring 1997), p. 4.
7 David Holmes, 'Virtual Identity: Communities of Broadcast, Communities of Interactivity', in David Holmes (ed.), *Virtual Politics: Identity and Community in Cyberspace* (London: Sage, 1997), pp. 6–7.
8 David Buckingham, 'News Media, Political Socialization and Popular Citizenship: Towards a New Agenda', in *Critical Studies in Mass Communication*, vol. 14, no. 4 (December 1997).

9 Theodor W. Adorno, *Culture Industry: Selected Essays on Mass Culture* (London: Routledge, 1991); and Deborah Cook, *The Culture Industry Revisited: Adorno on Mass Culture* (Lanham MD: Rowman & Littlefield Press, 1996).

10 Anthony Giddens, 'Living in a Post-traditional Society', in Ulrich Beck, Anthony Giddens and Scott Lash, *Reflexive Modernization: Politics, Tradition, and Aesthetics in the Modern Social Order* (Stanford CA: Stanford University Press, 1994).

11 As is argued, for example, by Robert Latham, 'Liberalism's Order/Liberalism's Other: A Genealogy of Threat', in *Alternatives*, vol. 20, no. 1 (January/March 1995), p. 120.

12 Iver B. Neumann, *Uses of the Other: "The East" in European Identity Formation* (Minneapolis: University of Minnesota Press, 1999); and Jürgen Habermas, *The Inclusion of the Other: Studies in Political Theory* (Cambridge MA: MIT Press, 1998).

13 Michel Foucault, *Foucault Live: Interviews 1966–84* (New York: Semiotext(e), 1989), especially Chapter 6 ('Rituals of Exclusion').

14 Quoted in Jennifer M. Welsh, 'The Role of the Inner Enemy in European Self-Definition: Identity, Culture and International Relations Theory', in *History of European Ideas*, vol. 19, no. 1–3 (1994), p. 53.

15 Ole Wæver, 'European Security Identities', in *Journal of Common Market Studies*, vol. 34, no. 1 (August 1996).

16 Russell Berman, 'Beyond Localism and Universalism: Nationhood and Solidarity', in *Telos*, no. 105 (Fall 1995).

17 Thomas Risse-Kappen (with Daniela Engelmann-Martin, Hans-Joachim Knopf and Klaus Roscher), 'To Euro or Not to Euro? The EMU and Identity Politics in the European Union', EUI Working Paper Series, no. 98–9 (Florence: European University Institute, 1998), p. 21.

18 Helmut Kohl, 'Speech at Leuven University, Belgium', 2 February 1996.

19 Thomas Risse-Kappen, 'A European Identity: Europeanization and the Evolution of Nation-State Identities', in Maria Green Cowles, James Caporaso and Thomas Risse-Kappen (eds), *Europeanization and Domestic Change* (Ithaca NY: Cornell University Press, 2000).

20 John S. Duffield, 'Political Culture and State Behavior: Why Germany Confounds Neorealism', in *International Organization*, vol. 53, no. 4 (Autumn 1999).

21 The debate was initiated by the German novelist Martin Walser in the autumn of 1998.

22 Slavoj Zizek, 'Die freie Wahl zwischen blauen und roten Tütchen: Warum wir es lieben, Haider zu Hassen', in *Süddeutsche Zeitung*, 9 February 2000.

23 Paul Ricoeur, *Oneself as Another* (Chicago: University of Chicago Press, 1994), as well as Peter Beyer, 'Identity and Character as Elective Strategies in Global Society', in *International Journal on World Peace*, vol. 14, no. 4 (December 1997).

24 James R. Andrews, 'The Rhetorical Shaping of National Interests: Morality and Contextual Potency in John Bright's Parliamentary Speech Against Recognition of the Confederacy', in *Quarterly Journal of Speech*, vol. 79, no. 1 (February 1993).

25 Anne Caldwell, 'Fairy Tales For Politics: The Other, Once More', in *Philosophy Today*, vol. 41, no. 1 (Spring 1997).

26 Julia Kristeva, *Strangers to Ourselves* (New York: Harvester Wheatsheaf, 1991); and Arwad Esber, 'In Quest of the Feminine: The Stranger Within Us (An Interview with Julia Kristeva)', in *Feminist Issues*, vol. 15, no. 1–2 (1997).

27 Marc Fumaroli, ' "I is an Other": Delusions of Identity', in *Diogenes*, vol. 45, no. 1 (Spring 1997), p. 122.

28 Charles E. Reagan, 'The Self as an Other', in *Philosophy Today*, vol. 37, no. 1 (Spring 1993), p. 20.

29 Iris Marion Young, 'Communication and the Other: Beyond Deliberative Democracy', in Seyla Benhabib (ed.), *Democracy and Difference: Contesting the Boundaries of the Political* (Princeton NJ: Princeton University Press, 1996), pp. 131–2.

30  Kathleen Bawn, 'Constructing "Us": Ideology, Coalition Politics, and False Consciousness', in *American Journal of Political Science*, vol. 43, no. 2 (April 1999).

31  Jean L. Cohen, 'Democracy, Difference, and the Right of Privacy', in Seyla Benhabib (ed.), *Democracy and Difference: Contesting the Boundaries of the Political* (Princeton NJ: Princeton University Press, 1996).

32  Denis-Constant Martin, 'The Choices of Identity', in *Social Identities*, vol. 1, no. 1 (1995), p. 11.

33  Judith Butler, *Gender Trouble: Feminism and the Subversion of Identity* (New York: Routledge, 1990), p. 145.

34  Welsh, 'The Role of the Inner Enemy in European Self-Definition', pp. 55–7.

35  Carlos A. Forment, 'Peripheral Peoples and Narrative Identities: Arendtian Reflections on Late Modernity', in Seyla Benhabib (ed.), *Democracy and Difference: Contesting the Boundaries of the Political* (Princeton NJ: Princeton University Press, 1996).

36  Aysegul Baykan, 'Issues of Difference and Citizenship for "New Identities": A Theoretical View', in *Innovation*, vol. 10, no. 1 (March 1997).

37  Iris Marion Young, 'The Ideal of Community and the Politics of Difference', in Linda J. Nicholson (ed.), *Feminism/Postmodernism* (London/New York: Routledge, 1990).

38  On Foucault's notion of heterotopia, see Thomas R. Flynn, 'Foucault and the Spaces of History', in *Monist*, vol. 74, no. 2 (April 1991).

39  For such a reading of postmodern society, see Walter Russell Mead, 'Trains, Planes, and Automobiles: The End of the Postmodern Moment', in *World Policy Journal*, vol. 12, no. 4 (Winter 1995). The quotation is from page 13.

40  R.B.J. Walker, 'Security, Sovereignty, and the Challenge of World Politics', in *Alternatives*, vol. 15, no. 1 (Winter 1990), p. 12.

41  Lene Hansen, 'A Case for Seduction? Evaluating the Poststructuralist Conceptualization of Security', in *Cooperation and Conflict*, vol. 32, no. 4 (December 1997), pp. 374–5.

42  Ole Wæver, 'Securitization and Desecuritization', in Ronnie D. Lipschutz (ed.), *On Security* (New York: Columbia University Press, 1995), pp. 50–1.

43  *Ibid.*, pp. 62–5.

44  Walker, 'Security, Sovereignty, and the Challenge of World Politics', p. 13.

45  James Der Derian, 'The Value of Security: Hobbes, Marx, Nietzsche, and Baudrillard', in Ronnie D. Lipschutz (ed.), *On Security* (New York: Columbia University Press, 1995), p. 33.

46  David Campbell, 'Apartheid Cartography: The Political Anthropology and Spatial Effects of International Diplomacy in Bosnia', in *Political Geography*, vol. 18, no. 4 (1999).

47  Cynthia Weber, *Simulating Sovereignty: Intervention, the State and Symbolic Exchange* (Cambridge: Cambridge University Press, 1995), p. 20.

48  Wæver, 'Securitization and Desecuritization', pp. 72–4.

49  In its efforts to write Europe's geopolitical space, the EU has adopted a Wittgensteinian approach, using the metaphor of *Familienähnlichkeiten* ('family resemblances') to illustrate the complex networks of similarities among Europe's peoples, who are nevertheless quite different in their essence. Ludwig Wittgenstein argued that, like the various resemblances between the members of a family, 'we see a complicated network of similarities overlapping and criss-crossing: sometimes overall similarities, sometimes similarities in detail' (Wittgenstein, *Philosophical Investigations* (Oxford: Blackwell, 1953), numbered remarks nos 66–7). In its semantic politics the EU has continuously applied this metaphor of family resemblances (the 'European family') to illustrate how Europe could relate to countries of Central and Eastern Europe (and *vice versa*). In doing so, the EU has rejected the framing of an undisputed definition of Europeanness and has not codified the unequivocal features and

characteristics of who belongs to Europe and who does not. Apart from an internalized culture of co-operation and a deeply ingrained willingness to make compromises, no check-list of criteria that will assure entry into this 'Club Europe' has been presented.

50  Weber argues that in International Relations theory, 'intervention is defined as the violation of one state's sovereignty by an uninvited intruder. It is rape on an international scale' (Cynthia Weber, *Faking It: US Hegemony in a "Post-Phallic" Era* (Minneapolis: University of Minnesota Press, 1999), p. 94.

51  Richard K. Ashley, 'Living on Borderlines: Man, Poststructuralism, and War', in James Der Derian and Michael J. Shapiro (eds), *International/Intertextual Relations: Postmodern Readings of World Politics* (Lexington MA: Lexington Books, 1989), p. 305.

52  Michael J. Shapiro, *Violent Cartographies: Mapping Cultures of War* (Minneapolis: University of Minnesota Press, 1997).

53  Ole Wæver, 'Identity, Integration and Security', in *Journal of International Affairs*, vol. 48, no. 2 (Winter 1995).

54  Aleksandar Boskovic, 'Hyperreal Serbia' (2 April 1996). Online. Available HTTP: http://www.ctheory.com (accessed 28 March 2000).

55  Weber, *Faking It*, p. 92.

56  Patrick Glynn, 'The Age of Balkanization', in *Commentary*, vol. 96, no. 1 (July 1993), p. 24.

57  Ronnie D. Lipschutz, 'Negotiating the Boundaries of Difference and Security at Millennium's End', in Ronnie D. Lipschutz (ed.), *On Security* (New York: Columbia University Press, 1995), p. 218.

58  Slavoj Zizek, 'Against the Double Blackmail', in *The Nation*, 24 May 1999, pp. 20–1.

59  Jean Baudrillard, *The Perfect Crime* (London: Verso, 1997), p. 135. See, on a similar theme, Campbell, 'Apartheid Cartography'.

60  Philip R. Schlesinger, 'Europe's Contradictory Communicative Space', in *Daedalus*, vol. 123, no. 2 (Spring 1994), p. 34.

61  David Harvey, 'Capitalism: The Factory of Fragmentation', in *New Perspectives Quarterly*, vol. 9, no. 2 (Spring 1992).

62  Stuart Ewen, 'Pragmatism's Postmodern Poltergeist', in *New Perspectives Quarterly*, vol. 9, no. 2 (Spring 1992).

63  Mel van Elteren, 'GATT and Beyond: World Trade, the Arts and American Popular Culture in Western Europe', in *Journal of American Culture*, vol. 19, no. 3 (Fall 1996).

64  Daniel R. White and Gert Hellerick, 'Nietzsche at the Mall: Deconstructing the Consumer' (1994). Online. Available HTTP: http://www.ctheory.com (accessed 29 March 2000).

65  Joyce Antler makes the case that in the American psyche the Holocaust appears entirely as a drama that occurred 'elsewhere'. Joyce Antler, 'The Americanization of the Holocaust', in *American Theatre*, vol. 12, no. 2 (February 1995).

66  Nathan Gardels, 'Interview With Jacques Delors', in *New Perspectives Quarterly*, vol. 13, no. 1 (Winter 1996).

67  Nathan Gardels, 'Interview With Costa-Gavras', in *New Perspectives Quarterly*, vol. 12, no. 4 (Fall 1995).

68  Martin Walker, 'The New American Hegemony', in *World Policy Journal*, vol. 13, no. 2 (Summer 1996), p. 21.

69  Perry Anderson, 'The Europe to Come', in Peter Gowan and Perry Anderson (eds), *The Question of Europe* (London: Verso, 1997), p. 139.

70  Heikki Mikkeli, *Europe as an Idea and an Identity* (New York: St Martin's Press, 1998), pp. 168–70.

71  Andrzej Walicki, *A History of Russian Thought: From the Enlightenment to Marxism* (Oxford: Clarendon Press, 1988), pp. 106–11.

72  Iver B. Neumann, *Russia and the Idea of Europe: A Study in Identity and International Relations* (London: Routledge, 1996), p. 38.

73 Elgiz Pozdnyakov, quoted *Ibid.*, p. 177.

74 Quoted in Judith Armstrong, 'Cultural Difference – Russia and the EU', in *Australia and World Affairs*, no. 25 (Spring 1995).

75 Quoted in *The Economist*, 15 June 1996.

76 Ola Tunander, 'Post-Cold War Europe: Synthesis of a Bipolar Friend–Foe Structure and a Hierarchic Cosmos–Chaos Structure?', in Ola Tunander, Pavel Baev and Victoria Ingrid Einagel (eds), *Geopolitics in Post-Wall Europe: Security, Territory and Identity* (London: Sage, 1997), p. 18.

77 For an overview, see Graham T. Allison, Owen R. Coté, Jr., Richard A. Falkenrath and Steven E. Miller, *Avoiding Nuclear Anarchy: Containing the Threat of Loose Russian Nuclear Weapons and Fissile Material* (Cambridge MA: MIT Press, 1996).

78 Franke Wilmer, 'Identity, Culture, and Historicity: The Social Construction of Ethnicity in the Balkans', in *World Affairs*, vol. 160, no. 1 (Summer 1997).

79 Iver B. Neumann, 'European Identity, EU Expansion, and the Integration/Exclusion Nexus', in *Alternatives*, vol. 23, no. 3 (July/September 1998), p. 406.

80 Eiki Berg, 'Writing Post-Soviet Estonia Onto the World Map', Copenhagen Peace Research Institute, COPRI Working Paper Series, no. 3 (2000).

81 Przemyslaw Grudzinski and Peter van Ham, *A Critical Approach to European Security: Identity and Institutions* (London: Cassell Academic, 1999), especially Chapter 9 ('Central Europe, *Mitteleuropa* and Identity: An Old Debate Revisited'); and Sergei Medvedev, ' "Zwischeneuropa": Historic Experiences, National Views and Strategic Alternatives', The Finnish Institute of International Affairs, UPI Working Paper Series, no. 6 (Helsinki, 1998).

82 Mikhail Gorbachev, *Perestroika: New Thinking for Our Country and the World* (London: Fontana, 1988), p. 190.

83 Grudzinski and Van Ham, *A Critical Approach to European Security*.

84 Edward W. Walker, 'No Peace, No War in the Caucasus: Secessionist Conflicts in Chechnya, Abkhazia and Nagorno-Karabakh', John F. Kennedy School of Government, Harvard University, Strengthening Democratic Institutions Project Paper Series (February 1998), especially pp. 3–11.

85 Ofer Zur has distinguished between two major types of Enemy: the 'worthy' and the 'evil'. Islam has mostly been Europe's evil Enemy, since it is understood to be so fundamentally different from 'us' that we can have little or nothing in common with it. See Ofer Zur, 'The Love of Hating', in *History of European Ideas*, vol. 13, no. 4 (1991).

86 Norman Davies, *Europe: A History* (Oxford: Oxford University Press, 1996), p. 257.

87 B.A. Roberson, 'Islam and Europe: An Enigma or a Threat?', in *Middle East Journal*, vol. 48, no. 2 (Spring 1994), p. 287.

88 Samuel P. Huntington, *The Clash of Civilizations and the Remaking of World Order* (New York: Simon & Schuster, 1996).

89 Edward W. Said, 'The Devil Theory of Islam', *The Nation*, 12–19 August 1996.

90 Roxanne L. Euben, 'Premodern, Antimodern or Postmodern? Islamic and Western Critiques of Modernity', in *Review of Politics*, vol. 59, no. 3 (Summer 1997).

91 M.M.J. Fischer, 'Is Islam the Odd-Civilization Out?', in *New Perspectives Quarterly*, vol. 9, no. 2 (Spring 1992).

92 Mohamed Sid-Ahmed, 'Cybernetic Colonialism and the Moral Search', in *New Perspectives Quarterly*, vol. 11, no. 2 (Spring 1994).

93 George Joffé, 'Democracy, Islam and the Culture of Modernism', in *Democratization*, vol. 4, no. 3 (Autumn 1997), p. 134.

94 Milton Viorst, 'The Muslims in France', in *Foreign Affairs*, vol. 75, no. 5 (September/October 1996).

95 For an overview, see Barry Buzan and Thomas Diez, 'The European Union and Turkey', in *Survival*, vol. 41, no. 1 (Spring 1999).

96  *Der Spiegel*, 14 October 1991. Quoted in David Kushner, 'Self-Perception and Identity in Contemporary Turkey', in *Journal of Contemporary History*, vol. 32, no. 2 (April 1997).
97  Sibel Bozdogan and Resat Kasaba (eds), *Rethinking Modernity and National Identity in Turkey* (Seattle: University of Washington Press, 1997).
98  Commentary in *Istanbul Milliyet*, 6 March 1997; Translated in *FBIS-WEU-97-053*.
99  Graham E. Fuller and Ian O. Lesser, *A Sense of Siege: The Geopolitics of Islam and the West* (Boulder CO: Westview Press, 1995), p. 63.
100  Fouad Ajami, 'In Europe's Shadows', in *New Republic*, 21 November 1994, p. 36.
101  Wolfgang Wessels, 'The Modern West European State and the European Union: Democratic Erosion or a New Kind of Polity?', in Svein S. Andersen and Kjell A. Eliassen (eds), *The European Union: How Democratic Is It?* (London: Sage, 1995), p. 69.
102  R.B.J. Walker, 'The Concept of Security and International Relations Theory', University of California, Institute of Global Conflict and Co-operation Working Paper Series, no. 3 (San Diego, 1988).
103  Kenneth Minogue, 'Does National Sovereignty Have a Future?', in *National Review*, vol. 48, no. 24 (23 December 1996), p. 37.
104  Frank Fischer, 'Beyond Empiricism: Policy Inquiry in Postpositivist Perspective', in *Policy Studies Journal*, vol. 26, no. 1 (Spring 1998), p. 132.

# Bibliography

Abou, Selim 'The Metamorphoses of Cultural Identity', in *Diogenes*, vol. 45, no. 1 (Spring 1997).

Ackelsberg, Martha A. 'Identity Politics, Political Identities: Thoughts Toward a Multicultural Politics', in *Frontiers*, vol. 16, no. 1 (1996).

Adler, Emanuel 'Imagined (Security) Communities: Cognitive Regions in International Relations', in *Millennium: Journal of International Studies*, vol. 26, no. 2 (Summer 1997).

—— 'Seizing the Middle Ground: Constructivism in World Politics', in *European Journal of International Relations*, vol. 3, no. 3 (September 1997).

Adorno, Theodor W. *Culture Industry: Selected Essays on Mass Culture* (London: Routledge, 1991).

Aggestam, Lisbeth 'The European Union at the Crossroads: Sovereignty and Integration', in Alice Landau and Richard G. Whitman (eds) *Rethinking the European Union: Institutions, Interests and Identities* (New York: St Martin's Press, 1997).

Agnelli, Giovanni 'The Europe of 1992', in *Foreign Affairs*, vol. 68, no. 4 (July/August 1989).

Ajami, Fouad 'In Europe's Shadows', in *The New Republic*, 21 November 1994.

Albert, Mathias ' "Postmoderne" und Theorie der internationalen Beziehungen', in *Zeitschrift für Internationale Beziehungen*, vol. 1, no. 1 (1994).

Aldersey-Williams, Hugh 'Symbols and Lies', in *New Statesman*, 10 July 1998.

Allison, Graham T., Owen R. Coté, Jr., Richard A. Falkenrath and Steven E. Miller *Avoiding Nuclear Anarchy: Containing the Threat of Loose Russian Nuclear Weapons and Fissile Material* (Cambridge MA: MIT Press, 1996).

Allott, Philip 'The Crisis of European Constitutionalism: Reflections on the Revolution in Europe', in *Common Market Law Review*, vol. 34, no. 3 (June 1997).

Alter, Karen J. 'Who Are the "Masters of the Treaty"? European Governments and the European Court of Justice', in *International Organization*, vol. 52, no. 1 (Winter 1998).

Andersen, Svein S., and Tom R. Burns 'The European Union and the Erosion of Parliamentary Democracy: A Study of Post-Parliamentary Governance', in Svein S. Andersen and Kjell A. Eliassen (eds) *The European Union: How Democratic Is It?* (London: Sage, 1995).

Andersen, Svein S. and Kjell A. Eliassen 'Democracy: Traditional Concerns in New Institutional Settings', in Svein S. Andersen and Kjell A. Eliassen (eds) *The European Union: How Democratic Is It?* (London: Sage, 1995).

—— (eds) *The European Union: How Democratic Is It?* (London: Sage, 1995).

Anderson, Benedict *Imagined Communities: Reflections on the Origin and Spread of Nationalism* (London: Verso, 1995).

Anderson, James 'The Shifting Stage of Politics: New Medieval and Postmodern Territorialities', in *Environment and Planning D*, no. 14 (1996).

Anderson, Jeffrey J. 'The State of the (European) Union', in *World Politics*, vol. 47, no. 3 (April 1995).

Anderson, Perry *Lineages of the Absolutist State* (London: New Left Books, 1974).

—— 'The Europe to Come', in Peter Gowan and Perry Anderson (eds) *The Question of Europe* (London: Verso, 1997).

Andrews, James R. 'The Rhetorical Shaping of National Interests: Morality and Contextual Potency in John Bright's Parliamentary Speech Against Recognition of the Confederacy', in *Quarterly Journal of Speech*, vol. 79, no. 1 (February 1993).

Ang, Ien (ed.) *Living Room Wars: Rethinking Media Audiences for a Postmodern World* (London: Routledge, 1995).

Antler, Joyce 'The Americanization of the Holocaust', in *American Theatre*, vol. 12, no. 2 (February 1995).

Appleyard, Bryan 'Post-Scientific Society', in *New Perspectives Quarterly*, vol. 10, no. 3 (Summer 1993).

Aram, John D. 'Challenges to the Social Foundations of Capitalism in an Age of Global Economics', in *Human Relations*, vol. 50, no. 8 (August 1997).

Archibugi, Daniele, and David Held (eds) *Cosmopolitan Democracy: An Agenda for a New World Order* (Cambridge: Polity Press, 1995).

Armstrong, Judith 'Cultural Difference – Russia and the EU', in *Australia and World Affairs*, no. 25 (Spring 1995).

Armstrong, Kenneth, and Simon Bulmer *The Governance of the Single European Market* (Manchester: Manchester University Press, 1998).

Ashley, Richard K. 'The Geopolitics of Geopolitical Space: Toward a Critical Social Theory of International Politics', in *Alternatives*, vol. 12, no. 4 (October 1987).

—— 'Untying the Sovereign State: A Double Reading of the Anarchy Problematique', in *Millennium: Journal of International Studies*, vol. 17, no. 2 (Summer 1988).

—— 'Living on Borderlines: Man, Poststructuralism, and War', in James Der Derian and Michael J. Shapiro (eds) *International/Intertextual Relations: Postmodern Readings of World Politics* (Lexington MA: Lexington Books, 1989).

Ashley, Richard K., and R.B.J. Walker 'Speaking the Language of Exile: Dissidence in International Studies', in *International Studies Quarterly*, vol. 34, no. 3 (September 1990).

—— 'Reading Dissidence/Writing the Discipline: Crisis and the Question of Sovereignty in International Studies', in *International Studies Quarterly*, vol. 34, no. 3 (September 1990).

Bader, Veit 'Citizenship and Exclusion', in *Political Theory*, vol. 23, no. 2 (May 1995).

Baier, Lothar 'Farewell to Regionalism', in *Telos*, no. 90 (Winter 1991).

Bakhtin, Mikhail M. 'Discourse in the Novel', in Mikhail M. Bakhtin, *The Dialogic Imagination: Four Essays* (Austin: University of Texas Press, 1981).

Ballmann, A., and J.H.H. Weiler *Certain Rectangular Problems of European Integration*, Project IV/95/02, Directorate General for Research of the European Parliament (1996). Online. Available HTTP: http://www.iue.it/AEL/EP/index.html (accessed 15 August 2000).

Barber, Benjamin R. *Jihad vs. McWorld* (New York: Times Books, 1995).

—— 'Three Challenges to Reinventing Democracy', in Paul Hirst and Sunil Khilnani (eds) *Reinventing Democracy* (Oxford: Blackwell, 1996).

—— 'Democracy at Risk: American Culture in a Global Culture', in *World Policy Journal*, vol. 15, no. 2 (Summer 1998).

Barnett, Anthony 'The Creation of Democracy', in Paul Hirst and Sunil Khilnani (eds) *Reinventing Democracy* (Oxford: Blackwell, 1996).

Bauböck, Rainer 'Citizenship and National Identities in the European Union', Harvard Law School, Jean Monnet Chair Working Paper Series, no. 4 (1997).

Baudrillard, Jean *Simulacra and Simulation* (Ann Arbor: University of Michigan Press, 1994).

—— *The Perfect Crime* (London: Verso, 1997).

Bauman, Zygmunt *Modernity and the Holocaust* (Ithaca NY: Cornell University Press, 1989).

—— *Modernity and Ambivalence* (Cambridge: Polity Press, 1991).

—— 'The Social Manipulation of Morality: Moralizing Actors, Adiaphorizing Action', in *Theory, Culture and Society*, vol. 8, no. 1 (1991).

—— 'Modernity, Postmodernity and Ethics – An Interview With Zygmunt Bauman' [no author], in *Telos*, no. 93 (Fall 1992).

—— *Intimations of Postmodernity* (London: Routledge, 1992).

—— *Postmodernity and Its Discontents* (New York: New York University Press, 1997).

—— *Globalization: The Human Consequences* (New York: Columbia University Press, 1998).

Bawn, Kathleen 'Constructing "Us": Ideology, Coalition Politics, and False Consciousness', in *American Journal of Political Science*, vol. 43, no. 2 (April 1999).

Bayard, Caroline, and Graham Knight 'Vivisecting the 90s: An Interview With Jean Baudrillard' (8 March 1995). Online. Available HTTP: http//www.ctheory.com/a24-vivisecting90s.html (accessed 28 March 2000).

Baykan, Aysegul 'Issues of Difference and Citizenship for "New Identities": A Theoretical View', in *Innovation*, vol. 10, no. 1 (March 1997).

Beck, Ulrich *Risk Society: Towards a New Modernity* (London: Sage, 1992).

—— 'The Reinvention of Politics: Towards a Theory of Reflexive Modernization', in Ulrich Beck, Anthony Giddens and Scott Lash, *Reflexive Modernization: Politics, Tradition and Aesthetics in the Modern Social Order* (Stanford CA: Stanford University Press, 1994).

Beck, Ulrich, and Elisabeth Beck-Gernsheim (eds) *Riskante Freiheiten: Zur Individualisierung von Lebensformen in der Moderne* (Frankfurt a/M: Suhrkamp, 1994).

—— 'Capitalism Without Work', in *Dissent*, vol. 44, no. 1 (Winter 1997).

—— 'The Cosmopolitan Manifesto', in *New Statesman*, 30 March 1998.

—— 'Das Demokratie-Dilemma im Zeitalter der Globalisierung', in *Aus Politik und Zeitgeschichte*, no. 38 (11 September 1998).

Beinart, Peter 'An Illusion For Our Time', in *The New Republic*, 20 October 1997.

Beiner, Ronald (ed.) *Theorizing Citizenship* (Albany: State University of New York Press, 1995).

Bell, Daniel *The Cultural Contradictions of Capitalism* (New York: Basic Books, 1996).

Benhabib, Seyla *The Reluctant Modernism of Hannah Arendt* (London: Sage, 1996).

—— 'On European Citizenship', in *Dissent*, vol. 45, no. 4 (Fall 1998).

Benko, Georges, and Ulf Strohmayer (eds) *Space and Social Theory: Interpreting Modernity and Postmodernity* (Oxford: Blackwell, 1997).

de Benoist, Alain 'The Idea of Empire', in *Telos*, no. 98–9 (Winter 1993).

Berg, Eiki 'Writing Post-Soviet Estonia onto the World Map', Copenhagen Peace Research Institute, COPRI Working Paper Series, no. 3 (2000).

Berger, Peter L. 'Four Faces of Global Culture', in *The National Interest*, no. 49 (Fall 1997).

Berman, George A. 'Subsidiarity in the European Community', in Paul Michael Lützeler (ed.) *Europe After Maastricht. American and European Perspectives* (Providence RI/Oxford: Berghahn Books, 1994).

Berman, Jerry, and Daniel J. Weitzner 'Technology and Democracy', in *Social Research*, vol. 64, no. 3 (Fall 1997).

Berman, Russell 'Beyond Localism and Universalism: Nationhood and Solidarity', in *Telos*, no. 105 (Fall 1995).

Bernstein, Richard J. *Beyond Objectivism and Relativism: Science, Hermeneutics, and Praxis* (Philadelphia: University of Pennsylvania Press, 1983).

Berten, André 'Identité européenne, une ou multiple? Réflexion sur les processus de formation de l'identité', in Jacques Lenoble and Nicole Dewandre (eds) *L'Europe au Soir du Siècle. Identité et Démocratie* (Paris: Esprit, 1992).

Beyer, Peter 'Identity and Character as Elective Strategies in Global Society', in *International Journal on World Peace*, vol. 14, no. 4 (December 1997).

von Beyme, Klaus 'Party Leadership and Change in Party Systems: Towards a Postmodern Party System?', in *Government and Opposition*, vol. 31, no. 2 (Spring 1996).

—— 'Shifting National Identities: The Case of German History', in *National Identities*, vol. 1, no. 1 (March 1999).

Bickford, Susan 'Anti-anti-identity Politics: Feminism, Democracy, and the Complexities of Citizenship', in *Hypatia*, vol. 12, no. 4 (Fall 1997).

Bifulco, Marco 'In Search of an Identity For Europe', Discussion Paper Series, no. 23 (Bonn: Rheinische Friedrich Wilhelms-Universität Zentrum für Europäische Integrationsforschung, 1998).

Birnbaum, Norman 'Democracy is as Democracy Does: An Inquiry', in *Salmagundi*, no. 116–17 (Fall 1997).

Blain, Neil, Raymond Boyle and Hugh O'Donnell *Sport and National Identity in the European Media* (Leicester: Leicester University Press, 1993).

Bleiker, Roland 'Forget IR Theory', in *Alternatives*, vol. 22, no. 1 (January/March 1997).

Bloom, William *Personal Identity, National Identity and International Relations* (Cambridge: Cambridge University Press, 1990).

den Boer, Monica 'Justice and Home Affairs: Co-operation Without Integration', in Helen Wallace and William Wallace (eds) *Policy-Making in the European Union* (Oxford: Oxford University Press, 1996).

Bogue, Ronald 'Art and Territory', in *South Atlantic Quarterly*, vol. 96, no. 3 (Summer 1997).

Bohman, James 'Citizenship and Norms of Publicity: Wide Public Reason in Cosmopolitan Societies', in *Political Theory*, vol. 27, no. 2 (April 1999).

Booth, W. James 'Communities of Memory: On Identity, Memory, and Debt', in *American Political Science Review*, vol. 93, no. 2 (June 1999).

Borgmann, Albert 'Society in the Postmodern Era', in *The Washington Quarterly*, vol. 23, no. 1 (Winter 2000).

Börzel, Tanja A. 'Does European Integration Really Strengthen the State? The Case of the Federal Republic of Germany', in *Regional and Federal Studies*, vol. 7, no. 3 (Autumn 1997).

—— 'Organizing Babylon – On the Different Conceptions of Policy Networks', in *Public Administration*, vol. 76, no. 2 (Summer 1998).

Boskovic, Aleksandar 'Hyperreal Serbia' (2 April 1996). Online. Available HTTP: http://www.ctheory.com/e39.html (accessed 28 March 2000).

Botwinick, Aryeh *Postmodernism and Democratic Theory* (Philadelphia: Temple University Press, 1993).

Boyce, Brigitte 'The Democratic Deficit of the European Community', in *Parliamentary Affairs*, vol. 46, no. 4 (October 1993).

Bozdogan, Sibel, and Resat Kasaba (eds) *Rethinking Modernity and National Identity in Turkey* (Seattle: University of Washington Press, 1997).

Bridges, Thomas *The Culture of Citizenship: Inventing Postmodern Civic Culture* (Albany: State University of New York Press, 1994).

Brown, Chris 'Turtles All the Way Down: Anti-Foundationalism, Critical Theory and International Relations', in *Millennium: Journal of International Studies*, vol. 23, no. 2 (Summer 1994).

Brown, Wendy 'Feminist Hesitations, Postmodern Exposures', in *Differences: A Journal of Feminist Cultural Studies*, vol. 3, no. 1 (Spring 1991).

—— 'Finding the Man in the State', in *Feminist Studies*, vol. 18, no. 1 (Spring 1992).

Brubaker, Rogers *Citizenship and Nationhood in France and Germany* (Cambridge MA: Harvard University Press, 1994).

Buckingham, David 'News Media, Political Socialization and Popular Citizenship: Towards a New Agenda', in *Critical Studies in Mass Communication*, vol. 14, no. 4 (December 1997).

Budge, Ian *The New Challenge of Direct Democracy* (Cambridge: Polity Press, 1996).

Bull, Hedley *The Anarchical Society: A Study of Order in World Politics* (London: Macmillan, 1997).

Bulmer, Simon J. 'The European Council and the Council of the European Union: Shapers of a European Confederation', in *Publius*, vol. 26, no. 4 (Fall 1996).

Burbules, Nicholas C., and Suzanne Rice 'Dialogue Across Differences: Continuing the Conversation', in *Harvard Educational Review*, vol. 61, no. 4 (November 1991).

Butler, Judith *Gender Trouble: Feminism and the Subversion of Identity* (New York: Routledge, 1990).

—— *Bodies That Matter. On the Discursive Limits of 'Sex'* (New York: Routledge, 1993).

—— *Excitable Speech: A Politics of the Performative* (New York: Routledge, 1996).

Buzan, Barry 'The Rise of "Lite" Powers: A Strategy for the Postmodern State', in *World Policy Journal*, vol. 13, no. 3 (Fall 1996).

Buzan, Barry, and Thomas Diez 'The European Union and Turkey', in *Survival*, vol. 41, no. 1 (Spring 1999).

Cafruny, Alan W., and Carl Lankowski 'Europe's Ambiguous Unity', in Alan W. Cafruny and Carl Lankowski (eds) *Europe's Ambiguous Unity: Conflict and Consensus in the Post-Maastricht Era* (Boulder CO: Lynne Rienner, 1997).

Caldwell, Anne 'Fairy Tales for Politics: The Other, Once More', in *Philosophy Today*, vol. 41, no. 1 (Spring 1997).

Calhoun, Craig J. (ed.) *Habermas and the Public Sphere* (Cambridge MA: MIT Press, 1993).

Calvocoressi, Peter 'The European State in the Twentieth Century and Beyond', in *International Relations*, vol. 14, no. 1 (April 1998).

Camilleri, Joseph A., and Jim Falk *The End of Sovereignty: The Politics of a Shrinking and Fragmenting World* (Aldershot: Edward Elgar, 1992).

Campbell, David 'Global Inscription: How Foreign Policy Constitutes the United States', in *Alternatives*, vol. 15, no. 3 (Summer 1990).

—— 'Political Prosaics, Transversal Politics, and the Anarchical World', in Michael J. Shapiro and Hayward R. Alker (eds) *Challenging Boundaries: Global Flows, Territorial Identities* (Minneapolis: University of Minnesota Press, 1996).

—— 'Apartheid Cartography: The Political Anthropology and Spatial Effects of International Diplomacy in Bosnia', in *Political Geography*, vol. 18, no. 4 (1999).

Canovan, Margaret 'Crusaders, Sceptics and the Nation', in *Journal of Political Ideologies*, vol. 3, no. 3 (October 1998).

Caporaso, James A. *The Structure and Function of European Integration* (Pacific Palisades CA: Goodyear, 1974).

Caporaso, James A., and John T.S. Keeler 'The European Union and Regional Integration Theory', in Carolyn Rhodes and Sonia Mazey (eds) *The State of the European Union: Building a European Polity?* (Boulder CO: Lynne Rienner, 1995).

—— 'The European Union and Forms of State: Westphalian, Regulatory or Postmodern?', in *Journal of Common Market Studies*, vol. 34, no. 1 (March 1996).

Carchedi, Bruno, and Guglielmo Carchedi 'Contradictions of European Integration', in *Capital and Class*, no. 67 (Spring 1999).

Cerny, Philip G. 'Globalization and Other Stories: The Search for a New Paradigm for International Relations', in *International Journal*, vol. 51, no. 4 (Autumn 1996).

—— 'Paradoxes of the Competition State: The Dynamics of Political Globalization', in *Government and Opposition*, vol. 32, no. 2 (Spring 1997).

Chambers, Simone *Reasonable Democracy: Jürgen Habermas and the Politics of Discourse* (Ithaca NY: Cornell University Press, 1996).

Cheah, Pheng, and Bruce Robbins (eds) *Cosmopolitics: Thinking and Feeling Beyond the Nation* (Minneapolis: University of Minnesota Press, 1998).

Chesnais, François *La Mondialisation du Capital* (Paris: Syros, 1994).

Chossudovsky, Michel 'Global Poverty in the Late 20th Century', in *Journal of International Affairs*, vol. 52, no. 1 (Fall 1998).

Chryssochoou, Dimitris N. *Democracy in the European Union* (London and New York: Tauris Academic Studies, 1998).

Clark, Ian 'Beyond the Great Divide: Globalization and the Theory of International Relations', in *Review of International Studies*, vol. 24, no. 4 (October 1998).

Clegg, Stewart R. *Frameworks of Power* (London: Sage, 1989).

Clinton, William J. 'Remarks at the World Trade Organization in Geneva, Switzerland', in *Weekly Compilation of Presidential Documents*, vol. 34, no. 21 (25 May 1998).

Close, Paul *Citizenship, Europe and Change* (London: Macmillan, 1995).

Coates, Crispin 'Spanish Regionalism and the European Union', in *Parliamentary Affairs*, vol. 51, no. 2 (April 1998).

Codd, Val 'Postmodernism Obfuscates Reality: No Room for Activism', in *Off Our Backs*, vol. 29, no. 8 (August/September 1999).

Cohen, Jean L. 'Democracy, Difference, and the Right of Privacy', in Seyla Benhabib (ed.) *Democracy and Difference: Contesting the Boundaries of the Political* (Princeton NJ: Princeton University Press, 1996).

Cohen, Michael P., James G. March and Johan P. Olsen 'A Garbage Can Model of Organizational Choice', in *Administrative Science Quarterly*, vol. 17, no. 1 (March 1972).

Connolly, William E. 'Tocqueville, Territory, and Violence', in Michael J. Shapiro and Hayward R. Alker (eds) *Challenging Boundaries: Global Flows, Territorial Identities* (Minneapolis: University of Minnesota Press, 1996).

Cook, Deborah *The Culture Industry Revisited: Adorno on Mass Culture* (Lanham MD: Rowman & Littlefield, 1996).

Coupland, Douglas *Life After God* (New York: Pocket Books, 1997).

Crawford, James 'Negotiating Global Security Threats in a World of Nation States', in *American Behavioral Scientist*, vol. 38, no. 6 (May 1995).

Crawford, Neta C. 'Postmodern Ethical Conditions and a Critical Response', in *Ethics and International Affairs*, vol. 12 (1998).

Cullet, Philippe 'Differential Treatment in International Law: Towards a New Paradigm in Inter-State Relations', in *European Journal of International Law*, vol. 10, no. 3 (1999).

Dahl, Robert A. *Who Governs? Democracy and Power in an American City* (New Haven and London: Yale University Press, 1961).

—— 'Power', in *International Encyclopaedia of the Social Sciences* (New York: Macmillan, 1968).

—— 'The Shifting Boundaries of Democratic Governments', in *Social Research*, vol. 66, no. 3 (Fall 1999).

Dahlgren, Peter *Television and the Public Sphere: Citizenship, Democracy and the Media* (London: Sage, 1995).

Dalby, Simon 'Security, Modernity, Ecology: The Dilemmas of Post-Cold War Security Dialogue', in *Alternatives*, vol. 17, no. 1 (Winter 1995).

Dammeyer, Manfred 'Speech at the Europe Conference of the European Movement in the Hague, the Netherlands', 10 May 1998.

Davies, Norman *Europe: A History* (Oxford: Oxford University Press, 1996).

—— 'The Euro is the Last Thing Europe Needs', in *The Sunday Times*, 24 May 1998.

Deeg, Richard E. 'Germany's *Länder* and the Federalization of the European Union', in Carolyn Rhodes and Sonia Mazey (eds) *The State of the European Union: Building a European Polity?* (Boulder CO: Lynne Rienner, 1995).

Deflem, Mathieu, and Fred C. Pampel 'The Myth of Postnational Identity: Popular Support for European Unification', in *Social Forces*, vol. 75, no. 1 (September 1996).

Deibert, Ronald J. ' "Exorcismus Theoriae": Pragmatism, Metaphors and the Return of the Medieval in IR', in *European Journal of International Relations*, vol. 3, no. 2 (June 1997).

Deleuze, Gilles, and Felix Guattari *Anti-Oedipus: Capitalism and Schizophrenia* (New York: Viking, 1977).

Dennard, Linda F. 'The Democratic Potential in the Transition of Postmodernism', in *American Behavioral Scientist*, vol. 41, no. 1 (September 1997).

Der Derian, James 'The (S)pace of International Relations: Simulation, Surveillance, and Speed', in *International Studies Quarterly*, vol. 34, no. 3 (September 1990).

—— *Antidiplomacy: Spies, Terror, Speed, and War* (Oxford: Blackwell, 1992).

—— 'The Value of Security: Hobbes, Marx, Nietzsche, and Baudrillard', in Ronnie D. Lipschutz (ed.) *On Security* (New York: Columbia University Press, 1995).

Derrida, Jacques *Of Grammatology* (Baltimore MD: Johns Hopkins University Press, 1998 – corrected edition).

Dery, David ' "Papereality" and Learning in Bureaucratic Organizations', in *Administration & Society*, vol. 29, no. 6 (January 1998).

Deutsch, Karl *Political Community and the North Atlantic Area* (Princeton NJ: Princeton University Press, 1957).

Diez, Thomas 'Postmoderne und europäische Integration: Die Dominanz des Staatmodells, die Verantwortung gegenüber dem anderen und die Konstruktion eines alternativen Horizonts', in *Zeitschrift für Internationale Beziehungen*, vol. 3, no. 3 (1996).

—— 'International Ethics and European Integration: Federal State or Network Horizon?', in *Alternatives*, vol. 22, no. 3 (Summer 1997).

—— *Die EU Lesen: Diskursive Knotenpunkte in der britischen Europadebatte* (Opladen: Leske & Budrich, 1999).

Dogan, Mattei 'Comparing the Decline of Nationalisms in Western Europe: The Generational Dynamic', in *International Social Science Journal*, vol. 45, no. 2 (May 1993).

Dogan, Rhys 'Comitology: Little Procedures with Big Implications', in *West European Politics*, vol. 20, no. 3 (July 1997).

Drezner, Daniel 'Globalizers of the World, Unite!', in *The Washington Quarterly*, vol. 21, no. 1 (Winter 1998).

Drucker, Peter F. 'The Post-Capitalist World: Toward a Knowledge-Based Society', in *The Public Interest*, no. 109 (Fall 1992).

Duffield, John S. 'Political Culture and State Behavior: Why Germany Confounds Neorealism', in *International Organization*, vol. 53, no. 4 (Autumn 1999).

Easton, David *The Political System: An Inquiry Into the State of Political Science* (New York: Knopf, 1953).

Eichener, V. 'Social Dumping or Innovative Regulation? Processes and Outcomes of European Decision-Making in the Sector of Health and Safety at Work Harmonization', EUI Working Paper Series, no. 92–28 (Florence: European University Institute, 1993).

Eisenstadt, S.N. 'Die Konstruktion nationaler Identitäten in vergleichender Perspektive', in Bernhard Giesen (ed.) *Nationale und kulturelle Identität* (Frankfurt a/M: Suhrkamp, 1991).

—— 'Modernity and the Construction of Collective Identities', in *International Journal of Comparative Sociology*, vol. 39, no. 1 (February 1998).

Eisenstadt, S.N., and B. Giesen 'The Construction of Collective Identity', in *Archives of European Sociology*, vol. 36 (1995).

Elkin, Stephen L., and Karol Edward Soltan (eds) *A New Constitutionalism: Designing Political Institutions for a Good Society* (Chicago: University of Chicago Press, 1993).

van Elteren, Mel 'GATT and Beyond: World Trade, the Arts and American Popular Culture in Western Europe', in *Journal of American Culture*, vol. 19, no. 3 (Fall 1996).

Emanuel, Susan 'A Community of Culture? The European Television Channel', in *History of European Ideas*, vol. 21, no. 2 (1995).

Emmerij, Louis 'Globalization, Regionalization and World Trade', in *Columbia Journal of World Business*, vol. 27, no. 2 (Summer 1992).

Epstein, Barbara 'Why Poststructuralism is a Dead End For Progressive Thought', in *Socialist Review*, vol. 25, no. 2 (1995).

Esber, Arwad 'In Quest of the Feminine: The Stranger Within Us (An Interview With Julia Kristeva)', in *Feminist Issues*, vol. 15, no. 1–2 (1997).

Eskelinen, Heikki, Ilkka Liikanen and Jukka Oksa (eds) *Curtains of Iron and Gold: Reconstructing Borders and Scales of Interaction* (Aldershot: Ashgate, 1999).

Euben, Roxanne L. 'Premodern, Antimodern or Postmodern? Islamic and Western Critiques of Modernity', in *The Review of Politics*, vol. 59, no. 3 (Summer 1997).

Eulau, Heiz *Micro-Macro Dilemmas in Political Science: Personal Pathways Through Complexity* (Norman OK and London: University of Oklahoma Press, 1996).

European Commission *First Report on the Consideration of Cultural Aspects in European Community Action* (Brussels, April 1996).

—— *Explicit Integration of Cultural Aspects Into Community Action and Policy* (Brussels, 1998).

European Parliament, Resolution on 'The Case of Andrei Babitsky, Freedom of the Media and Violations of Human Rights in Chechnya' (17 February 2000).

Ewen, Stuart 'Pragmatism's Postmodern Poltergeist', in *New Perspectives Quarterly*, vol. 9, no. 2 (Spring 1992).

Falk, Richard *Exploration at the Edge of Time: The Prospects for World Order* (Philadelphia: Temple University Press, 1993).

Farer, Tom 'New Players in the Old Game', in *American Behavioral Scientist*, vol. 38, no. 6 (May 1995).

Farmer, David John *The Language of Public Administration: Bureaucracy, Modernity, and Postmodernity* (Tuscaloosa: University of Alabama Press, 1995).

Featherstone, Mike 'Globalizing the Postmodern', in Mike Featherstone (ed.) *Undoing Culture: Globalization, Postmodernism and Identity* (London: Sage, 1995).

Feldman, Steven P. 'The Revolt Against Cultural Authority: Power/Knowledge as an Assumption in Organization Theory', in *Human Relations*, vol. 50, no. 8 (August 1997).

Ferguson, Kathy E. *The Feminist Case Against Bureaucracy* (Philadelphia: Temple University Press, 1985).

Fischer, Frank 'Beyond Empiricism: Policy Inquiry in Postpositivist Perspective', in *Policy Studies Journal*, vol. 26, no. 1 (Spring 1998).

Fischer, Joschka 'Europe's Choice: Full Unity or Old Balance-of-Power Wars', in *New Perspectives Quarterly*, vol. 14, no. 4 (Fall 1997).

Fischer, M.M.J. 'Is Islam the Odd-Civilization Out?', in *New Perspectives Quarterly*, vol. 9, no. 2 (Spring 1992).

Flax, Jane *Thinking Fragments: Psychoanalysis, Feminism, and Postmodernism in the Contemporary West* (Berkeley: University of California Press, 1991).

Flynn, Thomas R. 'Foucault and the Spaces of History', in *Monist*, vol. 74, no. 2 (April 1991).

Forland, Tor Egil 'Autonomy – Community – Suzerainty: Decision-Making Control and European Integration', in *Cooperation and Conflict*, vol. 32, no. 3 (September 1997).

Forment, Carlos A. 'Peripheral Peoples and Narrative Identities: Arendtian Reflections on Late Modernity', in Seyla Benhabib (ed.) *Democracy and Difference: Contesting the Boundaries of the Political* (Princeton NJ: Princeton University Press, 1996).

Forsberg, Tuomas 'Beyond Sovereignty, Within Territoriality: Mapping the Space of Late-Modern (Geo) Politics', in *Cooperation and Conflict*, vol. 31, no. 4 (December 1996).

Foucault, Michel 'Two Lectures', in Colin Gordon (ed.) *Power/Knowledge: Selected Interviews and Other Writings* (New York: Pantheon, 1980).

—— 'Disciplinary Power and Subjection', reprinted in Steven Lukes (ed.) *Power* (New York: New York University Press, 1986).

—— *Foucault Live: Interviews 1966–84* (New York: Semiotext(e), 1989).

—— 'Governmentality', in Graham Burchell, Colin Gordon and Peter Miller (eds) *The Foucault Effect* (Chicago: University of Chicago Press, 1991).

—— *The Order of Things: An Archeology of the Human Sciences* (New York: Vintage Books, 1994).

Fox, Charles J., and Hugh T. Miller *Postmodern Public Administration: Toward Discourse* (London: Sage, 1995).

Fraser, Nancy 'Rethinking the Public Sphere: A Contribution to the Critique of Actually Existing Democracy', in Craig J. Calhoun (ed.) *Habermas and the Public Sphere* (Cambridge MA: MIT Press, 1993).

Fredet, Jean-Gabriel 'France–US. The Cultural War is 50 Years Old', in *Le Nouvel Observateur* (26 February–4 March 1998).

Friedman, Thomas 'Turning Swords Into Beef-Burgers', in *The Guardian*, 19 December 1996.

Friedrich-Silber, Ilana 'Space, Fields, Boundaries: The Rise of Spatial Metaphors in Contemporary Sociological Theory', in *Social Research*, vol. 62, no. 2 (Summer 1995).

Fuchs, Gerhard 'The European Commission as Corporate Actor? European Telecommunications Policy After Maastricht', in Carolyn Rhodes and Sonia Mazey (eds) *The State of the European Union: Building a European Polity?* (Boulder CO: Lynne Rienner, 1995).

Fuller, Graham E., and Ian O. Lesser *A Sense of Siege: The Geopolitics of Islam and the West* (Boulder CO: Westview Press, 1995).

Fumaroli, Marc ' "I is an Other": Delusions of Identity', in *Diogenes*, vol. 45, no. 1 (Spring 1997).

Gabel, Matthew *Interests and Integration: Market Liberalization, Public Opinion, and European Union* (Ann Arbor: University of Michigan Press, 1998).

—— 'Public Support For European Integration: An Empirical Test of Five Theories', in *The Journal of Politics*, vol. 60, no. 2 (May 1998).

Gaddis, John Lewis 'International Relations Theory and the End of the Cold War', in *International Security*, vol. 17, no. 3 (Winter 1992).

Garcia, Soledad (ed.) *European Identity and the Search for Legitimacy* (London: Pinter, 1993).

Gardels, Nathan 'Interview With Costa-Gavras', in *New Perspectives Quarterly*, vol. 12, no. 4 (Fall 1995).

—— 'The Making of McWorld', in *New Perspectives Quarterly*, vol. 12, no. 4 (Fall 1995).

—— 'Interview With Jacques Delors', in *New Perspectives Quarterly*, vol. 13, no. 1 (Winter 1996).

Garrett, Geoffrey, and George Tsebelis 'An Institutional Critique of Intergovernmentalism', in *International Organization*, vol. 50, no. 2 (Spring 1996).

Garton Ash, Timothy 'Europe's Endangered Liberal Order', in *Foreign Affairs*, vol. 77, no. 2 (March/April 1998).

George, Jim 'International Relations and the Search for Thinking Space: Another View of the Third Debate', in *International Studies Quarterly*, vol. 33, no. 3 (September 1989).

—— 'Of Incarceration and Closure: Neo-Realism and the New/Old World Orders', in *Millennium: Journal of International Studies*, vol. 22, no. 2 (Summer 1993).

—— 'Understanding International Relations After the Cold War: Probing Beyond the Realist Legacy', in Michael J. Shapiro and Hayward R. Alker (eds) *Challenging Boundaries: Global Flows, Territorial Identities* (Minneapolis: University of Minnesota Press, 1996).

Giddens, Anthony 'Living in a Post-Traditional Society', in Ulrich Beck, Anthony Giddens and Scott Lash (eds) *Reflexive Modernization: Politics, Tradition, and Aesthetics in the Modern Social Order* (Stanford CA: Stanford University Press, 1994).

—— *Beyond Left and Right: The Future of Radical Politics* (Stanford CA: Stanford University Press, 1995).

—— 'Post-Traditional Civil Society and the Radical Center', in *New Perspectives Quarterly*, vol. 15, no. 2 (Spring 1998).

Gilbert, Alan 'Must Global Politics Constrain Democracy?', in *Political Theory*, vol. 20, no. 1 (February 1992).

Glynn, Patrick 'The Age of Balkanization', in *Commentary*, vol. 96, no. 1 (July 1993).

Goldblatt, David, David Held, Anthony McGrew and Jonathan Perraton 'Economic Globalization and the Nation-State: Shifting Balances of Power', in *Alternatives*, vol. 22, no. 3 (July/September 1997).

Goodman, John B. *Monetary Sovereignty: The Politics of Central Banking in Western Europe* (Ithaca NY: Cornell University Press, 1992).

Gorbachev, Mikhail *Perestroika: New Thinking for Our Country and the World* (London: Fontana, 1988).

Gordon, Philip H. ' "Rogue States" and Transatlantic Relations', in Frances G. Burwell and Ivo H. Daalder (eds) *The United States and Europe in the Global Arena* (London: Macmillan Press, 1999).

Gottdiener, M. *Postmodern Semiotics: Material Culture and the Forms of Postmodern Life* (Oxford: Blackwell, 1995).

Gray, John 'Globalization – The Dark Side', in *New Statesman and Society*, 13 March 1998.

Greenfeld, Liah 'Nationalism and Modernity', in *Social Research*, vol. 63, no. 1 (Spring 1996).

Greenfield, Matthew 'What We Talk About When We Talk About Culture', in *Raritan*, vol. 19, no. 2 (Fall 1999).

Gregory, Derek *Geographical Imaginations* (Oxford: Blackwell, 1993).

Gress, David *From Plato to NATO: The Idea of the West and Its Opponents* (New York: Free Press, 1998).

Grimm, Dieter 'Does Europe Need a Constitution?', in Peter Gowan and Perry Anderson (eds) *The Question of Europe* (London: Verso Books, 1997).

Grudzinski, Przemyslaw, and Peter van Ham *A Critical Approach to European Security: Identity and Institutions* (London: Cassell Academic, 1999).

Gunn, Giles 'Rorty's Novum Organum', in *Raritan*, vol. 10, no. 1 (Summer 1990).

Habermas, Jürgen *The Structural Transformation of the Public Sphere* (Cambridge MA: MIT Press, 1989).

—— 'What Does Socialism Mean Today?', in *New Left Review*, no. 183 (September 1990).

—— *Faktizität und Geltung* (Frankfurt a/M: Suhrkamp, 1992).

—— *Between Facts and Norms: Contributions to a Discourse Theory of Law and Democracy* (Cambridge MA: MIT Press, 1996).

—— *The Inclusion of the Other: Studies in Political Theory* (Cambridge MA: MIT Press, 1998).

Haltern, Ulrich 'Intergovernmentalism as a Way of Union Governance', Annex to A. Ballmann and J.H.H. Weiler *Certain Rectangular Problems of European Integration*, Project IV/95/02, Directorate General for Research of the European Parliament (1996). Online. Available HTTP: http://www.iue.it/AEL/EP/index.html (accessed 15 August 2000).

van Ham, Peter, and Przemyslaw Grudzinski 'Affluence and Influence: The Conceptual Basis of Europe's New Politics', in *The National Interest*, no. 58 (Winter 1999/2000).

—— 'Europe's New Defense Ambitions: Implications for NATO, the US, and Russia', Marshall Center Paper Series, no. 1 (Garmisch-Partenkirchen: June 2000).

Hammer, Dean C. 'Vaclav Havel's Construction of a Democratic Discourse: Politics in a Postmodern Age', in *Philosophy Today*, vol. 39, no. 2 (Summer 1995).

—— 'Incommensurable Phrases and Narrative Discourse: Lyotard and Arendt on the Possibility of Politics', in *Philosophy Today*, vol. 41, no. 4 (Winter 1997).

Hanke, Robert 'Theorizing Masculinity: With/In the Media', in *Communication Theory*, vol. 8, no. 2 (May 1998).

Hänsch, Klaus 'Reasserting the Political Will to Move Europe Forward'. The Robert Schuman Lecture at the European University Institute (Florence), 27 June 1996. Online. Available HTTP: http://www.iue.it/AEL/documents/haensch.html (accessed 15 August 2000).

Hansen, Lene 'A Case for Seduction? Evaluating the Poststructuralist Conceptualization of Security', in *Cooperation and Conflict*, vol. 32, no. 4 (December 1997).

—— 'R.B.J. Walker and International Relations: Deconstructing a Discipline', in Iver B. Neumann and Ole Wæver (eds) *The Future of International Relations: Masters in the Making?* (London: Routledge, 1997).

Hardy, Christianne 'European Political Parties and the European Union: Some Disintegrating Trends of Integration', in *World Affairs*, vol. 157, no. 1 (Summer 1994).

Hartley, John *The Politics of Pictures: The Creation of the Public in the Age of Popular Media* (London: Routledge, 1992).

Hartman, Geoffrey 'Public Memory and Its Discontents', in *Raritan*, vol. 13, no. 4 (Spring 1994).

Harvey, David 'Capitalism: The Factory of Fragmentation', in *New Perspectives Quarterly*, vol. 9, no. 2 (Spring 1992).

Hassard, John, and Martin Parker (eds) *Postmodernism and Organizations* (London: Sage, 1993).

Havel, Vaclav 'Speech to the Academy of Humanities and Political Science in Paris, France', 27 October 1992. Online. Available HTTP: http://www.hrad.cz/president/ Havel/speeches/1992/2710uk.html (accessed 2 August 2000).

—— 'Speech to the European Parliament in Strasbourg, France', 8 March 1994. Online. Available HTTP: http://www.hrad.cz/president/Havel/speeches/indexuk.html (accessed 15 August 2000).

Hedetoft, Ulf 'The State of Sovereignty in Europe: Political Concept or Cultural Self-Image', in Staffan Zetterholm (ed.) *National Cultures and European Integration: Exploratory Essays on Cultural Diversity and Common Policies* (Providence RI/ Oxford: Berg, 1994).

Heelas, Paul, and David Martin (eds) *Religion, Modernity and Postmodernity* (Oxford: Blackwell, 1998).

Held, David 'Democracy and Globalization', in *Global Governance*, vol. 3, no. 3 (September/December 1997).

Henderson, Hazel *Paradigms in Progress: Life Beyond Economics* (San Francisco CA.: Berrett-Koehler, 1995).

Herman, Edward S., and Noam Chomsky *Manufacturing Consent: The Political Economy of the Mass Media* (New York: Pantheon, 1988).

Hidien, Jürgen W. *Der bundesstaatliche Finanzausgleich in Deutschland* (Baden-Baden: Nomos, 1999).

Hirst, Paul, and Sunil Khilnani (eds) *Reinventing Democracy* (Oxford: Blackwell, 1996).

Hix, Simon 'Elections, Parties and Institutional Design: A Comparative Perspective on European Union Democracy', in *West European Politics*, vol. 21, no. 3 (July 1998).

Hobsbawm, Eric 'Language, Culture, and National Identity', in *Social Research*, vol. 63, no. 4 (Winter 1996).

Hodess, Robin B. 'The Role of News Media in European Integration: A Framework of Analysis for Political Science', in *Res Publica*, vol. 39, no. 2 (1997).

Hodgson, Godfrey 'Grand Illusion: The Failure of European Consciousness', in *World Policy Journal*, vol. 10, no. 2 (Summer 1993).

Hoffman, John *Sovereignty* (Minneapolis: University of Minnesota Press, 1998).

Hoksbergen, Roland 'Postmodernism and Institutionalism: Toward a Resolution of the Debate on Relativism', in *Journal of Economic Issues*, vol. 28, no. 3 (September 1994).

Holm, Hans-Henrik, and Georg Sorensen 'International Relations Theory in a World of Variation', in Hans-Henrik Holm and Georg Sorensen (eds) *Whose World Order? Uneven Globalization and the End of the Cold War* (Boulder CO: Westview Press, 1995).

Holmes, David 'Virtual Identity: Communities of Broadcast, Communities of Interactivity', in David Holmes (ed.) *Virtual Politics: Identity and Community in Cyberspace* (London: Sage, 1997).

Hood, C. Ellsworth 'Nietzsche Contra Postmodernism', in *Philosophy Today*, vol. 41, no. 3 (Fall 1997).

Hooghe, Liesbet, and Michael Keating 'The Politics of European Union Regional Policy', in *Journal of European Public Policy*, vol. 1, no. 3 (September 1994).

Hooghe, Liesbet, and Gary Marks 'Contending Models of Governance in the European Union', in Alan W. Cafruny and Carl Lankowski (eds) *Europe's Ambiguous Unity: Conflict and Consensus in the Post-Maastricht Era* (Boulder CO: Lynne Rienner, 1997).

—— 'Supranational Activists or Intergovernmental Agents? Explaining the Orientations of Senior Commission Officials Toward European Integration', in *Comparative Political Studies*, vol. 32, no. 4 (June 1999).

Höreth, Marcus 'The Trilemma of Legitimacy: Multilevel Governance in the EU and the Problem of Democracy', Discussion Paper Series, no. 11 (Bonn: Rheinische Friedrich Wilhelms-Universität, Zentrum für Europäische Integrationsforschung, 1998).

Hoskyns, C. 'Women, European Law, and Transnational Politics', in *International Journal of the Sociology of Law*, vol. 14 (1986).

Howe, Geoffrey 'Sovereignty and Interdependence: Britain's Place in the World', in *International Affairs*, vol. 66, no. 4 (October 1990).

Howe, Paul 'A Community of Europeans: The Requisite Underpinnings', in *Journal of Common Market Studies*, vol. 33, no. 1 (March 1995).

Humphreys, Peter J. *Mass Media and Media Policy in Western Europe* (Manchester: Manchester University Press, 1996).

Huntington, Samuel P. *The Clash of Civilizations and the Remaking of World Order* (New York: Simon & Schuster, 1996).

Ignatieff, Michael 'Nationalism and Toleration', in Richard Caplan and John Feffer (eds) *Europe's New Nationalism: States and Minorities in Conflict* (New York: Oxford University Press, 1996).

Immergut, Ellen M. 'The Theoretical Core of the New Institutionalism', in *Politics and Society*, vol. 26, no. 1 (March 1998).

Inglehart, Ronald *Cultural Shift in Advanced Industrial Society* (Princeton NJ: Princeton University Press, 1990).

—— *Modernization and Postmodernization: Cultural, Economic, and Political Change in 43 Societies* (Princeton NJ: Princeton University Press, 1997).

—— 'Globalization and Postmodern Values', in *The Washington Quarterly*, vol. 23, no. 1 (Winter 2000).

Inglehart, Ronald and Paul R. Abramson 'Economic Security and Value Change', in *American Political Science Review*, vol. 88, no. 2 (June 1994).

Jahabegloo, Ramin *Conversations With Isaiah Berlin* (London: Peter Halban, 1992).

James, Alan *Sovereign Statehood* (London: Allen & Unwin, 1986).

Jameson, Fredric *Postmodernism, or, the Cultural Logic of Late Capitalism* (Durham NC: Duke University Press, 1992).

—— *The Geopolitical Aesthetic: Cinema and Space in the World System* (Bloomington IN: Indiana University Press, 1995).

Jarvis, Darryl S.L. 'Postmodernism: A Critical Typology', in *Politics and Society*, vol. 26, no. 1 (March 1998).

—— *International Relations and the Challenge of Post-Modernism: Defending the Discipline* (Columbia SC: University of South Carolina Press, 2000).

Jauregui, José Antonio, 'The ECU as Vehicle of European Culture and Feelings', in Louis le Hardy de Beaulieu (ed.) *From Democratic Deficit to a Europe for Citizens*, Collection 'Perspectives' (Namur: Presses Universitaires de Namur, 1995).

Jepperson, Ronald L., Alexander Wendt and Peter J. Katzenstein 'Norms, Identity, and Culture in National Security', in Peter J. Katzenstein (ed.) *The Culture of National Security: Norms and Identity in World Politics* (New York: Columbia University Press, 1996).

Jervis, Robert 'The Future of World Politics: Will It Resemble the Past?', in *International Security*, vol. 16, no. 3 (Winter 1991).

Joerges, Christian 'States Without a Market? Comments on the German Constitutional Court's Maastricht-Judgement and a Plea for Interdisciplinary Discourses', in *European Integration online Papers* (*EIoP*), vol. 1, no. 20 (1997). Online. Available HTTP: http://olymp.wu-wien.ac.at/eiop (accessed 15 August 2000).

Joffé, George 'Democracy, Islam and the Culture of Modernism', in *Democratization*, vol. 4, no. 3 (Autumn 1997).

Johnston, Donald J. 'A New Global Age', in *OECD Observer*, no. 207 (August/September 1997).

Jordan, Grant, and William A. Maloney 'Accounting for Subgovernments: Explaining the Persistence of Policy Communities', in *Administration and Society*, vol. 29, no. 5 (November 1997).

Jordan, Tim 'The Philosophical Politics of Jean-François Lyotard', in *Philosophy of the Social Sciences*, vol. 25, no. 3 (September 1995).

Jörgensen, Knud Erik 'Beyond European Leviathans: Differentiating Layers of International Tranformation', in Nils Arne Sorensen (ed.) *European Identities: Cultural Diversity and Integration in Europe Since 1700* (Odense: Odense University Press, 1995).

—— (ed.) *Reflective Approaches to European Governance* (London: Macmillan, 1997).

Katz, Jon 'Birth of a Digital Nation', *Wired*, issue 5.04 (April 1997). Online. Available HTTP: http://www.wired.com/wired/archive/5.04/netizen.html (accessed 28 March 2000).

Kauffman, L.A. 'Democracy in a Postmodern World?', in *Social Policy*, vol. 21, no. 2 (Fall 1990).

Kaufman, Cynthia 'Postmodernism and Praxis: Weaving Radical Theory From Threads of Desire and Discourse', in *Socialist Review*, vol. 24, no. 3 (1994).

Kellner, Douglas 'Techno-Politics, New Technologies, and the New Public Spheres', in *Illuminations: The Critical Theory Website* (no date). Online. Available HTTP: http://www.uta.edu/huma/illuminations/kell32.htm (accessed 28 March 2000).

Keohane, Robert O. 'Hobbes's Dilemma and Institutional Change in World Politics: Sovereignty in International Society', in Hans-Henrik Holm and Georg Sorensen (eds) *Whose World Order? Uneven Globalization and the End of the Cold War* (Boulder CO: Westview Press, 1995).

Keohane, Robert O., and Stanley Hoffmann, 'Institutional Change in Europe in the 1980s', in Robert O. Keohane and Stanley Hoffmann (eds) *The New European Community: Decisionmaking and Institutional Change* (Boulder CO: Westview Press, 1991).

Kerber, Linda K. 'The Meanings of Citizenship', in *Dissent*, vol. 44, no. 1 (Fall 1997).

Klusmeyer, Douglas B. *Between Consent and Descent: Conceptions of Democratic Citizenship* (Washington DC: Carnegie Endowment for International Peace, 1996).

Kobrin, Stephen J. 'Back to the Future: Neomedievalism and the Postmodern Digital World Economy', in *Journal of International Affairs*, vol. 51, no. 2 (Spring 1998).

—— 'The MAI and the Clash of Globalization', in *Foreign Policy*, no. 112 (Fall 1998).

Kohl, Helmut 'Speech at Leuven University, Belgium', 2 February 1996.

Koslowski, Rey 'A Constructivist Approach to Understanding the European Union as a Federal Policy', in *Journal of European Public Policy*, vol. 6, no. 4 (December 1999).

Kostakopoulou, Theodora 'Why a "Community of Europeans" Could Be a Community of Exclusion: A Reply to Howe', in *Journal of Common Market Studies*, vol. 35, no. 2 (June 1997).

Kothari, Rajni 'Globalization: A World Adrift', in *Alternatives*, vol. 22, no. 2 (April/June 1997).

Krasner, Stephen D. 'Sovereignty: An Institutional Perspective', in *Comparative Political Studies*, vol. 21, no. 1 (April 1988).

Kratochwil, Friedrich 'Citizenship: On the Border of Order', in *Alternatives*, vol. 19, no. 4 (Fall 1994).

Kristeva, Julia *Strangers to Ourselves* (New York: Harvester Wheatsheaf, 1991).

Kushner, David 'Self-Perception and Identity in Contemporary Turkey', in *Journal of Contemporary History*, vol. 32, no. 2 (April 1997).

Laffan, Brigid 'Nations and Regions in Western Europe', Paper presented at the 2nd ECSA-World Conference, Brussels (May 1994).

—— 'The Politics of Identity and Political Order in Europe', in *Journal of Common Market Studies*, vol. 34, no. 1 (August 1996).

—— 'The European Union: A Distinctive Model of Internationalisation', in *European Integration online Papers (EIoP)*, vol. 1, no. 18 (1997). Online. Available HTTP: http://olymp.wu-wien.ac.at/eiop (accessed 15 August 2000).

Laitin, David D. 'The Cultural Identities of a European State', in *Politics and Society*, vol. 25, no. 3 (September 1997).

Lane, Jan-Erik 'Governance in the European Union', in *West European Politics*, vol. 20, no. 4 (October 1997).

Lang, Jack 'MAI is the Enemy', in *Le Monde*, 10 February 1998.

Lapham, Lewis H. 'Leviathan in Trouble', in *Harper's Magazine*, September 1988.

Lapid, Yosef, and Friedrich Kratochwil (eds) *The Return of Culture and Identity in IR Theory* (Boulder CO: Lynne Rienner, 1996).

Lapidoth, Ruth 'Redefining Authority', in *Harvard International Review*, vol. 17, no. 3 (Summer 1995).

Lapidus, Gail W., and Edward W. Walker 'Nationalism, Regionalism, and Federalism: Center–Periphery Relations in Post-Communist Russia', in Gail W. Lapidus (ed.) *The New Russia: Troubled Transformation* (Boulder CO: Westview Press, 1995).

Laswell, Harold *Politics: Who Gets What, When, How* (New York: Meridian Books, 1958).

Latham, Robert 'Liberalism's Order/Liberalism's Other: A Genealogy of Threat', in *Alternatives*, vol. 20, no. 1 (January/March 1995).

Latour, Bruno *Science in Action: How to Follow Scientists and Engineers Through Society* (Cambridge MA: Harvard University Press, 1987).

Lefort, Claude *Democracy and Political Theory* (Minneapolis: University of Minnesota Press, 1988).

Lehmbruch, Gerhard 'Institutional Linkages and Policy Networks in the Federal System of West Germany', in *Publius*, vol. 19, no. 4 (Fall 1989).

Leonard, Stephen T. *Critical Theory in Political Practice* (Princeton NJ: Princeton University Press, 1990).

Letamendia, Francisco 'Basque Nationalism and Cross-Border Co-operation Between the Southern and Northern Basque Countries', in *Regional and Federal Studies*, vol. 7, no. 2 (Summer 1997).

Lieven, Anatol 'Qu'est-ce qu'une Nation?', in *The National Interest*, no. 49 (Fall 1997).

Lijphart, Arend 'Consociational Democracy', in *World Politics*, vol. 21, no. 2 (January 1969).

Linklater, Andrew 'The Question of the Next Stage in International Relations Theory: A Critical-Theoretical Point of View', in *Millennium: Journal of International Studies*, vol. 21, no. 1 (Spring 1992).

—— 'The Transformation of Political Community: E.H. Carr, Critical Theory and International Relations', in *Review of International Studies*, vol. 23, no. 3 (July 1997).

—— *The Transformation of Political Community* (Columbia SC: University of South Carolina Press, 1998).

—— 'Transforming Political Community: A Response to the Critics', in *Review of International Studies*, vol. 25, no. 1 (January 1999).

Linstead, Stephen, and Robert Grafton-Small 'On Reading Organizational Culture', in *Organization Studies*, vol. 13, no. 3 (1992).

Lipschutz, Ronnie D. 'Negotiating the Boundaries of Difference and Security at Millennium's End', in Ronnie D. Lipschutz (ed.) *On Security* (New York: Columbia University Press, 1995).

Lister, Ruth 'Dialectices of Citizenship', in *Hypatia*, vol. 12, no. 4 (Fall 1997).

Lloyd, Trevor 'Union and Division in Europe', in *International Journal*, vol. 52, no. 4 (Autumn 1997).

Locke, John *Two Treatises of Government* [1690] (Cambridge: Cambridge University Press, 1988).

Lodge, Juliet 'Transparency and Democratic Legitimacy', in *Journal of Common Market Studies*, vol. 32, no. 3 (September 1994).

—— 'Federalism and the European Parliament', in *Publius*, vol. 26, no. 4 (Fall 1996).

Loughlin, John ' "Europe of the Regions" and the Federalization of Europe', in *Publius*, vol. 26, no. 4 (Fall 1996).

Lubbers, R.F.M. 'Globalisation and Value Systems', in Roberto Papini, Antonio Pavan and Stefano Zamagni (eds) *Living in the Global Society* (Aldershot: Ashgate, 1997).

Luke, Timothy W. 'Governmentality and Contragovernmentality: Rethinking Sovereignty and Territoriality After the Cold War', in *Political Geography*, vol. 15, no. 6–7 (July/September 1996).

—— 'Nationality and Sovereignty in the New World Order', in *AntePodium*, no. 3 (1996). Online. Available HTTP: http://www.vuw.ac.nz/atp (accessed 28 March 2000).

Lukes, Steven *Power: A Radical View* (London: Macmillan, 1974).

Lummis, C. Douglas *Radical Democracy* (Ithaca NY: Cornell University Press, 1996).

Lundquist, Karl-Johan, and Lars-Olof Olanter 'Regional Economies: A Threat to the Nation-State?', Paper presented at the Conference 'The Survival of the Nation State', Lund University, Sweden (30 March 1998).

Luttwak, Edward 'Central Bankism', in Peter Gowan and Perry Anderson (eds) *The Question of Europe* (London: Verso, 1997).

Lyotard, Jean-François *The Postmodern Condition: A Report on Knowledge* (Minneapolis: University of Minnesota Press, 1984).

—— *The Differend: Phases in Dispute* (Minneapolis: University of Minnesota Press, 1988).

—— *The Postmodern Explained: Correspondence, 1982–1985* (Minneapolis: University of Minnesota Press, 1992).

McClelland, J.S. *A History of Western Political Thought* (London: Routledge, 1996).

McKinlay, Patrick F. 'Postmodernism and Democracy: Learning From Lyotard and Lefort', in *Journal of Politics*, vol. 60, no. 2 (May 1988).

Maclaren, Roy, 'Government and National Parliaments: How Relevant is Economic Globalization and Regionalization in the Next Millennium', in *Vital Speeches of the Day*, 1 May 1998.

McLaughlin, Audrey, and Justin Greenwood 'The Management of Interest Representation in the European Union', in *Journal of Common Market Studies*, vol. 33, no. 1 (March 1995).

MacMillan, John, and Andrew Linklater (eds) *Boundaries in Question: New Directions in International Relations* (New York: St Martin's Press, 1995).

McNeil, Daniel, and Paul Freiberger *Fuzzy Logic: The Revolutionary Computer Technology That is Changing Our World* (New York: Simon & Schuster, 1993).

Majone, Giandomenico 'Independence vs. Accountability: Non-Majoritarian Institutions and Democratic Government in Europe', EUI Working Paper Series, no. 94–3 (Florence: European University Institute, 1994).

Malcolm, Derek 'You Silly Santer: Pass the Popcorn', in *The Guardian*, 9 April 1998.

Malcolm, Noel, 'Qu'est-ce qu'une Refutation/Reply', in *The National Interest*, no. 50 (Winter 1997/98).

Mander, Jerry 'The Dark Side of Globalization: What the Media are Missing', in *The Nation*, 15–22 July 1996.

Manent, Pierre 'On Modern Individualism', in *Journal of Democracy*, vol. 7, no. 1 (January 1996).

—— 'Democracy Without Nations', in *Journal of Democracy*, vol. 8, no. 2 (April 1997).

Marks, Gary, Liesbet Hooghe and Kermit Blank 'Integration Theory, Subsidiarity and the Internationalisation of Issues: The Implications for Legitimacy', EUI Robert Schuman Centre Working Paper Series, no. 95–7 (Florence: European University Institute, 1995).

Marks, Gary, Fritz Scharpf, Philippe C. Schmitter and Wolfgang Streeck *Governance in the European Union* (London: Sage, 1996).

Martin, Denis-Constant 'The Choices of Identity', in *Social Identities*, vol. 1, no. 1 (1995).

Martin, Laurence, and John Roper (eds) *Towards a Common Defence Policy* (Paris: WEU Institute for Security Studies, 1995).

Mattern, Douglas 'Democracy or Corporate Rule?', in *Humanist*, vol. 58, no. 4 (July/August 1998).

Mazey, Sonia, and Jeremy Richardson, 'Promiscuous Policymaking: The European Policy Style?', in Carolyn Rhodes and Sonia Mazey (eds) *The State of the European Union: Building a European Polity?* (Boulder CO: Lynne Rienner, 1995).

—— 'Policy Framing: Interest Groups and the Lead up to the 1996 Inter-Governmental Conference', in *West European Politics*, vol. 20, no. 3 (July 1997).

—— (eds) *Lobbying in the European Community* (Oxford: Oxford University Press, 1993).

Mazlish, Bruce *The Uncertain Sciences* (New Haven CT: Yale University Press, 1998).

Mead, Walter Russell 'Trains, Planes, and Automobiles: The End of the Postmodern Moment', in *World Policy Journal*, vol. 12, no. 4 (Winter 1995).

Medvedev, Sergei ' "Zwischeneuropa": Historic Experiences, National Views and Strategic Alternatives', UPI Working Paper Series, no. 6 (Helsinki: Finnish Institute of International Affairs, 1998).

Meehan, Elizabeth *Citizenship and the European Community* (London: Sage, 1993).

Meier, Kenneth J., and Richard W. Waterman 'Principal–Agent Models: An Expansion?', in *Journal of Public Administration Research and Theory*, vol. 8, no. 2 (April 1998).

Melchior, Josef 'Is a Transnational Political Community Possible?', Paper presented at the 1998 APSA annual meeting, Boston (September 1998).

Merritt, Deborah 'The Fuzzy Logic of Federalism', in *Case Western Reserve Law Review*, vol. 46, no. 3 (Spring 1996).

Mestrovic, Stjepan G. *The Balkanization of the West: The Confluence of Postmodernism and Postcommunism* (London/New York: Routledge, 1994).

Metcalfe, Les 'The European Commission as a Network Organization', in *Publius*, vol. 26, no. 4 (Fall 1996).

Michalski, Jerry 'What is a Virtual Community?', in *New Perspectives Quarterly*, vol. 12, no. 2 (Spring 1992).

Mikkeli, Heikki *Europe as an Idea and an Identity* (New York: St Martin's Press, 1998).

Millan, Bruce 'The Committee of the Regions: In at the Birth', in *Regional and Federal Studies*, vol. 7, no. 1 (Spring 1997).

Miller, David 'The Left, the Nation-State, and European Citizenship', in *Dissent*, vol. 45, no. 3 (Summer 1998).

Miller, Richard W. 'Cosmopolitan Respect and Patriotic Concern', in *Philosophy and Public Affairs*, vol. 27, no. 3 (Summer 1998).

Milward, Alan S. (with the assistance of George Brennan and Frederico Romero) *The European Rescue of the Nation-State* (Berkeley/Los Angeles: University of California Press, 1992).

Minc, Alain *The Great European Illusion: Business in the Wider Community* (Oxford: Blackwell, 1992).

Minogue, Kenneth 'Does National Sovereignty Have a Future?', in *National Review*, vol. 48, no. 24 (23 December 1996).

Mitchell, Mark, and Dave Russell 'Immigration, Citizenship and the Nation-State in the New Europe', in Brian Jenkins and Spyros A. Sofos (eds) *Nation and Identity in Contemporary Europe* (London/New York: Routledge, 1996).

Mitchell, Ronald B. 'Discourse and Sovereignty: Interests, Science, and Morality in the Regulation of Whaling', in *Global Governance*, vol. 4, no. 3 (July/September 1998).

Mittelman, James H. (ed.) *Globalization: Critical Reflections* (Boulder CO: Lynne Rienner, 1996).

Mlinar, Zdravko 'Individuation and Globalization: The Transformation of Territorial Social Organization', in Zdravko Mlinar (ed.) *Globalization and Territorial Identities* (Aldershot: Avebury, 1992).

Moïsi, Dominique 'The World Moves On', in *Financial Times*, 8 June 1998.

Moller, J. Orstrom *The Future European Model: Economic Internationalization and Cultural Decentralization* (Westport CT: Praeger, 1995).

Moravcsik, Andrew 'Negotiating the Single European Act: National Interests and Conventional Statecraft in the European Community', in *International Organization*, vol. 45, no. 1 (Winter 1991).

—— 'Preferences and Power in the European Community: A Liberal Intergovernmentalist Approach', in *Journal of Common Market Studies*, vol. 31, no. 4 (December 1993).

—— *The Choice for Europe: Social Purpose and State Power From Messina to Maastricht* (Ithaca NY: Cornell University Press, 1998).

Morson, Gary Saul 'Prosaics: An Approach to the Humanities', in *American Scholar*, vol. 57, no. 4 (Autumn 1988).

Mouffe, Chantal *The Return of the Political* (London: Verso, 1993).

—— 'Democracy, Power, and the "Political" ', in Seyla Benhabib (ed.) *Democracy and Difference* (Princeton NJ: Princeton University Press, 1996).

—— 'Decision, Deliberation, and Democratic Ethos', in *Philosophy Today*, vol. 41, no. 1 (Spring 1997).

Neack, Laura, and Roger M. Knudson 'Re-Imagining the Sovereign State: Beginning an Interdisciplinary Dialogue', in *Alternatives*, vol. 21, no. 1 (January/March 1996).

Neumann, Iver B., and Jennifer M. Welsh 'The Other in European Self-Definition', in *Review of International Studies*, vol. 17, no. 4 (1991).

—— 'Self and Other in International Relations', in *European Journal of International Relations*, vol. 2, no. 2 (June 1996).

—— *Russia and the Idea of Europe: A Study in Identity and International Relations* (London: Routledge, 1996).

—— 'European Identity, EU Expansion, and the Integration/Exclusion Nexus', in *Alternatives*, vol. 23, no. 3 (July/September 1998).

—— *Uses of the Other: 'The East' in European Identity Formation* (Minneapolis: University of Minnesota Press, 1999).

Neunreither, Karlheinz 'Governance Without Opposition: The Case of the European Union', in *Government and Opposition*, vol. 33, no. 4 (Autumn 1998).

Newhouse, John *Europe Adrift* (New York: Pantheon, 1997).

—— 'Europe's Rising Regionalism', in *Foreign Affairs*, vol. 76, no. 1 (January/February 1997).

Newman, Michael *Democracy, Sovereignty and the European Union* (New York: St Martin's Press, 1996).

Nietzsche, Friedrich *The Gay Science* [1882] (New York: Vintage Books, 1974).

Nolutshungu, Sam C. 'Introduction', in Sam C. Nolutshungu (ed.) *Margins of Insecurity: Minorities and International Security* (Rochester NY: University of Rochester Press, 1996).

Norton, Philip 'Legislatures in Perspective', in Philip Norton (ed.) *Parliaments in Western Europe* (London: Frank Cass, 1990).

Nye, Joseph S., Jr. *Bound to Lead: The Changing Nature of American Power* (New York: Basic Books, 1990).

O Tuathail, Gearoid 'At the End of Geopolitics? Reflections on a Plural Problematic at the Century's End', in *Alternatives*, vol. 22, no. 1 (January/March 1997).

O'Brien, Connor Cruise 'Toward European Disunion', in *Harper's Magazine*, July 1992.

O'Brien Hallstein, D. Lynn 'A Postmodern Caring: Feminist Standpoint Theories, Revisioning Caring, and Communication Ethics', in *Western Journal of Communication*, vol. 63, no. 1 (Winter 1999).

O'Sullivan, Noel, 'Nietzsche and the Agenda of Post-Modernity', in *History of European Ideas*, vol. 20, nos 1–3 (1995).

Obradovic, Daniela 'Policy Legitimacy and the European Union', in *Journal of Common Market Studies*, vol. 34, no. 2 (June 1996).

Odermatt, P. 'The Use of Symbols in the Drive for European Integration', in J. Th. Leersen and M. Spiering (eds) *National Identity: Symbol and Representation (Yearbook of European Studies)*, vol. 4 (Amsterdam: Radopi Press, 1991).

Ohmae, Kenichi *The End of the Nation-State: The Rise of Regional Economies* (New York: Free Press, 1995).

Orwell, George *Selected Essays* (London: Penguin, 1957).

Osterud, Oyvind 'Antinomies of Postmodernism in International Studies', in *Journal of Peace Research*, vol. 33, no. 4 (November 1996).

Ostner, I., and J. Lewis 'Gender and the Evolution of European Social Policies', in S. Leibfried and P. Pierson (eds) *European Social Policy: Between Fragmentation and Integration* (Washington DC: Brookings Institution, 1995).

Pahre, Robert 'Endogenous Domestic Institutions in Two-Level Games and Parliamentary Oversight of the European Union', in *Journal of Conflict Resolution*, vol. 41, no. 1 (February 1997).

Papcke, Sven 'Who Needs a European Identity and What Could It Be?', in Brian Nelson, David Roberts and Walter Veit (eds) *The Idea of Europe: Problems of National and Transitional Identity* (New York: Berg, 1992).

Parsons, Talcott 'Power and the Social System', in Steven Lukes (ed.) *Power* (New York: New York University Press, 1986).

Patomäki, Heikki 'How to Tell Better Stories About World Politics', in *European Journal of International Relations*, vol. 2, no. 1 (March 1996).

—— *The Tobin Tax: How to Make it Real*, Project Report by The Network Institute for Global Democratisation (NIGD), February 1999.

Pedler, R.H., and M.P.C.M. van Schendelen (eds) *Lobbying in the European Union: Companies, Trade Associations and Issue Groups* (Aldershot: Dartmouth, 1994).

Peerenboom, R.P. 'Reasons, Rationales, and Relativisms: What's at Stake in the Conversation over Scientific Rationality?', in *Philosophy Today*, vol. 34, no. 1 (Spring 1990).

Peters, B. Guy 'Bureaucratic Politics and the Institutions of the European Community', in Alberta M. Sbragia (ed.) *Euro-Politics: Institutions and Policymaking in the 'New' European Community* (Washington DC: Brookings Institution, 1992).

Peters, B. Guy, and John Pierre 'Governance Without Government? Rethinking Public Administration', in *Journal of Public Administration Research and Theory*, vol. 8, no. 2 (April 1998).

—— 'Institutions and Time: Problems of Conceptualization and Explanation', in *Journal of Public Administration Research and Theory*, vol. 8, no. 4 (October 1998).

Peters, B. Guy, and Donald J. Savoie 'Managing Incoherence: The Coordination and Empowerment Conundrum', in *Public Administration Review*, vol. 56, no. 3 (May/June 1996).

Peterson, John 'States, Societies and the European Union', in *West European Politics*, vol. 20, no. 4 (October 1997).

Pfaff, William 'The Reality of Human Affairs', in *World Policy Journal*, vol. 14, no. 2 (Summer 1997).

Pfetsch, Frank R. 'Die Problematik der europäischen Identität', in *Aus Politik und Zeitgeschichte*, no. 25–6 (12 June 1998).

Phillips, Anne *Democracy and Difference* (University Park: Pennsylvania State University Press, 1993).

Philpott, Daniel 'Sovereignty: An Introduction and Brief History', in *Journal of International Affairs*, vol. 48, no. 2 (Winter 1995).

Picht, Robert 'European Cultural Policy After Maastricht', in Paul Michael Lützeler (ed.) *Europe After Maastricht: American and European Perspectives* (Providence RI/Oxford: Berghahn Books, 1994).

Pickering, Andrew *Constructing Quarks: A Sociological History of Particle Physics* (Chicago: University of Chicago Press, 1999).

Pierson, Paul 'The Path to European Integration: A Historical Institutionalist Analysis', in *Comparative Political Studies*, vol. 29, no. 2 (April 1996).

Pijpers, Alfred *De Mythe van het Democratisch Tekort. Een Discussiebijdrage over de Europese Politiek* (The Hague: Instituut Clingendael, October 1999).

Pixley, Jocelyn *Citizenship and Employment: Investigating Post-Industrial Options* (Cambridge: Cambridge University Press, 1993).

Plescu, Andrei 'Welchen Patriotismus braucht Europa? Die verlorenen Söhne und ihre Sünden', in *Süddeutsche Zeitung*, 5 June 1997.

Pocock, J.G.A. 'What Do We Mean By Europe?', in *Wilson Quarterly*, vol. 21, no. 1 (Winter 1997).

Polanyi, Karl *The Great Transformation: The Political and Economic Origins of Our Time* (Boston: Beacon Press, 1957).

Posnock, Ross 'Before and After Identity Politics', in *Raritan*, vol. 15, no. 1 (Summer 1995).

Poster, Mark, 'Cyberdemocracy: The Internet and the Public Sphere', in David Holmes (ed.) *Virtual Politics: Identity and Community in Cyberspace* (London: Sage, 1997).

Postrel, Virginia 'Seattle Suprise', in *Reason*, vol. 31, no. 9 (February 2000).

Prodi, Romano '2000–2005: Shaping the New Europe', speech to the European Parliament in Strasbourg, France, 15 February 2000. Online. Available HTTP: http://europa.eu.int/comm/externalrelations/news/0200/speech0041.htm (accessed 15 August 2000).

Prosser, Jay *The Body Narratives of Transsexuality* (New York: Columbia University Press, 1998).

Puttnam, David *Movies and Money: The Undeclared War Between Europe and America* (New York: David McKay, 1998).

Ramonet, Ignacio 'The One Idea System' (21 February 1995). Online. Available HTTP: http://www.ctheory.com/e-oneideasystem.html (accessed 28 March 2000).

Rawls, John *Political Liberalism* (New York: Columbia University Press, 1993).

Reagan, Charles E. 'The Self as an Other', in *Philosophy Today*, vol. 37, no. 1 (Spring 1993).

Rees, Nicholas 'Inter-Regional Co-operation in the EU and Beyond', in *European Planning Studies*, vol. 5, no. 3 (June 1997).

Reif, Karlheinz 'Cultural Convergence and Cultural Diversity as Factors in European Identity', in Soledad Garcia (ed.) *European Identity and the Search for Legitimacy* (London: Pinter, 1993).

Reis, Raul 'The Impact of Television Viewing in the Brazilian Amazon', in *Human Organization*, vol. 57, no. 3 (Fall 1998).

Renan, Ernest 'What is a Nation?', in H.K. Bhaba (ed.) *Nation and Narration* (London: Routledge, 1990).

Renwick, Neil 'Re-reading Europe's Identities', in Jill Krause and Neil Renwick (eds) *Identities in International Relations* (London: Macmillan, 1996).

Rhodes, Carolyn, and Sonia Mazey 'Introduction: Integration in Theoretical Perspective', in Carolyn Rhodes and Sonia Mazey (eds) *The State of the European Union: Building a European Polity?* (Boulder CO: Lynne Rienner, 1995).

Rhodes, R.A.W. *Understanding Governance: Policy Networks, Governance, Reflexivity and Accountability* (Buckingham: Open University Press, 1997).

Richardson, Jeremy J. 'Policy-Making in the EU: Interests, Ideas and Garbage Cans of Primeval Soup', in Jeremy J. Richardson (ed.) *European Union: Power and Policy-Making* (London: Routledge, 1996).

Ricoeur, Paul 'Narrative Identity', in *Philosophy Today*, vol. 35, no. 1 (Spring 1991).

—— *Oneself As Another* (Chicago: University of Chicago Press, 1994).

—— 'Gedächtnis-Vergessen-Geschichte', in Klaus E. Müller and Jörn Rüsen (eds) *Historische Sinnbildung: Problemstellungen, Zeitkonzepte, Wahrnehmungshorizonte, Darstellungsstrategien* (Hamburg: Rowohlt, 1997).

Ripley, Randall B., and Grace A. Franklin *Congress, the Bureaucracy and Public Policy* (Homewood IL: Dorsey Press, 1984).

Risse-Kappen, Thomas 'A European Identity? Europeanization and the Evolution of Nation-State Identities', in Maria Green Cowles, James Caporaso and Thomas Risse-Kappen (eds) *Europeanization and Domestic Change* (Ithaca NY: Cornell University Press, 2000).

Risse-Kappen, Thomas (with Daniela Engelmann-Martin, Hans-Joachim Knopf and Klaus Roscher), 'To Euro or Not to Euro? The EMU and Identity Politics in the

European Union', EUI Working Paper Series, no. 98–9 (Florence: European University Institute, 1998).

Roberson, B.A. 'Islam and Europe: An Enigma Or a Threat?', in *Middle East Journal*, vol. 48, no. 2 (Spring 1994).

Robertson, Roland 'After Nostalgia? Wilful Nostalgia and the Phase of Globalization', in Bryan S. Turner (ed.) *Theories of Modernity and Postmodernity* (London: Sage, 1990).

Rorty, Richard *Truth and Progress: Philosophical Papers, Volume 3* (Cambridge: Cambridge University Press, 1998).

Rosecrance, Richard 'The Obsolescence of Territory', in *New Perspectives Quarterly*, vol. 12, no. 1 (Winter 1995).

—— 'The Rise of the Virtual State', in *Foreign Affairs*, vol. 75, no. 4 (July/August 1996).

Rosenau, James N. 'Governance, Order, and Change in World Politics', in James N. Rosenau and Ernst-Otto Czempiel (eds) *Governance Without Government: Order and Change in World Politics* (Cambridge: Cambridge University Press, 1992).

—— 'Governance in the Twenty-first Century', in *Global Governance*, vol. 1, no. 1 (Winter 1995).

Rosenau, Pauline Marie *Post-Modernism and the Social Sciences: Insights, Inroads and Intrusions* (Princeton NJ: Princeton University Press, 1992).

Rothfork, John 'Postmodern Ethics: Richard Rorty and Michael Polanyi', in *Southern Humanities Review*, vol. 29, no. 1 (Winter 1995).

Ruggie, John G. 'Continuity and Transformation in the World Polity: Toward a Neorealist Synthesis', in Robert O. Keohane (ed.) *Neorealism and Its Critics* (New York: Columbia University Press, 1986).

—— 'Territoriality and Beyond: Problematizing Modernity in International Relations', in *International Organization*, vol. 47, no. 1 (Winter 1993).

—— 'What Makes the World Hang Together? Neo-Utilitarianism and the Social Constructivist Challenge', in *International Organization*, vol. 52, no. 4 (Autumn 1998).

SACD *L'AMI: l'Ennemi* (Paris: SACD, 1998).

Said, Edward W. 'The Devil Theory of Islam', *The Nation*, vol. 263, no. 6, 12–19 August 1996.

Sandel, Michael J. *Democracy's Discontent: America in Search of a Public Philosophy* (Cambridge MA: Harvard University Press, 1996).

Sandholtz, Wayne, and John Zysman '1992: Recasting the European Bargain', *World Politics*, vol. 42, no. 1 (October 1989).

—— 'Choosing Union: Monetary Politics and Maastricht', in *International Organization*, vol. 47, no. 1 (Winter 1993).

Sassen, Saskia, and Kwame Anthony Appiah *Globalization and Its Discontents* (New York: New Press, 1998).

Schlesinger, Philip R. 'Wishful Thinking: Cultural Politics, Media, and Collective Identities in Europe', in *Journal of Communication*, vol. 43, no. 2 (Spring 1993).

—— 'Europe's Contradictory Communicative Space', in *Daedalus*, vol. 123, no. 2 (Spring 1994).

Schmidt, Vivien A. 'The Impact of European Integration on Member-States' Economic and Industrial Policies: Assessing the Loss of National Autonomy and Control From Globalization vs. Europeanization', Paper presented at the 1998 APSA annual meeting, Boston (September 1998).

Schmitter, Philippe C. 'The European Community as an Emergent and Novel Form of Political Domination', Juan March Institute Working Paper Series, no. 26 (Madrid, 1991).

—— 'Representation and the Future Euro-Polity', in *Staatswissenschaften und Staatspraxis*, vol. 3, no. 3 (1992).

—— 'The Future of Democracy: Could it Be a Matter of Scale?', in *Social Research*, vol. 66, no. 3 (Fall 1999).

Schott, Robin May 'Maternal Bodies and Nationalism', in *Philosophy Today*, vol. 41 (1997 – Supplement 'Remembrance and Responsibility').

Schulze, Gerhard *Die Erlebnisgesellschaft: Kultursoziologie der Gegenwart* (Frankfurt a/M: Campus, 1997).

Schuman, Robert *Pour l'Europe* (Paris: Nagel, 1964).

Schwartz, Regina 'Monotheism and the Violence of Identities', in *Raritan*, vol. 14, no. 3 (Winter 1995).

Sebinius, James K. 'Challenging Conventional Explanations of International Co-operation: Negotiation Analysis and the Case of Epistemic Communities', in *International Organization*, vol. 46, no. 1 (Winter 1992).

Selznick, Philip 'Institutionalism "Old" and "New" ', in *Administrative Science Quarterly*, vol. 41, no. 2 (June 1996).

Senelle, Robert 'The New Cultural Policy of the European Union', in Leonce Bekemans (ed.) *Culture: Building Stone for Europe 2002* (Brussels: College of Europe/European Interuniversity Press, 1996).

Sennett, Richard 'The New Capitalism', in *Social Research*, vol. 64, no. 2 (Summer 1997).

Severson, Kristin, and Victoria Stanhope 'Identity Politics and Progress: Don't Fence Me In (Or Out)', in *Off Our Backs*, vol. 28, no. 4 (April 1998).

Shackleton, Michael 'The Internal Legitimacy Crisis of the European Union', Europa Institute, University of Edinburgh, Occasional Paper Series, no. 1 (1994).

Shapiro, Michael J. *Violent Cartographies: Mapping Cultures of War* (Minneapolis: University of Minnesota Press, 1997).

Shaw, Josephine 'Citizenship of the Union: Towards Post-National Membership?', Harvard Law School, Jean Monnet Working Papers Series, no. 6 (1997).

Shephard, Mark 'The European Parliament: Laying the Foundations For Awareness and Support', in *Parliamentary Affairs*, vol. 50, no. 3 (July 1997).

Sheptycki, J.W.E. 'Policing, Postmodernism and Transnationalization', in *British Journal of Criminology*, vol. 38, no. 3 (Summer 1998).

Shetty, Sandhya '(Dis)figuring the Nation: Mother, Metaphor, Metonymy', in *Differences*, vol. 7, no. 3 (Fall 1995).

Shore, Chris 'Inventing the "People's Europe": Critical Approaches to European Community "Cultural Policy" ', in *Man* (London), vol. 28, no. 4 (December 1993).

Sid-Ahmed, Mohamed 'Cybernetic Colonialism and the Moral Search', in *New Perspectives Quarterly*, vol. 11, no. 2 (Spring 1994).

Silverstein, Ken 'Millions for Viagra, Pennies for Diseases of the Poor', in *The Nation*, vol. 269, no. 3 (19 July 1999).

Simeon, Richard 'Citizens and Democracy in the Emerging Global Order', in Thomas J. Courchene (ed.) *The Nation State in a Global/Information Era: Policy Challenges*, John Deutsch Institute for the Study of Economic Policy, Bell Canada Papers on Economic and Public Policy, no. 5 (Kingston, Ontario, 1997).

Sjolander, Claire Turenne 'The Rhetoric of Globalization: What's in a Wor(l)d?', in *International Journal*, vol. 51, no. 4 (Autumn 1996).

Smith, Anthony D. *National Identity* (London: Penguin, 1991).

—— *Nations and Nationalism in a Global Era* (Cambridge: Polity Press, 1995).

Smith, Huston 'The Ambiguity of Matter', in *Cross Currents*, vol. 48, no. 1 (Spring 1998).

Smith, Steve 'The Self-Images of a Discipline: A Genealogy of International Relations Theory', in Ken Booth and Steve Smith (eds) *International Relations Theory Today* (Cambridge: Polity Press, 1995).

—— 'Positivism and Beyond', in Steve Smith, Ken Booth and Marysia Zalewski (eds) *International Theory: Positivism and Beyond* (Cambridge: Cambridge University Press, 1996).

Sorensen, Georg 'An Analysis of Contemporary Statehood: Consequences For Conflict and Co-operation', in *Review of International Studies*, vol. 23, no. 3 (July 1997).

Spicer, Michael W. 'Public Administration, the State, and the Postmodern Condition', in *American Behavioral Scientist*, vol. 41, no. 1 (September 1997).

Spiering, Menno 'The Future of National Identity in the European Union', in *National Identities*, vol. 1, no. 2 (July 1999).

Spiro, Peter J. 'New Global Communities: Nongovernmental Organizations in International Decision-Making Institutions', in *The Washington Quarterly*, vol. 18, no. 1 (Winter 1995).

Spivak, Gayatri Chakravorty 'Translator's Preface' in Jacques Derrida *Of Grammatology* (Baltimore MD and London: Johns Hopkins University Press, 1998 – corrected edition).

Stam, Robert 'From Hybridity to the Aesthetics of Garbage', in *Social Identities*, vol. 3, no. 2 (June 1997).

Starr-Deelen, Donna, and Bart Deelen 'The European Court of Justice as a Federator', in *Publius*, vol. 26, no. 4 (Fall 1996).

Steel, Ronald 'The Bad News', in *New Republic*, 10 February 1997.

—— 'Who Is Us?', in *New Republic*, 14–21 September 1998.

Stone Sweet, Alec, and Thomas L. Brunell, 'Constructing a Supranational Constitution: Dispute Resolution and Governance in the European Community', in *American Political Science Review*, vol. 92, no. 1 (March 1998).

Strange, Susan 'An Eclectic Approach', in Craig N. Murphy and Roger Tooze (eds) *The New International Political Economy* (Boulder CO: Lynne Rienner, 1991).

—— *The Retreat of the State: The Diffusion of Power in the World Economy* (Cambridge: Cambridge University Press, 1996).

Swingewood, Alan *Cultural Theory and the Problem of Modernity* (New York: St Martin's Press, 1998).

Tassin, E. 'Europe: A Political Community', in Chantal Mouffe (ed.) *Dimensions of Radical Democracy: Pluralism, Citizenship, Community* (London: Verso, 1996).

Tate, John W. 'Kant, Habermas, and the "Philosophical Legitimation" of Modernity', in *Journal of European Studies*, vol. 27, no. 3 (September 1997).

Tehranian, Katherine Kia 'Global Communication and Pluralization of Identities', in *Futures*, vol. 30, no. 2–3 (March/April 1998).

Tempelman, Sasja 'Constructions of Cultural Identity: Multiculturalism and Exclusion', in *Political Studies*, vol. 47, no. 1 (March 1999).

Teschke, Benno 'Geopolitical Relations in the European Middle Ages: History and Theory', in *International Organization*, vol. 52, no. 2 (Spring 1998).

Tickner, J. Ann *Gender in International Relations: Feminist Perspectives on Achieving Global Security* (New York: Columbia University Press, 1992).

—— 'Introducing Feminist Perspectives Into Peace and World Security Courses', in *Women's Studies Quarterly*, vol. 23, no. 3–4 (Fall 1995).

Tilly, Charles 'Reflections on the History of European State-Making', in Charles Tilly (ed.) *The Formation of National States in Western Europe* (Princeton NJ: Princeton University Press, 1975).

de Tocqueville, Alexis *Democracy in America* [1835–40] (New York: Harper & Row, 1969).

Todorov, Tzvetan *Mikhail Bakhtin: The Dialogical Principle* (Minneapolis: University of Minnesota Press, 1984).

Tönnies, Ferdinand *Community and Association* (London: Routledge, 1974).

Traxler, Franz, and Philippe C. Schmitter 'The Emerging Euro-Polity and Organized Interest', in *European Journal of International Relations*, vol. 1, no. 2 (June 1995).

Tully, James *Strange Multiplicity: Constitutionalism in an Age of Diversity* (Cambridge: Cambridge University Press, 1995).

Tunander, Ola 'Post-Cold War Europe: Synthesis of a Bipolar Friend–Foe Structure and a Hierarchic Cosmos–Chaos Structure?', in Ola Tunander, Pavel Baev and Victoria Ingrid Einagel (eds) *Geopolitics in Post-Wall Europe: Security, Territory and Identity* (London: Sage, 1997).

Villa, Dana 'Postmodernism and the Public Sphere', in *American Political Science Review*, vol. 86, no. 3 (September 1992).

Viorst, Milton 'The Muslims in France', in *Foreign Affairs*, vol. 75, no. 5 (September/October 1996).

Voigt, Rüdiger 'Ende der Innenpolitik? Politik und Recht im Zeichen der Globalisierung', in *Aus Politik und Zeitgeschichte*, no. 29–30 (10 July 1998).

Wæver, Ole 'Identity, Integration and Security', in *Journal of International Affairs*, vol. 48, no. 2 (Winter 1995).

—— 'Securitization and Desecuritization', in Ronnie D. Lipschutz (ed.) *On Security* (New York: Columbia University Press, 1995).

—— 'European Security Identities', in *Journal of Common Market Studies*, vol. 34, no. 1 (August 1996).

Walicki, Andrzej *A History of Russian Thought: From the Enlightenment to Marxism* (Oxford: Clarendon Press, 1988).

Walker, Edward W. 'No Peace, No War in the Caucasus: Secessionist Conflicts in Chechnya, Abkhazia and Nagorno-Karabakh', John F. Kennedy School of Government, Harvard University, Strengthening Democratic Institutions Project Paper Series (February 1998).

Walker, Martin 'The New American Hegemony', in *World Policy Journal*, vol. 13, no. 2 (Summer 1996).

Walker, R.B.J. 'Genealogy, Geopolitics and Political Community: Richard K. Ashley and the Critical Social Theory of International Politics', in *Alternatives*, vol. 13, no. 1 (January 1988).

—— 'The Concept of Security and International Relations Theory', University of California, Institute of Global Conflict and Co-operation Working Paper Series, no. 3 (San Diego, 1988).

—— 'Security, Sovereignty, and the Challenge of World Politics', in *Alternatives*, vol. 15, no. 1 (Winter 1990).

—— 'On the Spatiotemporal Conditions of Democratic Practice', in *Alternatives*, vol. 16, no. 2 (Spring 1991).

—— *Inside/Outside: International Relations as Political Theory* (Cambridge: Cambridge University Press, 1993).

Wallace, Helen 'Politics and Policy in the EU: The Challenge of Governance', in Helen Wallace and William Wallace (eds) *Policy-Making in the European Union* (Oxford: Oxford University Press, 1996).

Wallace, William 'Government Without Statehood: The Unstable Equilibrium', in Helen Wallace and William Wallace (eds) *Policy-Making in the European Union* (Oxford: Oxford University Press, 1996).

Waltz, Kenneth N. *Man, the State and War. A Theoretical Analysis* (New York: Columbia University Press, 1959).

—— *Theory of International Politics* (New York: McGraw-Hill, 1979).

Weber, Cynthia *Simulating Sovereignty: Intervention, the State and Symbolic Exchange* (Cambridge: Cambridge University Press, 1995).

—— *Faking It: US Hegemony in a 'Post-Phallic' Era* (Minneapolis: University of Minnesota Press, 1999).

Weil, Simone *The Need For Roots: Prelude To a Declaration of Duties Toward Mankind* (London: Routledge, 1996 – reprint).

Weiler, J.H.H. 'Community, Member States and European Integration: Is the Law Relevant?', in *Journal of Common Market Studies*, vol. 21, no. 1–2 (September/December 1982).

Weiler, J.H.H., Ulrich R. Haltern and Franz C. Mayer 'European Democracy and Its Critique', in Jack Hayward (ed.) *The Crisis of Representation in Europe* (London: Frank Cass, 1995).

—— 'Europe After Maastricht – Do the New Clothes Have an Emperor?', Harvard Law School, Jean Monnet Chair Working Paper Series, no. 12 (1995).

—— 'The Selling of Europe: The Discourse of European Citizenship in the IGC 1996', Harvard Law School, Jean Monnet Chair Working Paper Series, no. 3 (1996).

—— 'Legitimacy and Democracy of Union Governance', in Geoffrey Edwards and Alfred Pijpers (eds) *The Politics of European Treaty Reform* (London: Pinter, 1997).

—— *The Constitution of Europe* (Cambridge: Cambridge University Press, 1999).

Welsh, Jennifer M. 'The Role of the Inner Enemy in European Self-Definition: Identity, Culture and International Relations Theory', in *History of European Ideas*, vol. 19, no. 1–3 (1994).

Wendt, Alexander, 'Anarchy is What States Make of It: The Social Construction of Power Politics', in *International Organization*, vol. 46, no. 2 (Spring 1992).

—— 'Collective Identity Formation and the International State', in *American Political Science Review*, vol. 88, no. 2 (June 1994).

—— *Social Theory of International Politics* (Cambridge: Cambridge University Press, 1999).

Wessels, Wolfgang 'The Modern West European State and the European Union: Democratic Erosion or a New Kind of Polity?', in Svein S. Andersen and Kjell A. Eliassen (eds) *The European Union: How Democratic Is It?* (London: Sage, 1995).

White, Daniel R., and Gert Hellerick 'Nietzsche at the Mall: Deconstructing the Consumer' (1994). Online. Available HTTP: http://www.ctheory.com/a-nietzsche_at_the_mall.html (accessed 29 March 2000).

Whitfield, Stephen J. *The Culture of the Cold War* (Baltimore MD: Johns Hopkins University Press, 1991).

Wight, Martin *International Theory: The Three Traditions* (New York: Holmes & Meier, 1992).

Wilber, Charles K. 'Globalization and Democracy', in *Journal of Economic Issues*, vol. 32, no. 2 (June 1998).

Wilks, Michael *The Problem of Sovereignty in the Later Middle Ages* (Cambridge: Cambridge University Press, 1964).

Williams, Michael C. 'Identity and the Politics of Security', in *European Journal of International Relations*, vol. 4, no. 2 (June 1998).

Williams, Michael C., and Keith Krause 'Preface: Toward Critical Security Studies', in Keith Krause and Michael C. Williams (eds) *Critical Security Studies* (Minneapolis: University of Minnesota Press, 1997).

Wilmer, Franke 'Identity, Culture, and Historicity: The Social Construction of Ethnicity in the Balkans', in *World Affairs*, vol. 160, no. 1 (Summer 1997).

Wilson, Louise 'Cyberwar, God and Television: Interview With Paul Virilio' (1 December 1994). Online. Available HTTP: http://www.ctheory.com/a-cyberwargod.html (accessed 29 March 2000).

Wintle, Michael 'Cultural Identity in Europe: Shared Experience', in Michael Wintle (ed.) *Culture and Identity in Europe: Perceptions of Divergence and Unity in Past and Present* (Aldershot: Avebury, 1996).

Wittgenstein, Ludwig *Philosophical Investigations* (Oxford: Blackwell, 1953).

Worsham, Jeff, Marc Allen Eisner and Evan J. Ringquist 'Assessing the Assumptions: A Critical Analysis of Agency Theory', in *Administration and Society*, vol. 28, no. 4 (February 1997).

Wyschogrod, Edith, and John D. Caputo 'Postmodernism and the Desire For God: An E-Mail Exchange', in *Cross Currents*, vol. 48, no. 3 (Fall 1998).

Yarbrough, Beth V., and Robert M. Yarbrough 'Regionalism and Layered Governance: The Choice of Trade Institutions', in *Journal of International Affairs*, vol. 48, no. 1 (Summer 1994).

Young, Iris Marion 'The Ideal of Community and the Politics of Difference', in Linda J. Nicholson (ed.) *Feminism/Postmodernism* (London/New York: Routledge, 1990).

—— 'Communication and the Other: Beyond Deliberative Democracy', in Seyla Benhabib (ed.) *Democracy and Difference: Contesting the Boundaries of the Political* (Princeton NJ: Princeton University Press, 1996).

Young, James E. 'Germany's Memorial Question: Memory, Counter-Memory, and the End of the Monument', in *South Atlantic Quarterly*, vol. 96, no. 4 (Fall 1997).

Zielonka, Jan *Explaining Euro-Paralysis: Why Europe is Unable to Act in International Politics* (New York: St Martin's Press, 1998).

Zizek, Slavoj 'For a Leftist Appropriation of the European Legacy', in *Journal of Political Ideologies*, vol. 3, no. 1 (February 1998).

—— 'Against the Double Blackmail', in *The Nation*, vol. 268, no. 19, 24 May 1999.

—— 'Die Freie Wahl zwischen blauen und roten Tütchen: Warum wir es lieben, Haider zu hassen', in *Süddeutsche Zeitung*, 9 February 2000.

Zur, Ofer 'The Love of Hating', in *History of European Ideas*, vol. 13, no. 4 (1991).

Zürn, Michael 'The Challenge of Globalization and Individualization: A View From Europe', in Hans-Henrik Holm and Georg Sorensen (eds) *Whose World Order? Uneven Globalization and the End of the Cold War* (Boulder CO: Westview Press, 1995).

# Index